KU-201-216

*of photo copying*

# Comparing Media Systems

This book proposes a framework for comparative analysis of the relation between the media and the political system. Building on a survey of media institutions in eighteen West European and North American democracies, Hallin and Mancini identify the principal dimensions of variation in media systems and the political variables that have shaped their evolution. They go on to identify three major models of media system development, the Polarized Pluralist, Democratic Corporatist, and Liberal models; to explain why the media have played a different role in politics in each of these systems; and to explore the forces of change that are currently transforming them. It provides a key theoretical statement about the relation between media and political systems, a key statement about the methodology of comparative analysis in political communication, and a clear overview of the variety of media institutions that have developed in the West, understood within their political and historical context.

Daniel C. Hallin is a Professor of Communication and an Adjunct Professor of Political Science at the University of California, San Diego. He has written widely on media and politics, including studies of media and war, the shrinking soundbite in television news, the history of professionalism in American journalism, and the media and the process of democratization in Mexico, as well as earlier studies of U.S. and Italian news with Professor Mancini. His previous books include *The "Uncensored War": The Media and Vietnam* and *We Keep America on Top of the World: Television Journalism and the Public Sphere*. His articles have appeared in the *Journal of Communication, Political Communication, Media Culture & Society*, the *Journal of Politics*, and the *Columbia Journalism Review*, among other publications, and have been translated into many languages. He has served as editor of *The Communication Review* and as an at-large board member of the International Communication Association.

Paolo Mancini is presently a full professor at the Dipartimento Istituzioni e Società, Facoltà di Scienze Politiche, Università di Perugia. He is also the Director of Centro Interuniversitario di Comunicazione Politica (Interuniversity Center of Political Communication).

He received his Laurea degree from the Facoltà di Scienze Politiche and his Dea at the Ecole des Hautes Etudes en Science Sociales of Paris. Professor Mancini went on to teach at various institutions in Italy and abroad including the University of California, San Diego, and Università di Perugia and was a Fellow at the Shorenstein Center on the Press, Politics, and Public Policy, Harvard University. Professor Mancini is the author of a number of books including his most recent, *Il sistema fragile* (2000). With David Swanson he edited *Politics, Media and Modern Democracy*. Professor Mancini is also corresponding editor of many journals including *European Journal of Communication, Press/Politics, The Communication Review, Political Communication*, and *Journalism Studies*.

LIVERPOOL JMU LIBRARY

3 1111 01453 1220

# COMMUNICATION, SOCIETY, AND POLITICS

## Editors

W. Lance Bennett, *University of Washington*
Robert M. Entman, *North Carolina State University*

### Editorial Advisory Board

Larry M. Bartels, *Princeton University*
Jay G. Blumer, Emeritus, *University of Leeds*
Daniel Dayan, *Centre National de la Recherche Scientifique Paris*, and
*University of Oslow*
Paolo Mancini, *Università di Peruia*
Pippa Norris, *Harvard University*
Barbara Pfetsch, *Wissenschaftszentrum Berlin für Socialforschung*
Philip Schlesinger, *University of Stirling*
David L. Swanson, *University of Illinois at Urbana-Champaign*
Gadi Wolfsfeld, *The Hebrew University of Jerusalem*
John Zaller, *University of California, Los Angeles*

Politics and relations among individuals in societies across the world are being transformed by new technologies for targeting individuals and sophisticated methods for shaping personalized messages. The new technologies challenge boundaries of many kinds – between news, information, entertainment, and advertising; between media, with the arrival of the World Wide Web; and even between nations. *Communication, Society, and Politics* probes the political and social impacts of these new communication systems in national, comparative, and global perspective.

# Comparing Media Systems

## THREE MODELS OF MEDIA AND POLITICS

**Daniel C. Hallin**
*University of California*

**Paolo Mancini**
*Università di Perugia*

**CAMBRIDGE**
UNIVERSITY PRESS

CAMBRIDGE UNIVERSITY PRESS
Cambridge, New York, Melbourne, Madrid, Cape Town, Singapore,
São Paulo, Delhi, Dubai, Tokyo, Mexico City

Cambridge University Press
The Edinburgh Building, Cambridge CB2 8RU, UK

Published in the United States of America by Cambridge University Press, New York

www.cambridge.org
Information on this title: www.cambridge.org/9780521543088

© Daniel C. Hallin and Paolo Mancini 2004

This publication is in copyright. Subject to statutory exception
and to the provisions of relevant collective licensing agreements,
no reproduction of any part may take place without the written
permission of Cambridge University Press.

First published 2004

*A catalogue record for this publication is available from the British Library*

ISBN 978-0-521-83535-0 Hardback
ISBN 978-0-521-54308-8 Paperback

Cambridge University Press has no responsibility for the persistence or
accuracy of URLs for external or third-party internet websites referred to in
this publication, and does not guarantee that any content on such websites is,
or will remain, accurate or appropriate. Information regarding prices, travel
timetables, and other factual information given in this work are correct at
the time of first printing but Cambridge University Press does not guarantee
the accuracy of such information thereafter.

# Contents

# List of Figures and Tables

## FIGURES

## TABLES

# List of Acronyms

| | |
|---|---|
| AGI | Agencia Giornalistica Italia |
| ASNE | American Society of Newspaper Editors |
| BBC | British Broadcasting Corporation |
| CBC | Canadian Broadcasting Corporation |
| CSA | Conseil Superieur de l'Audiovisuel |
| DNVP | German National People's Party |
| DR | Danmarks Radio |
| EBU | European Broadcasting Union |
| ECU | European Currency Unit |
| EU | European Union |
| FCC | Federal Communications Commission |
| IBA | Independent Broadcasting Authority |
| ITC | Independent Television Commission |
| ITV | Independent Television |
| IU | Izquierda Unida |
| NOS | Dutch Broadcasting Foundation |
| NUJ | National Union of Journalists |
| ORTF | Office de Radiodiffusion-Télévision Française |
| PASOK | Panhellenic Socialist Party of Greece |
| PBS | Public Broadcasting System |
| PCC | Press Complaints Commission |
| PCI | Partido Comunista Italiana |
| PP | Partido Popular |
| PSOE | Spanish Socialist Workers Party |
| RAI | Radiotelevisione Italiana |
| RTF | Radio Télévision Française |

| | |
|---|---|
| RTVE | Grupo Radio Televisión Española |
| TUC | Trades Union Congress |
| WAN | World Association of Newspapers |
| WTO | World Trade Organization |

# Preface

We don't remember exactly when the idea of this book was born. Probably at the moment we were finishing our first joint enterprise, "Speaking of the President," which was published in 1984, we already had a strong sense that this kind of research was extremely promising and that we should try to do it more systematically and on a broader scale. Little by little, through other experiences of comparative studies on particular subjects, we conceived the idea of this project. Briefly, what we have set out to do is to find out whether it is possible to identify systematic connections between political and mass media structures. We were curious, in particular, whether it made sense to think in terms of distinct models of journalism and of the media-politics relationship. This has been an ambition in the field of communication since *Four Theories of the Press*, and it also seemed to us, as we began to survey the variety of media systems in Western Europe and North America, that there really were clusters of media system characteristics that tended to co-occur in distinct patterns. We introduce a schema centered around three models of journalism and media institutions in the pages that follow – though with plenty of qualifications about the variation that exists within and between actual media systems belonging to these three models. We have tried to carry out this effort at comparative analysis empirically, without having in mind any ideal professional model of reference against which other systems would be measured – eschewing the normatively centered approach that, as we will argue in the pages that follow, has held back comparative analysis in communication. At the same time, we will try in this book to assess weaknesses and strengths of each media system model as a support for democracy; this much of the normative orientation of communication theory is certainly worth maintaining.

For methodological and practical reasons that we explain in the following text, we chose to confine this study to a limited set of countries that have much in common in terms of their history, culture, and institutions, those of Western Europe and North America. We do believe that much of the analysis will be of interest to those studying other regions, and we will say a little about how we see our models in relation to the rest of the world; we will also stress that we don't intend any of this analysis simply to be applied to other systems without modification.

Our experience carrying out this project was genuinely exciting: We discovered interesting peculiarities we didn't expect, and similarities appeared where we had expected differences. We enjoyed stimulating discussions with colleagues in different parts of the world. We challenged our linguistic abilities, and spent many hours trying to interpret one another's drafts and forge our separate ideas into a single, coherent argument. (We know that university review committees sometimes believe that co-authoring a book is only half as much work as writing a single-authored one, but we can assure them that this is not the case!) This book was written partially in San Diego and partially in Perugia. Jet lag was a common challenge, and long transoceanic flights were often the occasion for new ideas and improvements. In the end we don't claim to have presented a fully finished analysis; the state of comparative study in communication is too primitive for that, both conceptually and in terms of available data and case studies. We believe we can offer important results, but more than anything else we think we have been able to point to possible areas and strategies for future research.

The "official" beginning of the project was a conference organized in Berkeley in 1998; during and since that seminar we have taken advantage of the suggestions of many colleagues and the help of several institutions. We would like to acknowledge their help here. The University of California, San Diego, has supported both of us with travel grants and teaching opportunities that were important occasions for discussing and writing this book. The Center for German and European Studies of the University of California, Berkeley, made possible the organization of the 1998 conference, as well as funding some of our content analysis and a graduate seminar we taught jointly at the University of California, San Diego. Grants from Università di Perugia, progetti d'Ateneo, provided additional resources for traveling. A grant from RAI, Radiotelevisione Italiana, made possible the collection of much of the documentary data. A seminar organized by the Institut für Journalistik at the University of

Dortmund in connection with the Erich Brost Stiftungsprofessor provided an important opportunity for discussion of some of our early results. A visiting professorship at the University of Düsseldorf, funded by the Deutsche Forschungsgemeinshaft and organized by Professor Karin Böhme-Dürr, provided important opportunities for research, as did a United States Information Agency (USIA) Academic Specialist grant for travel to Greece. Meetings organized at the Universidade Nova de Lisboa, the Universidad Complutense de Madrid, and by the Journalists Union of Macedonia and Thrace were also very useful.

Stlianos Papathanassopoulos, Ralph Negrine, Winfried Schultz, Wolfang Donsbach, José Luis Dader, Michael Gurevitch, Peter Humphreys, Erik Neveu, Katharina Hadamik, and Gerd Kopper attended seminars during which we discussed our project, and they have been very helpful in providing both information and critiques of our ideas. We bored other colleagues in various parts of the world asking them to read parts of the book and to correct our mistakes. The reactions of Peter Humphreys, James Curran, Lennart Weibull, Raimo Salokangas, Robert Hackett, Winfried Schultz, Kees Brants, Jay Blumler, Stylianos Papathanassoupolos, José Luis Dader, Isabel Fernández, and Erik Neveu to our drafts have been very useful. We asked many colleagues to help us with information we lacked about particular countries. In addition to those we have mentioned, we received help from Els de Bens, Monika Djerf-Pierre, Tom Olsson, Jan Ekecrantz, Yuezhi Zhao, Rudi Renger, Nelson Traquina, Eric Darras, Yoram Peri, and Sigurd Høst. At various times we discussed the content of this book with Cees Hamelink, Peter Dahlgren, Kaarle Nordenstreng, Klaus Schoenbach, Rod Benson, Partick Champagne, Dominique Marchetti, Holli Semetko, and J. M. Nobre-Correia. Raquel Fernández, Llucia Oliva, Juan Diez Nicolas, and Maria-Teresa Cordero were very helpful in arranging interviews in Spain. Many journalists, media regulators, and others in a number of countries were also willing to give their time for our questions. Rod Benson and Mauro Porto did the coding and helped to develop the content analysis reported here. Alain Cohen and Ferruh Yilmaz provided help with translations.

# ONE

# Introduction

"In the simplest terms," Siebert, Peterson, and Schramm wrote in *Four Theories of the Press* (1956), "the question behind this book is, why is the press as it is? Why does it apparently serve different purposes and appear in widely different forms in different countries? Why, for example, is the press of the Soviet Union so different from our own, and the press of Argentina, so different from that of Great Britain?"

Nearly half a century later the field of communication has made limited progress in addressing this kind of question. Though there have been attempts, particularly since the 1970s, to push the field in the direction of comparative analysis, such a research tradition remains essentially in its infancy.[1] We attempt in this book to propose some tentative answers to the questions posed by Siebert, Peterson, and Schramm – though not on such a grand scale. We confine ourselves to the developed capitalist democracies of Western Europe and North America. We attempt to identify the major variations that have developed in Western democracies in the structure and political role of the news media, and to explore some ideas about how to account for these variations and think about their consequences for democratic politics. We place our primary focus on the relation between media systems and political systems, and therefore emphasize the analysis of journalism and the news media, and, to a somewhat lesser extent, media policy and law.

---

[1] Some important statements of this ambition in communication include Blumler, McLeod, and Rosengren (1992), Blumler and Gurevitch (1995), and Curran and Park (2000).

## WHY COMPARATIVE ANALYSIS?

It is worth dwelling for a moment on one of the most basic insights of Siebert, Peterson, and Schramm: the idea that if we want to address a question such as "Why is the press as it is?" we must turn to comparative analysis. The role of comparative analysis in social theory can be understood in terms of two basic functions: its role in concept formation and clarification and its role in causal inference.[2]

Comparative analysis is valuable in social investigation, in the first place, because it sensitizes us to variation and to similarity, and this can contribute powerfully to concept formation and to the refinement of our conceptual apparatus. Most of the literature on the media is highly ethnocentric, in the sense that it refers only to the experience of a single country, yet is written in general terms, as though the model that prevailed in that country were universal. This, at least, is true in the countries with the most-developed media scholarship, including the United States, Britain, France, and Germany. In countries with less developed traditions of media research, another pattern often emerges: a tendency to borrow the literature of other countries – usually the Anglo-American or the French literature – and to treat that borrowed literature as though it could be applied unproblematically anywhere. We believe this style of research has often held media researchers back from even posing the question, "Why are the media as they are?" Important aspects of media systems are assumed to be "natural," or in some cases are so familiar that they are not perceived at all. Because it "denaturalizes" a media system that is so familiar to us, comparison forces us to conceptualize more clearly what aspects of that system actually require explanation. In that sense comparative analysis, as Blumler and Gurevitch (1975: 76) say, has the "capacity to render the invisible visible," to draw our attention to aspects of any media system, including our own, that "may be taken for granted and difficult to detect when the focus is on only one national case." Our own comparative work began with the experience of exactly this type of insight. Comparing U.S. and Italian TV news in the early 1980s, familiar patterns of news construction, which we had to some extent assumed were the natural form of TV news, were revealed to us as products of a particular system. We were thus forced to notice and to try to account for many things we had passed over, for

---

[2] Basic works on the comparative method, beyond those cited in the text, include Marsh (1964), Przeworski and Teune (1970), Tilly (1984), Dogan and Pelassy (1990), and Collier (1993).

example, the highly interpretive character of American compared with Italian TV news, a characteristic that contradicted common assumptions about "objective" journalism in the American system (Hallin and Mancini 1984).

Comparative analysis makes it possible to notice things we did not notice and therefore had not conceptualized, and it also forces us to clarify the scope and applicability of the concepts we do employ. Comparative studies, as Bendix (1963: 535) puts it, "provide an important check on the generalizations implicit" in our concepts and forces us to clarify the limits of their application. Sociologists, for example, had assumed "urbanization" to be so closely associated with secularism and Western forms of individualism that the latter could be treated as part of the very notion of urbanism – a generalization that, Bendix argued, fell apart when we looked at India or other non–Western societies. In a similar way we will try to clarify the conceptual definitions of a number of key concepts in media studies – journalistic professionalization, for example – and to use comparative analysis to discover which aspects of those concepts really do vary together and which do not.

If comparison can sensitize us to variation, it can also sensitize us to similarity, and that too can force us to think more clearly about how we might explain media systems. In the United States, for example, media coverage of politicians has become increasingly negative over the past few decades. We typically explain that change by reference to historical events such as Vietnam and Watergate, as well as changes in the conduct of election campaigns. This trend is not, however, unique to the United States. Indeed, it is virtually universal across Western democracies. The generality of this change, of course, suggests that particular historical events internal to the United States are not an adequate explanation. Comparative analysis can protect us from false generalizations, as Bendix says, but can also encourage us to move from overly particular explanations to more general ones where this is appropriate.

Of course, comparative analysis does not automatically bring these benefits. It can be ethnocentric itself, imposing on diverse systems a framework that reflects the point of view of one of these – though this is probably most true of work that, similar to *Four Theories of the Press*, purports to be comparative but is not in fact based on comparative analysis. We will argue later in this chapter that ethnocentrism has been intensified in the field of communication by the strongly normative character of much theory. Comparison can indeed be ethnocentric. We believe, however, the comparative method properly applied provides a basis for systematic critique of work that falls into these patterns of overgeneralization and conceptual narrowness.

The second reason comparison is important in social investigation is that it allows us in many cases to test hypotheses about the interrelationships among social phenomena. "We have only one means of demonstrating that one phenomenon is the cause of another: it is to compare the cases where they are simultaneously present or absent," wrote Émile Durkheim (1965) in *The Rules of Sociological Method*. This has become the standard methodology in much of the social sciences, particularly among those interested in analyzing social phenomena at the system level, where variation will often not exist in a single-country study. There are, of course, many epistemological debates surrounding the effort to find "sociological rules" in Durkheim's sense. Some believe social theory should follow the natural sciences in the search for laws that are "always and everywhere the case"; others believe that the generalizations of social theory will necessarily be relative to particular systems and historical contexts. Some believe explanation requires a clear identification of cause and effect, "dependent" and "independent" variable; others think in terms of identifying patterns of coevolution of social phenomena that might not always be separated into cause and effect. In the field of communication, those who do analysis at the system level often tend to be skeptical of "positivism"; the "positivists" in the field tend to be concentrated among people working at the individual level. For many years empirical research in communication was almost synonymous with the media effects paradigm, which was concerned not with larger media structures but with the effects of particular messages on individual attitudes and beliefs. This may be one reason systematic use of comparative analysis has developed slowly. We believe, however, that it is not necessary to adopt strong claims of the identity between natural and social science to find comparative analysis useful in sorting out relationships between media systems and their social and political settings.

Let us take one example here. Jeffrey Alexander, in an unusual and very interesting attempt to offer a comparative framework for the analysis of the news media, poses the question of how to explain the particular strength of autonomous journalistic professionalism in the United States. One hypothesis he offers is that "it is extremely significant that no labor papers tied to working class parties emerged on a mass scale in the United States" (1981: 31). He goes on to contrast U.S. press history with that of France and Britain, and advances the claim that the absence of a labor press in the United States explains the development of autonomous professionalism. We will discuss Alexander's important theoretical framework in greater detail in Chapters 4 and 8. As for the particular hypothesis about the labor press, comparative analysis allows us fairly easily to dismiss it, once we go beyond the comparison between the United States and France. There are a number of cases in Europe where a strong labor press and strong professional autonomy of journalists both developed; indeed we argue that this pattern is typical of most of Northern Europe. What other factors might account for journalistic autonomy we take up later (as well as a number of questions about how to define it).

The use of comparative analysis for causal inference belongs to a relatively advanced stage in the process of analysis. Our own study is primarily exploratory in character, using comparative analysis to serve the first cluster of purposes previously outlined, for conceptual clarification and theory development, much more than for the second, for hypothesis testing and causal inference. Our purpose here is to develop a framework for comparing media systems and a set of hypotheses about how they are linked structurally and historically to the development of the political system, but we do not claim to have tested those hypotheses here, in part because of severe limitations of data underscored in the following text.

Comparative analysis, particularly of the broad synthetic sort we are attempting here, is extremely valuable but difficult to do well, especially when the state of the field is relatively primitive. It is risky to generalize across many nations, whose media systems, histories, and political cultures we cannot know with equal depth. This is why we have undertaken this project as a collaboration between an American and a European. Some might wonder why we did not try to organize a broader collaboration. There are, of course, many practical difficulties in such an enterprise, but the fundamental reason is that our purpose in this book is to produce a cogent theoretical framework – or at least to move toward one. Multinational collaborations in our field have often tended to fall back on the least common denominator in terms of theory, or to leave theoretical differences unresolved. We hope that scholars will find our general arguments interesting enough to excuse occasional errors or lack of subtlety in dealing with particular cases. In comparative research, much of the real collaboration is of course indirect. Our study builds on a growing body of scholarship across Europe and North America, and we hope that many of these scholars will eventually carry the ideas proposed in this volume much further than we can do here.

## SCOPE OF THE STUDY

This study covers the media systems of the United States, Canada, and most of Western Europe, excluding only very small countries (e.g., Luxembourg, much of whose media system is actually directed toward audiences in neighboring countries). Our study is thus based on a "most similar systems" design. As Lijphart (1971) stresses, one of the greatest problems in comparative analysis is the problem of "many variables, few cases." One of the principal means of solving that problem, he notes, is to focus on a set of relatively comparable cases, in which the number of relevant variables will be reduced. This approach will reduce the number of cases; but in a field such as communication, where the existing literature and available data are limited, this is often a benefit as well in the sense that it is impossible for analysts to handle competently more than a limited number of cases. One of the problems of *Four Theories of the Press*, as we noted, is that its scope is so grand that it is almost inevitably superficial: like a photo with too much contrast, it obscures too much of the detail we need to see.[3] By limiting ourselves to North America and Western Europe we are dealing with systems that have relatively comparable levels of economic development and much common culture and political history. This is a limitation, obviously: the models developed here will not apply without considerable adaptation to most other areas of the world, though we hope they will be useful to scholars working on other regions as points of reference against which other models can be constructed. One advantage of this focus is the fact that the media models that prevail in Western Europe and North America tend to be the dominant models globally; understanding their logic and evolution is therefore likely to be of some use to scholars of other regions not only as an example of how to conduct comparative research but also because these models have actually influenced the development of other systems.

Our study, as mentioned previously, is an exploratory one, and the main purpose of the "most similar systems" design is not to hold certain variables constant for purposes of demonstrating causality, but to permit careful development of concepts that can be used for further comparative analysis, as well as hypotheses about their interrelations. The fact that

---

[3] Another example is Martin and Chaudhary (1983), which attempts a global analysis of media systems, dividing the world into "three ideological systems," the Western, Communist, and Third World – a noble attempt to cover the whole world, but obviously one that involves huge generalizations within these groups. There are also collections that impose little in the way of a common analytical framework, for example Nimmo and Mansfield (1982).

it is an exploratory study also means that the geographical definition of its scope is in some ways arbitrary: we did not already have a theoretical framework that could provide the basis for selection of cases. Instead we followed the familiar strategy of limiting the study to a region on the assumption that this would result in a reasonably comparable set of cases. "Comparability," as Lijphart (1971: 689) says, "is not inherent in any given area, but it is more likely in an area than in a randomly selected set of countries." The area approach also made the study more manageable in a practical sense – we were able to visit the countries more easily, for instance, and to take advantage of the relatively large amount of comparable data compiled on European media systems. We could probably have added Australia and New Zealand – whose historical connections make them very similar to Western European countries – to our study without making the conceptual framework significantly more complex. We suspect, however, that most other cases we might have added would have introduced important new variables, straining our ability to master the relevant literatures and present the resultant framework in a coherent way. In Chapter 4 we introduce a triangular drawing on which each of our cases is represented in relation to three media-system models. Any significant multiplication of cases would probably have made such a two-dimensional representation impossible!

The desire to "reduce the property space of the analysis," in Lijphart's terms, is also reflected in our decision to focus primarily on news media and media regulation. A comparative analysis of media systems certainly could include much more about cultural industries – film, music, television and other entertainment; telecommunication; public relations; and a number of other areas. But this would involve other literatures and require very different sets of concepts and we will not try to take it on here.

## THE LEGACY OF *FOUR THEORIES OF THE PRESS*

Since we began with *Four Theories of the Press*, a work that remains remarkably influential around the world as an attempt to lay out a broad framework for comparative analysis of the news media, it makes sense to follow Siebert, Peterson, and Schramm's argument a bit further.[4]

---

[4] Many variations of the Siebert, Peterson, and Schramm schema have been proposed over the years, for example by Altschull (1995), Hachten (1996), Mundt (1991), and Picard (1985), who proposes to add a model that corresponds more or less to what we will call the Democratic Corporatist Model. McQuail (1994: 131–2) summarizes a number of the revisions of *Four Theories*.

"The thesis of this volume," they continue, "is that the press always takes on the form and coloration of the social and political structures within which it operates. Especially, it reflects the system of social control whereby the relations of individuals and institutions are adjusted. We believe that an understanding of these aspects of society is basic to any systematic understanding of the press" (1–2). Here again, we think the problem is well posed. We shall follow the agenda set out by Siebert, Peterson, and Schramm in attempting to show how different media models are rooted in broader differences of political and economic structure. We will argue that one cannot understand the news media without understanding the nature of the state, the system of political parties, the pattern of relations between economic and political interests, and the development of civil society, among other elements of social structure.

On one point, we will leave matters a bit more open than the authors of *Four Theories of the Press*. Note that Siebert, Peterson, and Schramm seem to assume that the media will always be the "dependent variable" in relation to the "system of social control," which it "reflects." In this sense, their formulation is ironically similar to a traditional Marxist base and superstructure theory (though as we shall see in a moment they quickly stand Marx on his head). In many cases it may be reasonable to assume that the media system essentially "reflects" other aspects of social structure – the party system, for example. But there is good evidence that media institutions have an impact of their own on other social structures.

There is also historical variation in the degree to which media are reflective or independently influential, and many scholars have argued that there is an important trend in the direction of greater media influence, particularly in relation to the political system. The belief that the media have become an important "exogenous" variable affecting other political institutions is one reason scholars in comparative politics have begun to pay attention to media institutions they previously ignored. It is worth noting that, just as communication scholars have paid little attention to comparative analysis, scholars of comparative politics have paid little attention to the media. One can search the index of the classic works on political parties and find virtually nothing on the press or media, even though politicians have certainly been preoccupied by – and occupied in – the latter as long as political parties have existed, and even though those classic works often *define* parties as communicative institutions (Deutsch 1966; Sartori 1976), a theoretical perspective that would seem to suggest they would have an important pattern of relationships with other institutions of communication.

Today this is beginning to change, due in part to a growing feeling that the media are less "reflective" than they once were. Sometimes this change may actually be exaggerated. Media scholars – following the tradition of McLuhan – often tend to have a professional bias toward over-stressing the independent influence of media. And scholars from other fields sometimes do so as well, perhaps out of a sense that the media are "overstepping their bounds" as they become more powerful relative to other sorts of institutions. Bourdieu's recent work, *On Television* (1998), might be an example here, as well as much speculation in comparative politics about "videocracy." In Chapter 8, we will address the question of the reciprocal influences of the media and the political system, and try to sort out some of the arguments about the relative influence of media system change in shaping contemporary European political systems.

Siebert, Peterson, and Schramm go on:

> To see the differences between press systems in full perspective, then, one must look at the social systems in which the press functions. To see the social systems in their true relationship to the press, one has to look at certain basic beliefs and assumptions which the society holds: the nature of man, the nature of society and the state, the relation of man to the state, and the nature of knowledge and truth. Thus, in the last analysis the difference between press systems is one of philosophy, and this book is about the philosophical and political rationales or theories which lie behind the different kinds of press we have in the world today (2).

At this point, we part company with Siebert, Peterson, and Schramm. To be sure, we too believe that political culture is important, and we will try to show how differences in media systems are connected with socially shared conceptions about state and society, objectivity, the public interest, and the like. But the focus on "philosophies" of the press – or as one might also call them, "ideologies" of the press – points to what we see as a key failing of *Four Theories of the Press*. Siebert, Peterson, and Schramm did not, in fact, empirically analyze the relation between media systems and social systems. They looked neither at the actual functioning of media systems nor at that of the social systems in which they operated, but only at the "rationales or theories" by which those systems legitimated themselves. "In arguing that 'in the last instance the difference between

9

press systems is one of philosophy' the book disregards the material existence of the media" (Nerone 1995: 23).

Nor was their analysis actually comparative. In part, this was because of the background of the Cold War: because it is so preoccupied with the dichotomy between the contending U.S. and Soviet models, *Four Theories of the Press* has little room for the actual diversity of world media systems. In tracing the origins of the four theories, for example, Siebert, Peterson, and Schramm make reference almost exclusively to three countries – the United States, to which they trace the libertarian and social responsibility theories; Britain, to which they trace both the authoritarian and, along with the United States, the libertarian theories; and the Soviet Union. All the models, moreover, are really "defined . . . from within one of the four theories – classical liberalism" (Nerone 1995: 21). The four theories are of limited use in understanding the European experience. One could say that Western Europe has combined the libertarian model (manifested in the relatively unregulated commercial and party press and the tradition of advocacy journalism); the social responsibility model (public broadcasting, right-of-reply laws, press subsidies, press councils); and the authoritarian tradition (Gaullist state broadcasting or the British Official Secrets Act, as well as the controls exercised in periods of real dictatorship). One could probably say that *any* system combines these elements in some way. But this is far too thin a framework to begin a real comparative analysis.

*Four Theories of the Press* has stalked the landscape of media studies like a horror-movie zombie for decades beyond its natural lifetime. We think it is time to give it a decent burial and move on to the development of more sophisticated models based on real comparative analysis.[5]

## MEDIA SYSTEM MODELS

One reason *Four Theories of the Press* has proved so influential over so many years is that there is a great deal of appeal in the idea that the world's media systems can be classified using a small number of simple, discreet models. Is it possible to replace the four theories with a new set of models, better-grounded empirically but sharing something of the parsimony of the originals? Only with great caution. We will in fact introduce three media system models. These will be elaborated more fully

---

[5] A discussion of the historical background of the book and further critical analysis can be found in Nerone (1995).

in the following chapter, but briefly they are the Liberal Model, which prevails across the Britain, Ireland, and North America; the Democratic Corporatist Model, which prevails across northern continental Europe; and the Polarized Pluralist Model, which prevails in the Mediterranean countries of southern Europe. The Liberal Model is characterized by a relative dominance of market mechanisms and of commercial media; the Democratic Corporatist Model by a historical coexistence of commercial media and media tied to organized social and political groups, and by a relatively active but legally limited role of the state; and the Polarized Pluralist Model by integration of the media into party politics, weaker historical development of commercial media, and a strong role of the state. We will try to show that the characteristics that define these models are interrelated, that they result from a meaningful pattern of historical development, and do not merely co-occur accidentally. We will also use these models to organize the discussion of the media systems of individual countries, trying to show how each country's media system does and does not fit these patterns.

Many qualifications must be introduced as soon as we begin to use these models. They are ideal types, and the media systems of individual countries fit them only roughly. There is considerable variation among countries that we will be grouping together in our discussion of these models. The British and American media systems (which we will discuss as examples of the Liberal Model) are in fact quite different in many ways, even though it is common to talk about the Anglo-American model of journalism as though it were singular. Italy, with a "consensus" political system and a full half-century of democratic government is quite different from Spain, with a majoritarian system and a much later transition to democracy, though both are close to the Polarized Pluralist Model in many characteristics. We will discuss Germany in relation to the Democratic Corporatist Model, though it is quite different from the small democracies that represent the classic cases of that model. We will discuss France in relation to the Polarized Pluralist Model of the Mediterranean countries, but we shall see that it is something of a mixed case between the Polarized Pluralist and Democratic Corporatist Models, as Britain is a mixed case between the Liberal and Democratic Corporatist Models. In part we hope that the models will be useful precisely in bringing these variations to light. It should be stressed that their primary purpose is not classification of individual systems, but the identification of characteristic patterns of relationship between system characteristics.

It is also important to note that media systems are not homogeneous. They are often characterized by a complex coexistence of media operating according to different principles. "In most countries," as McQuail (1994: 133) puts it, "the media do not constitute any single 'system,' with a single purpose or philosophy, but are composed of many separate, overlapping, often inconsistent elements, with appropriate differences of normative expectation and actual regulation." In Britain, for example, it could be said that there historically have been three distinct cultures of journalism, sharing some common characteristics, to be sure, but diverging sharply on others – the tabloid press, the quality press, and broadcasting. Our models are in this way quite different from those of *Four Theories of the Press*. They describe not a common philosophy but an interrelated system (McQuail declines to use the term *system*, but its use does not really imply homogeneity) that may involve a characteristic division of labor or even a characteristic conflict between media principles.

Finally, the models should not be understood as describing static systems. The media systems we are describing here have been in a process of continual change, and were very different in 1960 than in 1990. If Britain historically has had three journalistic cultures (others actually can be identified if we go back further in history) they are much less distinct today than they were twenty years ago. The models, we hope, will be seen not as describing a set of fixed characteristics, but as identifying some of the underlying systemic relationships that help us to understand these changes.

We will pay considerable attention to history in this analysis. Media institutions evolve over time; at each step of their evolution past events and institutional patterns inherited from earlier periods influence the direction they take. We shall see, for example, that there is a strong correlation between literacy rates in 1890 and newspaper circulation rates today, and that where mass circulation newspapers exist they almost always trace their origin to this era. North (1990) has called this "path dependence." Path dependence means only that the past has a powerful influence. It does not mean present or future institutions must essentially *resemble* those of the past, or that change is absent. We shall see that the media systems of Western Europe and North America have in fact changed very substantially in recent years. We shall see in particular that globalization and commercialization of the media has led to considerable convergence of media systems.

One question we cannot answer is whether the distinct models we identify here, which emerged in Western democracies in the mid-twentieth century, will eventually disappear altogether. Media systems have historically been rooted in the institutions of the nation state, in part because of their close relationship to the political world. National differentiation of media systems is clearly diminishing; whether that process of convergence will stop at a certain point or continue until national differentiation becomes irrelevant we cannot yet know.

## DO WE NEED NORMATIVE THEORIES OF THE MEDIA?

The field of communication, and most particularly the study of journalism, has always been heavily normative in character. This is due in part to its rooting in professional education, where it is more important to reflect on what journalism *should be* than to analyze in detail what and why it *is*. Thus a book such as *The World's Great Dailies: Profiles of Fifty Newspapers* (Merrill and Fisher 1980) obviously includes not those newspapers most typical of journalism in their respective countries or those with the highest circulation, but "great" newspapers, those that are in some sense models of professional practice. *Four Theories of the Press* is also clearly normative in character (its subtitle is *The Authoritarian, Libertarian, Social Responsibility and Communist Concepts of What the Press Should Be and Do*) judging world press systems in terms of their distance from the liberal ideal of a neutral "watchdog" press free from state interference. Much subsequent comparative analysis, especially in the United States, was tied to modernization theory, which similarly compared world press systems against the liberal ideal, only with underdevelopment rather than totalitarianism as the opposing pole.[6]

The Liberal Model enshrined in normative theory, based primarily on the American and to a somewhat lesser extent the British experience, has become so widely diffused around the world – partly, as Blanchard (1986) points out, as a result of campaign mounted by the U.S. government and press in the early years of the Cold War – that other conceptions of journalism often are not conceptualized clearly even by their own practitioners. Even within the United States, the normative ideal of the neutral independent watchdog leads to blind spots in journalists' understanding of what they do, obscuring many functions – for example, that of celebrating consensus values (Hallin 1986: 116–18) – that fall outside the normative model. The gap between ideal and reality is far

---

[6] This is true, for example, of the studies summarized in Edelstein (1982). See the critical discussion of comparative research in Hardt (1988).

greater in countries such as Italy or Spain where journalists will express allegiance to the Liberal Model of neutrality and objectivity, while the actual practice of journalism is deeply rooted in partisan advocacy traditions. In scholarship, too, the Anglo-American Liberal Model has been conceptualized much more fully – even by its critics – than other media system models. And there is a strong tendency for comparative discussions to privilege normative judgments, often in a rather Manichaean mode (like *Four Theories of the Press*). Again, this is true of defenders of the Liberal Model, Alexander (1981), for example, and critics such as Chalaby (1998), who recounts French and British media history as a shift toward what for him is the anti-ideal of depoliticized commercial media.

We are interested here not in measuring media systems against a normative ideal, but in analyzing their historical development as institutions within particular social settings. We want to understand why they developed in the particular ways that they did; what roles they actually play in political, social, and economic life; and what patterns of relationship they have with other social institutions. Our models of journalism are intended as empirical, not normative models.

This does not mean that we are uninterested in normative questions, nor, certainly, that we mean to adopt an attitude of functionalist relativism, assuming that any media institutions that exist must *ipso facto* be assumed to perform positive functions for the society as a whole. We will try to show, in fact, that comparative analysis can be extremely useful in addressing the kinds of normative questions that legitimately concern communication scholars. Does commercialization support or undercut the independence of the media? Is the diversity of voices in a plural society better represented in a media system with external or internal pluralism – that is, news media that represent distinct political orientations or news media that seek to report the news in a "balanced" way? Which is more responsive to new voices emerging in society: a professionalized commercial press or one more closely tied to the political system? Comparative analysis can help us to address these kinds of questions, first, by giving us a clearer sense of the range of different kinds of institutional arrangements that have evolved to deal with the problems of communication in a democratic society and, second, by allowing us to assess the actual consequences of these institutional structures for the values we consider important – diversity; openness and responsiveness; independence; and accuracy and completeness of information.

We suspect that in most cases comparative analysis would suggest complex answers to these kinds of questions. That is, it would help us specify *under what circumstances* commercialization leads to media independence, under what circumstances it undercuts it, and under what circumstances other institutional arrangements might be more conducive to the realization of that value. And we will insist in addressing normative questions that these questions can never be answered in a purely abstract and universal way. It is not clear that media models that "work" in one context would also "work" in another very different one. It is not clear that one could have transplanted American neutral commercial journalism, for instance, or British tabloid journalism to 1950s Netherlands or 1970s Italy and expect it to have had any credibility to audiences or any relevance to democratic politics as it was actually conducted in those contexts. Similarly, we may judge party newspapers to be of little relevance to the democratic process in Western Europe at the beginning of the twenty-first century, but this does not mean we can dismiss their significance in the different political context in which they flourished some decades ago – or, perhaps, deny that in some other political system they might play an important role today. Any judgment we make about a media system has to be based on a clear understanding of its social context – of such elements as the divisions existing within society, the political process by which they were (or were not) resolved, and the prevailing patterns of political belief.

## LIMITATIONS OF DATA

"Writing in 1975, nobody could claim to be able to paint an assured portrait of the field of investigation to be discussed in this essay." So wrote Blumler and Gurevitch (1975 [1995]) in an early effort to develop a framework for comparative analysis in political communication. "It is not only that few political communication studies have yet been mounted with a comparative focus. More to the point, there is [no] settled view of what such studies should be concerned with ... (59)." Things are a little better today. A number of genuinely comparative studies have been done, and scholarly communication across national boundaries has increased substantially (this is manifested, for example, in the creation of the *European Journal of Communication* in 1985). Nevertheless, the basic situation is as Blumler and Gurevitch described it in 1975: limitations of comparative data impose severe restrictions on our ability to draw any firm conclusions about the relations between media and social systems.

In some ways, comparative research in communication may be inherently harder than in some fields. Those who study comparative politics, for example, can take advantage of the structured choices that characterize electoral politics to generate quantitative data that are relatively easy to compare across systems. It is easy enough to come up with comparable quantitative data on things such as newspaper circulation, state subsidies to the press, or (slightly more difficult) ownership concentration. Although even when dealing with very concrete kinds of information – whether particular countries had right-of-reply laws, for example, or whether they allowed paid political advertising – we were surprised at how difficult it could be to find information on all the countries in our study, and often found contradictions in the published literature or between that literature and scholars we consulted in each country. The situation is far more difficult with something such as the day-to-day flow of political discourse in the media, the significance of which is often dependent on subtle cultural cues that may be inherently harder to study comparatively than much of the subject matter of comparative politics and certainly harder to quantify. We would stress here that comparative research by no means requires quantitative data, though such data can often be extremely useful. To a large extent what we need in communication is more qualitative case studies based, for example, in discourse analysis or field observation – case studies carried out with a theoretical focus that gives them broader significance for the comparative understanding of media systems.[7] This brings us back to the fundamental problem identified by Blumler and Gurevitch in 1975: the fact that we are still so unclear on what to look for when we do comparative research on media systems. It is toward this conceptual problem that our book is directed. Given the limitations of the existing research, we cannot claim to test most of the hypotheses we raise here. Neither will we attempt to fill the gap of comparative research. Our analysis is based primarily on existing published sources and we make only very limited attempts at new empirical research. It is our intent instead to propose a theoretical synthesis and a framework for comparative research on the media and political systems.

---

[7] On the role of case studies in comparative analysis see Lijphart (1971), George (1979), George and McKeowan (1985).

## PLAN OF THE BOOK

The remainder of the book is divided into three parts. Part I introduces the theoretical framework. In Chapter 2 we propose a set of dimensions for comparing media systems and address a number conceptual issues that arise in relation to those dimensions. In Chapter 3 we focus on characteristics of the political system and of sociopolitical history that we believe are important to understanding the development of media systems, and propose a number of hypotheses about links between political and media system characteristics. In Chapter 4 we introduce the three models, then go on to discuss the relation of these models to more general perspectives in social theory, particularly differentiation theory, which – we will argue – is implicit in much communication theory that assumes the Liberal Model as a norm, and critics of differentiation theory, particularly Habermas and Bourdieu.

Part II discusses the three models in detail: the Mediterranean or Polarized Pluralist Model in Chapter 5; the North/Central European or Democratic Corporatist Model in Chapter 6; and the North Atlantic or Liberal Model in Chapter 7. Here we examine the historical development and the structural and cultural logic of each system, consider how particular cases fit the general model, and attempt to establish the plausibility of the framework we propose in Part I.

Part III concludes our study by focusing on the transformations currently under way in media systems in Western Europe and North America. Chapter 8 focuses on homogenization or convergence of media systems, addressing the forces of change that are eroding the differences among three media systems we explore here – and generally pushing them in the direction of the Liberal Model – as well as the limits of these forces. Chapter 8 also returns to the theoretical debate over differentiation, to consider to what extent the language of "modernization" connected to differentiation theory can serve as a framework for understanding media system convergence. In the concluding chapter we assess what we have learned from this study, and what we propose for the future of comparative analysis of media and political systems.

PART I

# Concepts and Models

LIVERPOOL JOHN MOORES UNIVERSITY
LEARNING SERVICES

# TWO

# Comparing Media Systems

In this chapter we propose a framework for comparing media systems. We propose, specifically, four major dimensions according to which media systems in Western Europe and North America can usefully be compared: (1) the development of media markets, with particular emphasis on the strong or weak development of a mass circulation press; (2) political parallelism; that is, the degree and nature of the links between the media and political parties or, more broadly, the extent to which the media system reflects the major political divisions in society; (3) the development of journalistic professionalism; and (4) the degree and nature of state intervention in the media system. Note that each of these can be seen in some sense as a single, quantitative dimension. That is, we can speak about high or low levels of press circulation, political parallelism, journalistic professionalism, or state intervention. But we shall also see that each of these dimensions is complex and that many more subtle qualitative distinctions become important as we begin to analyze concrete media systems. In many cases we will also introduce related, minor dimensions along which media systems may vary. Ours is not, of course, the first attempt to set forth a framework of this sort. We have tried to build on previous work, refining it based on our attempt to make sense of the patterns of difference and similarity we have found among the countries covered here, and to link these patterns to the social and political context in which they evolved. One version particularly close to our own is that of Blumler and Gurevitch (1995). Blumler and Gurevitch proposed, originally in 1975, four dimensions for comparative analysis: (1) degree of state control over mass media organization; (2) degree of mass media partisanship; (3) degree of media-political elite integration; and (4) the nature of the legitimating creed of media institutions. Their first dimension coincides with our fourth; their second and third dimensions we treat as related components of political parallelism; and their fourth dimension essentially coincides with our professionalization dimension.

What we will try to do in this chapter is to define these four dimensions, along with a number of concepts related to them, to clarify some of the more problematic concepts and to illustrate some of the kinds of variation that can be found among media systems. In doing this we will often give illustrations drawn from our analysis of particular media systems. These illustrations, of course, cannot be fully developed here, and will be explained at much greater length in Part II.

## THE STRUCTURE OF MEDIA MARKETS: THE DEVELOPMENT OF A MASS PRESS

One of the most obvious differences among media systems has to do with the development of the mass circulation press. In some countries mass circulation newspapers developed in the late nineteenth and early twentieth century. In others they did not. That historical difference is reflected today in sharply different rates of newspaper circulation, from a high of 720 per thousand adult population in Norway to a low of 78 per thousand in Greece. As can be seen in Table 2.1, high rates of newspaper circulation are characteristic of Scandinavia and other parts of Northern Europe, and low rates characteristic of Southern Europe.

The distinction here is not only one of quantity. It is also a distinction in the nature of the newspaper, its relation to its audience and its role in the wider process of social and political communication. The newspapers of Southern Europe are addressed to a small elite – mainly urban, well-educated, and politically active. They are both sophisticated and politicized in their content, and can be said to be involved in a *horizontal* process of debate and negotiation among elite factions. The newspapers of Northern Europe and North America, by contrast, tend to be addressed to a mass public not necessarily engaged in the political world. They are, in this sense, involved in a *vertical* process of communication, mediating between political elites and the ordinary citizen, though they may at the same time play a role in the horizontal process of interelite communication.

The newspapers of Southern Europe, with their relatively low circulations, have not historically been profitable business enterprises, and have often been subsidized by political actors, a fact that has important implications for the degree of political parallelism and of journalistic professionalism discussed in the following text. The high-circulation

Table 2.1 *Newspaper Sales per 1,000 Adult Population, 2000*

| | |
|---|---|
| Norway | 719.7 |
| Finland | 545.2 |
| Sweden | 541.1 |
| Switzerland | 453.7 |
| United Kingdom | 408.5 |
| Germany | 375.2 |
| Austria | 374.3 |
| Denmark | 347.1 |
| Netherlands | 345.9 |
| United States | 263.6 |
| Canada | 205.7 |
| Ireland | 191 |
| France | 190 |
| Belgium | 186.5 |
| Spain | 129.4 |
| Italy | 121.4 |
| Portugal | 82.7 |
| Greece | 77.5 |

*Source:* World Association of Newspapers, *World Press Trends.*

newspaper markets of Northern Europe, on the other hand, have sustained strong commercial media enterprises, though as we shall see in many high-circulation countries commercial media have coexisted with media rooted more in the world of politics: the growth of a mass circulation press is by no means synonymous with commercialization.

One interesting manifestation of this difference in patterns of development of the press is the fact that there are large gender differences in newspaper readership in Southern Europe, while these differences are small or nonexistent in the other regions covered here. This pattern is shown in Table 2.2, which shows gender gaps ranging from a 35 percent difference between male and female readership in Portugal, to only 1 percent in Sweden. This reflects historical differences in literacy rates, as well as differences in the function of the media. Because the media were closely tied to the political world in Southern Europe, and because women were historically excluded from that sphere, the habit of newspaper reading never developed among women there.

Table 2.2 *Gender Differences in Newspaper Reach, 2000*

|  | Men | Women | Male/Female |
|---|---|---|---|
| Portugal | 58.3 | 24.1 | 2.41 |
| Spain | 47 | 26.2 | 1.79 |
| Italy** | 50.2 | 29.8 | 1.68 |
| Greece | 22.5 | 17.2 | 1.31 |
| Belgium | 57.9 | 47.5 | 1.21 |
| Canada | 64.6 | 54.9 | 1.17 |
| Netherlands | 70.8 | 60.7 | 1.16 |
| United States | 59 | 52 | 1.13 |
| Switzerland | 78 | 72 | 1.08 |
| Austria | 78.4 | 73.2 | 1.07 |
| France | 34.3 | 32 | 1.07 |
| United Kingdom* | 84 | 79 | 1.06 |
| Denmark | 76.1 | 72.1 | 1.06 |
| Ireland | 59 | 56 | 1.05 |
| Finland | 87 | 84 | 1.04 |
| Norway | 87 | 85 | 1.02 |
| Sweden | 89 | 88 | 1.01 |

*Source:* World Association of Newspapers, *World Press Trends.*
*National dailies only.
**1999.

The differential development of mass circulation newspapers is naturally accompanied by differences in the relative roles of print and electronic media. In countries where mass circulation newspapers are absent, the mass public relies heavily on electronic media for information about political affairs. Table 2.3 shows the relative importance of newspapers and television as sources of news (notice that the audience for television varies much less than the audience for newspapers).

OTHER ASPECTS OF MEDIA MARKET STRUCTURE. We place particular emphasis in this book on the wide differences in newspaper readership. These differences have deep historical roots. So far as we know no country that did not develop mass circulation newspapers in the late nineteenth to early twentieth century has ever subsequently developed them, even if its levels of literacy and pattern of political and economic development have converged with those of the high-circulation countries. And we will argue that the presence or absence of a mass circulation press has deep implications for the development of the media as political institutions.

Table 2.3 *Proportion of Public Watching or Reading News Every Day, and the Ratio of Television to Newspaper Consumption, European Union Countries, 2001*

|  | Television | Newspapers | TV/Newspapers |
|---|---|---|---|
| Greece | 65 | 13 | 5 |
| Portugal | 64 | 20 | 3.20 |
| Spain | 72 | 24 | 3 |
| Italy | 83 | 30 | 2.77 |
| France | 62 | 26 | 2.38 |
| Belgium | 60 | 30 | 2 |
| United Kingdom | 71 | 47 | 1.51 |
| Ireland | 67 | 46 | 1.46 |
| Denmark | 70 | 51 | 1.37 |
| Netherlands | 77 | 60 | 1.28 |
| Finland | 79 | 67 | 1.17 |
| Germany | 68 | 59 | 1.15 |
| Austria | 61 | 55 | 1.11 |
| Sweden | 69 | 70 | 0.99 |

*Source: Eurobarometer: Public Opinion in the European Union.* Report No. 55, October 2001. Brussels: European Commission.

However, there are a number of other aspects of the structure of media markets that will enter into our analysis from time to time. One of these, closely related to the development of a mass circulation press, is the distinction between media systems characterized by a clear separation between a sensationalist mass press and "quality" papers addressed to an elite readership (Britain is the strongest example) and those that lack such stratification of the newspaper market (or where it is developed to only a limited extent), either because they lack a mass circulation press altogether or because they are dominated by newspapers that serve elite and mass readerships simultaneously. Newspaper markets also vary in the balance of local, regional, and national newspapers. Some (Britain, Austria, Italy, Spain) are dominated by a national or super-regional press, some by local papers (the United States, Canada, Switzerland) and some (Germany, France, Scandinavia) have a combination of both. National newspaper markets, as we shall see, tend to produce a more politically differentiated press. Some media markets are simply bigger than others, which can have important implications for the number of media outlets, and hence for both state regulation of media and the relation of media outlets with political actors. Language factors can also be important, dividing media markets into separate segments (as in Switzerland or Belgium) or increasing the importance of competition from outside a particular national market (as in Ireland, Canada, Austria, and Belgium).

## POLITICAL PARALLELISM

Journalism has always had many functions: it provides information for economic actors about prices and events such as shipwrecks, wars, or technological innovations that might affect their interests, and it provides entertainment in the form of human interest stories and the print equivalent of gossip. From the beginning of the print era, particularly from the time of the Reformation, political advocacy was also a central function of print media, and by the late eighteenth to early nineteenth century, when the newspaper began to emerge as a force in political life, this became its principal function in every country in this study. The political journalist was a publicist who saw it as his or her role to influence public opinion in the name of a political faction or cause, and in many cases newspapers were established on the initiative of political parties or other political actors, or supported by them. By the late nineteenth century a contrasting model of political journalism was beginning to emerge, in which the journalist was seen as a neutral arbiter of political communication, standing apart from particular interests and causes, providing information and analysis "uncolored" by partisanship. This was often connected with the development of a commercial press, whose purpose was to make money rather than to serve a political cause, and that was financed by advertising rather than by subsidies from political actors. It was also often connected with the development of journalistic professionalism, which is discussed in the following text.

No serious media analyst would argue that journalism anywhere in the world is literally neutral. A tremendous body of research has been devoted to debunking that notion, showing that even where journalists may be sincerely committed to a professional ideology of "objectivity," news incorporates political values, which arise from a range of influences, from routines of information gathering to recruitment patterns of journalists and shared ideological assumptions of the wider society. Neither would it be correct to draw too sharp a dichotomy between a commercial press and a politicized one: as we shall see, commercial media can be politically partisan, and noncommercial media – even those supported by political parties – can adopt norms of political balance. Nevertheless, important differences have persisted among media systems in the strength of connections between the media and political actors and in the balance between the advocacy and neutral/informational traditions of political journalism.

One of the most obvious differences among media systems lies in the fact that media in some countries have distinct political orientations, while media in other countries do not. Ask anyone who follows politics closely to give you a road map of the press, and, in many European countries, they are likely to move on fairly quickly to identifying newspapers by their political orientations – in Germany, the *Frankfurter Allgemeine* is right of center, the *Süddeutsche Zeitung* left of center; *Die Welt* further still to the right and the *Frankfurter Rundschau* further to the left. Even though the true party press has almost disappeared, and even if the political tendencies of European newspapers are fuzzier today than they were a generation ago, distinct political tendencies persist, more in some countries than in others – and not only in newspapers, but in many cases in electronic media as well. In the United States, no one could coherently map the politics of the media in this way; those on the left of the spectrum are likely to tell you that all the media slant to the right, and those on the right that they slant to the left.

This distinction is expressed by the concept of *party-press parallelism*, proposed in some of the earliest work on comparative analysis of media systems (Seymour-Ure 1974; Blumler and Gurevitch 1975), and which we will adapt by referring to the broader concept of *political parallelism*. What Seymour-Ure and other early comparative analysts meant by party-press parallelism was the degree to which the structure of the media system paralleled that of the party system. It exists in its strongest form when each news organization is aligned with a particular party, whose views it represents in the public sphere, as, for example in Denmark in the early twentieth century, when each town had four newspapers, representing the four major political parties. This kind of one-to-one connection between media and political parties is increasingly uncommon today, and where media are still differentiated politically, they more often are associated not with particular parties, but with general political tendencies: the *Frankfurter Allgemeine* is a paper of the right-center, not narrowly of the Christian Democratic party; the *Süddeutsche Zeitung* of the left-center, not narrowly of the Social Democrats, etc. In the Netherlands, Van der Eijk (2000: 320) describes *Die Volkskrant* as "oriented toward postmaterial values such as education, multiculturalism and socioeconomic equality." We will therefore use the more general term of *political parallelism*, while recognizing that party-press parallelism in the stricter sense does in some cases persist.

Political parallelism has a number of different components, and there are a number of indicators that can be used to assess how strongly it is present in a media system.[1] Perhaps most basically, it refers to *media content* – the extent to which the different media reflect distinct political orientations in their news and current affairs reporting, and sometimes also their entertainment content.

Historically, another of the most important components of political parallelism is *organizational connections* between media and political parties or other kinds of organizations, including trade unions, cooperatives, churches, and the like, which are often linked to political parties. Through much of the twentieth century many media organizations were connected to such institutions, which funded and helped to distribute them and whose goals the media served in a variety of ways. These kinds of organizational connections have mostly died out, though we will argue that their influence can still be seen in the media institutions of countries where they were once strong. Another, closely related component of political parallelism is the *tendency for media personnel to be active in political life*, often serving in party or public offices. This is also much less common today. Somewhat more common is a *tendency in some systems for the career paths of journalists and other media personnel to be shaped by their political affiliations*, in the sense that they work for media organizations whose politics coincide with their own, or get their jobs in part because their media organizations want to balance the representation of different political tendencies, or get the assignments they do because their political affiliations open certain political doors for them.

Political parallelism is also often manifested in the *partisanship of media audiences*, with supporters of different parties or tendencies buying different newspapers or watching different TV channels.

Finally, it is manifested in *journalistic role orientations and practices*. Journalists in some systems, and some historical periods, retain more of the "publicist" role that once prevailed in political journalism – that is, an orientation toward influencing public opinion. Journalists in other systems or periods, meanwhile, are more likely to see themselves as providers

---

[1] One attempt to measure political parallelism across systems is Patterson and Donsbach (1993).

of neutral information or entertainment, an orientation we would associate with a low level of political parallelism. These differences are connected with differences in emphasis on commentary or analysis versus news gathering. It is hard to imagine their German, Italian, or French contemporaries endorsing the claim of Joseph and Stuart Alsop (1958: 5), two of the most prominent American columnists of the 1950s (and thus among the few journalists of their age granted the privilege of writing commentary) that "His feet are a much more important part of a reporter's body than his head." To most continental European journalists in this period analysis and commentary were absolutely central to the function of the journalist. These kinds of differences in journalistic culture are associated with differences in writing style and other journalistic practices, with colorful or erudite commentary favored in some systems while a telegraphic informational style is favored in others; commentary rigidly segregated from news in some countries, and mixed more freely in others. These differences are also manifested in the organization of journalistic labor, with journalists in some systems moving fairly freely between the roles of reporter and commentator – if indeed the distinction has meaning to them at all – while in others those roles tend to be segregated. We will argue that the strength of advocacy traditions in journalism is connected with the history of institutional ties between the media and the system of parties and organized social groups, and we will treat these characteristics of journalistic culture also as indicators of political parallelism. In systems where political parallelism is strong, the culture and discursive style of journalism is closely related to that of politics.

Closely related to the concept of political parallelism is the distinction between two manners in which media systems handle diversity of political loyalties and orientations, which are referred to in the literature as internal and external pluralism. *External pluralism* can be defined as pluralism achieved at the level of the media system as a whole, through the existence of a range of media outlets or organizations reflecting the points of view of different groups or tendencies in society. Systems characterized by external pluralism will obviously be considered to have a high level of political parallelism. The contrary term, *internal pluralism*, is defined as pluralism achieved within each individual media outlet or organization. The term is actually used in two different ways in the media studies literature. We will generally use it to refer to cases where media organizations both avoid institutional ties to political groups and attempt to maintain neutrality and "balance" in their content. A system characterized by internal pluralism in this sense will have a low level of political parallelism. Internal pluralism is also sometimes used to refer to media organizations – usually broadcasting organizations – that formally represent a variety of political forces within the structure and content of a single organization (Hoffmann-Riem 1996). This could be understood as an intermediate level of political parallelism, as it means that political divisions are reflected in the structure of the organization, and often in the content, in the sense that, for instance, one current-affairs program may be run more by journalists from one political orientation, and one by journalists from another orientation.

## POLITICAL PARALLELISM IN BROADCAST GOVERNANCE AND REGULATION

Because they are public bodies, public broadcasting systems and the regulatory agencies responsible for supervising commercial broadcasting obviously have a significant relationship to the political system. These relationships vary significantly in form, however, and could also be said to reflect different degrees and forms of political parallelism. Four basic models can be distinguished for the governance of public broadcasting (c.f. Humphreys 1996: 155–8), and in most countries regulatory authorities tend to follow fairly similar patterns:

(1) The *government model* in which public broadcasting – which in this case approaches state broadcasting – is controlled directly by the government or by the political majority. The classic case of this form is French broadcasting under DeGaulle, which fell under the control of the Ministry of Information formally until 1964, and, in practice, through government control of appointments to the board of the formally independent Office de Radiodiffusion-Télévision Française (ORTF) from 1964 into the 1980s. Many European countries approached this model in an early phase of the history of broadcasting, but most eventually developed alternative institutional forms that would insulate public service broadcasting to a substantial degree from control by the political majority. It does still exist in more or less modified form, however, in the newest democracies of Western Europe, Greece, Portugal, and Spain. In the latter case, directors of public broadcasting are appointed by Parliament, not directly by the government, but this in the end gives the majority party effective control.

(2) The *professional model* is exemplified above all by the British Broadcasting Corporation (BBC), where a strong tradition developed that broadcasting should be largely insulated from political control and run by broadcasting professionals. As we shall see, this model is also characteristic of the Canadian Broadcasting Corporation (CBC), Irish public broadcasting, some Scandinavian countries, and public broadcasting in the United States.

(3) In the *parliamentary* or *proportional representation* model control over public broadcasting is divided among the political parties by proportional representation, as part of what is known in Italy as the *lottizzazione* or in German-speaking countries as the *proporz* principle. The classic example here would be Radiotelevisione Italiana (RAI) in the 1980s, where not only was the board of directors appointed by proportional representation, but the three channels were also divided among the parties: RAI 1 under the control of the Christian Democrats, RAI 2 under the control of the "secular" parties, and RAI 3 under the control of the Communist Party. Lower-level appointments within RAI also largely followed the principle of proportional representation. The parliamentary model is only really distinct from the government model in systems where coalition government and power sharing are typical – a distinction that will be explained further in the following text. In a majoritarian political system, even if public broadcasting is formally under the authority of parliament and not directly supervised by the government, appointment of the governing board by proportional representation results in control by the political majority, as in Spain.[2]

(4) The *"civic"* or *"corporatist"* model is similar to the parliamentary model in the sense that control of public service broadcasting is distributed among various social and political groups, but differs in that representation is extended beyond political parties to other kinds of "socially relevant groups" – trade unions, business associations, religious organizations, ethnic associations, and the like. The Dutch "pillarized" system, in which broadcasting was run directly by associations rooted in diverse religious and ideological subgroups, is the purest example of such a system. This model can also be seen

---

[2] In fact, as we shall see, the government parties in Italy had the predominant position; in this sense Italy, like other Southern European countries, shaded toward the government model.

in certain forms of community radio in Europe and in German broadcasting councils, which represent "socially relevant groups" along with political parties.

Kelly (1983) proposes a three-way distinction, to which we will also refer. Kelly distinguishes among what she calls politics-over-broadcasting systems, formally autonomous systems, and politics-in-broadcasting systems. What we have called the professional model is obviously a formally autonomous system; the government model is a politics-over-broadcasting system; and the parliamentary and civic models are typically politics-in-broadcasting systems, though some power-sharing systems are further along the spectrum toward politics-over-broadcasting systems, where the parties are particularly insistent on maintaining control. It should also be noted that the civic model can collapse into the parliamentary model where the "socially relevant groups" have close ties to political parties. The distinctions introduced by Kelly underline an important difference of philosophy. The professional, parliamentary, and civic/corporatist models are all, in some sense, solutions to the problem of how to keep public broadcasting, or a regulatory authority, from falling under the control of the most powerful political force and failing to serve a politically diverse society. The professional model solves the problem by attempting to insulate broadcasting from political interests in order to keep the parties and other organized interests *out* of the process of producing television and radio. The parliamentary and civic/corporatist models, which, as we shall see are typical of power-sharing or "consensus" political systems, attempt to solve the problem by making sure that all the major groups within society are included *in* the process. In terms of political parallelism, the professional model is obviously toward the low end of the spectrum, the government model toward the high end, and the other two models – the politics-in-broadcasting systems – are in between.

These models are not mutually exclusive, and in the real world they are almost always combined. Many systems, for example, combine proportional representation in appointments to the board of directors of public broadcasting with a culture and often legal norms that grant substantial autonomy to broadcasting professionals. Most systems in northern Europe can be understood as combinations of the parliamentary or civic/corporatist and the professional model. All modern broadcasting systems require professionals to run them and no system can work adequately if these professionals do not enjoy some degree of independence. All modern broadcasting systems are also subject to political pressures from the government, and in a pluralist political system all must have mechanisms for responding to the demands of various social and political groups. The particular ways in which these models are combined, however, do differ significantly between systems.

It should also be noted that distinguishing among these models requires looking beyond formal structures to the norms and practices that govern their actual operation as institutions. The BBC is a good example of this. The director general of the BBC is appointed by the prime minister. In its formal structure the BBC is not distinguishable from state-controlled broadcasting. Its distinctiveness, as we shall see, is rooted in the informal norms expectations that govern the selection of the director general, his or her relation to the government and opposition, and the role of journalists and other broadcasting professionals within the organization.

As noted, similar differences can be found in the governance of the regulatory authorities that oversee privately owned broadcasting. In particular a distinction can be made between more party-politicized authorities, in which the role of political parties is central, and those organized as independent public agencies (similar to a central bank) largely under the control of legal and technical experts.

## PROFESSIONALIZATION

The concepts of "professionalism" and "professionalization" – like many others in social science – have always been subject to sharp debate. Their boundaries are ambiguous and their core definitions have been subject to repeated reinterpretation. The ideal type of professionalization that has anchored most of the debate is based on the history of the classic "liberal" professions, above all medicine and law. Journalism departs substantially from that ideal type. One of the central criteria of this model is that the practice of a profession is "based on systematic knowledge or doctrine acquired only through long prescribed training" (Wilensky 1964: 138). Journalism has no such systematic body of knowledge or doctrine. Formal "professional" training has become increasingly common, and does often play an important role in defining journalism as an occupation and social institution. But it is clearly not essential to the practice of journalism, and there is not a strong correlation between professionalism as we define it here and formal training. In the United States, journalism degrees are actually less common at the most prestigious news organizations – whose journalists in other ways fit the concept of professionalization most closely – than those of less prestigious ones. Journalists in Spain, meanwhile, are much more likely to have journalism degrees than those in Germany, but this clearly does not mean that Spanish journalism is characterized by a higher level of professionalization than German journalism. Because formal training is unnecessary, moreover, entry to the profession of journalism is not formally regulated. Ironically, the only exception in Western Europe or North America is Italy, where membership in the Order of Journalists is based on an examination and is mandatory for practice of the profession. By other criteria, however – as we shall see subsequently – Italian journalism has a particularly *low* level of professionalization.

The focus of this section is specifically on *journalistic* professionalism. It is most often in relation to journalism rather than to other media-related occupations that the issue of professionalization is raised. However, it should be noted that similar questions can be raised about other kinds of media professionals. In public broadcasting systems, particularly, where all broadcast programming has been seen in some sense as a public service, it is quite relevant to raise similar issues about the degree of professional autonomy of television producers.

*DIMENSIONS OF PROFESSIONALIZATION.* As much as it departs from the ideal type of the liberal professions, journalism has come to share important characteristics with them, and it can be very useful to compare media systems in terms of the degree and form of professionalization of journalism. We will focus primarily on three fairly closely related dimensions of professionalization.

(1) *Autonomy.* Autonomy has always been a central part of the definition of professionalism. This is one of the key reasons why many occupations try to "professionalize" themselves, to justify greater control over their work process. The classic case is medicine: even if bureaucratization has limited the autonomy doctors enjoyed in the era when virtually all (at least in the classic U.S. and British cases) were "free" professionals,[3] there is still a strong presumption that certain kinds of decisions can only be made by medical professionals, and that outside interference is inappropriate. Journalism has never achieved a comparable degree of autonomy. The autonomy of doctors or lawyers, for one thing, is based on the "esoteric" character

---

[3] In continental Europe, some professionals have more typically been civil servants rather than participants in a market for services (McClelland 1990). But this does not necessarily mean they were less "professionalized" by the criteria we develop here.

of medical or legal knowledge. Journalists lack esoteric knowledge, though their strategic position in the flow of information sometimes provides a partial substitute. Unlike doctors and lawyers who provide personal services, moreover, journalists work in an industry where mass production is the norm. They almost never own their own means of production, but are salaried employees of large enterprises. In some sense, the professionalization of journalism begins precisely when the first hired reporters enter the picture, and the occupation of the journalist thus begins to become differentiated from that of printer or politician/owner. Aside from a few historical moments and the special cases that we will explore below, journalists have rarely asserted and almost never achieved the right to control media organizations outright. Nevertheless, they have often been successful in achieving significant relative autonomy within those organizations. Or to put it in another way, control of the work process in journalism is to a significant extent collegial, in the sense that authority over journalists is exercised primarily by fellow journalists. (It should be noted that the autonomy we are talking about here is not necessarily the autonomy of *individual* journalists, but of the *corps* of journalists taken as a whole.)

The degree of journalistic autonomy varies considerably over time, across media systems, and often within media systems, from one type of news organization to another (e.g., "quality" versus "popular" press, press versus broadcasting). Thus Donsbach and Patterson (1992), when they asked journalists in the United States, Germany, Britain, and Italy about the importance of "pressures from management" on "the job one does," found that 27 percent of Italian journalists said that such pressures were "very" or "quite" important, while only 7 percent of German journalists answered similarly.

(2) *Distinct professional norms.* Professions, as Collins (1990) puts it, "are occupations which organize themselves 'horizontally,' with a certain style of life, code of ethics, and self-conscious identity and barriers to outsiders." An important part of this "horizontal" organization is the existence of a set of shared norms distinct to the profession. In the case of journalism these norms can include ethical principles such as the obligation to protect confidential sources or to maintain a separation between advertising and editorial content, as well as practical routines – common standards of "newsworthiness," for example – and criteria for judging excellence in professional practice and allocating professional prestige. Professionalization of

journalism is thus likely to be manifested in criteria of newsworthiness on which journalists will agree regardless of their political
orientations, as well as a tendency for journalists to define their
standing in the field in terms of the opinions of fellow journalists, rather than those of outsiders – political party leaders, for example, or stockholders. Obviously the existence of distinct professional norms is related to autonomy, in the sense that such norms
could not govern the practice of journalism if that practice were
controlled by outside actors. We shall see that there are important
variations in the degree to which distinctively journalistic norms
have evolved, the degree of consensus they enjoy among those who
practice journalism, and their relative influence on news-making
practices.

(3) *Public service orientation.* Another important element of the concept of "professionalism" is the notion that professions are oriented
toward an ethic of public service. This has been a particularly controversial point in the sociology of the professions. Parsons (1939)
stressed the public service orientation of professionalism as part of a
critique of the Marxist idea that the development of capitalism dis-
places all motivations other than those of "cold calculation." Siebert,
Peterson, and Schramm's social responsibility theory of the press
belongs to this era in the scholarship on professionalism. A wave
of revisionist scholarship beginning in the 1960s stressed against
Parsons that the "altruism" of the professions needed to be understood as an ideology that often concealed other ends, serving,
particularly, to justify the economic monopoly and social power of
professionals. Much of the classic sociology of journalism of this era
was similarly concerned with the critique of the ideology of journalistic professionalism, and certainly it would be naïve in the extreme
to accept the claims of journalists to serve the public purely at face
value.

Nevertheless, the adoption of an ideology of journalism as a "public trust" is an important historical development and should not be
dismissed as "mere ideology" any more than it should be accepted as
pure altruism. It is a historically specific conception of the journalist's role in society with important consequences for the practice of
journalism and the relation of the media to other social institutions;
and its differential development in different societies needs to be explained. The ethic of public service may be particularly important in
the case of journalism, compared with other occupations claiming

36

professional status: because journalism lacks esoteric knowledge, journalists' claims to autonomy and authority are dependent to a particularly great extent on their claim to serve the public interest. One of the clearest manifestations of the development of an ethic of public service is the existence of mechanisms of journalistic self-regulation, which in some systems are formally organized, in the form, for instance, of "press councils" (or sometimes for the electronic media "audiovisual councils") and sometimes operate informally, and that vary considerably in strength, regardless of whether they are formally organized.

INSTRUMENTALIZATION. We will often draw a contrast in the pages that follow between professionalization and *instrumentalization* of the media. What we mean by instrumentalization is control of the media by outside actors – parties, politicians, social groups or movements, or economic actors seeking political influence – who use them to intervene in the world of politics. A political party paper is in some sense an instrument for the party's intervention in the political world, though as we shall see many party-linked papers eventually drifted away from a purely instrumental conception of their social function. We shall also see that privately owned papers have been established primarily or partly to serve as vehicles for political intervention. Obviously, to the extent that media organizations are instrumentalized in this way, professionalization as previously defined will be low: journalists will lack autonomy, political rather than distinctively journalistic criteria will guide the practice of journalism, and media will serve particular interests rather than functioning as a "public trust."

We will use the term *instrumentalization* in the pages that follow to refer specifically to *political* instrumentalization. It should be noted that media can also be "instrumentalized" for commercial purposes: advertising is essentially this, and media organizations are often subject to broader forms of commercial instrumentalization, ranging from more blatant examples such as product placement in film and television programming and demands from advertisers for influence over editorial content, to more subtle kinds of pressures. As we shall see there is considerable debate about the relation between commercialization of the media and professionalization. Some see them as essentially in harmony, arguing that commercialization undercuts political instrumentalization. We will generally take the view that professionalization can be threatened either by political instrumentalization or by commercialization, and indeed in many cases by both at once.

*PROFESSIONALIZATION AND POLITICAL PARALLELISM.* One question that might be raised here is why we have treated the degree of professionalization and political parallelism as separate dimensions. As we noted in Chapter 1, the "Anglo-American" or Liberal media model is typically taken as the norm against which other media systems are measured, and one corollary of that conceptual framework is the idea that professionalization is essentially synonymous with "objectivity" and political neutrality. In this view, a system in which media have ties to organized social and political groups, and in which journalists retain elements of a publicist conception of their role, is by definition a system in which professionalization is weakly developed. If journalists are to serve the public rather than particular interests, if they are to act according to specifically journalistic standards of practice rather than following agendas imposed from outside, they must act as neutral information providers and avoid identification with particular points of view, according to this interpretation.

Clearly the two dimensions of political parallelism and professionalization are in fact related. One way to think about professionalization is in terms of differentiation theory: a high degree of professionalization of journalism means that journalism is differentiated as an institution and form of practice from other institutions and forms of practice – including politics; or to put it in terms of Bourdieu's sociology, professionalization exists where journalism is developed as a distinct field with significant autonomy from other social fields, including the political field. (We will go more deeply into both differentiation theory and Bourdieu's field theory in Chapter 4.) Where political parallelism is very high, with media organizations strongly tied to political organizations, and journalists deeply involved in party politics, professionalization is indeed likely to be low: journalists are likely to lack autonomy, except to the extent that they enjoy it due to high political positions, and journalism is likely to lack a distinct common culture and distinct sense of social purpose, apart from the purposes of the political actors with which media are affiliated. Or to put it the other way around, it is clear that historically the development of journalistic professionalization eroded political parallelism in important ways, diminishing the control of parties and other political organizations over the media, and creating common practices that blurred the political distinctions among media organizations. Nevertheless, we believe that the empirical relationship between these two dimensions is only rough, and that there is no convincing justification for treating them as conceptually synonymous.

Because this issue helps to clarify the distinctions involved in both of these dimensions, it is worth elaborating a bit further here. We will consider two examples drawn from outside the region that is the primary focus of this book.

One of the more interesting discussions of the nature of journalistic professionalism is Curry's (1990) analysis of journalists in communist Poland – interesting in part because the structural conditions of the media in Poland were not those we usually associate with the professionalization. Curry argues that despite an official ideology that conceived the media as instruments of the party, Polish journalists developed a strong professional culture. This was in some sense, of course, a failed professionalism: external conditions – the prevalence of censorship, state ownership of the media and political repression – meant that journalists were routinely thwarted in attempting to act according to a professional conception of their role. Nevertheless they did clearly have such a conception: they had a strong sense of distinct identity and of a distinct role in society, and resisted intrusions of outsiders into journalistic work, including the "worker and peasant correspondents" of the early Stalinist years, high-level political figures who wrote political commentary but were refused membership in the journalists' union, and Solidarity officials who wanted control when dissident papers emerged. They placed a high value on autonomy, had a strong sense of professional solidarity that persisted even in periods of sharp political conflict, and a hierarchy of prestige based on peer judgments that cut across political differences.

At the same time, Polish journalists clearly saw journalism as a "political profession," as Max Weber once put it. They conceived it as part of their role to shape policy and solve social problems. They considered the mere reporting of facts not to be real professional work, and practiced a style of writing that placed heavy emphasis on commentary. This conception of journalism seems to have carried over to the independent media of the post-Communist period. Adam Michnik, editor of the *Gazeta Wyborcza* – originally a paper connected to the Solidarity trade union and now Poland's major daily – while emphasizing that his paper sought to avoid narrow partisanship and to provide a high degree of internal pluralism, wrote in 1995, "I always wanted *Gazeta* to have a clearly defined line. It resulted from the identity of the Solidarity democratic opposition and workers' social ethics . . . (76)." And he quoted the legendary Polish journalist Ksawery Pruszynski as saying "The task of the journalist . . . is to voice what he has arrived at in his reasoning (78)."

39

Another interesting example comes from Israel (whose journalism can trace its historical roots in part to central Europe). In 1989, the Canadian publisher Hollinger, Inc. bought *The Jerusalem Post*, and quickly moved to establish control over the political line of the English-language paper. *The Jerusalem Post* had for many years been owned by economic institutions connected with the Labor party – a common pattern in Europe as well; Conrad Black, then the owner of Hollinger, is politically conservative. The editor, Erwin Frenkel, objected to the new publisher's attempts to interfere with journalistic decisions and soon resigned, as did thirty other journalists.[4] He explained his resignation in a column in the *Post* this way:

Journalism is an enterprise in social judgment. The object of that judgment is the historical present, the fast flood of daily events. Journalism plucks from this infinite flow those events deemed worthy of public regard, reporting them as honest witness. That it calls news. It assigns such news events weights of importance and interest. And it seeks, by further interpretive judgment, to help place those events in a more explicit context of narrative understanding.

It does all this on behalf of the society of which it is a part, in the conviction that the "news" it so delivers is essential feedback in helping that society best steer itself. In that sense, journalism is guardian of a public trust.

In a newspaper this process of judgment is a collective effort. It has checks and balances. But judgment it remains. For that reason all newspapers have a character of their own, telling the story of the present as they perceive it.

To give that collective judgment coherence and to protect it from influences that would divert it in their favour, there is the editor and his authority. In the end, it is his voice, his judgment over what is fit to print, that would save this collective process from chaos or corruption. So long as his judgment of what is fit to print is not subject to fear or favour.

---

[4] The case produced an interesting judgment in Court of Labour Disputes: granting severance compensation to journalists. The judge expressed the view – common as we will see in many countries in Northern and Central Europe where it is sometimes referred to as internal press freedom – that press freedom requires that editors and reporters have freedom of expression and limits the right of media owners to interfere with their work.

Now this process of journalist judgment may not precisely describe a profession. But it does describe a commitment. A commitment to its own integrity.

The key elements of journalistic professionalization are clearly present in Frenkel's statement: the notion of journalism as a "public trust," the existence of shared standards of professional practice (Frenkel's "checks and balances"), and the emphasis on journalistic autonomy. If Frenkel's account is accurate the latter was particularly strongly developed at *The Jerusalem Post*, where, he says, the functions of editor and publisher were never separated, and the editor's independence was "absolute," thus guaranteeing "the preeminence of the journalistic interest in the operations and policies of the newspaper and the company." At the same time, Frenkel emphasizes the importance of "interpretive judgment" and believes that "all newspapers have a character of their own, telling the story of the present as they perceive it." He clearly conceives the expression of a distinct point of view to be not contrary to but in fact intimately connected with the notion of journalistic independence and journalism as a public trust: this is what it means to be an "honest witness," to tell the "story of the present" as the journalist perceives it; this is how journalism serves the public; and this is why journalistic autonomy matters – to preserve not neutrality, but the integrity of this process of "social judgement."

This is quite different from the North American conception of professionalism as political neutrality or "objectivity." It would be a familiar point of view to many journalists in continental Europe, however, and it seems an essentially coherent view of the journalist's social role – and obviously a view that casts doubt on the idea that journalistic professionalism and political parallelism cannot coexist. We will argue that in much of Northern and Central Europe, especially, a relatively high level of political parallelism did coexist for most of the twentieth century with a high degree of journalistic professionalism, and indeed to some extent these continue to coexist.

## THE ROLE OF THE STATE

The state plays a significant role in shaping the media system in any society. But there are considerable differences in the extent of state intervention as well as in the forms it takes. The most important form of state intervention is surely public service broadcasting, which has been present

Table 2.4 *Public Broadcasting Systems*

| | Revenues per Capita (in ECU) | Revenues as % of GDP | % Commercial Revenues | TV Audience Share |
|---|---|---|---|---|
| | (1997)[a] | (1997)[b] | (1998)[c] | (2000)[d] |
| Denmark | 104.5 | 0.37 | 34.8 | 69 |
| United Kingdom | 103.7 | 0.30 | 15.8 | 39 |
| Switzerland | 99.7 | 0.36 | 26.2 | |
| French | | | | 32 |
| German | | | | 32 |
| Italian | | | | 25 |
| Austria | 88.6 | 0.39 | 49.9 | 57 |
| Germany | 85.5 | 0.38 | 17.2 | 42 |
| Norway | 72 | 0.23 | 0 | 41 |
| Ireland | 69.8 | 0.36 | 66 | 48 |
| Finland | 68.8 | 0.34 | 25.4 | 43 |
| Sweden | 67.4 | 0.30 | 7.3 | 44 |
| Belgium | 56.3 | | | |
| Flemish | | | 33.4 | 32 |
| French | | | 27.6 | 25 |
| France | 55.8 | 0.21 | 45.5 | 44 |
| Italy | 49.2 | 0.20 | 43 | 48 |
| Netherlands | 45 | 0.22 | 22.5 | 37 |
| Spain | 33.9 | 0.28 | 77.6 | 33 |
| Canada | 23.8 | 0.13 | 32 | 9 |
| Greece | 17.9 | 0.18 | 43.1 | 12 |
| Portugal | 12.5 | 0.15 | 55.5 | 34 |
| United States | 5.8 | 0.02 | 13 | 2 |

[a] *Source:* Teodosi and Albani (2000: 193); figure for Belgium is from *2002 Statistical Yearbook of the European Audiovisual Observatory* and is for 2000.
[b] *Source:* Teodosi and Albani (2000: 193).
[c] *Source:* For Europe, Schulz (2002); for United States and Canada (Teodosi and Albani 2000: 192); U.S. and Canada figures are for 1997.
[d] *Source:* For Europe, Schulz (2002); for Canada, Lorimer and Gasher (2001: 141); for United States Hoynes (1994: 17).

in every country in Western Europe and North America except the smallest (e.g., Luxembourg), and in most countries has until recently been the only or the primary form of broadcasting. There has, of course, been a strong shift toward commercial broadcasting in recent years, but public service broadcasting remains quite significant in most of the countries in this study. Table 2.4 shows funding revenues for public broadcasting systems both per capita and as a percent of GDP, the percent of those revenues that come from advertising and other commercial sources, and the percent of the television audience captured by public service broadcasting in 2000. In only one of the European countries covered here does the audience share of public service broadcasting fall below 20 percent, and in most cases it is in the range of 30 to 50 percent – in contrast to 9 percent in Canada and 2 percent in the United States. Funding levels are also much higher in Europe than in the United States. The purity of public broadcasting systems, in the sense of their dependence on commercial revenue, on the other hand, varies considerably within Europe.

Public broadcasting has been the most important form of state ownership of media (in most countries the state until recently also ran the telecommunication infrastructure). However, in many countries the state has also owned news agencies, newspapers, or other media-related enterprises, either directly or through state-owned enterprises. Press subsidies have also been present in most of the countries covered here, and have played an important role in many. These can be direct or indirect (e.g., reduced postal, telecommunication, or VAT rates), and can be directed either at news organizations or at individual journalists (e.g., in the form of reduced tax rates or fares on public transport).[5] The state, and in many cases state-owned enterprises, are also advertisers, in many cases very important ones. Subsidies for the film industry are also very common.

Other forms of state intervention include:

- Libel, defamation, privacy, and right-of-reply laws;
- Hate speech laws;
- Professional secrecy laws for journalists (protecting the confidentiality of sources) and "conscience laws" (protecting journalists when the political line of their paper changes);

---

[5] Picard (1984) summarizes the basic forms of state financial intervention in the newspaper industry. He also attempts a ranking of countries in terms of such intervention, but not very successfully, as his ranking only takes into account the presence or absence of a particular kind of state support, not its magnitude or the policy governing its allocation (which may or may not, for instance, allow authorities discretion to reward or punish particular papers for their political support or opposition).

- Laws regulating access to government information;
- Laws regulating media concentration, ownership, and competition;
- Laws regulating political communication, particularly during election campaigns; and
- Broadcast licensing laws and laws regulating broadcasting content, including those dealing with political pluralism, language, and domestic content.

In the broadest terms, a distinction can be made between relatively liberal media systems, in which state intervention is limited and the media are left primarily to market forces, and systems in which social democratic or *dirigiste* traditions are manifested in a larger state role in the ownership, funding, and regulation of media. The extreme case of a liberal system is of course the United States, where the unique legal priority of the First Amendment limits many of the forms of media regulation that are common in Europe – though we shall see that the state's role in the United States is quite important in its own way. There are also subtler variations in the particular mixes of media policy that have evolved in different systems, usually closely connected with broader patterns in the relation of state and society that we will introduce in the following chapter. Systems also vary in the *effectiveness* of media regulation: a weaker state role can result either from a deliberate policy favoring market forces or from failure of the political system to establish and enforce media policy. This phenomenon, as we shall see, is particularly common in the recent history of broadcasting Southern Europe; Traquina (1995) refers to it as "savage deregulation."

Apart from issues of media ownership, funding, and regulation, the state always plays an important role as a source of information and "primary definer" of news (Hall et al. 1978), with enormous influence on the agenda and framing of public issues. These two roles are not necessarily correlated – that is, it is not clear that the state is less a "primary definer" in systems with liberal media policy than in systems with a stronger state intervention in media ownership, funding, and regulation.

## CONCLUSION

We would suggest that the four dimensions outlined here cover most of the major variables relevant to comparing the media systems of Western Europe and North America, at least from the point of view of media and politics. We conceive of these dimensions as clusters of media-system characteristics that tend to vary together – for example, the several components of journalistic professionalism or of political paralellism, though we shall certainly see that they do not do so in perfectly even and predictable ways; and for example, some systems may develop some components of journalistic professionalization more fully than others, or the state may play a strong role in some respects and not in others. Each of these dimensions probably also has other correlates (e.g., with characteristics of news content) many of which can be identified only with further research. We also conceive of the four dimensions as ultimately irreducible to one another. We have argued this explicitly in the case of journalistic professionalism and political paralellism – that the two influence one another in important ways, but also vary independently. We suspect that the same is probably true of any pair of dimensions. We hope that the analysis that follows will establish the plausibility of this framework, though clearly much more research will be needed to refine and assess it fully.

The following chapter identifies the principal dimension of the political system that we consider essential for comparative analysis of media and politics, and outlines a number of hypotheses about the relations between these variables and the media-system dimensions introduced here.

# THREE

# The Political Context of Media Systems

In Chapter 1 we argued that media systems are shaped by the wider context of political history, structure, and culture. In this section we will discuss some of the principal characteristics of political systems that can influence the structure of media institutions. We have taken from the literatures on comparative politics and political sociology a number of concepts that we believe are useful for understanding the evolution of media systems. We summarize these concepts relatively briefly here – and apologize to specialists in these fields for what may seem like an overly elementary discussion, and at the same time to media scholars unfamiliar with them for what may seem like an overly quick one. We hope that for both groups, the discussion will deepen and the meaning of the concepts will become clearer as we go on to apply them to the analysis of concrete cases. We also outline in this chapter a set of hypotheses that emerge from our research about how these political system variables are connected with the media system variables introduced in the preceding chapter. In the final section of this chapter we introduce an argument that common historical roots shape the development of both media and political systems, and are crucial to understanding the relation between the two. All the arguments introduced here are developed at greater length as we analyze the evolution of particular systems.

The concepts we have taken from political sociology and comparative politics were in most cases developed without any thought about their application to the study of the media, and we may select from them or adapt them in ways that will seem slightly odd to people in those fields, though we hope we can show that our adaptations make sense in the subsequent analysis. One of the challenges for the comparative study of media systems – which we can only begin to take up in this book – is to sort out which elements of the frameworks used in comparative politics are actually relevant to understanding the media, and how they have to be adapted conceptually for this purpose.

In some sense, the political system variables discussed here could be called the "independent variables" in our analysis of the relation between media and political systems, as many are more general and deeply rooted aspects of social structure and culture than are the media-system characteristics outlined previously. As we noted in Chapter 1, however, we see the relation between media and political systems more in terms of coevolution than of strict causal ordering. Indeed, the relative influence of the media system on political institutions and vice versa may vary historically, with political forces dominating the media system in some periods, while in other periods the media system is more independent (or more determined by economic forces), and may exercise greater autonomous influence on the political world. This issue we will take up in detail in Chapter 8.

## INTERACTION WITH ECONOMIC VARIABLES

We introduce in this chapter a number of hypotheses about the way political variables are connected with media system variables. It is important to keep in mind, however, that the relationships are only rough, and we are not proposing any kind of one-to-one correspondence between political and media-system characteristics. This is true both because of the complexity of real political systems and because political variables interact with a number of other influences on media systems. The media are in a very important sense a political institution, but they are also (increasingly often) businesses and are shaped by many economic factors.[1] We have already mentioned, in the previous chapter, some important characteristics of media market structure that will play a role in our analysis: we noted, for example, that national newspaper markets are more likely than local markets to be compatible with external pluralism in the press. Relatively little work has been done to develop conceptual frameworks for understanding these factors in comparative perspective,

---

[1] Media are also cultural institutions. Because our focus in this book is primarily on the news media and the relation of media to the political system, it is political culture, specifically, something that is intimately connected with the kinds of structural factors considered in this chapter, that is relevant to our analysis. If we were doing a comparative analysis that focused more fully on cultural industries, other kinds of cultural factors would also need to be taken into account.

and we will not try to fill the gap here. But it is worth giving just a couple of examples of the kinds of factors that may be relevant.

One extremely important factor is clearly the development of the advertising industry, which in turn is linked to historical patterns in the sociology of consumption and of business. Pilati (1990: 47), for example, makes these observations about the differences between the United States, where the use of media for marketing developed early and strongly, and Europe:

> In Europe markets have national [as opposed to continental] dimensions which are therefore much smaller than those in America: this means a greater cultural homogeneity and therefore weaker motivations to standardize collective customs through communication; at the same time, in many cases, it confines firms to modest dimensions which result in much lower advertising revenues than those associated with larger-scale business organization. Branding makes it possible to reduce or neutralize risks and weaknesses resulting from the large size of American business: elevated organizational costs of coordination; lower levels of local advantage; high costs of research on new products. . . . [T]he range of products which by tradition remain excluded from industrial production (from fresh pasta to gelato and from bread to dining out) is much larger in Europe. Also local producers, who exploit commercial factors (capillary networks of distribution, price) and are favored by the lesser coverage of large-scale distribution networks, maintain consistent operating potential.

Pilati's point is that a variety of cultural and economic factors have made brand-name marketing and therefore advertising less central to European business, and this has affected the development of media in a variety of ways. Even the prevalence of public broadcasting in Western Europe may in part be attributed to this fact.

Another factor that we suspect is relevant is the degree of concentration of capital, both in the media industry specifically and in the economy generally. It seems likely that where capital is highly concentrated there will be a relatively high degree of interrelationship between the state and media owners, either through subsidy and regulation or in the form of clientelist ties and partisan alliances, and also – other factors being equal – a tendency for media to be influenced by outside business interests. We shall see in Chapter 5, for instance, that in Spain a relatively small number of banks that command much of the country's capital have exercised great influence over the media.

In the balance of the chapter we will focus specifically on the political context of media systems.

## THE ROLE OF THE STATE

The differing roles the state can play as owner, regulator, and funder of the media are clearly rooted in more general differences in the role of the state in society. At the most basic level, a distinction can be made between *liberal democracies* – with the United States as the most obvious example – and the *welfare state democracies* that predominate in Europe, especially on the continent. The difference is obviously not absolute, as the state plays a significant but also limited role in all capitalist democracies. Nor is it a dichotomy: there are many shades of difference within Europe, with Switzerland, for example, considerably in the direction of the liberal pattern, compared with Sweden, Norway, or neighboring Austria. But there is clearly an important distinction between the relatively restricted role of the state in the U.S. and European traditions of more active state intervention, and this distinction is strongly reflected in the relation of the state to the media system. Just as the state in Europe takes responsibility for funding health care; higher education; cultural institutions such as symphony orchestras and operas; and often political parties and churches, so it takes responsibility for funding television and to a significant degree the press. The media have been seen in Europe, for most of the twentieth century, as first social institutions and only secondarily, if at all, private businesses. Just as the state in Europe is expected to play an active role in mediating disputes between capital and labor or in maintaining the health of national industries, it is expected to intervene in media markets to accomplish a variety of collective goals from political pluralism and improving the quality of democratic life (Dahl and Lindblom 1976; Gustafsson 1980) to racial harmony and the maintenance of national language and culture. The difference between the United States and Europe in the degree of state intervention may in fact be sharper in the case of the media than in other areas of social life, as the American legal tradition gives press freedom – understood in terms of the freedom of private actors from state intervention – unusual primacy over other social values. One clear manifestation of this difference can be seen in the fact that European countries generally regulate political communication: many ban paid political advertising;

some limit the length of campaign periods; some regulate the time given to politicians on public service and/or commercial television. In the United States such regulations are held by the courts to violate the First Amendment.

The European tradition of an active state has complex historical roots. It arises both out of a preliberal tradition of aristocratic rule and out of the more modern tradition of social democracy. In the media sphere as in other spheres, it involves a combination of more authoritarian or paternalistic and more participatory and pluralist elements. The British Official Secrets Act and interventions by various Spanish governments to influence media ownership might be taken as examples of the former, and the Swedish press ombudsman or German rules on representation of social groups on broadcasting councils as examples of the latter. Though many institutional structures and practices – French laws regulating foreign-language content might be an example – combine both elements.

Beyond the distinction between welfare state and liberal democracy, many other distinctions can be made in the role of the state in society. Katzenstein (1985) for example, makes a three-way distinction among liberalism in the United States and Britain, statism in Japan and France, and corporatism in the small European states and to a lesser extent in Germany. We will come back to this distinction in discussing the Democratic Corporatist Model. It should also be noted that three of the countries in our study, Greece, Spain and Portugal, shifted from authoritarian to democratic systems relatively recently. They have been characterized for most of their history by statism without social democracy – a strong state role in the economy and in society generally, but not a strong welfare state. This history, combined with the tradition of clientelism discussed in the following text, makes these Southern European countries historically distinctive in important ways.

## CONSENSUS VS. MAJORITARIAN DEMOCRACY

Lijphart's (1984, 1999) distinction between consensus and majoritarian democracy is widely used in comparative politics and is probably of considerable use in understanding relations between the political and media systems, particularly along what Lijphart calls in his later formulations the executive-parties dimension. Lijphart's contrasting models are summarized in Table 3.1.

Table 3.1 *Consensus vs. Majoritarian Politics*

| Majoritarian Politics | Consensus Politics |
| --- | --- |
| 1. Winning party concentrates power | Power sharing |
| 2. Cabinet dominance | Separation of power between legislative and executive |
| 3. Two-party system | Multiparty system |
| 4. Plurality voting system | Proportional representation |
| 5. Clear distinction between government and opposition | Compromise and cooperation between opposing forces |

Majoritarianism, as we will try to show in Chapter 7 when we discuss the Liberal systems where this pattern prevails, tends to be associated with the notion of the journalist as a neutral servant of the public as a whole, rather than as a spokesperson of a particular political tendency or social group, and with internal rather than external pluralism, though as we shall see the British press deviates significantly from this pattern. It is part of the political culture of a majoritarian system – at least of a long-standing majoritarian democracy – that the parties compete not to gain a greater share of power for their particular segment of society, but for the right to represent the nation as a whole, and it may be that in this sense the notion of neutral professionalism is more natural in a majoritarian system. Majoritarianism probably also tends to be associated with the development of catch-all political parties with vague ideological identities, appealing to a wide public across social divisions, though this is much more true of the American presidential system than of the British Westminster system. Where catch-all parties predominate, it makes sense that catch-all media should also develop. Consensus systems, on the other hand, are typically multiparty systems, and external pluralism (as defined in the previous chapter) is more likely in the media system of multiparty polities, along with other characteristics of political parallelism.

There is a particularly clear and direct connection between patterns of consensus or majoritarian rule and systems of broadcast governance and regulation that tend to follow patterns similar to those that prevail in other spheres of public policy. The most basic feature of politics in consensus systems is power sharing, and the strongest examples of power sharing in broadcast governance can be found in systems that tend toward the consensus model, either in the form of the parliamentary model (Italy, Belgium) or the civic/corporatist model (Netherlands, Germany).

As for majoritarian systems, Humphreys (1996: 11) argues that there "we might expect the publicly-owned media to be more vulnerable to capture by the dominant political tendency." And indeed, what we have called the "government model" of broadcast regulation is typically to be found in majoritarian systems: France before the 1980s and contemporary Spain, Portugal, and Greece. Often the same institutional arrangements for broadcast governance produce different political results in consensus and in majoritarian systems: a governing board appointed by parliament according to proportional representation will result in power sharing in a consensus system such as Italy, and in effective government control in a majoritarian system such as Spain. As Humphreys also notes, however, the quintessential majoritarian system, the British Westminster system, is characterized not by capture of public broadcasting by the majority but by separation of broadcasting from political control, a deviation from the expected pattern that he attributes to the relatively strong liberal tradition of limited government in Britain.

In fact it seems likely that the professional model of broadcast government is quite commonly associated with majoritarianism. In a pluralist political system direct control of broadcasting by the political majority is difficult to sustain. It almost always creates intense political conflict and damages the credibility of the media system. Most European countries started out, in the early days of broadcasting, with something resembling the government model, but eventually had to devise alternatives. One alternative is power sharing, but this conflicts with the basic political structure and culture of majoritarian systems; the logical solution in such systems would seem to be the professional model. Canada and Ireland fit this pattern. Sweden might also be cited as an example. Sweden is a mixed case in terms of the consensus/majoritarian distinction. But it is characterized by one-party governments through most of the late twentieth century, and like Britain it is characterized by a high degree of separation between broadcasting and politics. Our argument, then, is that where majoritarian systems start out with the government model of broadcast governance and regulation, they are likely to move over time to the professional model, as enough alternations of power take place that the major parties accept their inevitability and are willing to give up hope of controlling broadcasting when they are in power, knowing that they will someday again be in opposition and would prefer not to have their rivals in control.

## INDIVIDUAL VS. ORGANIZED PLURALISM; LIBERALISM VS. CORPORATISM

One of the dimensions of Lijphart's distinction between majoritarian and consensus rule has to do with the political role of interest groups. "The typical interest group system of majoritarian democracy," he notes, "is a competitive and uncoordinated pluralism of independent groups, in contrast with the coordinated and compromise-oriented system of corporatism that is typical of the consensus model" (1999: 171). We would connect this distinction to a broader contrast between systems in which political representation is conceived and organized in terms of the relation between governing institutions and individual citizens, along with a multiplicity of competing "special interests" – which we will call *individualized pluralism* – and those in which organized social groups are more central to the political process – which we will call *organized pluralism*. Organized pluralist systems are characterized by strongly institutionalized social groups representing different segments of the population, which often play a central role in mediating their members' relations with the wider society and may be formally integrated into the process of making public policy. A classic example of organized pluralism would be the "pillarized" system that prevailed in the Netherlands through the early to middle twentieth century, in which the different subcommunities – Protestant, Catholic, Socialist, and Liberal – developed their own educational, cultural, social, and political institutions – ranging from sports clubs to trade unions and political parties. The Catholic and Communist subcultures in Italy similarly developed dense webs of organizational structures, on which individuals depended, to a large extent, for everything from leisure activities and cultural life to jobs and government services. In cases where these organized subcommunities structure most aspects of social life, and social institutions are separated by subcommunity – as was true in the Netherlands before the 1960s – this is referred to in the comparative politics literature as *segmented pluralism*.

The formal integration of social groups into the political process is what is known as *corporatism*. As Katzenstein (1985: 32) has argued, the smaller states of Europe, particularly Scandinavia, the Low countries, and Switzerland, developed a characteristic form of politics early in the twentieth century that was "distinguished by three traits: an ideology of social partnership expressed at the national level; a relatively centralized and concentrated system of interest groups; and voluntary and informal coordination of conflicting objectives through continuous political bargaining between interest groups, state bureaucracies and political parties." Katzenstein contrasts this form of *democratic corporatism*, which was also adopted in significant part by Germany and Austria after World War II, with *liberalism*. We will argue in Chapter 6 that the concept of democratic corporatism is extremely useful for understanding the media systems of Northern and West-Central Europe. The kinds of group structures associated with segmented pluralism and corporatism have broken down to a very significant extent in Western Europe, giving way to a more individualized pattern of social belonging. But they played a central role in the development of both political and media systems in much of Europe, and significant differences do persist in the extent to which they continue to affect political life.

It is worth adding here that systems also differ in the extent to which political parties play a dominant role relative to other kinds of organized social groups. A strong role of political parties tends to be characteristic of systems that tend to polarized pluralism – a concept that will be explained in the following text. These systems usually have a history of weaker development of civil society and parties have tended to fill the organizational void.

Where organized pluralism was strongly developed, the media were always integrated to a significant extent into the institutions of group representation. The Dutch pillars, for example, had their own newspapers, and Dutch broadcasting was similarly organized into a pillarized system of broadcasting organizations representing the different subcultures. Organized pluralism is thus clearly associated with external pluralism and political parallelism: media tied to political parties, trade unions, and churches, and the notion of journalism as a vehicle for the representation of groups and ideologies develops most strongly in societies characterized by organized pluralism. These societies also tend to have some version of a politics-in-broadcasting system – either the parliamentary or the civic/corporatist model – because democracy is conceived as requiring direct representation of social interests. One interesting manifestation of the way this difference in political culture affects broadcasting policy can be found in the different rules introduced by Britain and by Scandinavian countries for the granting of licenses for community radio:

Britain forbade the granting of licenses to churches and political parties. Scandinavian countries expressly included them (De Bens and Petersen 1992). It should be noted, finally, that in societies that typically have strong, centralized organizations representing social groups, journalists will also have such organization. As we shall see, the democratic corporatist societies of Northern Europe are characterized by a particularly strong formal organization of the profession of journalism.

## RATIONAL-LEGAL AUTHORITY AND CLIENTELISM

Max Weber defined *rational-legal authority* as a form of rule based on adherence to formal and universalistic rules of procedure. The characteristic institution of a rational-legal system, for Weber, was bureaucracy – that is, an administrative apparatus that is autonomous of particular parties, individuals, and social groups, acts according to established procedures and is conceived as serving society as a whole. Among the key characteristics of autonomous administration are civil-service recruitment based on merit, adherence to formal rules of procedure, and "corporate coherence" within the civil-service corps, which enforces adherence to established procedures and protects the administrative process from outside interference not in accordance with them.[2] The key institutional development in the formation of autonomous public administration is the establishment of a civil-service system that governs the hiring, promotion, and tenure of administrative personnel, separating that process from monopolization by particular status groups and from party patronage. Historically, according to Shefter (1977), bureaucratic autonomy originated in the United States and Europe in one of two ways. In some countries it began to develop in the seventeenth and eighteenth centuries, as monarchs felt the need for larger-scale armies and regulatory apparatuses, and attempted to create "a modern, centralized bureaucratic state to replace the decentralized *standestaat* [which involved monopolization of administrative positions by the traditional landholding class]" (417). In other countries it was established in the nineteenth century by a "rationalizing bourgeoisie," which sought to provide the kind of flexible,

---

[2] Despite its importance in the seminal work of Weber, the notion of rational-legal authority does not seem that strongly developed in the contemporary literature on West European politics. One important recent statement, on which we have drawn here is Evans (1997). Evans, however, is primarily interested in the development of the "Weberian state" in newly industrializing countries, and does not deal much with its different patterns of development in Western Europe or North America.

rule-governed regulatory system in which dynamic modern capitalism could develop. In addition to bureaucracy, the other principal institution of a rational-legal order is an autonomous judicial system. There are also important cultural components to rational-legal authority, manifest, for example, in the degree to which citizens, businesses, and other actors are willing to follow rules, or alternatively seek to evade them, and whether public officials, technical experts, and other authorities are seen as serving a general "public interest" transcending particular interests.

As with other elements of political structure the most obvious and direct implication of the development of rational-legal authority for the media system can be found in public broadcasting systems and in the agencies that regulate private broadcasting, allocate press subsidies, and so forth. Where rational-legal authority is strongly developed, these institutions, similar to other public agencies, are likely to be relatively autonomous from control by government, parties, and particular politicians, and to be governed by clear rules and procedures. This does not necessarily mean broadcasting governance will follow the formally autonomous, professional model. As we shall see, many of the democratic corporatist countries of Northern and Central Europe have strong rational-legal authority, but follow broadcasting-in-politics models of media regulation. Bureaucracies of course are not intended to be entirely autonomous, but to be responsive to elected political leadership; the negative connotations of the term *bureaucracy* have their origins in complaints about administrative apparatuses losing accountability. All bureaucracies therefore have some degree of political control and penetration, particularly at the top levels (Suleiman 1984). But where rational-legal authority is strong, this will always be balanced more or less strongly by the professional autonomy of civil servants, including, in the case of public broadcasting, journalists. In countries where rational-legal authority is less strongly developed – principally, as we shall see, in Southern Europe – party control and penetration of public broadcasting and regulatory institutions tends to be stronger and deeper.

The development of rational-legal authority also affects media systems in broader though more indirect ways. Systems of rational-legal authority, for one thing, require formal codification of procedures and information, and their public accessibility, and thus provide relatively fertile ground for the development of journalism. Habermas, in his account of the origins of the public sphere, notes that the institution of formalized public administration along with a need to address ordinances and announcements to a large body of citizens, played an important role in the origin of the press (1989: 21–2).

Instrumentalization of the media, as defined in the previous chapter, is less likely in systems with strong rational-legal authority: media owners are less likely to have strong and stable alliances with particular political parties, and less likely to use their media properties as instruments to intervene in political affairs. The independence of administrative and judicial institutions and the rule-governed character of public policy means that in systems where rational-legal authority is strong businesses do not depend too heavily on arbitrary decisions of particular officials, who may, for example, favor an enterprise with which they are allied politically, nor are their fates affected too dramatically by which party happens to be in power at the moment. This does not mean that business will lack influence on public policy in a system with strong rational-legal authority, nor that their interests will be disfavored: on the contrary, a system of rational-legal authority will often institutionalize this influence, though depending on the balance of political forces in society it may also provide other interests with access to the policy process. But it does mean that business owners will have less need for particularistic political alliances, and this implies that media owners will find it easier to keep their distance from party politics.

Professionalization of journalism is also more common where rational-legal authority is strong. In fact, the development of journalistic professionalism arises to a large extent from the same historical forces that produced autonomous administrative and legal systems – particularly in the phase of "bourgeois rationalization" – and these developments historically influenced one another in many ways. Journalistic professionalism began to develop in Europe and North America in the second half of the nineteenth century, as there was a general shift toward professionalism as a model of social organization in many areas of social life, including public administration. Journalistic and administrative professionalism involve similar world views, including the notion of an autonomous institution serving the common good, and an emphasis on rational and fact-centered discourses. "Bureaucracy has a 'rational' character," Weber wrote, "rules, means, ends and matter-of-factness dominate its bearing" (Gerth and Mills 1946: 244). The same can clearly be said of the new forms of information-oriented journalism. In many cases journalists, who also tended to come from the progressive middle class, were deeply involved in the reform movements that established modern administrative systems. Those systems in turn provided the kinds of politically "neutral" information sources on which new forms of information-based journalism would be built, and relied to a large extent on publicly accessible proceedings and documents that became the subject matter for much of the news.

A contrasting form of organization is *political clientelism*, which remained strong in Southern Europe through much of the twentieth century, and whose legacy, we will argue, is still important to understanding media systems in that region. Clientelism refers to a pattern of social organization in which access to social resources is controlled by patrons and delivered to clients in exchange for deference and various forms of support (Mouzelis 1980, Eisenstadt and Lemarchand 1981, Roniger and Günes-Ayata 1994, Piattoni 2001, Hallin and Papathanassopoulos 2002). It is a particularistic form of social organization, in which formal rules are less important relative to personal connections or, in later forms of clientelism, connections mediated through political parties, the Church, and other organizations. While rational-legal authority tends to be associated with a political culture that enshrines the notion of the "common good" or "public interest" (we leave aside here the question of whether policies pursued in the name of the "common good" really are in the interest of all), in a clientelist system commitment to particular interests is stronger and the notion of the "common good" weaker. All societies saw the development of clientelism at some point in their history, and clientelist relationships continue to exist to some degree everywhere (Legg 1975). These relationships, however, were the target of the reform movements that sought to strengthen rational-legal authority, and where those movements were successful clientelism receded in importance.

Clientelism tends to be associated with instrumentalization of both public and private media. In the case of public media, appointments tend to be made more on the basis of political loyalty than purely professional criteria. Private business owners also will typically have political connections, which are essential to obtaining government contracts and concessions (including broadcast licenses) and in many other ways necessary for the successful operation of a business. These owners will often use their media properties as a vehicle for negotiation with other elites and for intervention in the political world; indeed in many cases this will be the primary purpose of media ownership. For these reasons political parallelism tends to be high where the tradition of clientelism is strong.

Adherence to legal norms is generally weaker where clientelism is strong; actors will expect to be able to use their connections to avoid inconvenient regulations. This contributes to the phenomenon of "savage deregulation" mentioned in Chapter 2, as regulatory authorities are in many cases unsuccessful in enforcing broadcast regulation. It also contributes to instrumentalization. The fact that laws are often honored in the breach offers many opportunities and incentives for particularistic pressures. Politicians can pressure media owners by selectively enforcing broadcasting, tax, and other laws. Media owners, and in some cases perhaps prominent journalists as well, can exert pressures of their own by threatening selectively to expose wrongdoing by public officials.

Clientelism is also associated with lower levels of professionalization of journalism. Journalists tend to be integrated into clientelist networks, and their ties to parties, owners, or other patrons weaken professional solidarity. It is commonly noted in the literature on clientelism that it tends to break down "horizontal" forms of social organization, and professionalism is one such form. Because the political culture does not emphasize the separation between the public good and particular interests, or the following of abstract norms, the cultural basis for professionalization is weaker. In this sense there is a connection between the fact that Italians don't wear seat belts, even though it is required by law, and the fact that Italian journalists don't follow journalistic codes of ethics, even though their union did create one recently.

Clientelism, finally, is associated with private rather than public communication patterns. The need of ordinary citizens for information about public affairs is relatively small; as Piattoni (2001: 202) writes, "Clientelism is...simple: a vote for a benefit." At the top, meanwhile, the process of political communication tends to be closed: public hearings and documents are less important to the political process, closed negotiations among elites more so. Access of journalists to relevant political information is thus more dependent on their political ties, and it is more likely that political communication will tend to serve the process of negotiation among elites rather than providing information for the mass public.

## MODERATE VS. POLARIZED PLURALISM

Another basic distinction in the field of comparative politics is between *moderate* and *polarized pluralism*. In polarized pluralism, according to Sartori (1976: 135) "cleavages are likely to be very deep...consensus is surely low, and...the legitimacy of the political system is widely questioned. Briefly put, we have polarization when we have ideological

Table 3.2 *Effective Number of Political Parties
and Index of Polarization, Average Figures
for 1945–89*

|  | Polarization | Parties |
|---|---|---|
| France | 5.1 | 4.8 |
| Portugal* | 4.7 | 3.6 |
| Finland | 3.9 | 5.5 |
| Italy | 3.7 | 4 |
| Greece* | 3.7 | 3.2 |
| Netherlands | 3.6 | 4.9 |
| Germany | 3.6 | 2.9 |
| Spain* | 3.4 | 4 |
| United Kingdom | 3.3 | 2.7 |
| Norway | 3.2 | 3.9 |
| Sweden | 3.2 | 3.4 |
| Austria | 2.4 | 2.5 |
| Denmark | 2.4 | 4.8 |
| Belgium | 2.1 | 5 |
| Switzerland | 1.6 | 5.6 |
| Ireland | 0.9 | 3.1 |

*Source:* Lane and Ersson 1991: 184–5.
*Democratic periods only.

distance. . . ." Polarized pluralism is characterized by the existence of significant antisystem political parties. In Italy, for example, both Fascist and Communist parties have been important throughout the democratic period, with the Communists typically getting 25 to 30 percent of the vote. The political spectrum is wide, and parties tend to have distinct and sharply opposed ideologies. In moderate pluralism tendencies toward the center are stronger, ideological differences among the parties are less great and often less distinct, and there is greater acceptance of the fundamental shape of the political order.

The classic pattern of polarized pluralism to which Sartori referred has existed only in a limited number of cases: Italy (in the period when he developed the term), Fourth Republic France, and Weimar Germany among them. But the underlying distinction between systems in which ideological polarization and diversity are relatively great or more limited is much more broadly useful, we believe, for understanding the development of media systems. Table 3.2 shows differences among European countries in terms of ideological polarization (reported by Lane and Ersson 1991 and measured through analyses of party manifestos) and the number of political parties. The degree of ideological polarization is related to historical differences, summarized in part in the final section of this chapter – polarized pluralism developed where conservative opposition to liberalism was strong, and the transition to liberalism long and conflictual. Later in our analysis, we will extend the term *polarized pluralism* to refer to this broader pattern of political development – and thus apply it to countries such as Spain and Portugal, which had a form of polarized pluralism only during brief periods of democracy early in the twentieth century (after which pluralism was suppressed for half of the twentieth century by dictatorship), but that share much of the pattern of historical development of Sartori's Italy.

Polarized pluralism tends to be associated with a high degree of political parallelism: newspapers are typically identified with ideological tendencies, and traditions of advocacy and commentary-oriented journalism are often strong. The notion of politically neutral journalism is less plausible where a wide range of competing world views contend. Similar to clientelism, with which it has common historical roots, polarized pluralism tends to undermine a conception of the "common good" transcending particular ideological commitments. Sartori argues that Polarized Pluralist systems tend to have political cultures that emphasize "ideology understood as a way of perceiving and conceiving politics, and defined, therefore, as a distinctly doctrinaire, principled and high-flown way of focusing on political issues (137)."[3] In such a culture it is not surprising that a tradition of advocacy or commentary-oriented journalism would be strong. Polarized pluralist societies are also characterized historically by sharp political conflicts often involving changes of regime. The media typically have been used as instruments of struggle in these conflicts, sometimes by dictatorships and by movements struggling against them, but also by contending parties in periods of democratic politics. This history similarly pushes toward the politicization of the media. Moderate pluralism, on the other hand, is more conducive to the development of commercialized and/or professionalized media with less political parallelism and instrumentalization.

---

[3] Sartori connects this ideological style to a "mentality of rationalism as opposed to the empirical and pragmatic mentality (137)," though he does not explore the historical roots of this cultural difference. As we shall see in Chapter 5, Putnam (1973) attributes it more to the simple fact of polarization – to the fact that political life is highly conflictual.

## HISTORICAL ROOTS

European political institutions developed out of a series of conflicts rooted in major social transformations: the Protestant Reformation, the industrial revolution, the democratic revolution, and the formation of the nation-state. Media systems also developed out of these transformations and the conflicts and cleavages that resulted from them. Early mass media – newspapers, books, pamphlets, handbills – were deeply implicated in these conflicts, and the modern mass media are to a significant extent associated with certain poles in them. The modern newspaper, especially, is most characteristically an institution of a secular, urban, national, democratic, capitalist social order. The particular patterns through which these transformations and the associated conflicts were played out are thus crucial to understanding the relationships between media and political systems.

In the chapters that follow, we will deal in much greater detail with the historical co-development of particular media and political systems in their social contexts. Here we would like point to one broad distinction between those countries where liberal, bourgeois institutions triumphed relatively early over the feudalism and patrimonialism, and those where the conflict between the forces of liberalism and traditional conservatism remained unresolved until well into the twentieth century. This historical difference accounts to a large extent for the quite distinct patterns of media system development that prevail in Northern and Southern Europe. In much of Northern Europe, the landed interests that were the social basis of the old order in Europe were relatively weak, and liberal forces consolidated their hegemony relatively early. Where this pattern prevailed, one usually finds moderate pluralism and a strong development of rational-legal authority in the political sphere, combined with a strong development of mass circulation media and of journalistic professionalism. The United States, as Tocqueville pointed out, was a liberal society from the beginning, and subsequent political conflicts – between labor and capital and over slavery and race – were carried out on the ground of liberal hegemony; in this sense the United States also fits this pattern.

In Southern Europe the landed interests and the Catholic Church were much stronger; industrialism and the market developed later, and sharp political conflict over the basic shape of the political system continued much longer. Polarized pluralism, clientelism, and statism resulted in the political field. In the media system, discouraged by the counterreformation cultural tradition, by political authoritarianism, and by weaker development of the market and the nation-state, mass-circulation newspapers never developed and journalistic professionalism was limited by clientelism. What did emerge, once democracy took root, was a wide spectrum of media closely tied to the diverse political factions that contended for power – a system marked by a high degree of political parallelism.

One good illustration of the importance of history for understanding contemporary media systems is the fact that rates of newspaper circulation still reflect patterns established at the end of the nineteenth century, when the mass-circulation newspaper first developed. Figure 3.1 shows the correlation between literacy rates in 1890 and newspaper circulation rates in 2000, for thirteen countries on which we have data. The correlation between the two (using a log transformation of circulation rates) is about .8. The split between Northern and Southern Europe is clear in these figures, with low circulation rates across Southern Europe reflecting their literacy rates in 1890. The point here is not that literacy rates cause the development of mass-circulation newspapers (to some extent the causality may even run the other way). As Cipolla (1969: 18) puts it, "literacy is in fact only one aspect of a complex socio-cultural reality"; the development of a mass-circulation press is another aspect of that same reality.

Of course, there are many variations among individual countries, as we shall see in subsequent chapters, which complicate the simple division we have used here between those countries where liberal institutions were consolidated early and those where the transition was more protracted. Germany and France, in particular, are very much mixed cases in terms of this historical distinction. And though the liberal countries of the north Atlantic – Britain, Ireland, the United States, and Canada – share many characteristics with Northern European countries where liberal institutions also developed relatively early, they also diverge from them in important aspects of their subsequent political and media history. In Part II we will try to give a more nuanced view of the historical context of media systems.

## CONCLUSION

In this chapter we have identified a number of political system variables that we believe are relevant to the comparative analysis of media systems. These variables, derived and in some cases adapted from the literatures

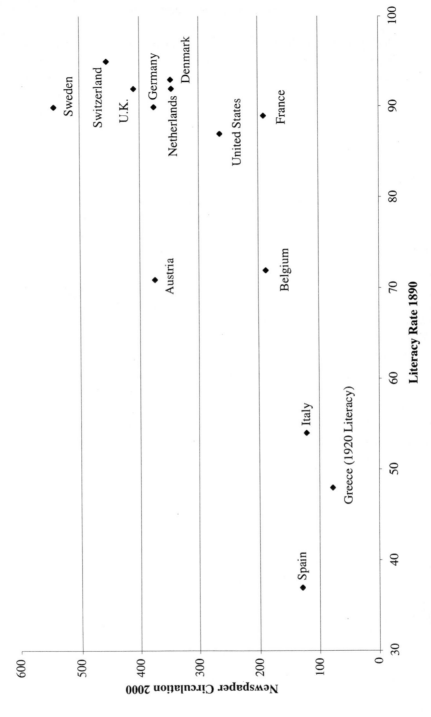

*Figure 3.1* Relation Between Literacy Rate in 1890 and Newspaper Circulation in 2000.

on comparative politics and political sociology, can be summarized in terms of five principal dimensions: the relation of state and society, and particularly the distinction between liberal and welfare-state democracy; the distinction between consensus and majoritarian government; the distinction, related to consensus and majoritarian patterns of government, between organized pluralism or corporatism, and liberal pluralism; the development of rational-legal authority; and the distinction between moderate and polarized pluralism. We believe that these, and the related characteristics of political structure and culture summarized here, have regular patterns of association with important characteristics of the media system, and we have summarized the patterns of association that emerged in our research. The relationships proposed here must be considered as hypotheses, given the preliminary nature of this research. Nevertheless we will make as strong a case as we can for them as we discuss the development of particular media systems in Part II. We have also argued that these relationships can be traced in large part to common historical roots that underlie the development of both media and political systems, including, most centrally, the early or late development of the bourgeois institutions of market and political democracy.

In the following chapter we introduce the three media system models that will organize our discussion of the development of particular systems, and discuss some broad theoretical issues that underlie the analysis of these three media systems.

# FOUR

# Media and Political Systems, and the Question of Differentiation

In Chapters 2 and 3 we introduced a framework for comparing media systems and a set of concepts adapted from comparative politics and political sociology that, we argued, have important relationships with the media system. In Chapter 3 we also introduced a number of hypotheses about how particular political system variables were related with particular media system variables. In the remainder of this book, we will try to analyze these relationships in a more synthetic and historical way, exploring the broader patterns of relationship that have developed in North America and Western Europe; the reasons why particular sets of characteristics have tended to co-occur; and why these patterns occur when and where they do. This chapter will begin this process of analysis, first, by introducing three models of the relation between media and political systems that will organize our empirical discussion of the media systems of particular countries, and second, by posing the question whether the patterns observed here can be understood in terms of differentiation theory. The discussion of differentiation theory will lead us into a deeper look at an issue posed in the introduction to this volume, the use of the Liberal Model as a standard for measuring media systems; it will also carry us forward to a discussion, in Chapter 8, of convergence or homogenization of media systems, and whether this can be understood as a process of "modernization."

## THE THREE MODELS INTRODUCED

Our discussion of the patterns of interrelationship among the political and media system characteristics discussed in this chapter will be organized around three models, which are summarized in Tables 4.1 and 4.2. The basic characteristics of these models are described here. In Part II

Table 4.1 *The Three Models: Media System Characteristics*

| | Mediterranean or Polarized Pluralist Model | Northern European or Democratic Corporatist Model | North Atlantic or Liberal Model |
|---|---|---|---|
| | France, Greece, Italy, Portugal, Spain | Austria, Belgium, Denmark, Finland, Germany, Netherlands, Norway, Sweden, Switzerland | Britain, United States, Canada, Ireland |
| Newspaper Industry | Low newspaper circulation; elite politically oriented press | High newspaper circulation; early development of mass-circulation press | Medium newspaper circulation early development of mass-circulation commercial press |
| Political Parallelism | High political parallelism; external pluralism, commentary-oriented journalism; parliamentary or government model of broadcast governance – politics-over-broadcasting systems | External pluralism especially in national press; historically strong party press; shift toward neutral commercial press; politics-in-broadcasting system with substantial autonomy | Neutral commercial press; information-oriented journalism; internal pluralism (but external pluralism in Britain); professional model of broadcast governance – formally autonomous system |
| Professionalization | Weaker professionalization; instrumentalization | Strong professionalization; institutionalized self-regulation | Strong professionalization; noninstitutionalized self-regulation |
| Role of the State in Media System | Strong state intervention; press subsidies in France and Italy; periods of censorship; "savage deregulation" (except France) | Strong state intervention but with protection for press freedom; press subsidies, particularly strong in Scandinavia; strong public-service broadcasting | Market dominated (except strong public broadcasting in Britain, Ireland) |

Table 4.2 *The Three Models: Political System Characteristics*

| | Mediterranean or Polarized Pluralist Model | North/Central European or Democratic Corporatist Model | North Atlantic or Liberal Model |
|---|---|---|---|
| | France, Greece, Italy, Portugal, Spain | Austria, Belgium, Denmark, Finland, Germany, Netherlands, Norway, Sweden, Switzerland | Britain, United States, Canada, Ireland |
| Political History; Patterns of Conflict and Consensus | Late democratization; polarized pluralism | Early democratization; moderate pluralism (except Germany, Austria pre-1945) | Early democratization; moderate pluralism |
| Consensus or Majoritarian Government | Both | Predominantly consensus | Predominantly majoritarian |
| Individual vs. Organized Pluralism | Organized pluralism; strong role of political parties | Organized pluralism; history of segmented pluralism; democratic corporatism | Individualized representation rather than organized pluralism (especially United States) |
| Role of the State | Dirigisme, strong involvement of state and parties in economy; periods of authoritarianism, strong welfare state in France, Italy | Strong welfare state; significant involvement of state in economy | Liberalism; weaker welfare state particularly in United States |
| Rational Legal Authority | Weaker development of rational legal authority (except France); clientelism | Strong development of rational-legal authority | Strong development of rational-legal authority |

of this book we will explore each in detail, showing its inner logic and historical evolution. We have identified the three models both by the geographical region in which they predominate and by a key element of the political system that we consider crucial to understanding the distinctive characteristics that mark the media-politics relationship in each model: the Mediterranean or Polarized Pluralist Model, the North/Central European or Democratic Corporatist Model, and the North Atlantic or Liberal Model. Table 4.1 focuses on the media system and Table 4.2 summarizes relevant characteristics of the political system and political history.

We will argue that these models identify patterns of development that are both coherent and distinct, and that the sets of countries we have grouped together under these headings share many important characteristics. Nevertheless, it is important to keep in mind that these are "ideal types." We hope they will prove useful as conceptual devices for organizing a discussion of media and political systems in comparative perspective, but they are far from capturing the full complexity either of the media systems of particular countries, or of the patterns of relationships among the major variables we have identified.

The tables, in particular, are extreme simplifications, affected in part by the simple need to fit the information on single pages. We hope they will be useful to the reader in getting an overview of the framework we are proposing. At the same time we hope they will be interpreted in light of the more nuanced discussion of the three models and of particular countries presented in the chapters that follow. We would reiterate here a number of qualifications introduced in Chapter 1. First, the groups of countries we discuss under each of the models are heterogeneous in many ways, and it is not our intent to minimize the differences among them. In certain cases, indeed, those differences will be central to our argument. Although the United States and Britain, for example, are often lumped together – with good justification up to a point – as Liberal systems we will try to show that they are very different in important ways, and that the common idea of an "Anglo-American" model of journalism is in part a myth. Britain could actually be conceived as lying somewhere between the ideal type of the Liberal Model and the Democratic Corporatist Model that prevails in northern continental Europe. France is also a mixed case, and can be conceived as lying between the Polarized Pluralist and Democratic Corporatist models. In terms of newspaper circulation, to take just one example, it is higher than all the other "Mediterranean" countries, but lower than the rest of Europe – a difference that reflects

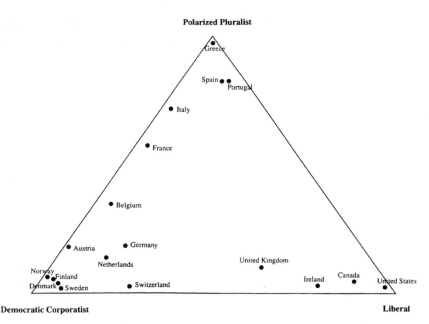

*Figure 4.1* Relation of Individual Cases to the Three Models.

a particularly contradictory media history, marked by dramatic ups and downs in the development of the mass-circulation press. Belgium might be said to have important similarities with the Mediterranean countries on certain dimensions – the relatively strong involvement of political parties in public broadcasting, for example. Sweden might be said to have certain similarities with the Liberal systems – strong insulation of public broadcasting from political party control, for instance – but also differs particularly sharply in some ways. Germany, which was very much a polarized pluralist system until the *stunde null* of 1945 (when both the political and media systems were rebuilt from the ruins of Nazism), is distinct in important ways from the small democratic corporatist states of Northern Europe. Spain and Portugal, which had consolidated dictatorships for half the twentieth century, have to be distinguished from Italy and France, which have a much longer history of democratic politics. We will deal with some, though certainly not all of these variations among individual countries in the chapters that follow, and try to show how they can be understood, in many cases, in terms of the variables introduced in the preceding chapters.

Figure 4.1 represents these variations graphically, showing each model as one corner of a triangle, and the various countries as points in a space defined by that triangle. The placements of the individual countries represent our tentative judgments about their similarity or difference from the ideal types represented by the three models. Germany, for example, shares many characteristics with the other countries we have classified as Democratic Corporatist – high newspaper circulation and strong involvement of organized social groups in policy, including media policy. But we have placed it toward the middle of the triangle, closer to both the Polarized Pluralist and Democratic Corporatist Models for a number of reasons. It shares with the Polarized Pluralist countries a history of sharp ideological conflict, has a more confrontational political style than the smaller Democratic Corporatist states, and, as in the Polarized Pluralist countries, political parties play a particularly strong role in social life, as they do also in the media. Similar to the Liberal systems, it lacks press subsidies and tends to give strong emphasis to the privileges of private ownership in much media policy. Spain and Portugal are shown as further from the Democratic Corporatist and closer to the Liberal Model than Italy because they have weaker welfare states, manifested in less state support for both the press and public broadcasting. In principle, it would be possible to place countries in such a space on the basis of some set of quantitative indices, but the limitations of data noted in Chapter 1 and, more importantly, conceptual problems about how to weight various criteria that might be used to construct such indices make that approach seem more misleading than enlightening. Of course, these conceptual problems mean that the placement of particular countries is very much subject to debate. The representation of these media systems in a two-dimensional space obviously abstracts from a tremendous amount of complexity and is not meant to substitute for the more complex discussion that appears in Part II.

It is also important to keep in mind that the media systems of individual countries are not homogeneous. Actually countries themselves are not homogenous. Many, for example, are characterized by regional variations in both media and political systems: the media in Quebec and Catalonia are distinct in a number of ways from the media in the rest of Canada or Spain, and the history, current economy and political culture, and media markets of Northern and Southern Italy are very different. We take the nation-state as our primary unit of analysis here – and media systems have to a large extent been organized at this level over the past couple of centuries – but it is important to keep in mind that this is in some ways misleading. It is also important to remember that not every element of a given media system operates according to the same logic, with the same kinds of relationships with the political world. (This is one of the weaknesses of *Four Theories of the Press*, which tends to assume that each society has a certain world view that will be expressed in each element of its media system.) In most systems the press and broadcasting operate according to different logics – the press will often be characterized by external pluralism, for example, and broadcasting by internal pluralism. In many cases broadcasting was deliberately organized *not* to follow the pattern that prevailed in the press. Different sectors of the press often operate by different logics as well – national newspapers are often more politicized, for example, while the regional press is more strictly commercial and politically unaligned.

Finally, it is important to keep in mind that media systems are not static, but characterized by substantial historical change. These historical changes are not easy to represent on the tables presented here, but they will be a central focus of the chapters that follow. Many argue, of course, that the main historical shift underway is essentially a convergence of European media systems toward the Liberal Model, a change that has probably been underway for some time, but which has accelerated greatly since the commercialization of European broadcasting began in the 1980s. Certainly the three groups of countries we are discussing differed much more dramatically in their media systems in 1970 than they do today. We will focus on the issue of convergence in Part III. To some extent, in Part II we will place relatively greater emphasis on the *differences* among media systems, both historical and present, in an effort to show the distinct logics of the patterns that have developed among liberal democratic systems, which, as we argued in Chapter 1, have never been fully conceptualized by media scholars.

Some may wonder why the models we are proposing involve geographically contiguous countries. There is certainly no reason *a priori* that this should be true. Is it just a strange historical coincidence? This was something that puzzled us in the early phases of the analysis: the differentiation of media systems really did seem to follow a geographical pattern, but we were not sure we could explain why. By the time we had done the actual analysis, it was clear to us that there were deep reasons for this. There were, in the first place, geographical patterns in European historical development that accounted for the similarities of groups of countries – Protestantism and industrialization, for example, occurring together in the north rather than the south. Secondly, there were important patterns of influence between different groups of countries: British political, economic, and media institutions were exported to Ireland, Canada, and the United States; France had enormous influence on Italy and the Iberian Peninsula resulting from the Napoleonic invasion, which introduced journalism to this region; and a dense web of interactions also connected the countries of Northern and Central Europe. If the eighteen countries covered here were eighteen independent "cases" it would be statistically unlikely that we would have observed the geographical pattern of similarity that we did—but of course they are not really independent cases; their development was deeply intertwined, and the relations among them did clearly follow geographical patterns.

With those qualifications, here are summaries of the principal characteristics of the three models, focusing first on media system characteristics and second on the political context in which they developed.

The **Mediterranean** or **Polarized Pluralist Model** is characterized by an elite-oriented press with relatively small circulation and a corresponding centrality of electronic media. Freedom of the press and the development of commercial media industries generally came late; newspapers have often been economically marginal and in need of subsidy. Political parallelism tends to be high; the press is marked by a strong focus on political life, external pluralism, and a tradition of commentary-oriented or advocacy journalism persists more strongly than in other parts of Europe. Instrumentalization of the media by the government, by political parties, and by industrialists with political ties is common. Public broadcasting tends to follow the government or parliamentary models outlined in Chapter 3. Professionalization of journalism is not as strongly developed as in the other models: journalism is not as strongly differentiated from political activism and the autonomy of journalism is often limited, though, as we shall see, the Mediterranean countries are characterized by particularly explicit conflicts over the autonomy of journalists – power and authority within news organizations has been more openly contested in the Polarized Pluralist systems. The state plays a large role as an owner, regulator, and funder of media, though its capacity to regulate effectively is often limited. Many Mediterranean countries are characterized by a particularly rapid and uncontrolled transition from state controlled to commercial broadcasting. Or as Traquina says, they are characterized by "savage deregulation."

We have chosen to refer to this as the Polarized Pluralist Model because we believe that these patterns are rooted to a large extent in the high degree of ideological diversity and conflict that characterizes these

LIVERPOOL JOHN MOORES UNIVERSITY
LEARNING SERVICES

Southern European countries, and which in turn is rooted in delayed development of liberal institutions. The delayed development of liberalism is connected with a strong role of the state in society (often in an authoritarian form), a strong role of political parties once the transition to democracy is achieved, a continuing importance of clientelism, and a weaker development of rational-legal authority. Under this model we will discuss France, Greece, Italy, Portugal, and Spain. France is an exception in important ways, characterized by polarized pluralism and a strong role of the state, certainly, and by a history of strong political parallelism in the media, but also by stronger industrialization and stronger development of the mass-circulation press and of rational-legal authority.

The **North/Central European** or **Democratic Corporatist Model** is characterized by early development of press freedom and the newspaper industry, and very high newspaper circulation. It is also characterized by a history of strong party newspapers, and other media connected to organized social groups. This political press coexisted with the commercial press through much of the twentieth century, though by the 1970s it was fading. Political parallelism is historically high and, though it is diminishing, a moderate degree of external pluralism and a legacy of commentary-oriented journalism persists, mixed with a growing emphasis on neutral professionalism and information-oriented journalism. Journalistic professionalism is high, and marked by a high degree of formal organization. Media are seen to a significant extent as social institutions for which the state has responsibility, and press freedom coexists with relatively strong state support for and regulation of media. Public broadcasting systems tend to follow the parliamentary or civic/corporatist model with parties and organized social groups involved in broadcast governance, but professional autonomy in broadcasting is also normally high. It is important to note that a number of sets of media system characteristics that are often assumed to be incompatible have historically coexisted in the Democratic Corporatist countries. Strong commercial media industries have coexisted with politically linked media and a high degree of political parallelism; high political parallelism has also coexisted with a high degree of journalistic professionalization; and a strong liberal tradition of press freedom and freedom of information has coexisted with strong state intervention in the media sector as in other sectors of society.

Liberal institutions generally developed early in the Democratic Corporatist countries. These countries also tended to have strongly organized social groups; some have histories of strong segmented pluralism. In the first half of the twentieth century (except in Austria and Germany, where its introduction occurred after World War II) democratic corporatism emerged as a system that integrated these groups into the political process. They are characterized today by moderate pluralism (though with greater ideological diversity than the Liberal counties) and by consensus politics. The welfare state is strong, though with significant variations in its extent. Rational-legal authority is also strongly developed. Under this model we will discuss Austria, Belgium, Denmark, Finland, Germany, the Netherlands, Norway, Sweden, and Switzerland.

The **North Atlantic** or **Liberal Model**, similar to the Democratic Corporatist Model, is characterized by early development of press freedom and the mass-circulation press, though newspaper circulation today is lower than in the Democratic Corporatist societies. Commercial newspapers dominate, political parallelism is low, and internal pluralism predominates – with the important exception of the highly partisan British press. Professionalization of journalism is relatively strong, though without the kind of formal organization that prevails in the Democratic Corporatist countries. Journalistic autonomy is more likely to be limited by commercial pressures than by political instrumentalization, though the latter is more common in Britain. Information-oriented journalism predominates, with a bit stronger commentary tradition in Britain. The role of the state is limited, though more so in the United States than in Ireland and Canada, where concerns about national culture have given the state a large role, and Britain, where public broadcasting and the regulation of commercial broadcasting have both been very strong. Public broadcasting and broadcast regulation is organized according to the professional model, with relatively strong insulation from political control.

Liberal institutions of course developed relatively early in these societies, where the role of the market is traditionally strong and the role of the state relatively limited, though more so in the United States than the others. All are characterized by moderate pluralism and tend toward majoritarianism, and none have the strongly organized social groups that are often important in continental Europe, though again Britain does to a larger extent than the United States. Rational-legal authority is strongly developed in all the Liberal countries.

## DIFFERENTIATION AND DE-DIFFERENTIATION

At a very general level we could summarize the differences among these systems by saying that in the Liberal countries the media are closer to the world of business, and further from the world of politics. In the Polarized Pluralist systems they are relatively strongly integrated into the political world, while in Democratic Corporatist countries the media have had strong connections to both the political and economic worlds, though with a significant shift away from political connections particularly in recent years. As we shall see in detail in Chapter 8, there is a trend in all countries toward commercialization of the media and professionalization of journalism and other media-related occupations, and a corresponding separation of the ties that once connected the media to the world of politics – most particularly to political parties and other organized social groups. There is, in this sense, a convergence toward the Liberal Model.

One theoretical perspective that is of obvious relevance to the analysis of this pattern of differences among systems and their subsequent convergence is the tradition of differentiation theory, originating with Durkheim and passing through the systems theory of Talcott Parsons. Differentiation theory is not very often employed explicitly in contemporary media studies. It was, however, in an earlier era: Much of the of the work on comparative media systems in the 1960s was tied to the "modernization" framework that had close connections to differentiation theory (e.g., Pye 1963). Many assumptions drawn from differentiation theory are embedded in the conventional wisdom about media systems, particularly in the view that the Liberal Model is the most "modern," and that convergence toward that model is to be understood as "modernization." In this section we elaborate the assumptions of differentiation theory more explicitly, contrast it with alternative frameworks for understanding media systems and media system change at the macrosociological level, and position our own analysis in relation to these perspectives. In Chapter 8, where we discuss convergence of media systems, we will return to this discussion to draw further conclusions about the applicability of differentiation theory to the study of media systems.

*THE PERSPECTIVE OF DIFFERENTIATION THEORY.* Durkheim, in *The Division of Labor in Society* (1893), spoke of the separation of professions as a kind of horizontal differentiation of society: Modern societies, he argued, become increasingly complex as functions are divided among social bodies that specialize in particular functions. This idea of Durkheim, that increased complexity of society requires functional differentiation of social roles and institutions, is central to the evolutionist theory of Parsons. Parsons (1971: 26) defines differentiation as "the division of a unit or structure of a social system into two or more units or structures that differ in their characteristics and functional significance for the system," and describes a process of social change from primitive to modern societies as one in which social functions initially fused are separated: politics, for example, is differentiated from religion and from economics.

There are at least three major points of Parsons's thought that have been applied by his followers to media analysis. First, Parsons points out the importance of the evolutionary process: from an original unity of functions, societies progress to a condition of specialization. Second, the increased specialization of functions requires integrative mechanisms to interconnect different subsystems, and communication systems are identified as performing this integrative role. Third, differentiation increases the adaptive abilities of each subsystem, and therefore of the whole society. This evolutionist view, of course, implies the necessity and superiority of modernity, and this is the focus of much criticism of Parsons and of structural-functionalism as conservative and ethnocentric, as an apology, essentially, for the existing social order.

Another influential version of differentiation theory is that of Niklas Luhmann. Luhmann's version is more strictly functionalist than Parsons's evolutionary view, and one might say more cynical.[1] Luhmann claims that the difference between social knowledge produced by a specialized mass media system and that produced by "sages, priests, the nobility, the city, by religion or by politically and ethically distinguished ways of life . . . is so stark that one can speak neither of decline nor of progress" (2000: 85). In this sense he differentiates his view from Parsons by disavowing a claim that modernity is superior. In many other ways, however, his views are quite similar.

Public opinion, Luhmann argues in a well-known paper bearing that title, must be conceived functionally as a means to select themes around which public discussion will be focused. These themes are understood to be sets of meanings about which "one can discuss, have the same or

---

[1] Cynical, in the sense that Luhmann rejects any notion of enlightened public opinion; the media, in Luhmann's view provide not enlightenment (even as an ideal goal) but "irritation."

different opinions" (Luhmann 1978: 94). In this sense Luhmann argues that public opinion in the more traditional sense of a common opinion "may not exist." At the level of microgroups, themes allow dialogue between different partners and, in a wider systemic perspective, organize and make public discussion possible. For Luhmann a theme of opinion must have certain characteristics: it has to be general, so as to simplify public discussion without breaking it up into several contrasting streams. There should also be a precise distinction between theme (information about a certain topic) and opinion (judgment and evaluation of the same topic). If the two are not kept apart, a proper discussion between the partners will not be possible: they will not be able to conduct dialogue on an equal level and will be subject to manipulation.

Luhmann places great emphasis on what he calls (2000: 37) the "self-referential character" of the process of public communication and argues that the media "are autonomous in the regulation of their own selectivity" (2000: 23–4). The generation of communication themes has a specific place in the functional distribution of tasks among the various social subsystems. Luhmann makes a distinction, in particular, between attention rules and decision rules, the former belonging to the field of communication, the latter to political institutions. Through the mass media, communication themes are brought to attention, analyzed, and proposed to the political system. It is the function of public opinion, organized by the media system, to draw attention to important problems, but government and more broadly the political system has the responsibility to make decisions about those problems – the media and the public discuss but do not decide. The organization of public discussion around themes simplifies social complexity, which would otherwise be unmanageable. To perform this function the means of communication need to be independent from other systems, particularly from the political system for which they develop a thematic agenda.

Another, more explicitly comparative statement on the media from the perspective of differentiation theory is that of Alexander (1981). For Alexander, a society is considered "modern" if its journalistic information system is autonomous from other social systems:

> In a modernizing and differentiating society, the media are a functional substitute for concrete group contact, for the now impossible meeting of the whole. Indeed . . . media emerge only with social differentiation itself, and the more "modern" a society is the more important its media. . . . The very possibility of a flexible normative

production is dependent on the autonomy of news media from control by groups and institutions in other social subsystems. If the news is controlled by political authorities it will be unable to evaluate or characterize political events in relation to competing political and normative perspectives. The news media must also be independent, in a relative sense of course, of more general value-producing institutions, like the church, university and party. Finally, there must be differentiation from structures in the economic dimension, particularly social classes.

Alexander analyzes the development of news media in western society – focusing particularly on the United States and France – as a process of progressive differentiation of media from other social bodies: political groups, the state, religion, etc. In "rational-legal societies" (in his terms), journalism follows a path parallel to that of the state: both struggle for their freedom of movement in relation to other social institutions. The progressive differentiation of the news media, according to Alexander, is the consequence of three major forces: demands for more universalistic information put forward by new social groups against forms of advocacy journalism linked to the preexisting social order; the growth of professional norms and self-regulation leading toward the development of journalistic autonomy; and "the degree of universalism in national civil cultures" (the latter, as we will try to show in subsequent chapters, is connected with rational-legal authority, with moderate pluralism, and, though less exclusively, with majoritarianism). Alexander is also very explicit in indicating that the Liberal Model, particularly as found in the United States, is close to the ideal of a differentiated media system. (Notice that Luhmann, in his stress on separation of news and opinion, seems also to endorse the Liberal Model.)

The concept of differentiation is unquestionably useful for understanding differences among media systems. Many of the concepts we have employed can be connected to it. Professionalization is a central concept in differentiation theory, and can clearly be understood in terms of the degree of differentiation of journalism from other occupations and forms of social practice. Many elements of political parallelism, organizational links between parties and media most obviously, can be understood in terms of the degree of differentiation or lack of differentiation between the media and the political system, though it is not clear that *any* form of political parallelism can be seen as indicating a lack of differentiation of the media system – not clear, for example, that some degree of external pluralism is incompatible with differentiation of the media system. The fact that media make judgments independently does not necessarily mean that they must all make the same judgments, and cannot have distinct ideological orientations. Similarly some, though not all, of our analysis of the role of the state can be understood in terms of the differentiation or lack of differentiation between media and state. How active the state is in relation to other social institutions is a different question from whether it is structurally differentiated from them; a strongly differentiated state is often a very active one, and the fact that it is active does not necessarily threaten the differentiation of other social subsystems, any more than an active media system necessarily threatens differentiation. Press subsidies, for example, could threaten the autonomy of media from the state, but in societies with strong rational-legal authority, where the allocation of subsidies is governed by clearly stated criteria, they do not generally have this effect.

In terms of the three models, the Liberal Model is characterized by a high degree of differentiation of the media from "other social bodies," particularly those historically active in the political sphere – parties, interest groups, and in some cases religious groups. The Polarized Pluralist and Democratic Corporatist systems, on the other hand, are characterized by lower levels of differentiation of media from such organized social and political groups, with a more recent trend toward differentiation particularly in the Democratic Corporatist countries. This trend toward differentiation from the political system, as we shall see in Chapter 8, is present in all the countries of our study to varying degrees and is indeed connected with the three forces Alexander identifies: demands for more universalistic information put forward by new social groups, the growth of professional norms and autonomy, and development of universalistic political cultures.

At the same time, there are many problems with differentiation theory, and particularly with the notion that media history can be understood as a unilinear movement toward greater differentiation. Here it will be useful to introduce two contrasting perspectives on the role of the media in the social system, those of the Critical Theory, particularly that of Habermas, and of Bourdieu and French media sociologists drawing on Bourdieu. In each case we introduce these perspectives relatively briefly and return in Chapter 8 to assess them more systematically against differentiation theory.

*CRITIQUES OF DIFFERENTIATION THEORY: HABERMAS AND BOURDIEU.* For Habermas, the history of the public sphere is characterized not by differentiation but by de-differentiation. The nascent sphere of "collective will-formation," in which public issues could be discussed and an autonomous public opinion created, emerged in the early days of the development of liberal institutions and later collapsed into the market as commercial mass media developed, and into the system of political power as political parties, the state, and other large and powerful organizations used their control of social resources and political power, as well as the techniques of public relations, to dominate the process of public communication. The de-differentiation of the public sphere is part of what Habermas refers to as the "colonization of the lifeworld" by the systems of political and economic power. From this point of view it is not necessarily clear that the Liberal Model – where the commercialization of the media is much more advanced, as is the use of systematic public relations – represents a higher level of differentiation or "modernity" than the other models.

Bourdieu, like Habermas, shares with Parsonian systems theory the crucial elements of the problematic of differentiation theory, derived from Weber and Durkheim. In Bourdieu's field theory, a "field" is a sphere of social action with its own "rules of the game," standards of practice, and criteria of evaluation. To say that journalism or the media have emerged as a field is to say that they have become differentiated from other fields as a sphere of action. Bourdieu clearly expresses a normative preference for the autonomy of fields. He differentiates fields into what he calls "heteronomous" and "autonomous" poles, the former being those parts of the field that are most strongly influenced by other fields.

> In Bourdieu's model total domination exists when one field dominates all others and there exists only one acceptable "definition of human accomplishment" for the entire society. A field's autonomy is to be valued because it provides preconditions for the full creative process proper to each field and ultimately resistance to the "symbolic violence" exerted by the dominant system of hierarchization (Benson 1998: 465).

Bourdieu does not, however, assume an evolutionary process of development toward greater differentiation: fields change through a process of struggle among the agents working within them, and the direction of change is not predetermined. What has actually happened in contemporary France, according to media scholars who have applied Bourdieu's theory, is that the French media field has become more distant from the field of politics but closer to the increasingly dominant field of economics[2] (as we shall see in more detail in Chapter 8, differentiation theorists usually say relatively little about commercialization, and this is one of the greater ambiguities in the application of differentiation theory to the media). The autonomous pole within the media field, moreover – which was represented by the elite print press – has lost ground to the heteronomous pole represented above all by commercial television. Finally, the media themselves, consistent with Luhmann, Alexander et al., have become more important in society – but with the consequence, according to Bourdieu, that other cultural fields have lost autonomy, as they are increasingly influenced by the mass media. (Bourdieu argues particularly that the growing prestige of the mass media has distorted the academic field, which is increasingly dominated by "heteronomous" intellectuals whose prestige derives from outside academia.) Bourdieu and other French scholars working in this tradition thus paint a complex picture in which media change involves a substantial degree of de-differentiation.

THE QUESTION OF POWER. One of the criticisms most commonly leveled against differentiation theory is that it pays no attention to power. Differentiation theory is generally concerned with relations among social institutions, not among agents or social interests, and it tends to imply that with the process of differentiation power essentially withers away, or becomes diffused to the point that it is not a significant social issue. As it has been applied to the study of the media, differentiation theory suggests that power should be most diffused and least concentrated – therefore least significant – in the highly differentiated Liberal system. Do we in fact find significant differences in the distribution of power in the three systems we have outlined? Are there important differences across systems in the degree of inequality regarding access to the media and in the representation of interests and points of view?

There are literatures dealing with the relation of media to structures of social and political power within various national traditions, but there has really been no attempt to study this sort of question in a systematic comparative way, so it is unfortunately difficult to answer these questions with much certainty.[3] All of the systems considered in this book

---

[2] Summaries of Bourdieu's field theory and its application to media studies can be found in Benson (1998), Marliere (1998), Benson (2000), and Neveu (2001). Bourdieu never wrote much directly on the media, only the relatively slight *On Television* (1998). But there is a large community of media scholars, to a large extent concentrated in sociology, who draw on his ideas.

[3] Interestingly there seems to be more media-studies literature focused on power in the Liberal countries than in others. British or American media scholars, for example, are much more likely to use Gramsci than Italians. Ironically one reason for this is that

are pluralist, democratic systems. In each, a wide variety of political parties, social groups and movements (both organized and unorganized), individuals and institutions compete for voice and power, and the media systems reflect, incorporate, and shape this pluralism in a variety of ways. At the same time, all are systems of power. In each system, there are structured inequalities in the relations among these actors; some have much greater access to resources or are better positioned to exercise influence than others. The media must be seen not only as part of a process of democratic competition but also as a part of this structure of power. Alongside the conventional wisdom about the superiority of the Liberal Model, there is also a tendency for media critics in each system to believe that the grass is surely greener on the other side of the fence. Thus in the Liberal countries, media critics often look to the Democratic Corporatist system – particularly to Scandinavia, with its tradition of media tied to organized social groups – as a more democratic alternative to the commercial media that dominate their own system. But what British or Americans might see as a wonderful form of pluralism, the Scandinavian researchers will see more as a form of control of the media by the elites of established interests in society. Critics in the Polarized Pluralist countries, meanwhile, will look to the "watchdog" press of the Liberal system as more democratic, while scholars in the Liberal countries see the same commercial forces and professional routines as constraints that limit news coverage within relatively narrow ideological bounds. There are, no doubt, complex patterns of difference in which kinds of groups or ideas will have access and which will have dominance and under what conditions. These would be very important to study, given the limited state of research in the area; however, we will only be able to touch on these differences in the pages that follow. We are very skeptical, however, of the idea that the three models could be arranged into any kind of hierarchy of openness of the public sphere. We are also skeptical that convergence toward the Liberal Model can be seen as a separation of media from systems of power. As we shall see in Chapter 8, it is possible that the disruption of the old bonds between media and organized social groups that characterized much of Europe would lead to greater imbalance in the representation of social interests, rather than greater openness and diversity.

the "Anglo-American" tradition of quantitative empirical research, which generally stays away from questions of power, is probably more dominant in a lot of continental Europe than in English-speaking countries, where the "critical" tradition has been a significant influence since the 1970s.

If it is very difficult to say whether power is more or less equally distributed in different media systems, a bit more can be said about *how power works* in different systems. Within the Democratic Corporatist countries, for example, the relation of media to organized social groups has historically been extremely important, while in the Liberal countries both market forces (e.g., that make the media more responsive to some segments of the audience than to others) and routines by which journalists interact with individual political actors have been more central. One important general distinction is worth raising here. In neo-Marxist state theory a distinction was introduced in the 1970s between "structuralist" and "instrumentalist" theories of the state (e.g., Jessop 1982; Block 1987).[4] Instrumentalist theories were those that focused on power exercised by particular actors, usually in a conscious and direct way, through threats, inducements, personal ties, and the like. Structuralist theories were those that focused on impersonal mechanisms or structures that biased the political process, giving actors unequal access or constraining the outcome of the political process without necessarily requiring intervention by any particular actor.[5] "Structuralist" theories of the state also tended to emphasize the "relative autonomy" of the state from social classes and other actors, stressing that the state tended to operate to a significant extent by a logic of its own, rather than being governed purely by the logics of other social spheres – particularly the economic logic of relations between social classes. This literature generally treated structuralist theories as more sophisticated than instrumentalist ones, which were seen as simple-minded "conspiracy" theories. Most of this literature, however, focused on the experience of North American and Northern European systems; in other contexts instrumentalist theories might be perfectly adequate.

A similar distinction is probably useful in the study of the media. The Polarized Pluralist countries, as we have seen, tend to be characterized by a relatively high degree of instrumentalization of the media. Instrumentalization certainly is not absent in the Liberal and Democratic Corporatist systems; the political role of Rupert Murdoch in Britain, Conrad

---

[4] These works describe the so-called Poulantzas-Miliband debate of the 1970s. Miliband (1969) included an early but not unsophisticated Marxist analysis of the role of media in the system of political power.

[5] This distinction is connected with the distinction Lukes (1974) makes among three "faces" of power: power exercised directly by actors with greater access to resources, power that results from biases in institutional structure, and power that results from effects of the dominant culture.

Black in Canada, or Axel Springer in Germany can be seen to a significant extent in instrumentalist terms. And clearly "structural" forms of power exist in the Polarized Pluralist system as well.[6] But in general structural mechanisms are probably more important in the Liberal and Democratic Corporatist countries, where the relative autonomy of the media is greater. Central among these mechanisms are professional routines of journalism, which, according to substantial literatures particularly developed in the United States, Britain, and Canada, can be seen as embedding in the process of news production both differential relationships of the media to various news sources, and cultural and ideological criteria of newsworthiness and interpretation.

## CONCLUSIONS

In this chapter we have introduced the three models that will structure our discussion of the eighteen countries whose media systems form the empirical basis for this book. In Part II, we will explore in detail the logic and historical evolution of the three models, the connections between the media system and political system variables that can be seen in these patterns of development, and the ways in which particular countries do or do not fit the three models.

We have also introduced the debate over differentiation theory as a framework for understanding the differences among these models and their historical development. We have argued that differentiation theory takes us a certain distance in understanding the broad differences in media systems, particularly in its emphasis on the historical fusion of media systems with the system of political parties and social groups based on class, religion, ethnicity, and the like, and the different degrees to which systems have moved away from these relationships. At the same time, there are good reasons to doubt that the history of media in Western Europe and North America can be seen as a unilinear movement toward differentiation, or that the three models can be organized into a neat hierarchy in terms of differentiation. We will elaborate on this argument more fully after analyzing the three models and their histories in Part II, and after discussing more fully the trend toward convergence in media systems in Part III. For now it is worth noting that our use of a triangle in Figure 4.1 to represent the three models suggests an important

---

[6] Sampedro (1997), for example, analyzes the coverage of the movement in opposition to compulsory military service in Spain essentially in institutional or structuralist terms.

disagreement with differentiation theory. If we believed that media systems developed along a unilinear path toward greater differentiation, we would collapse our triangle into a single line, with the Polarized Pluralist countries at one end, the Liberal countries at the other, and the Democratic Corporatist countries at various places in between. In fact, we think the reader will see in subsequent pages that the differences among the systems do not justify this kind of representation.

PART II

# The Three Models

In Part II we examine the media systems of each of our three groups of countries in detail, exploring the logic and the historical evolution of each of the three models introduced in Part I. We discuss the Mediterranean or Polarized Pluralist Model in Chapter 5; the North/Central European or Democratic Corporatist Model in Chapter 6; and the North Atlantic or Liberal Model in Chapter 7. In each case, we try to stress both the common elements that define our three models, and the ways in which the media systems of individual countries vary from the three ideal types. Each of the three chapters in Part II begins with a discussion of the historical origins of the press, continues to discuss the characteristics of the media system, and moves in the final section to a discussion of the political context in which each media system evolved and an analysis of the links between the media system variables introduced in Chapter 2 and the political system variables introduced in Chapter 3. The discussions of the three media system models are essentially organized around the four variables proposed in Chapter 2: the development of media markets and particularly of the mass circulation press, political parallelism, journalistic professionalism, and the role of the state. The exact structures of the chapters vary somewhat, however, because different issues require extended discussion in the different cases. In the case of the Polarized Pluralist Model, for example, we move from an initial discussion of journalistic professionalization into an extended discussion of instrumentalizaton of the media; in the case of the Democratic Corporatist Model we include a special discussion of the complex relation between commercial media markets and political parallelism.

# FIVE

# The Mediterranean or Polarized Pluralist Model

In 1974 and 1975 Greece, Portugal, and Spain threw off the last three authoritarian regimes in Western Europe and began successful transitions to liberal democracy. Those transitions motivated an increased interest on the part of historians and social scientists in "Southern Europe" as a region with a distinct historical experience (e.g., Gunther, Diamandouros, and Phule 1995). Southern Europe is usually understood to include the three countries that moved to democracy in the mid-1970s, plus Italy, which made that transition earlier but shares many historical and structural characteristics with the other three countries. France is often mentioned in discussions of Southern Europe, though almost always treated as a marginal case. What distinguishes Southern Europe – and to a lesser degree France – from the rest of Western Europe and from North America is most basically the fact that liberal institutions, including both capitalist industrialism and political democracy, developed later. The forces of the *ancien régime* – the landholding aristocracy, the absolutist state, and the Catholic or Orthodox Church – were stronger there, and liberalism triumphed only after a protracted political conflict that continued in many cases well into the twentieth century. One important legacy of this history is the fact that the political spectrum remained wider and political differences sharper in Southern Europe than in Northern Europe or North America. As we have seen in Chapter 3, this is what political scientists refer to as polarized pluralism, and we will return in the last section of this chapter to explore more systematically how this political context has shaped the media systems of Southern Europe.

We argue that the late and contested transition to democracy in the Mediterranean region of Western Europe has produced distinct patterns of relationship between the media and the political world. The mass media in the Mediterranean countries were intimately involved in the political conflicts that mark the history of this region, and there is a strong tradition of regarding them as means of ideological expression and political mobilization. At the same time, the development of commercial media markets was relatively weak, leaving the media often dependent on the state, political parties, the Church, or wealthy private patrons, and inhibiting professionalization and the development of the media as autonomous institutions. These patterns are changing: the forces of globalization, commercialization, and secularization that, as we shall see in greater detail in Chapter 8, are transforming the media across Europe are strongly at work in the Mediterranean region. Nevertheless, the media in the Mediterranean countries remain distinctive in important ways that are connected with this history.

In its media system, as in its political history and social structure, France is clearly a borderline case; in terms of our three models it can be seen as falling somewhere between the Polarized Pluralist and Democratic Corporatist models. We have made the decision to include France with the Mediterranean countries for two reasons. First, we believe that the tendency for the media to be dominated by the political sphere that is characteristic of the Polarized Pluralist systems is strong enough in French media history that France fits this model more closely than any other. Second, there is a strong and direct historical connection between the French media and those of other Southern European countries. It was the Napoleonic invasion that brought the modern newspaper to Italy and the Iberian peninsula, and French journalism was in many ways the paradigm case on which the journalism of the region was based.

## THE POLITICAL AND LITERARY ROOTS OF JOURNALISM

The media developed in Southern Europe as an institution of the political and literary worlds more than of the market. In Northern Europe and North America, the commercial bourgeoisie, whose success in a market economy depended on a steady flow of reliable information about trade, navigation, technology, and politics, played a key role in the development of the first newspapers. A mass circulation press then began to develop as increasing numbers of the middle, working, and agrarian classes – including both males and females – entered the market and – through the development of mass political parties – the political process.

Certain elements of this process did, of course, take place in the Mediterranean countries, especially in France and in northern Italy. Venice, in fact, was the most important center of the European printing industry at one time, and early newspapers developed there as they did in the trading cities of Northern Eurpope. The onset of the Counter-Reformation, however, undermined the print industry of Venice, which was eclipsed by Amsterdam as a center of printing (Briggs and Burke 2002: 57–8). In general, the development of the bourgeoisie was weaker in Southern Europe, and early newspapers were tied more to the aristocracy, whose wealth was based in land rather than trade. The literary salons described in Habermas's work on the public sphere were attended more by aristocrats than by the bourgeoisie, and the period of the "literary public sphere" lasted relatively long in Southern Europe. The world of journalism described in Balzac's *Illusiones Perdues* or Maupassant's *Bel Ami* was frequented to a large extent by aristocrats. The same was true of Italian journalism in the early nineteenth century (the time when the "penny papers" were beginning to develop in the United States). The clergy in Italy, also closely associated with the landholding aristocracy, played a particularly central role (Murialdi 1986; Farinelli et al. 1997). Describing the readership of nineteenth-century Italian newspapers, Ricuperati (1981: 1087) writes, "we find a world of literary people, that is a public made up of erudites, theologians, university professors, members of scientific academies: a strong and important presence of clergymen." Ricuperati estimates that half the journalists working in Italian newspapers in this period were members of the clergy. The purpose of the nineteenth-century newspaper in Southern Europe was the expression of ideas, both literary and political. Balzac described the "press" as

> the word adopted to express everything which is published periodically in politics and literature, and where one judges the works both of those who govern, and of those who write, two ways of leading men (quoted in Ferenczi 1993: 28).

Scholars across the region describe the origins of journalism in similar terms: Alberto Asor Rosa (1981), an Italian historian, speaks of two *filoni* (veins) in the history of Italian journalism, the literary and the political; and Neveu (1991) speaks of a *"tropisme litteraire"* and a *"tropisme politique"* in the history of French journalism (see also Chalaby 1996).

Commercial newspapers did emerge, and newspaper circulation began to rise in Southern Europe beginning in the 1880s, at the same time mass circulation newspapers were developing in Northern Europe, North America, and East Asia. But a true mass-circulation press never fully emerged in any of the Mediterranean countries. The process went furthest in France, and this is one important way in which France is a borderline case. Today newspaper circulation is higher in France than in all the other Mediterranean countries, but lower than in all the rest of Western Europe. The history of the French press is characterized by sharp ups and downs both in the achievement of press freedom and in readership. The revolution and the Declaration of the Rights of Man and the Citizen ushered in an early period of press freedom. Newspaper circulation soared to a total that might be as high as 300,000 a day, close to the limit of what could be produced with the technology of the day, and higher than anywhere in the world. The newspaper public, multiplied by the location of newspapers in public places such as cafes, reached substantially beyond the aristocratic and bourgeois readers of earlier periods, though it still remained restricted by later standards – perhaps three million out of an adult population of fourteen million (Popkin 1990: 82–6). By 1802, however, the total press run of Paris papers had fallen back to 33,000.

Press freedom was reestablished in France in 1881, and the period from 1881 until World War I is generally referred to as the Golden Age of the French Press. Commercial newspapers modeled in part on the American penny press (*Le Matin* was run by an American) played an important role in this period, and put French newspapers again at the top rank in terms of circulation. By the beginning of World War I *Le Petit Parisien*, with distribution across much of France and a circulation over two million, was the largest-selling newspaper in the world. France had a circulation rate of 244 newspapers sold per 1,000 inhabitants, about the same as the United States at 255 per thousand, and higher than Britain at 160 per thousand (Albert 1983: 24–5). But the commercial press, which claimed to have no politics, did not displace the press of opinion in the way it did in the Liberal countries. In 1914 80 percent of Paris papers were still papers of opinion (Thogmartin 1998: 95), though by circulation these papers were much less significant. Most important, the mass circulation press of the French "Golden Age" did not develop into a powerful and lasting newspaper *industry*. Though their circulations were large, the French commercial papers were never as profitable as their U.S. or British counterparts. The advertising market in France remained small, and in 1936 French newspapers were estimated to have about one sixth to one eighth the advertising revenue of their British or American counterparts (Thogmartin 1998: 107; Neveu 2001: 11–12). By the 1930s the French newspaper industry, much of it controlled by a cartel and riddled with corruption, was in serious decline. Repression and collaboration during the Nazi era further damaged its development and it only partly recovered after World War II.

The French experience had a very direct impact on the rest of the Mediterranean region, and the pattern of media development is essentially similar, though the commercial press was weaker than in France. In Italy and the Iberian peninsula, the press began to grow in the wake of the Napoleonic invasion, and newspapers served primarily to fight out the battles between tradition and modernity that extended over most of the following century and a half. In Spain and Italy a vigorous opinion press emerged in the nineteenth century and the press played a key role in the institution of a liberal state during the Italian Risorgimento and the Canovite Restoration in Spain (Ortiz 1995). In both cases important political leaders – Cánovas and Canalejas in Spain; Cavour and Mazzini in Italy – were journalists as well as politicians: newspapers were essential tools for the organization of the movements they led. Commercial press markets also developed to a limited extent in the period from about 1880–1920, and newspapers experimented with information-oriented journalism of the sort that had developed in the United States and Britain. But the economic and social base of the press always remained narrow. The development of the market economy was limited, compared with the Liberal or Democratic Corporatist countries. Literacy rates were low except in France (Cipolla 1969), where the state played a strong role in the expansion of education (Weber 1976). In Spain over 70 percent of the population was illiterate in 1887, and this was true of about a third of the population in 1940 (Ortiz 1995: 216). Italy had not only a relatively high illiteracy rate – a bit less than 60 percent at the time of unification in 1870 – but also substantial linguistic diversity. Only 2 to 3 percent of the population could understand the Tuscan dialect established as the official language at unification (Vincent 2000: 139).[1] It was television that eventually brought linguistic standardization to Italy (De Mauro 1979). By the 1920s–30s, the development of the press was disrupted by dictatorship, for many decades in the Spanish and Portuguese cases.

The first Greek newspapers were exile papers published under Turkish occupation, which lasted until the 1830s. Greek history is marked by sharp political conflict and frequent alternation between dictatorship – or occupation – and democracy. Greek newspapers have for the most part developed as political papers with limited readership. Until the

---

[1] Illiteracy diminished in all of the Southern European countries following World War II and today is not much different from the rest of Europe.

1960s they were published in a literary form of Greek different from the *demotike* spoken in everyday life, and the dictatorship that ruled from 1967–74 banned the use of *demotike* in the press (Zaharapoulos and Paraschos 1993). Freedom of the press was introduced in Portugal in 1820, but frequently interrupted throughout the nineteenth century. The most important period of press freedom lasted from the overthrow of the monarchy in 1910 until the start of the Salazar dictatorship in 1926. By the time of the revolution in 1974 the Portuguese press was the weakest in Europe (Seaton and Pimlott 1980; Agee and Traquina 1984).

The development of the commercial press in Southern Europe was, in sum, limited in comparison with the Liberal and Democratic Corporatist countries whose histories we will explore in the following chapters. In Italy and in France, on the other hand, a strong party press developed in the early twentieth century, which for both countries was part of a long period of political democracy. In this way their media history is similar to that of the Democratic Corporatist countries. The Italian Communist party (PCI) was one of the quintessential mass parties, along with the German Social Democrats. Like the mass parties of Northern Europe, it had a dense network of institutions that involved citizens in its organizational and cultural life – social and sports clubs, cultural organizations, libraries, economic institutions, and, of central importance, communications media. *L'Unità*, the main paper of the PCI, was established under the influence of Antonio Gramsci in 1924 and reached a top circulation of about 300,000 in the 1960s and a circulation of 700,000 for its Sunday edition – the highest of any Italian paper (Murialdi 1986). It remained important into the 1990s, and still exists as a paper of the left, though it is no longer an official party paper. *L'Unità* played a central role in the large political subculture that developed around the Communist party in Italy. Among its activities was the organization of the Festa del'Unità, an annual festival that still takes place in cities around Italy and has always been an important part of the collective social life of the left. The party was at the same time crucial to the success of the paper, providing not only subsidized funding but also distribution through the party's organizational network. Other parties also established their own newspapers – *Il Popolo* of the Christian Democrats and *l'Avanti* of the Socialists, among the most important. These newspapers were crucial to the ability of mass parties to communicate with the public, particularly given the control of most of the press by industrialists with their own political ties and ambitions, which we will explore a bit later.

Fascism interrupted the development of a pluralist party press; but it reemerged strongly in the immediate post-liberation period as party papers joined other politically oriented papers, often connected with the resistance (in France, e.g., *Combat*, directed by philosopher Albert Camus, survived until 1974) as pioneers of the new democratic media. Fifty percent of the Italian newspapers in the late 1940s were party papers. A strong party press also developed in France (Barbrook 1995). *L'Humanité*, the paper of the Communist Party, had the largest circulation of all French papers in 1947. By 1996 its circulation was down to less than 60,000, though it is still seen as a significant political voice. The value placed in French culture on the survival of this kind of ideological newspaper is suggested by the fact that in 2001, when *L'Humanité* was forced to sell shares in an effort to stay alive, the main commercial television company, TF1, became an investor.

In Spain and Portugal long periods of dictatorial rule choked off the development of mass parties and the party press (both countries have very low rates of party membership). Spain did have the "Prensa del Movimiento" connected with Franco's "Movimiento Nacional," but party papers have not had a significant role in the democratic period. The Salazar dictatorship in Portugal never was a mobilizing regime, and never placed much emphasis on the press, or has a significant party press developed in the democratic period. In Greece, for somewhat different reasons connected with the persistence of political clientelism, mass parties did not really develop until the 1970s. So again, a true party press has never been strong – though privately owned papers, as we shall see, are typically fiercely partisan.

Church-linked media have played a significant role in the Mediterranean countries, as they have in some of the countries of the Democratic Corporatist Model (e.g., the Netherlands). The Catholic-owned paper *Ya* was the highest-circulation paper in Spain for a while in the 1970s; the liberal Catholic paper *La Croix* has played an important role in France. The Church owns important radio networks in Spain and Portugal, and for a while a television network in the latter. Catholic dailies are even more important in Italy: *L'Osservatore Romano* is the official paper of the Catholic Church; *L'Avvenire* was the daily of the organization of Italian Bishops and still is linked to the Church organization; and local churches own a number of papers in Northern Italy.

Newspapers in the Mediterranean countries – whether commercially owned or linked to parties or the Church – have been directed for the most part to an educated elite interested in the political world. The Italian journalist Forcella expressed this particularly well in a 1959 essay titled "*Millecinquecento lettori*" – "Fifteen hundred readers":

A political journalist, in our country, can count on fifteen hundred readers: the ministers and subsecretaries (all of them), members of parliament (some), party and trade union leaders, the top clergy and those industrialists who want to show themselves well-informed. The rest don't count, even if a newspaper sells three hundred thousand copies. First of all it is not clear whether the common readers read the first page of the paper, and in any case their influence is minimal. The whole system is organized around the relation of the journalist to that group of privileged readers.

Starting in the 1970s or 1980s, to be sure, all the Mediterranean countries saw a shift toward a more market-oriented print press. *La Repubblica* in Italy, *Público* in Portugal, *El País, Diario 16* (in the 1970s and 1980s) and *El Periódico de Catalunya* in Spain, and *Libération* in France all have tried aggressively to expand circulations with forms of journalism that combine the old focus on politics with more human interest, more feature news, a more graphic presentation, and so on. Spain and Portugal were among the only countries in the world with increases in aggregate newspaper circulation in the 1990s. If they are no longer directed at fifteen hundred readers, however, these papers still reach affluent, educated minorities with a very particular political and cultural identity within society (e.g., Delberghe 2000). A look back at Table 2.1 will confirm that newspaper circulation in the Mediterranean region remains the lowest in Europe, ranging from 78 copies per thousand population in Greece (for 2000) to 190 per thousand in France. Two additional characteristics of the press market in the Mediterranean countries are worth noting. Gender differences in newspaper readership are quite large, reflecting the closeness of the press to the world of politics and the traditional exclusion of women from the latter, as well as historically high rates of female illiteracy (70 percent in Spain in 1910 [Vincent 2000: 10]). Table 2.2 shows Portugal, Spain, Italy, and Greece had larger gender differences in newspaper reach than any of the other countries in this study. In the Spanish case, for example, 47 percent of men and 26 percent of women reported reading newspapers daily. Newspaper industries in the Mediterranean region are also highly dependent on newsstand sales rather than subscription – over 90 percent of papers are sold in newsstands in all of the Mediterranean countries except France, as compared with 59 percent in Britain, 28 percent in Sweden, or 10 percent in the Netherlands (World Association of Newspapers 2001).

Tabloid or sensationalist popular newspapers are virtually absent in the Mediterranean region except for *France Soir*, which has declined substantially in circulation since the 1980s.[2] Attempts to establish sensationalist papers in Spain, one involving the German publisher Axel Springer and another involving the *Daily Mirror*, have failed on a number of occasions (Barerra 1995: 137–9). The role of the popular press is in part filled in Southern Europe by sports dailies, which are important in every country, and in some cases by what the Spanish call the *prensa del corazón*, weekly publications with predominantly female audiences focusing on celebrities and human-interest stories.[3] Sports dailies had combined circulations at the time this book went to press of more than 800,000 in Italy, 650,000 in Spain, and 200,000 in Portugal (as against 280,000 for the four main general-interest papers). It should be noted that the figures for circulation per thousand reported in Chapter 2 include the sports press, and thus could be said to overstate newspaper circulation in Southern Europe. The local press is also relatively undeveloped, except in France, where it accounts for about 70 percent of newspaper circulation; its readership is less elite and less male in character than the national press. The largest selling paper in France is a provincial daily, *Ouest France*, at about 700,000.

Mass circulation newspapers never developed in Southern Europe in part because the economic and political conditions for the development of media markets were not present until the mid–twentieth century – when radio had already become an important medium and television was beginning to emerge. It seems unlikely that any country that did not develop mass circulation newspapers in the late nineteenth century ever will have them. The only true mass media of Southern Europe are electronic media, and their importance for the formation of mass public opinion is therefore particularly great.

---

[2] *Le Parisien* was also once a sensationalist paper, though it has since repositioned itself as a respectable regional paper for the Paris area. Neither *Le Parisien* nor *France Soir* was ever as sensationalist as British tabloids.

[3] The most significant is *¡Hola!*, which goes back to the 1930s. Felipe Gonzáles gave his first interview as president to *¡Hola!* (Barrera 1995: 177). The company also publishes *Hello!* in Britain. *¡Hola!* is less sensationalist than British tabloids. In one case it bought nude pictures of Lady Di so that other publications couldn't get them and did not publish them.

## POLITICAL PARALLELISM

As the history suggests, the media in the Mediterranean countries are relatively strongly politicized, and political parallelism is relatively high. The style of journalism tends to give substantial emphasis to commentary. Newspapers tend to represent distinct political tendencies, and this is reflected in the differing political attitudes of their readerships. At times newspapers play an activist role, mobilizing those readers to support political causes. Public broadcasting tends to be party-politicized. Both journalists and media owners often have political ties or alliances, and it remains fairly common for journalists to become politicians and vice versa.

Greece is a strong example of this pattern. From the time of the exile press, Greek newspapers have always been political instruments above all, rooted culturally in passionate ideological divisions, and often tied to the state and/or parties, which have provided financial subsidies, help with distribution, and other forms of assistance. The many Athens newspapers, especially, still reflect a wide range of ideologies, and their writing is often highly polemical. Zaharapoulos and Paraschos (1993) give examples of their headlines when U.S. President George Bush visited Greece in 1991, ranging from "National Success, the Cyprus Issue Is Solved," to "Frigid Bush: Cyprus Is Not Kuwait, said the Caesar." Greek journalists tend to be strongly opinionated and politically engaged, and often run for political office.

The political identification of French newspapers varies, from clearly ideological papers such as *L'Humanité* and *La Croix* to relatively apolitical regional papers. The major Paris dailies reflect broad political tendencies, *Le Monde* and *Libération* representing the left-center, and *Le Figaro* and *France-Soir* the right-center. The polemical style that can often be found in Greece and could once be found in France is mostly gone (Charon 1990). Still, as Albert (1983) put it:

> French Journalism has always been more a journalism of expression than a journalism of observation: it gives precedence to the chronicle and the commentary over summary and reportage. As much as in the presentation of facts, it has always been interested in the exposition of ideas. . . . In this, it is fundamentally different from Anglo-Saxon journalism, for which news always has priority over commentary.

Ferenczi argues that when the mass circulation press began to develop in France, key elements of the news- and information-based

Table 5.1 *Functions of Paragraphs in U.S. and French News Stories*

|  | Reporting Only | Background | Interpretation | Opinion |
|---|---|---|---|---|
| *Le Monde* | 76.6% | 7.5 | 17.1 | 6.6 |
| *Le Figaro* | 70.0 | 11.3 | 13.4 | 5.2 |
| *The New York Times* | 90.3 | 4.5 | 4.8 | 0.4 |

Anglo-American model were embraced. Articles of pure "doctrine or reflection" gave way to a form of journalism that combined reporting and commentary. But a strong emphasis on commentary remained, as did an emphasis on style, creating a French model of journalism distinct from the Anglo-American. Information-oriented journalism, as we shall see in greater detail near the end of this chapter, has made even greater inroads into French journalism in the last couple of decades of the twentieth century, as investigative reporting, for example, has become common. But French journalism still includes a relatively strong emphasis on commentary that reflects its political roots. Table 5.1 shows the results of a content analysis of *The New York Times, Le Monde,* and *Le Figaro,* with samples from coverage of national politics in the 1960s and 1990s, showing the percent of paragraphs devoted to four journalistic functions: reporting events and statements, giving background, giving interpretation (usually involving comments about the motives, causes, or consequences of an action or event), and giving opinions.[4] In all three papers, the reporting function predominated, accounting for 90 percent of *The New York Times* paragraphs and more than 70 percent of those in the French papers. The French press, however, clearly put more emphasis on background, interpretation, and opinion, the latter, for example, accounting for 6.6 percent of paragraphs in *Le Monde* and less than 1 percent in *The New York Times.* When *Times* stories were coded for opinion it usually involved the journalist drawing conclusions about disputed facts; in the French press it was more likely to involve policy advocacy or value judgments about political actions. We did not find

---

[4] The sample includes 318 stories and 1,479 paragraphs from *Le Monde*; 308 stories and 1,350 paragraphs from *Le Figaro*; and 358 stories and 3,189 paragraphs from *The New York Times.* Dates were selected randomly from 1965–7 and 1995–7, and every other story dealing with national politics was coded. Paragraphs were coded for their predominant function and in paragraphs that clearly had multiple functions, more active forms of journalism were coded over less active forms – opinion over interpretation, over background, over simple reporting. Coding of the French papers was done by Rod Benson and coding of the U.S. paper was done by Mauro Porto.

consistent differences between the two decades we studied, the 1960s and 1990s.

Here is a fairly typical example of commentary-oriented political reporting in the French press. On June 21, 1991, the lead story in *Le Monde* concerned a "polemic on immigration" between Socialist Prime Minister Edith Cresson and conservative President Jacques Chirac. Under the headline was a *"chapeau"* or "hat," a paragraph reporting what American journalists would call the "peg" for the story, a statement the previous day by Cresson criticizing Chirac. Below it was a story by Bruno Frappat, one of the paper's top political editors, which began like this (insofar as a translation can do justice to the typically literary French style!):

> Yes, immigration poses a problem for France. No, over thirty years, governments have neither seen it coming nor been able to prepare themselves properly [*n'ont rien vu venir ni rien su maîtriser*]. Yes, ineffectiveness is general and imagination failed, except at the base [i.e., at lower levels of society]. Yes, economic gloom augments the bitterness of the tensions.
>
> Against a background of impotence two discourses confront one another: denial and hysteria. The angelic left cannot hide its discomfort with the stubborn facts. Right wing extremists are gaining ground every day with their simplistic local-bar-style "send'em back where they came from" solutions.
>
> What's new: the right, its eye fixed on ballot box, is falling into line behind a common message. The 19th of June, in Orléans, Jacques Chirac spoke of an "overdose" and complained of the "French worker," same-floor neighbor of immigrants, driven "crazy" by the "noise and the smell." Michel Poiniatowski [a conservative politician] flatters himself, in [an interview in] *Le Figaro*, to have gone "further" than Jean Marie Le Pen [leader of the anti-immigrant National Front].
>
> There are words which emit a foul odor.

In Italy – as also in France – earlier traditions of a politicized press were reinforced by the experience of Fascist dictatorship and the Liberation. Under Fascism, of course, the media were expected to serve political ends – Mussolini was a journalist. And with the Liberation the first newspaper licenses went to anti-Fascist political forces. As we have seen, the party press was extremely important in the immediate post liberation period. As commercial papers reemerged, they too would have political orientations, for reasons we will explore a bit later.

Commentary-oriented journalism was the rule. To quote Forcella (1959) once again:

> When I first started doing journalism, I thought journalism was be-fore all else information, facts, news. . . . But I sadly learned, slowly, too slowly, that I was greatly deceived. Facts for a political journalist never speak by themselves. They either say too much or too little. When they say too much you have to make them speak more softly, when they say too little you have to integrate them to give them their proper meaning. Clarity in this work is a cumbersome virtue (454).

The dominant form of political reporting through the fifties and six-ties was a kind of article known as the *pastone*, written by the most prestigious journalists and appearing on the front page (Dardano 1976), which combined a review of the major political developments of the day with comments by the journalist (a form similar in many ways to what the French call the *chronique* and the Spanish call the *crónica*). Even as more market-oriented papers emerged, beginning in the 1970s, they did not abandon political identities or commentary-oriented journal-ism (Mancini 2000a; Roidi 2001). *La Repubblica* was the pioneer in the shift toward a more market-oriented newspaper industry in Italy. It in-troduced more colorful writing and graphic presentation; broadened its agenda to include more entertainment and culture and eventually sports and crime; hired women reporters; and increased female readership. Yet it is clearly a paper of the left and a prime example of a paper that offers "orientation rather than just news facts," in the words of its founder, Eugenio Scalfari (quoted in Poggioli 1991: 6). In the first issue of *La Repubblica* (January 14, 1976, p. 6), Scalfari wrote:

> This newspaper is a bit different from others: it is a journal of information that doesn't pretend to follow an illusory political neutrality, but declares explicitly that it has taken a side in the political battle. It is made by men who belong to the vast arc of the Italian left.

In the 1990s two other Italian papers, *L'Indipendente* and *Il Giornale*, moved toward a still higher level of sensationalism in the search for read-ers, characterized by screaming headlines of a sort previously unknown. Both are also highly political – *L' Indipendente*, close to the right-wing Northern League and *Il Giornale*, the voice of Berlusconi's Forza Italia. The history of *L'Indipendente* is very illustrative of Italian journalistic

Table 5.2 *Party-Press Parallelism in Italian Newspaper Readership, 1996*

| | Communist Refounding | Democrats of the Left | Popular Party | Northern League | Forza Italia | National Alliance |
|---|---|---|---|---|---|---|
| *Corriere della sera* | 64 | 89 | 120 | 100 | 111 | 100 |
| *La Repubblica* | 124 | 156 | 122 | 54 | 34 | 62 |
| *La Stampa* | 71 | 105 | 81 | 215 | 98 | 65 |
| *Il Giornale* | 28 | 22 | 8 | 57 | 260 | 188 |
| *Il Giorno* | 0 | 75 | 61 | 246 | 164 | 93 |
| *La Nazione* | 84 | 70 | 193 | 0 | 88 | 153 |
| *Il Mattino* | 97 | 88 | 135 | 13 | 99 | 162 |
| *Resto del Carlino* | 126 | 111 | 135 | 56 | 83 | 85 |
| *Gazzetta Mezzogiorno* | 50 | 87 | 27 | 0 | 97 | 203 |
| *L'Unità* | 165 | 245 | 19 | 19 | 19 | 35 |
| *L'Avvenire* | 47 | 47 | 613 | 60 | 27 | 60 |

*Source:* Sani (2001: 205).
Figures show the number of voters of a given party that read each paper, per hundred readers of that paper in the population as a whole. Thus figures over 100 indicate that voters of that party are overrepresented in the paper's readership; figures below 100 indicate that they are underrepresented.

culture: it was started to be the Italian counterpart of the Anglo-Saxon "objective," neutral newspaper, with "cold" headlines and a very low level of news dramatization. But the attempt was not successful. Its circulation remained small and soon its editor and founder was forced to resign and the owners appointed a new editor, Vittorio Feltri, well known as a combative journalist willing to take part in political struggle. Soon the daily became the "unofficial voice" of the Northern League. Some Italian papers, *La Stampa* or *Il Corriere della Sera*, especially, tilt more toward information and less toward commentary than papers such as *La Repubblica*. But in general, commentary-oriented journalism has survived the shift toward a stronger market orientation in the Italian press. Indeed it could be argued that partisanship has been particularly intense in the Italian press since media mogul Berlusconi entered politics.

One common manifestation of political parallelism is a significant differentiation of media in terms of the political orientations of their audience. Table 5.2 shows the political orientations of the readerships of Italian papers from 1996. The figures make clear that the choices of Italian newspaper readers are still strongly influenced by politics.

Italian newspapers have also often taken an activist role, mobilizing their readers to support political causes and participate in political events. Of course, this role was central to the party press; but it was never exclusive to them. Commercial papers as well often include information on how to get to a political demonstration, and will at times campaign for political causes. In 1974, to take a particularly dramatic example, when a key referendum was being held to overturn Italy's new law permitting divorce, the entire front page of *Il Messaggero* was taken up with the word "**No!**" Individual journalists often play activist roles; the head of the journalists' union led a demonstration protesting the actions of the police against protestors at the World Trade Organization meeting in Genoa in 2001.

In Spain and Portugal, the tradition of a pluralistic and politically engaged press was cut off by dictatorship. In Portugal, it reemerged dramatically with the revolution of 1974. As the revolution radicalized, newspapers and radio stations were taken over by politicized journalists; the Journalists' Union described their role in these terms:

> Newspapers should be defined as organs of anti-fascist, anti-colonial and anti-imperialist combat, intransigently on the side of the interests and struggles of laborers, workers, peasants, popular masses and the exploited (quoted in Agee and Traquina 1984: 13).

Eventually, as political parties developed, newspapers became aligned with them, and often were funded by parties or by the state – many newspapers had been owned by banks before the revolution, and became state property when the banks were nationalized. In the 1980s, however, state-owned newspapers were privatized, the press and radio industries moved more into the commercial sphere, and the degree of party-politicization has declined considerably.

The Spanish transition to democracy was a more gradual, elite-managed transition. In the absence of fully formed democratic institutions, "media served as conduits for information about the strategy for political change being implemented by the reformist Suárez government, as well as platforms for the articulation of political demands by newly emerging political and trade union organizations" (Gunther, Montero, and Wert 2000: 45). This new pluralist press, the so-called *Parlamento de Papel* (Parliament of Paper) emerged in a commercial context, though with strong political ties. The key event was the launching of *El País* by the commercial media conglomerate PRISA in 1976; "its principal stockholders included all the representatives of the political families that would govern during the transition to democracy" (Gunther, Montero, and Wert 2000: 45). *El País* was joined several months later by *Diario 16*. In the transition period, an advocacy orientation was common among Spanish journalists, who often saw it as their role to promote the new democratic regime and to oppose Francoism. Canel, Rodriguez, and Sánchez (2000: 128–32) and Canel and Piqué (1998) found that in the late 1990s 40 to 50 percent of Spanish journalists still considered it an important part of the journalists role to "promote certain values and ideas" and to "influence the public"; advocacy orientations were most common among older journalists who had worked during the transition period.

While political parallelism has declined in most of Europe in the last decades of the twentieth century, it is reasonable to argue that it has increased in the new Spanish democracy, resulting in a division of most of the media into two rival camps. In this sense there is a parallel with the Italian case, where media partisanship has also increased in recent years. When the Spanish Socialist Workers Party (PSOE) came to power in 1982, ending the initial phase of transition to democracy, PRISA, which also included the most important radio network, publishing, and eventually television interests, became fairly closely aligned with the new governing elite, as its owner was an important advisor to President Felipe González. Eventually an opposition camp began to form around the traditional conservative newspaper *ABC* (historically associated with the monarchist movement), the Church-owned radio network COPE, and a new newspaper, *El Mundo*, which was formed in 1989 following a conflict within *Diario 16* and was read while the PSOE was in power by supporters of the two principal opposition groupings, the conservative Partido Popular (PP) and Izquierda Unida (IU), the United Left, whose core is the Communist Party. Gunther, Montero, and Wert (2000) report figures from a Spanish election survey – reproduced in Table 5.3 – that show that in Spain, as in Italy, the readerships of national newspapers continue to reflect political divisions. *El Mundo* built its popularity as an opposition newspaper to a significant extent by breaking a series of scandals involving PSOE finances and human-rights violations in the war against Basque terrorists, and Gunther, Montero, and Wert also show that readers of *El Mundo* and *ABC* were much more likely to consider corruption a serious problem than readers of *El País*.

Both media partisanship and government pressures increased as elections became increasingly competitive in the 1990s. After 1996, when the Partido Popular came to office, media grouped around PRISA became the opposition camp. A progovernment camp formed around *El Mundo*,

Table 5.3 *Party-Press Parallelism in Spanish Newspaper Readership, 1993 (percentages down)*

| | Newspaper Read Most Frequently | | |
| --- | --- | --- | --- |
| | El País | ABC | El Mundo |
| Voted for PSOE | 36% | 13% | 10% |
| Voted for PP | 14 | 74 | 38 |
| Voted for IU | 24 | 3 | 21 |
| Voted for other party | 7 | 5 | 2 |
| Did not vote | 19 | 5 | 29 |

*Source:* 1993 Spanish CNEP Survey reported in Gunther, Montero, and Wert (2000: 46).

COPE, and the privatized state telecommunications company, Telefónica de España (headed by a childhood friend of President José María Aznar), which gained control of the private television company Antena 3 and the radio network Onda Cero, and launched a rival satellite television operation to compete with PRISA's Canal Plus (Bustamante 2000). Among major national media, only the private television channel Tele 5, largely owned by foreign capital, has remained more or less outside of these camps. Regional media reflect the often special political alignments of the autonomous regions – the Barcelona paper *La Vanguardia*, for example, being close to the Catalan Nationalist CiU.[5]

With the tradition of the political press interrupted in Spain, the influence of the American form of professionalism has been fairly great, at least as far as the newer papers are concerned (the traditional conservative paper *ABC* has been characterized by a much more explicitly ideological style).[6] The Style Book of *El País* (1996) says on its first page, "information and opinion shall be clearly differentiated from one another." Nevertheless, even at the newer Spanish papers, advocacy traditions coexist with the influence of neutral professionalism. Pedro J. Ramírez, director of *El Mundo*, for example, wrote in his initial article introducing the paper that it would be "un órgano radical en la defensa de sus convicciones" – "a radical organ in defense of its convictions" (quoted in Barrera 1995: 126).

[5] Barrera (1995: 106ff) gives a much more detailed discussion of the evolution of its political orientation during the period of PSOE rule.
[6] Gunther, Montero, and Wert (2000: 55) argue that both *ABC* and *El Mundo* mix news and opinion more than *El País*.

On contentious issues one can often see sharp political differences in the Spanish media, manifested in contentious headlines, patterns of selection and emphasis (including both articles and photography) and bitter polemics in editorials. To take one typical example – a fairly subtle one by Spanish standards – when Spanish judge Balthasar Garzón moved to bring former Chilean dictator Augusto Pinochet to trial in Spain, the media belonging to the different camps treated the case in widely varying ways: the Left in Spain thinks of the Right as still in some sense Fascist at heart, so the Pinochet case had important ideological implications. Thus when Spanish Foreign Minister Matutes commented on the decision of Chilean President Frei to contest the Spanish extradition order in the World Court of Justice (September 20, 1999), *El País* carried the headline, "Matutes applauds the decision of Chile to take to the Tribunal of the Hague the 'Pinochet case'" – associating the Partido Popular government with the defense of Pinochet. *El Mundo* saw no such defense of Pinochet in the Minister's statement: "Matutes says Frei acted under pressure in the 'Pinochet case.'" One survey of Spanish journalists found that more than 85 percent believed information and opinion were often mixed (Ortega and Humanes 2000: 168).

## POLITICAL PARALELLISM IN PUBLIC BROADCASTING

Public broadcasting systems in the Mediterranean countries have also tended to be party-politicized, "politics over broadcasting" systems. French television under de Gaulle was the quintessential case of what we called in Chapter 2 the "government model" of broadcast organization. De Gaulle considered control of television essential to effective government. The top personnel of the public broadcasting company Radio Television Française (RTF) were appointed directly by the Minister of Information until 1964 and were under tight political control even later (Kuhn 1995). Through the 1960s and 70s changes in government in France would be reflected directly in the personnel and policies of public broadcasting, as in any other agency of government. After a series of reforms in the 1980s that failed to establish an independent broadcasting regulator – mainly because governments were unwilling to make appointment on a basis other than political loyalty – France moved significantly away from government control with the formation of the Conseil Supérieur de l'Audiovisuel (CSA) in 1989 (Kuhn 1995; Hoffmann-Riem 1996). One third of the members of the CSA are appointed by the president of the Republic and one third each by the presidents of the Senate and Assembly, a formula based on that used for the Constitutional Court. A third of the members are replaced every two years, breaking the association between the appointment of the CSA and the formation of governments, and appointments have tended to emphasize expertise above political loyalty. According to the analysis of Dagnaud (2000: 37–9), new governments still press successfully to name directors at the public television channels. But the mediating role of the CSA, which must appoint them, limits considerably the ability of the government to intervene in the management of those channels.

In Greece, Portugal, and Spain the political majority has effective control of public broadcasting, though that control is more limited in the Iberian countries. In Greece, like Gaullist France, control is direct, with directors of the state broadcasting company ERT under the authority of the Minister of the Press and the Mass Media. A more broadly representative National Radio-Television Council, its members nominated by the parties in Parliament according to proportional representation, has advisory authority. Portuguese public television is a corporation whose capital is held by the state. The government names its directors. However, a High Authority for Social Communication with greater independence – modeled to some degree on French institutions – has some oversight authority and is supposed to approve appointments of news directors. There is also an advisory Opinion Council on which "socially relevant groups" are represented, similar to the German system – though only advisory in character. In Spain, the governing body of the Grupo Radio Televisión Española (RTVE) is appointed by the parties in Parliament, and must be approved by a two-thirds majority. Spain is essentially a majoritarian system (see Chapter 3) – the PSOE governed with an absolute majority and the PP gained an absolute majority after the 2000 election – so appointment by Parliament according to proportional representation means majority control, though the requirement of a two-thirds majority requires serious negotiation with the opposition. The board appointed following the 2000 election included six representatives of the Partido Popular (four of them, incidentally, journalists), one each from Catalan and Canary Islands nationalist parties allied with the majority and four from the opposition PSOE, with the IU and the Basque Nationalists excluded from representation. Board members are unambiguously appointed as party representatives, and both the PSOE and the PP governments have pursued interventionist policies toward public broadcasting. Political coverage cannot ignore the variety of Spanish political forces, but clearly has a slant toward the political interests of the governing party (Bustamante 1989; on election coverage Rospir 1996; Fernández and Santana 2000). Similar systems prevail with public broadcasting at the regional level, though the political majority will vary from region to region. Survey data reported by Gunther, Montero, and Wert (2000) show that, as with newspaper readerships, viewers of different television news programs – on TVE or the various commercial broadcasters – differ in their political preferences. The same is true with radio listeners. Spanish radio is characterized by highly polemical political discussion programs – *tertulias* – that are widely regarded as having an important political influence.

France, Greece, Spain, and Portugal are all essentially majoritarian systems. Italy is a consensus system, and the politicization of broadcasting has taken a different form there. Through the 1950s and 1960s, the Catholic culture remained dominant in Italian social life and the Christian Democrats dominated Italian politics. The Italian public broadcaster RAI reflected this Catholic dominance. By the 1970s secularization of Italian society led to a shift in the political balance; Christian Democratic dominance was eroded and the Christian Democrats increasingly had to share power with the so-called "secular parties" and even, to some extent, with the Communist opposition. Control of RAI shifted from the government to Parliament and RAI was increasingly integrated into the *lottizzazione* by which the parties divided power and resources, though the government parties continued to have the predominant position (Chiarenza 2002).

By the 1980s a system had emerged that gave control of the first channel of RAI to the Christian Democrats, RAI 2 to the secular parties, and RAI 3, intended originally as a regional channel, to the Communist opposition. The *lottizzazione* affected not only appointments to the Administrative Council of RAI and the heads of the three channels, but appointment of much of the personnel down through the organization as well as the allocation of time in public affairs programming. The system was actually a complex mixture of external pluralism – in the sense that the different political forces had their "own" channels – and internal pluralism, both in the sense that RAI was still governed by a common body and in the sense that each channel still had personnel from a variety of different parties (Monteleone 1992). News programs on each channel reflected the full spectrum of Italian political parties: the typical form of television news reporting in this period was to summarize events and then to present the comments of the various political parties (Hallin and Mancini 1984). This is also true in the other Mediterranean countries, even if they don't have the *lottizzazione* in management of the different channels. Other kinds of current affairs programs, on the other hand, typically have clear political orientations and offer journalists the opportunity to engage in active commentary of a sort that is usually not possible on news broadcasts.[7]

The collapse of the Italian party system in the early 1990s – all of the old parties were destroyed following financial scandals and the end of the Cold War – has changed this system to a degree. The governing board of RAI now has only five members, which means that it cannot be appointed by strict proportional representation. It includes three representatives of the majority and two of the opposition and in a sense reflects a more majoritarian logic (Marletti and Roncarolo 2000). Personnel are still appointed to a significant extent according to the *lottizzazione*, though there is not as clear a division as before among the channels. Top directors also still tend to be intimately involved in politics. The director of TG1 at the time this book was written was close to the majority (he had been a journalist, then became a deputy for Berlusconi's Forza Italia before being named director) and the director of TG3 was close to the opposition.

In all of the Mediterranean countries political logic tends to play a large role in broadcasting, particularly – though not exclusively – in publicly owned media, and of course particularly in news and public affairs programming. This is perhaps most clearly illustrated by the fact that the news agenda is not considered to be governed purely by journalistic judgments of "newsworthiness," but is a question of political policy. France and Italy both have formal systems for monitoring representation of political parties in broadcasting (Caruso 2000). In the French case the "rule of three thirds" has been in force since 1969, specifying that one-third of the time given to political representatives to speak should go to the government, one-third to the parliamentary majority, and one-third to the opposition (and during election campaigns, equally divided between the candidates). When the rule was renewed in 2000, a provision was added that small parties not represented in Parliament should also get some air time, though the exact criteria have not yet been developed. This rule applies to all television broadcasters, public and commercial, and the CSA monitors compliance each month.

---

[7] In Spain a *lottizzazione* was proposed (using the Italian word) by the UCD, the governing party in the early 1980s, but rejected by the opposition PSOE (Fernández and Santana 2000: 101) – which no doubt knew that it would soon be in the majority and would be better off rejecting power sharing according to the Italian model.

## PROFESSIONALIZATION

Journalism, as we have seen, originated in the Mediterranean countries as an extension of the worlds of literature and politics. The corps of journalists was an "unformed aggregate of authors and editors" and journalism a "route of passage, not a place of arrival" (Ferenczi 1993: 29, 41; Chalaby 1996). Newspapers typically "valued more highly writers, politicians and intellectuals," and journalism was "a secondary occupation, poorly paid and to which one aspired often as a springboard to a career in politics" (Ortega and Humanes 2000: 125) or in literature. In Spain it was commonly said that there were only two routes to a career in politics – through the military or through journalism (Ortiz 1995). This began to change with the development of the commercial press and the "new journalism" in the last two decades of the nineteenth century. The number of people making a full-time, permanent living from journalism increased dramatically. New genres of writing were being developed that could be considered distinctively journalistic and a sense of a distinct professional identity clearly began to emerge.

In many ways, this history of journalistic professionalization is closely parallel to what occurred in the Liberal and Democratic Corporatist countries. The process did not develop as strongly in the Mediterranean countries, however, as in the North. The political and literary roots of journalism were deeper, and the political connections persisted much longer. Limited development of media markets meant that newspapers were smaller and less likely to be self-sustaining. And state intervention, particularly in periods of dictatorship, interrupted the development of journalism as a profession. The level of professionalization thus remains lower in the Mediterranean countries, though it increased in important ways in the last couple of decades of the twentieth century.

It is important to make clear what we mean when we say the level of professionalization is lower. This does not, for example, mean that journalists in the Mediterranean countries are less educated than those elsewhere. Spanish journalists are *more* likely to have university degrees today than those in Britain or Germany (Weaver 1998). The close connection of journalism with the political and literary worlds and the orientation of newspapers to educated elites has meant that journalism has in some sense been a more elite occupation in Southern Europe than in other regions. In Italy famous writers and intellectuals have often been journalists as well: the film director and writer Pasolini was a commentator for *Il Corriere della Sera*, for example, where the writer Barzini (the author of *The Italians*) also worked. In France, writing books has always been important to the prestige of journalistic stars (Rieffel 1984). It also does not mean that journalists in the Mediterranean countries are not as good at what they do as those in other regions. How one judges professionalization from a normative point of view is a complex issue, and we will explore it from different angles in various parts of this book. But one could certainly make an argument that the quality of the writing and the sophistication of political analysis are higher in papers such as *Le Monde, El País, La Vanguardia*, and *La Repubblica* than in American newspapers – not to mention British tabloids. Again it is important to remember that Mediterranean newspapers have smaller and more sophisticated readerships.

Padioleau (1985: 310–11), in a comparative study of *Le Monde* and *The Washington Post* at the beginning of the 1980s, pointed to the following characteristics of French journalism, in making the argument that the level of professionalization was lower there than in other systems:

> ... weak [*chétives*] professional organizations except in the form of competing trade unions; limited social recognition of the Press as a collective, autonomous and legitimate social actor; a limited system of common professional ethics; limited agreement on journalistic standards; weak prestige of training institutions, etc.

He adds that journalists at *Le Monde* had a strong sense of commitment to the social role of their own paper, but it was not a commitment they shared with journalists at other news organizations – in this sense they were part of an institution but not exactly of a profession.

Certain things have changed, of course, since Padioleau studied *Le Monde* in the early 1980s. The rise of *Libération* as a professional competitor, the increasing importance of the regional papers, and above all the increasing centrality of electronic media to the journalistic "field" have made *Le Monde* less unique, and the prestige of the media as a social actor has surely increased. Nevertheless, the characteristics noted by Padioleau apply to a significant degree across the Mediterranean region.

Professional organizations and journalists' unions are generally weak, at least in comparison with the strong organizations of the Democratic Corporatist countries. In France and Spain where trade unions are affiliated with political parties, union membership among journalists is limited. In Spain about 60 percent of journalists belong to a professional association left over from the days of fascist corporatism, but "nowadays membership is just a matter of tradition" (as well as providing some material benefits); 4 percent belong to trade unions (Canel and Piqué 1998: 306; on France, McMane 1998). Italy, Greece, and Portugal do have journalists' unions that cut across political lines and in the Italian case it has become quite a significant force, with influence on media policy and, as we shall see, a role in the very recent move to establish a code of ethics. In this sense Italy is closer than some of the other Polarized Pluralist countries to the Democratic Corporatist Model.

The Polarized Pluralist countries also have significant forms of state recognition of the profession of journalism, though these can be considered more a manifestation of the closeness of journalism to the state than its development as an autonomous profession. Italy is the strongest case here. In 1963 an Order of Journalists was established by law, giving journalists a legal status similar to that of lawyers, doctors, engineers, and other professionals. All journalists must belong to it to practice the profession. But if it plays an important role in controlling access, it has not played an equivalent role in advancing common standards of professional conduct. France also has formal organization in the form of the *Comission de la Carte*, which issues credentials to journalists, but its functions are mainly limited to regulating access to benefits provided journalists by the state – discussed in the following text – and enforcing minimum wage regulations. Portugal has a commission similar to that of France. Regulation of access to the profession has been discussed in Spain, in part because intense competition for jobs often leaves many media industry workers in a precarious and marginal employment situation (Fernández 1997; the increase in temporary and part-time employment of journalists has also occurred in other countries). Employers have fiercely opposed such control, however.

Formal education in journalism developed relatively late in all the Mediterranean countries. Bechelloni (1995) argues that because one typically entered journalism through a friendship or family relationship, journalism education did not develop in Italy until the 1980s.

Formal accountability systems are essentially absent in the Mediterranean countries. None has a Press Council at the national level; the only real press council in Southern Europe is the Consell de la Infomació de Catalunya, established as a self-regulatory body, modeled after the British Press Complaints Commission, in 1996. The absence of such institutions reflects the general lack of consensus on ethical standards in the media of Southern Europe to which Padioleau referred (also Rieffel 1984: 26). Attempts to establish codes of ethics have certainly taken place. In France for example, the Syndicat National des Journalistes established one in 1935. But such codes have not become strongly institutionalized in the culture and practice of journalism. In Italy, serious efforts to codify journalistic ethics date essentially to the 1990s. A 1997 survey showed that less than 30 percent of Italian journalists knew the provisions of the major codes well, and that large numbers of journalists rejected them (Mancini 2000: 123). It is also worth noting that the Mediterranean countries tend to have relatively weak protection for professional confidentiality of information collected by journalists (a bit stronger, probably, in France and Portugal),[8] reflecting limited recognition of the profession by the wider society.

## JOURNALISTIC AUTONOMY VS. INSTRUMENTALIZATION

Weak consensus on journalistic standards and limited development of professional self-regulation reflect the fact that journalism in the Mediterranean region has to a significant extent not been an autonomous institution, but has been ruled by external forces, principally from the worlds of politics and of business. One well-known Italian journalist, Pansa (1977), used the phrase "*giornalista dimezzato*" – the journalist cut in half – by which he meant that the Italian journalist belonged only half to himself and the other half belonged to powers outside journalism: media owners, financial backers, and politicians. The rules of the game of Italian journalism have traditionally been above all political rules: they have to do with the process of bargaining among political elites, which journalism for the most part has served. In the last section of this chapter we will consider more systematically the nature of this bargaining process, the role of the media within it, and the nature of a democratic system based on this form of political communication. Here we will focus on the conflicts over journalistic autonomy and "instrumentalization" of the media that have been an important part of media history in Southern Europe.

One of the most characteristic patterns of the Mediterranean region is the use of the media by various actors as tools to intervene in the political world. This takes many forms. Media tied to political parties and the Church obviously are established in large part to facilitate the intervention of these institutions. In periods of dictatorship the media

---

[8]  Errea (1993); Rodriguez Ruiz (1993); Mendes (1999). It should be noted that systematic comparative analyses of media law are hard to find. Obviously, legal practices are not fully described by the texts of the laws.

have served the political and cultural ends of authoritarian elites. Public broadcasting – even under democratic regimes – has to a significant degree also served the ends of the state, whether in the form of promoting national culture, reinforcing state authority in a climate of polarized politics (as in Gaullist France), or promoting political pluralism and compromise (as in the case of RAI under the *lottizazzione*). In some cases – most notoriously in France between the two world wars – journalists and newspaper owners took payments from both political and private interests to place publicity or propaganda disguised as news. Newspapers also sometimes extorted payments by threatening unfavorable publicity.

Probably the most significant form of instrumentalization, however, has been the use of media by commercial owners – sometimes private and sometimes state-linked, as in the case of state-owned enterprises – to wield influence in the political world. In Italy the development of large-scale nationally circulated newspapers took place early in the twentieth century, with the backing of industrial and financial enterprises, the most important being two steel companies, Ilva and Perrone (Castronovo 1976). These newspapers were not profitable, and were subsidized by their owners primarily as a means of enhancing their political influence. Ilva, for example, was a strong proponent of an interventionist military policy. This pattern was substantially recreated in the post–World War II period. The Milan daily *Il Giorno*, for example, was founded in 1956 by Enrico Mattei, president of the state-owned oil company ENI, with the intent of giving the interests of the state sector a political voice. Mattei was close to sectors of the Socialist and Christian Democratic parties. Giovanni Agnelli of Fiat controls *La Stampa*; Cesare Romiti, now a fashion mogul, once general manager of Fiat, controls *Il Corriere della Sera*; Carlo DeBenedetti of Olivetti controls *L'Espresso* and *La Repubblica* (*La Repubblica* started out as a "pure publisher," but De Benedetti's Mondadori acquired it in 1989); and Raul Ferruzi of Montedison Chemicals controlled *Il Messaggero* for many years (now it belongs to a real-estate concern). Each is a player in Italian politics and control of a newspaper plays a key role in his ability to influence the political process. Private television, of course, is dominated by Silvio Berlusconi, who has used his media empire as a springboard to create his own political party and win the prime ministership. Berlusconi also controls *Il Giornale* (through his brother) and made an unsuccessful attempt in 1989 to take over *La Repubblica*.

The Greek situation is very similar: industrialists with interests in shipping, travel, construction, telecommunication, and oil industries dominate media ownership, and a long tradition of using media as a means of pressure on politicians continues. As Papathanassopoulos (2000) notes, "give me a ministry or I will start a newspaper" is a traditional political threat in Greece. Newspaper owners are well-known figures and are often decisive actors in the political world (Dimitras 1997: 101).

In France, there was a move in the immediate post-Liberation era to prevent industrial control of the press – a reaction to the corruption and instrumentalization of the interwar period – and establish some sort of public service system. The French Press Federation said in 1945, "The press is not a means of commercial profit. It is free only when it is not dependent on either the government or the money powers, but only on the conscience of its journalists and readers" (Thogmartin 1998: 144). No such system was established, however, and important elements of the old pattern reasserted themselves. The most important example of control by a politically ambitious private owner has been Robert Hersant, owner of *Le Figaro* and *France-Soir*, among other media properties. Hersant was a member of both the French parliament (1956–78) and later the European parliament, and in the 1986–8 National Assembly there were twelve members who worked for some Hersant entity (Tunstall and Palmer 1991: 145). In Spain, unlike Italy or Greece, media conglomerates – rather than companies based in other industries – overwhelmingly dominate media ownership. This is the trend in Southern Europe, as media markets grow and media properties become profitable. Hersant's empire is also based within media industries. Nevertheless, as we have seen, the Spanish media owners do have clear political alliances. In the Spanish case banks also play an important role as investors. Barrera (1995: 350) writes of their motivations:

> It is not only a business deal they seek in the media, especially when, in many cases, as is true today in commercial TV, these have barely reached the threshold of profitability. It is their capacity for influence, in terms of political power and public opinion....

An obvious correlate to instrumentalization is the relatively low level of journalistic autonomy to which Pansa's phrase *giornalista dimezzato* refers. This has not been entirely unchallenged in the Mediterranean countries. In fact, the issue of control of editorial content has been posed more explicitly in Mediterranean countries than Northern Europe or North America. In the latter, journalists have never seriously contested the right of owners to control commercial media organizations. They

have accepted limited professional autonomy within a hierarchy ultimately based on property rights. In Polarized Pluralist systems – where,
in general, property rights have been subject to more radical challenges –
journalists have at times aspired to more radical forms of autonomy.

The most important case is France after the Liberation when, as we
have seen, the political left briefly advanced a vision of a public service
press system outside the control of private capital. The strongly politicized press of the immediate post-Liberation period was quickly eclipsed
and industrialists regained control of most newspapers. But important
echoes of this era sounded through the subsequent history of the French
media. *Le Figaro* was licensed to resume publication after the war under
the direction of journalist Pierre Brisson. A dispute eventually arose between Brisson and the prewar owner of the paper over its editorial line,
which was resolved by splitting the organization into two companies,
one managing the business affairs of the paper and one the journalistic content. Brisson actually headed both; in general in the 1950s and
1960s the directors of French papers (equivalent to an American editor-
in-chief) enjoyed considerable autonomy in relation to owners (Frieberg
1981). Conflicts over control of *Le Figaro* reemerged in the wake of the
political turmoil of 1968 and eventually the paper was bought by Robert
Hersant, who canceled the agreement separating the two sides of the
organization. Many journalists went on strike and eventually exercised
their right to leave the paper with compensation under the *clause de
conscience*, which gives French journalists the right to such compensation when the ideological line of their paper is changed by management.
Conscience clauses are distinctive to Polarized Pluralist systems where
conflict over the political line of news media is relatively sharp. Italy
and Spain also have such laws (as does Israel), which do not exist in the
Liberal or Democratic Corporatist countries, at least in the form they
take in the Polarized Pluralist system.[9] Hersant had the following to say
on the journalistic autonomy:

> For me, pluralism does not mean a diversity of political views within
> a particular newspaper. If a journalist joins *L'Humanité* it is to
> produce a newspaper that tallies with the wishes of the Communist
> Party. The press, by its very nature, has to make policy choices and

[9] Countries fitting the Democratic Corporatist Model sometimes have a sort of conscience clause that gives journalists the right to refuse particular assignments that
would violate their principles.

journalists must choose to work for newspapers that accord with their political views (Tunstall and Palmer 1991: 145).

Journalists in French public television also went on strike following the 1968 rebellion, protesting restrictions on the reporting of political events; many were fired following the strike.

Only at *Le Monde* and *Libération* (the latter founded as a cooperative radical paper following the 1968 uprising) did a form of the journalists' control envisaged in post-Liberation France survive. Control of *Le Monde* was eventually placed in the hands of the Société des Rédacteurs, the Journalists' Corporation, which had the right to elect the director, and was backed financially by a Corporation of Readers and by a group of "moral guarantors" who held nonvoting shares. The journalists' ownership of the company has eroded significantly over time, but they do retain the right to elect the director, and in this sense *Le Monde* remains a highly unusual example of journalistic autonomy. *Le Monde* has also until recently followed a policy of limiting the percent of revenue derived from advertising, which was seen as protecting the newspaper from outside influence. At *Libération* the nonhierarchical culture of its early years as a radical alternative paper was institutionalized in a Société Civil des Personels similar to that of *Le Monde*. In 1996 most of the shares of the paper were sold to a commercial company, Chargeurs, S.A., with the employees retaining 20 percent ownership and the right to veto the appointment of a new director.

In Portugal following the revolution journalists also challenged ownership control of the media, taking over most of them for a while – not in the name of professional autonomy, in this case, but as instruments of class struggle. The radical phase of the Portuguese revolution ended in part because of a public reaction against the journalists' takeover of the Catholic radio station Radio Renaçensa. In Italy, as well, activist journalists sometimes challenged ownership prerogatives during the 1970s. The cover of *Il Messaggero* urging a No vote on the divorce referendum was printed in defiance of the owner. In both Italy and Portugal, owners eventually reasserted control. But a legacy of this period exists in the form of editorial councils that give journalists the right to be consulted on certain decisions, usually including the appointment of the director. *El País*, also founded in the 1970s in a period of social activism, has such a council as well.

In general, however, the level of journalistic autonomy is lower in the Mediterranean countries compared with both Democratic Corporatist and the Liberal systems. It is not surprising that a survey of journalists in Italy, Germany, Britain, and the United States (Donsbach and Patterson 1992) found Italian journalists substantially more likely to report that pressures from senior editors or management were "very" or "quite important" as limitations on their jobs: 27 percent of Italian journalists described pressures from management as important, as opposed to 15 percent in Britain, 13 percent in the United States, and 7 percent in Germany. Italian journalists were also more likely to report that their work was changed by others in the newsroom for political reasons. Data are also available from Spain and Greece that suggest that journalists are often called upon to "render unto Caesar that which is Caesar's."[10]

---

[10] Greek journalists asked whether "journalists exercise their profession freely nowadays or are they subject to intervention," answered overwhelmingly that they were subject to intervention: 7.9 percent said they exercised their profession freely, 65.7 percent said that they were subject to intervention, and 24.3 percent said that they censored themselves. Nearly 75 percent also responded that the "line taken by owners of media enterprises" determined the "image and politics of the mass media" (see Hallin and Papathanassopoulos 2000). For Spain, Canel and Piqué (1998) report 21.9 percent of journalists describing "pressures from my boss" an "important" or "very important" part of their jobs, and 4.9 percent of journalists saying the same about pressures from owners. Another survey of Spanish journalists found 69.3 percent disagreeing that "journalists are independent of political power," and 76.6 percent disagreeing that they are independent of economic power (Ortega and Humanes 2000: 168). Canel and Piqué describe the 21.9 percent of journalists they found complaining about intervention as a low rate of concern about autonomy, and point out that the journalists in their survey felt much more constrained by deadline pressures, lack of space, and other problems mostly related to the logistics of reporting. Do their findings contradict the argument that journalistic autonomy is comparatively more limited in Southern Europe? Certainly they remind us not to exaggerate the degree of instrumentalization. In any modern media system, intervention by owners is an occasional thing. Most of the time journalists go about their work in a routine way, and owners, or even editors cannot be bothered to monitor what they are doing. Tensions and conflicts over direct interference are rare, but might be said to be the tip of an iceberg that cannot be ignored in analysis of the political role of journalism – in every society, but probably more in Southern than Northern Europe. In part, tensions are rare because many stories do not affect the owners' important political interests. Spanish newspapers can be blatantly partisan on certain stories – an example would be the reporting of a recent conflict between judges Liaño and Garzón, a case that involved proceedings against the owner of El País. On some stories their partisanship is more subtle and on others, absent. In part, tensions are limited because journalists accept as natural the fact that different media have different political positions to which they must adapt. One Spanish journalist explained to us in an interview that a journalist is a sort of chameleon: if you work for El País you may write a story one way, for El Mundo you may write it another way. This is simply part of the job. Many journalists also share the political orientation of the news organization they work for (this is perhaps especially true of more senior journalists) and on sensitive stories these will be the journalists assigned.

The special case of journalistic autonomy in public broadcasting should also be noted here. Because public broadcasting in Southern Europe is controlled fairly closely by the political parties, the role of the journalist is circumscribed. In the following chapter we will see that television journalists in many of the Democratic Corporatist countries shifted during the late 1960s and early 1970s toward a stance more critical of established political and social institutions. In Italy, by contrast, even though there was a strong shift in the general culture toward more critical orientations, a change strongly reflected in the print press, television journalists did not play this role. In general, public television journalists in Italy, as in the other Mediterranean countries, tend to report in a relatively passive way, at least on news bulletins (as opposed to current affairs programs, where commentary is the rule), a form of journalism ironically similar in many ways to the very constrained form of "objective journalism" that prevailed in the United States before the shift toward more active forms of journalism in the late 1960s. They leave both agenda setting and the interpretation of political reality to other political actors, particularly representatives of political parties and other organized groups, whose comments usually dominate the news (Hallin and Mancini 1984; on Spain, Gunther, Montero, and Wert 2000). The primary form of election coverage on Spanish public TV consists of live reports from the campaigns of the different parties, which leaves the journalists with minimal roles as mediators. The highly formalized monitoring of time given to different political actors in Italy and France also has limited the autonomy of television journalists, though today in France the CSA enforces the rule of three thirds only loosely.

## THE MEDIA AND THE STATE

The state has always played a large role in the social life of Southern Europe and its role in the media system is no exception. The role of the state is also complex: it reflects a combination of authoritarian traditions of intervention and democratic traditions of the welfare state similar to those that prevail in the Democratic Corporatist countries. It is also made complex by the fact that the state's grasp often exceeds its reach: The capacity of the state to intervene effectively is often limited by lack of resources, lack of political consensus, and clientelist relationships that diminish its capacity for unified action.

Through much of history, of course, that state has played the role of censor. The direct authoritarian control of the years of dictatorship is presumably a thing of the past, but some remnants carried over into the democratic period. French law gives the State the right to seize publications under certain circumstances, a power used in the 1950s and 1960s during the conflict over Algeria, and at the beginning of the 1970s, when editors of some of the many radical papers that sprung up following the May 1968 political rebellion were arrested. De Gaulle invoked a law prohibiting "offenses to the chief of state" 350 times while he was in office (Eisendrath 1982). In Spain, legal actions against journalists were common in the late 1970s and early 1980s (Fernández and Santana 2000), and as we shall see in the following text legal pressures on owners continue to be an important political tactic. The remnants of authoritarianism are strongest today in Greece, where journalists are still sometimes prosecuted for defamation against public officials (the result is usually a small fine or suspended sentence), and the law gives the state the right to seize and shut down publications, for offenses against religion or against the President of the Republic among other things (Dimitras 1997: 100).

The state has also played an important role as an owner of media enterprises. As in the rest of Europe, broadcasting has been mainly state owned through most of its history. But the state has also had significant ownership in commercial media in the Mediterranean countries, including the print press. Authoritarian governments – the Franco regime in Spain, for example – often had state-owned newspapers. News agencies – Agence France Presse, the Agencia Giornalistica Italia (another Italian agency ANSA, is a cooperative run by news organizations, though it is state subsidized), and the Spanish agency EFE – have been primarily state owned, with varying degrees of insulation from government control.[11] Publicly funded news agencies function both to maintain the presence of the national press on the world scene and as a subsidy to domestic news media that use the service. France also had a publicly owned advertising agency, Havas, that controlled most advertising sales in the interwar period and was privatized only in 1987, and for many years a publicly owned newsprint company. State-owned enterprises have at times played an important role in financing media owners' acquisitions, most notably in the 1970s when state-owned banks helped to finance the expansion of Robert Hersant's media empire. And the French government held large blocks of shares for many years in the *périphériques* – radio stations

---

[11] Agence France Presse is generally regarded as fairly independent, though there have often been political debates over the appointment of its head (Thogmartin 1998: 146ff). At EFE, Alfonso Sánchez-Palomares, who headed the agency for ten years, was a close personal friend of Felipe González.

outside French borders that played an important role in the French radio market during the public service "monopoly." The Spanish government owned 25 percent of each of the major radio networks until the early 1990s, and the Portuguese government (like the French government immediately after the liberation) owned most newspapers in the first years after the transition to democracy (the Spanish government also initially inherited Franco's Prensa del Movimiento). In Italy parastatal enterprises have often owned or had investments in print media. Both *Il Giorno* and *Il Messaggero* have been owned by such entities, which of course are also important advertisers. SIPRA, RAI's advertising sales unit, handles sales for many commercial newspapers (Castronovo and Tranfaglia 1994).

Italy and France have the highest levels of state subsidies to the press in Europe (Humphries 1996: 105–6). Direct subsidies have gone primarily toward economically marginal papers considered important to maintaining political diversity – party and ideological papers – though in Italy during the 1980s all newspapers received them. Extensive indirect subsidies have been provided to the press as a whole in the form of tax breaks, reduced utility rates, and the like. Total subsidies have been estimated to amount to about 12 to 15 percent of the revenue of the press. There are also subsidies to journalists as individuals; French journalists get a 30 percent tax reduction and such benefits as free admission to national museums. Italian journalists get cheap train tickets and, through the Ordine di Giornalisti, better pension and health benefits than most Italian workers.

Other countries have less extensive subsidy systems, though these have been significant in some periods. Portugal has reduced postal rates for newspapers, reduced rates for journalists' transportation, and subsidies for training and technological modernization. Spain had substantial press subsidies for a while in the 1980s, but does not currently. However, government advertising is an important form of subsidy, particularly for smaller local newspapers, many of which would not exist without it. Unlike formal press subsidies in France, Italy, or the Democratic Corporatist countries, government advertising is fairly often used in Spain as a form of political pressure. In Greece state subsidies to the press are not governed by a clear legal framework, consistent with the clientelist nature of Greek politics that will be discussed in the following text. They take the form of "soft" loans, subsidies both overt and covert, and state jobs offered to many journalists (Dimitras 1997: 102–3).

Like the other European countries, and, as we shall see in Chapter 7, in contrast to the relatively pure liberal system in the United States, the

Mediterranean systems treat the media as a social institution properly subject to a substantial regulation in the public interest. All but Greece, for example, have right-of-reply laws for the press, giving people criticized in the media a right of access to answer criticisms against them (all European Union [EU] countries are required by European law to have right-of-reply laws for broadcasting). Most have hate speech regulations – these are particularly strong in France (Bird 1999) – as well as regulations on political communication during election campaigns, including bans on paid political advertising in France, Spain, Portugal, and Italy and regulations on the publication of polls (poll results cannot be publicized, for example, in the week prior to the election in France). Privacy laws are strong in France, inhibiting investigative reporting, but also providing recourse for individuals who feel they have been harmed by the media and, along with the right of reply, providing a substitute through the legal system to the institution of press councils in the Democratic Corporatist countries. There are also a variety of regulations affecting commercial broadcasting in general, though as we shall see in the following section they are generally less extensive and less effective than in the Democratic Corporatist countries. Regulations limiting concentration of media ownership have also been relatively weak in the Mediterranean countries. The political alliances media owners have built with politicians and the often extremely close personal relationships among them are surely a central reason for this.

An important phenomenon in the recent political history of the Mediterranean countries is the rise of political scandals, a phenomenon that reflects significant changes in the relation of the media to the state. The central role of the state in Mediterranean media systems has historically limited the tendency of the media to play the "watchdog" role so widely valued in the prevailing liberal media theory. The financial dependence of media on the state, and the persistence of restrictive rules on privacy and on the publication of official information have combined with the intertwining of media and political elites and – especially in the French case – with a highly centralized state not prone to "leaks" of information to produce a journalistic culture cautious about reporting information that would be embarrassing to state officials. This never meant – aside from periods of authoritarianism – that political criticism and debate were absent from the media, which would make no sense in polarized pluralist systems where parties with a wide range of political ideologies contend and their debates are central to the content of the news. But investigative reporting and the exposure of corruption, incompetence, and conflict of interest were indeed rare.

This changed dramatically in the 1980s and 1990s, as most of the Mediterranean countries experienced numerous political scandals. In the Italian case the Tangentopoli or "bribe city" scandal, which involved revelations of bribes paid by businessmen and corporations to most prominent politicians, produced a radical change of the political structure of Italian democracy, with the disappearance of almost all of the parties that ruled Italy for half a century – the Christian Democratic, Socialist, Liberal, and Republican parties – and the imprisonment of many important political leaders. The exact dynamics of these scandals, and the role of the media in them, varies from country to country. But in all cases it involves important changes in the relation of the media to the state: media become less deferential and their relations with political elites more adversarial. In the French case, the exposure by *Le Monde* of the role of the French State in an attack on the Greenpeace ship the *Rainbow Warrior*, which was protesting French nuclear testing in the Pacific, is often seen as a watershed event in the shift toward a less deferential attitude toward the state. It came against the background of heightened competition between *Le Monde* and *Libération*, at a time when *Le Monde*, whose prestige had been based in part on its role as the main oppositional newspaper when the Right was in power, was in danger of being seen as an "official" paper under a Socialist government. Information on this sort of affair had previously been published outside the mainstream press, usually by the satirical weekly *Le Canard Enchaîné* (as it was published in Spain for a while by the soft-porn magazine *Interviú*).

In Italy, the scandals have been driven less by investigative reporting on the part of journalists than by judges – in the case of Tangentopoli a group of activist judges from Milan – who have used the media to build support for their investigations (Pizzorno 1998).[12] Though the media did not initiate the revelations, their role was clearly important. From early in the scandal, almost all journalists took sides with the judges against the "corrupt political class" that ruled Italy. Through extensive

---

[12] In France, too, the rise of investigative journalism is partly due to the arrival, at the end of the 1960s, of "new generations of investigating magistrates (*juges d'instruction*), (the 'red judges'), who more often came from the middle classes and as carriers of '68er' attitudes, were more focused on human rights" (Marchetti 2000: 31). These judges organized, insisted on greater autonomy of the judicial system relative to the political parties, and carried out many investigations that provided fertile ground for the growth of scandal-centered journalism.

and often emotional news coverage, public opinion assumed the role of the "incorruptible judge" theorized by Jeremy Bentham, and judges were able to produce changes that would have been inconceivable in an earlier era of Italian politics. Both the judiciary and the media became more powerful in relation to the political parties, as both claimed to speak for a public opinion that transcended partisanship. In Spain, as we have seen, *Diario 16* and later *El Mundo* played an important role in revealing both financial scandals similar to Tangentopoli and a scandal involving extra-legal actions against radical Basque nationalists.[13] In the Spanish case, investigative reporting was more closely tied to party politics in the sense that media revealed scandals about their partisan enemies. Nevertheless it clearly made the media more central as a political actor than in the past.

In all of the Mediterranean countries there is an increased tendency to frame events as moral scandals, and for journalists to present themselves as speaking for an outraged public against the corrupt political elite. These changes are not unique to the Mediterranean countries. They are connected with the growth of powerful, market-based media, with a cultural shift toward "critical professionalism" in journalism, and with a deeply rooted decline of traditional loyalties to political parties, the dynamics of which we will explore in more general terms in Chapter 8. The changes have, however, been particularly dramatic in the Polarized Pluralist countries, given the historically close relations between the media and the state.

### "SAVAGE DEREGULATION"

Traquina (1995, 1997) refers to Portuguese media policy in the 1980s and 1990s as one of "savage deregulation." His argument is that Portugal introduced commercial broadcasting in an uncontrolled way, without imposing significant public-service obligations on commercial broadcasters and without any framework that would protect the interests public broadcasting systems were intended to serve: providing information to citizens about public affairs, providing access to a wide range of political views, promoting the national language and culture, encouraging national audio-visual production, and so on. Portugal eliminated the license fee for public broadcasting in 1991. Patterns of development of

---

[13] The media in the Mediterranean, as also in the Democratic Corporatist countries, have stayed away from the kinds of scandal about politicians' personal lives that are common in the Liberal countries. In Southern Europe, sex is not a scandal!

broadcasting differ considerably among the five countries covered in this chapter, but the pattern of "savage deregulation" applies to some degree across the Mediterranean region except for France: despite the strong role the state has traditionally played in these countries – or in some ways perhaps because of it – the "commercial deluge" came to Southern Europe more suddenly and with fewer restraints than to Northern Europe.

Italy might be said to be the classic case of "savage deregulation." In contrast to Greece, Spain, and Portugal, Italy shares with the Democratic Corporatist countries a strong history of regarding broadcasting as a public service, even if the notion was tainted in practice by the strength of party control. Under the Christian Democrats this was motivated by a liberal Catholic conception of the mass media as a means of raising the cultural level of the population. Early Italian television had a heavy emphasis on classic Italian and world literature, music, and art. By the 1970s the rising political left had become aware of the importance of television and was advancing a conception of the media as part of the welfare state, a means of promoting pluralism and wider access to the public sphere. Nevertheless, it could be said that the "commercial deluge" in European broadcasting began in Italy in the 1970s. The Italian Constitutional Court invalidated RAI's monopoly in 1976, and from 1976 to 1990 Italy had no law regulating commercial broadcasting. One Italian government resigned during that period because of its inability to reach agreement on a broadcasting law and even when a law was finally passed in 1990 three ministers resigned because they felt it favored Berlusconi, whose monopoly of commercial television was built during this long regulatory vacuum.

Greece also fits the model of savage deregulation strongly: pirate radio and then television stations began to proliferate in the late 1980s (often introduced by local governments ruled by other parties than the Panhellenic Socialist Party [PASOK] then in power in Athens). The government was forced to move toward legalization, but hundreds of broadcast stations continued to operate without authorization as the government was unable to establish licensing procedures. Public broadcasting, meanwhile, which always lacked independence from the state, has dropped to the lowest audience share in Europe (8 percent). The level of sensationalism is extremely high in Greek commercial television (Papathanassopoulos 1997; 2001).

In Spain, as also in Greece and Portugal, public service broadcasting in the full sense of the word never really existed (Bustamante 1989).

The Franco dictatorship was concerned about political and ideological control of broadcasting, but otherwise state broadcasting operated essentially as a commercial enterprise; there was never a license fee. Spanish television was always supported by advertising, from 1982–92 exclusively so; since then its deficits have meant a need for state subsidies (de Mateo 1997: 204). Radio was always a mixed commercial and state-owned system. Spain also differed from the Italian pattern – to which the PSOE government pointed in the 1980s as an example to avoid – in that state never lost control of broadcast licensing, though it is true that regional governments moved to establish local radio and TV before central government had authorized them (Maxwell 1995; Fernández and Santana 2000) and that some pirate broadcasting did develop. The Spanish state did, however, maintain tight control of broadcast licensing in general, paying careful attention to the political affinities of licensees (Barrera 1995; Fernández and Santana 2000) (broadcast licenses are granted directly by the government, rather than by an independent regulatory agency). On the other hand, although terrestrial broadcasting is still defined in theory as an "essential public service" in Spanish law, public service regulations are weak compared with those in Britain or the Democratic Corporatist countries and also tend to be weakly enforced. Market forces are heavily dominant and not much less so at RTVE than at commercial broadcasters. One thing that is striking in reading the history of debates over media policy in Spain is the weakness of the discourse of public service: intervention by the state in media markets is almost always seen – and with much reason – as a cynical attempt at political control. Democracy, of course, was restored in Spain, Portugal, and Greece at a time when the welfare state was on the defensive in Europe and global forces of neoliberalism were strong. These countries missed the historical period when social democracy was at its strongest and instead have a history of a very different sort of state intervention.

The notion of "savage deregulation" cannot really be extended to France, though certain elements of the pattern could be said to apply. Dagnaud (2000) points out that although France has always had a particularly strong rhetoric about the importance of public service broadcasting as an institution of national culture, it was never as pure a public service system as some. It was a mixed-revenue system, funded in part by advertising, and public funding was limited compared with much of the rest of Europe: thirty ECU per inhabitant, compared with fifty-one in the United Kingdom and seventy-two in Germany (Spain and Portugal were both at eleven ECU per inhabitant).[14] The French state decided to join the *périphériques* – by investing in them – rather than fight them. And France moved rapidly into the commercial age: "Coming among the first European countries to commercial television, France was taken with vertigo, seized with the enthusiasm of skeptics suddenly converted" (Dagnaud 2000: 76). The most important result of this enthusiasm was the privatization of the first channel of public service broadcasting. France also went through a period in the 1980s when regulatory authorities had a good deal of difficulty enforcing regulations on private broadcasters.

In general, however, France was much more successful than the other Mediterranean countries in developing an effective centralized state, and the *dirigiste* tradition of state intervention in the market to accomplish national ends can be seen in the media sphere in recent years, even if the focus of *dirigisme* in media policy has moved from promoting culture to a greater emphasis on building competitive national media industries, and even if French regulators do not always win their battles with troublesome youth radio stations (Dauncy and Hare 1999). There remains a strong consensus in France on the basic principle of broadcasting as a national institution. France has particularly strong rules on language and on European-produced content, and the Conseil Supérieur de l'Audiovisuel is a strong and active regulatory agency by world standards. It has substantial authority over programming decisions of private broadcasters. A good example would be its intervention to require that the producers of the reality show *Loft Story* give the participants some periods of time when they were off camera.

## POLITICAL HISTORY, STRUCTURE, AND CULTURE

In this section, we will try to connect the media system characteristics previously described with the history, social and political structure, and culture of the countries of Southern Europe. The key theoretical concepts employed here – particularly polarized pluralism and clientelism – are introduced in more general terms in Chapter 3; here we will discuss their concrete manifestation in Southern Europe.

Freedom of the press, as we have seen, was introduced to Italy and the Iberian peninsula following the Napoleonic invasion. Liberal

[14] Dagnaud (2000: 230, n. 4). Dagnaud is quoting figures from an internal document of the Observatoire Europeén de l'Audiovisuel.

institutions, as Carr (1980) says of Spain, were imposed "on an economically and socially 'backward' and conservative society." Industrialism and the market were developed only to a limited extent, and their
growth would continue to be slow and uneven through the nineteenth
and early twentieth centuries. In 1930 47 percent of the working population of Portugal, Spain, Italy, and Greece was still engaged in agriculture,
as compared with 20 percent in Germany. France stood in between, at
29 percent agricultural (Malefakis 1995: 41). At the time liberalism was
introduced, with the Napoleonic invasion, social and political structures
were essentially feudal and patrimonial in character, based on landed
property and an absolutist state, albeit one with weak penetration into
the countryside. Cultural life was dominated by the Church. The social
forces that would form the political constituency for liberalism – the industrial and commercial bourgeoisie and the urban working and middle
classes – were relatively weak. In Greece, a similar importation of liberal
institutions began in 1821, when Turkish rule was overthrown, and liberal ideas introduced by exiled nationalist leaders "unavoidably clashed
with a pre-existing institutional setting characterized by a pre-capitalist,
underdeveloped economy, a patrimonial structure of political controls,
and the anti-enlightenment, anti-western ideology of the Christian Orthodox Church" (Mouzelis 1995). In France, the sociological base for the
development of liberal institutions was considerably stronger, though
French history is characterized by sharper conflict between tradition
and modernity than that of most of the Liberal and Democratic Corporatist countries. The late, uneven and conflictual development of liberal
institutions in Southern Europe is fundamental to understanding the
development of the media in this region.

The weakness of liberal social and economic institutions, first of all,
limited the development of the mass circulation press. The counteren-
lightenment tradition discouraged the development of literacy, and the
cultures of Southern Europe can probably still be said to remain oral
cultures to a larger extent than those of Northern Europe and North
America. Limited development of the market economy restricted both
the resources available to commercial newspapers and the need for the
kind of information-oriented content that was crucial to their social
function elsewhere: in a market economy publicly circulated information on prices, technology, legal regulations, and political and business
developments on a national and international scale are crucial. In traditional economies information flows are more private and more local. Political instability and repression also made the development of

commercial media more risky. And limited development of political democracy meant a limited constituency for political news. Spain, for example, had an electoral system in the late nineteenth century, the *turno* system, in which parties made up of small cliques of notables agreed to alternate in office and political bosses controlled the votes of a dependent rural population. Collusion among political elites was characteristic of the early periods of liberal rule in Southern Europe.

This history is not, of course, uniform within each country: there were important regional variations, and the legacy of these variations can be seen in the contemporary media systems. As Putnam (1993) stresses in his well-known study of regional government in Italy, parts of northern and central Italy had very different social systems in medieval and early modern Europe from the typical pattern of Southern Europe. These were the regions where the communal republics developed self-governing urbanized communities with significant market economies in which, as Putnam shows, a dense network of civic associations as well as relatively professionalized administrative structures developed. Self-government was lost in these regions by the seventeenth century, but Putnam argues that the habits of civic life remained part of the culture and are an important part of the explanation for the success of regional government in these areas. It is in these same regions that newspaper circulation is most extensive. Putnam includes newspaper readership in the index of Civic Community that is his primary explanatory variable. In Spain, liberal institutions were stronger in the Basque country, Madrid, and Catalonia than in most of the rest of the country – many historians refer to the "two Spains" – and again this can be seen in the contemporary media system, both in newspaper readership and in such phenomena as the development of the only press council in Southern Europe in Catalonia. In France, too, there were important sociological and cultural differences between north and south, but the centralized French state diminished the significance of these differences.

## POLARIZED PLURALISM

The strength of conservative forces in Southern Europe ensured that politics in the region would be sharply polarized and conflictual. Supporters of the old order continued to resist liberal modernization from the right. As the socialist and sometimes anarchist working-class movement developed, the strength of the right prevented its incorporation into a consolidated liberal order and a radicalized opposition became entrenched on the left as well. The stakes of political conflict were high, as there was no consensus on the basic structure of the social order. Liberal democracy was not finally consolidated in Southern Europe until relatively late, and when it was achieved, it tended toward the form Sartori (1976) called *polarized pluralism*, with many political parties, distinct in their ideological orientations, ranging over a wide political spectrum and including "antisystem" parties on the right and left. France and Italy had the strongest Communist parties in Western Europe, parties that are still important in the twenty-first century; both also have significant right-wing parties. As we saw in Chapter 3, Lane and Ersson's (1991) index of polarization, which reflects the ideological distances between parties and the strength of antisystem parties, shows France with an average score of 5.1 for the period from 1945–89, Portugal 4.7, Greece and Italy 3.7, and Spain 3.4 (Portugal and Spain included only from 1975), as compared with a European average of 3.1.

Polarization has surely diminished in Southern Europe during the last couple of decades of the twentieth century. This is part of the process of "secularization" we will discuss in Chapter 8, though as we shall see it is not without some countertrends, including the growth of the anti-immigrant extreme right in France. The two main Spanish parties today are catch-all parties not greatly different in their policy views, though the antagonisms between them are greater than the policy differences might suggest.[15] Putnam (1993: 33) gives data on changing political attitudes of local government officials in Italy, showing, for example, that while in 1970 50 percent believed that "to compromise with one's political opponents is dangerous because it usually leads to betrayal of one's own side," only 29 percent expressed this view in 1989. And across the region, while significant minorities still expressed sympathy for authoritarianism in the 1970s, antidemocratic views are no stronger today in the Mediterranean countries than in the rest of Europe (Gunther and Montero 2001).

Nevertheless, the development of the media in the region has been deeply affected by the political patterns of polarized pluralism.

---

[15] The Socialist party followed essentially free-market policies while it was in power and similar to the Partido Popular is basically a catch-all party. The United Left still remains as an ideological party and radical nationalist parties also exist. But beyond this, Spanish politics probably has more of the style and tone of polarized pluralism than the actual ideological differences suggest: those on the left tend to associate the Partido Popular with Francoism, while the Populares believe that the PSOE tried during its fourteen-year rule to monopolize power. The two parties have only exchanged roles, between government and opposition, once since the transition to democracy, and Spanish politics still has something of the feel of an all or nothing struggle for power.

Newspapers, and eventually some electronic media as well, were principal participants in struggles among diverse ideological camps, especially as champions of liberalism in the nineteenth century, but eventually on all sides. This cemented the ties between the media and the world of politics. The sharpness of ideological divisions and the high stakes of political conflict made it difficult for the media system to become differentiated from politics; difficult for a professional culture and organization of journalism to develop across party lines, for example; and difficult for public broadcasting to be separated from party politics. Chalaby (1996: 310) stresses this point in his comparison of the histories of French and Anglo-American journalism:

> In [the United States and Britain] political struggles were confined within the limits of parliamentary bipartism. Journalists could claim to be "neutral" simply by proclaiming to support neither of the political parties and to be "impartial" by giving an equal amount of attention to both parties. This efficient codification of the political struggle facilitated the development of a discourse based on news and information rather than political opinions. . . . During much of the [French] Third Republic, political positions spanned from communism to royalism. The principles these parties put into question (private property and universal suffrage) were both taken for granted in Washington and London.

At the same time, a strong positive value was often placed on political engagement of the media and on ideological diversity. This is particularly clear in the immediate post-Liberation period in France and Italy, when an idealistic vision of a diverse and politically engaged press predominated. And as Putnam (1973: 81–2) pointed out, in a comparative study of political elites in Britain and Italy, a distinctive discursive style prevailed in Italy – and the same is clearly true of all the Polarized Pluralist countries – one that emphasized "rational consistency, 'synthetic' comprehensiveness [and] adherence to explicit social and moral principles," a style that is also connected with higher levels of partisanship. "Intense social conflict," he adds, "calls for and seems to justify generalized explanations of social affairs." In journalism, this style is reflected in the fact that facts are not seen as speaking for themselves, commentary is valued, and neutrality appears as inconsistency, naïveté, or opportunism.

Another, contrasting effect of polarized pluralism may have been to dampen the enthusiasm of journalists for the "watch-dog" role, as journalists worried about endangering political stability and democratic legitimacy. Eisendrath (1982: 79) quotes French sociologist Robert Escarpit, who founded one of the first schools of journalism, as saying,

> Why should we bring out all the facts? This is an ancient country, with a past full of feuding. Some of us make mistakes; we all live in glass houses. For instance, I'm from the Resistance. I could walk down the street in Paris and point out those who collaborated . . . who was responsible for deaths. What if I did that? What if we all did that? How could we all live together as a nation?

Padioleau (1985: 320) quotes a top political editor as saying – in the same post-Watergate period – "Is it necessary to feed the anti-parliamentarism of the French with scandals?" Polarized pluralism has also limited the legitimacy of media institutions, particularly public broadcasting, which because of the sharpness of ideological cleavages and the unwillingness of conflicting factions to let it out of their control has always been the subject of polemics and public scrutiny.

Polarized pluralist systems are typically complex political systems, with many contending parties, often themselves made up of contending factions. This results in a public sphere that is structured differently from the liberal public sphere in which the central element of political communication is assumed to be the appeal of political actors to a mass public of individual citizens. In a multiparty system of this sort, the most important element of political communication is the process of bargaining that takes place among parties, factions, and other social actors allied with them.[16] Much of this process of communication takes place outside of the open public sphere, or enters it only tangentially or in coded, cryptic form. The negotiating process is delicate and messy and generally succeeds better if carried out informally, outside of the public arena. The media in such a system – especially newspapers – have historically served and participated in this process of bargaining. They are an important means by which elites follow and comment on the progress of negotiations, establish an agenda, signal positions and commitments, pressure one another, and arrive at an agreement. Many key characteristics of the media in Southern Europe are connected with this pattern: the

---

[16] Piattoni (2001: 194) associates this pattern also with clientelism, which is discussed later in this chapter: "In fragmented democracies, political decision-making often takes the form of ceaseless bargaining, with only minimal agreement on the rules of the game, and decisions often have the quality of horse-trading. . . ." The fact that agreement on the rules of the game is so limited is one of the key things that divides the Polarized Pluralist countries from the Democratic Corporatist ones, where bargaining is also central, but more rule-based.

closeness of the relationship between political actors and the media, the heavy focus of the media on political life, and the relatively elitist nature of journalism, addressed to political insiders rather than to a broad mass public. This pattern has been most characteristic of Italy. In the other Mediterranean countries it has been modified by majoritarianism, though it still applies to a significant degree. It is something the Mediterranean countries share in important ways with Democratic Corporatist systems, particularly those that tend toward polarized pluralism.

Also similar to the Democratic Corporatist countries, the political systems of the Mediterranean region have been characterized by "affiliational" rather than "issue" voting. That is, individuals have tended to "cast their vote as a statement of subjective identification with a political force they believe to be integrally, and not just representatively, identified with their own social group," (Parisi and Pasquino 1977: 224) rather than evaluating the specific issue positions or candidates of each party. This has again been more true of some countries than others – less true for example of Spain, where the two biggest parties are catch-all parties and social roots of political parties are more shallow (though the parties of the left, whose histories go back to the pre-Franco period, have more "affiliational" attachment of their voters). Where the pattern has been strong it has meant that political communication has been less a matter of winning over an uncommitted mass public and more a matter of mobilizing particular political groups, expressing their positions to other groups, and, again, conducting the process of bargaining with those other groups. In contrast to the Democratic Corporatist countries, moreover, the bargaining process is not guided by a conception of the general interest: what comes first is the particular interest of the group to which each medium is linked.

## THE ROLE OF THE STATE

The late development of capitalism in Southern Europe is also connected with the strong role played by the state. With the market poorly developed, the state played a particularly central role in the accumulation of capital. In the absence of a strong bourgeoisie and civil society, it also played a central role in organizing modern social life. In Greece and Spain, for instance, the army often substituted in the nineteenth century for the middle class as a center of initiative for social change (Malefakis 1995). In France and Italy, the consolidation of democracy led to the development of a strong welfare state similar to that of the Democratic Corporatist societies of Northern Europe. Particularly in Italy, this has been manifested in public policies supporting the press and an attempt to build public service broadcasting as an arena open to all social and political groups. These ideals, however, have been confounded with a political culture more inclined toward particularism than the general interest, so the result has been very different than in the Democratic Corporatist countries. In Spain, Portugal, and Greece the welfare state is weaker, reflecting both more limited resources and a later transition, coming at a time when neoliberalism was on the rise globally.[17]

The strong role played by the state in the development of the media reflects this general pattern. Bechelloni (1980: 233–4) writes,

> In Italy . . . all cultural undertakings were economically fragile, requiring, with some exceptions, help from the state or from private patrons in order to survive. This had two important consequences: there never were many economically self-sufficient cultural or journalistic enterprises, and intellectuals and journalists . . . always lived in a state of financial uncertainty and hence enjoyed little autonomy. The state, which was in control of this situation, always had ample opportunities for maneuver and interference. . . .

The centrality of the state in Southern Europe means not only that the state intervenes relatively strongly in the media institutions, but also to some extent the reverse. Because the state is so important, other social actors have a strong stake in influencing state policy, and one of the principal ways they do this is through the media. Business, in particular, often has a powerful stake in access to state contracts, subsidies, waivers of regulations, and so on. This is one of the reasons business owners

[17] The following table gives the rankings of the Mediterranean countries among sixteen West European countries in two measures of the size of the state sector, for 1985,

|  | Government Disbursements As % of GDP | Total Tax Revenues As % of GDP |
|---|---|---|
| France | 6 | 6 |
| Greece | 9 | 12 |
| Italy | 11 | 13 |
| Portugal | 13 | 15 |
| Spain | 15 | 16 |

Greece was relatively high in total government expenditure at the time represented in these figures. However, its social expenditure was the lowest and its military expenditure the highest in Western Europe, as a percent of GDP (Lane and Ersson 1991: 328–35).

have traditionally been willing to subsidize economically marginal media enterprises.

A strong state, combined with the history of political conflict previously discussed, has also contributed in much of Southern Europe to a broad politicization of society. Mouzelis (1995: 22) writes about Greece:

> In the same way that nothing can be done in Greece without stumbling over the all-pervasive state bureaucracy, so nothing is said, thought or otherwise expressed without being colored by strong political connotations and considerations. From dinner parties of fashionable middle and upper-class Athenian society to everyday coffeeshop gatherings in villages, the main mode of social interaction and cultural exchange is the impassioned discussion of political happenings and personalities. . . . [T]his predilection for the logic of the political . . . permeates all institutional spheres, from sport to religion and from education to popular theater.

Something similar could be said about Italy, which is also a country with a historically high level of politicization, reflected in high levels of voting turnout and party membership. No doubt this has contributed to the high level of politicization of even commercial media in these countries. This level of politicization does not extend to Spain and Portugal, perhaps due to the demobilization that took place during the dictatorship – both have relatively low levels of mass involvement in politics.

## CLIENTELISM AND RATIONAL-LEGAL AUTHORITY

The late development of liberal institutions in Southern Europe is also connected with the importance of clientelism and the relatively slow development of rational-legal authority (Hallin and Papathanassopoulos 2002). Clientelism, as explained in Chapter 3, is a pattern of social organization in which access to resources is controlled by patrons and delivered to clients in exchange for deference and various kinds of support. It developed in Southern Europe as the traditional institutions of feudal society broke down, persisted because of the weakness of the universalistic forms of social organization associated with liberalism – the market, the bureaucratic state, and representative democracy. The earliest forms of clientelism, which involved the personal dependence of the rural population on landowners who controlled their access to resources of all kinds, has been transformed with modernization, without being entirely displaced. With the development of mass parties, the old political bosses were displaced to a significant extent, and their monopoly of power gave way to a more competitive structure. But the parties incorporated many of the particularistic forms of patronage that had been part of classic clientelism. Clientelism is generally seen as destructive of "horizontal" forms of organization such as mass parties and voluntory organizations, but it might be argued that forms of "democratic clientelism" that aided the growth of such organizations did sometimes emerge in Southern Europe, as they also did when mass parties first developed in the United States in the nineteenth century.

France is an exception to this pattern of persistence of clientelist relationships and weakness of rational-legal authority. This is one of the principal reasons we have described France as a marginal case lying at the boundary between the Polarized Pluralist and Democratic Corporatist systems. It has a strong cultural tradition of the state as an embodiment of the "general will," and a long history of professionalized administration going back even to the *ancien régime* and the École Nationale des Ponts et Chauseés, the National School of Bridges and Roads, which functioned to train and select competent administrators. The École Nationale d'Administration now performs that function, producing an administrative elite selected on meritocratic rather than political criteria, with a strong *ésprit de corps* and substantial autonomy. French civil servants are less rigidly separated from party politics than those in other countries. They can and often do run for office without resigning from the civil service. But the common norms and culture of the administrative elite remain strong (Suleiman 1984).[18] The negative stereotype of bureaucracy as an administrative apparatus following its own rules and intractable to control from the outside is actually based on the French case. French journalists often share with civil servants training at the Institut des Etudes Politiques in Paris, and in some sense are thus part of a common elite culture.

In all the countries covered here, clientelism has been undermined in recent years by many forces, from economic growth to European integration (which imposes common standards of rational-legal authority) to the rise of journalism education, which tends to replace particularistic ties and subcultures with a common professional culture and recruitment network. Nevertheless the historical strength and continuing relevance of clientelism has a number of consequences for the media systems of Southern Europe. In clientelist systems, information is treated

---

[18] Italy, by contrast, has a neutral civil service, but without the strong system for recruiting and forming an elite corps and without the importance in the political process of French administrators (Cassese 1984).

as a private resource, not shared publicly, and this is one of the reasons journalism was slow to develop as an institution. Barrera (1995: 161), for instance, argues that business journalism developed very late in Spain in part because of the lack of transparency of Spanish business.[19] Clientelism increases the importance of particularistic ties among social actors, especially – given the centrality of the state and the assumption by political parties of many of the functions of the individual patrons of an earlier era – ties to political parties. One of the key differences between the Mediterranean countries and the Liberal or Democratic Corporatist systems is that political institutions are more party-politicized. The bureaucracy and judiciary are less separate from party politics than in systems where rational-legal authority is more fully developed and ties to parties or factions within them are particularly important to any actor who needs the cooperation of the state. The regulation of broadcasting is a good example here: Berlusconi had strong ties to Italy's Socialist party, which were crucial to protecting his interests as he built his television empire. The licensing of commercial broadcasters in Spain has similarly followed a strongly political logic.

Another good example of the effect of clientelism on the media can be found in the frequency in Southern Europe of legal proceedings against media owners. The legacy of clientelism is associated both with a relatively party-politicized judicial system and with a tradition of evasion of the law, "the attitude . . . that if one group of people had discovered a profitable evasion, then other groups had better look to their own interests" (Dennis Mack Smith, quoted in Putnam 1993: 143). In this context, it is relatively easy for governments to use the legal system to pressure private actors, including media owners, by threatening selectively to enforce tax laws and other regulations. In Spain charges were brought against Jesús de Polanco, owner of PRISA, once his Socialist allies were out of power, and Antonio Asensio maintains that he was threatened with prison if he did not sell Antena 3 television to Telefónica de España (in both cases the PSOE had previously ignored laws on media ownership to allow the media empires of these businessmen to expand). Juan Villalonga, the head of Telefónica after its privatization, similarly came under investigation

---

[19] He adds that modern multimedia groups have maintained financial papers even when they have not been profitable because of the "growing importance of economic information in the business and political life of the country: to possess a voice in the market, to possess information for the defense of their own interests is vital for economic groups . . . which act in sectors which are certainly strategic. Information is power, we must remember."

for securities trading irregularities after falling out of favor with President Aznar, who had installed him in that position. Berlusconi has faced charges on a number of occasions in Italy. This obviously increases the stakes for media owners – as for other private actors – in having strong political ties and in seeing the appropriate faction prevail politically. On the other side, media actors have the ability to pressure political figures by selectively exposing corruption, thus increasing incentives for politicians to be concerned about control of the media. The patterns of politicization, instrumentalization, and state intervention we have seen previously are clearly rooted to a significant extent in these characteristics of Southern European politics. As the example of Berlusconi's ties to the Socialist party suggest, the persistence of clientelism also means that, although the state aspires to intervene strongly in the media sphere in the Mediterranean countries, it often fails to act effectively: particularistic ties weaken its ability to act in a centralized and consistent fashion, thus contributing to the pattern of "savage deregulation" of broadcasting.

Clientelism is also connected with a political culture that is relatively cynical about the notion of a general public interest transcending particular interests. "Savagely closed to the external world," as Bellah (1974) put it in an analysis of Italy, this culture "implies forms of loyalty to family and clan, to groups of pseudo family like the Mafia, to village and town, to faction and clique . . . weakening every real commitment to liberal democratic values." This view of Italian political culture has been widely criticized as too simplistic (e.g., Sciolla 1990). It ignores the high (though uneven) level of political engagement discussed previously and the strong value placed on plurality and debate, characteristics of Italian political culture that were just in some sense reaching their peak when Bellah's essay was written. Nevertheless it is correct that an important element of particularism in the political culture of Italy, as of other countries with strong histories of clientelism, tends to undermine the notion of a transcendent "public interest." This, we believe, is an important reason for the slower development of journalistic professionalism in Southern Europe. As we shall see in the following chapters, professionalization is connected in the Liberal and Democratic Corporatist systems with the displacement of earlier patterns of clientelism by rational-legal institutions.

## CONCLUSION

The long and conflicted transition to capitalism and bourgeois democracy in Southern Europe produced a media system closely tied to the world of politics. Once democracy was consolidated, a high degree of political parallelism prevailed, with the media serving to represent the wide range of political forces that contended for influence, both in their bargaining with one another and in their efforts to consolidate their own political voices. The commercial press did not develop as strongly as in either the Liberal or Democratic Corporatist systems. Newspaper circulation remained relatively low and electronic media correspondingly central. Broadcasting too has tended to be party-politicized, with France moving away from that pattern in the 1980s. Journalistic professionalism is less developed than in the Liberal or Democratic Corporatist systems, with political loyalties often superseding commitments to common professional norms and institutions. Instrumentalization of the media by the state, parties, and private owners with political ties is relatively common. The state has tended to play an interventionist role in many ways, though clientelism and political polarization have often undercut its effectiveness as a regulator, except in France.

The media of the Mediterranean countries deviate in many ways from the dominant liberal norm of neutral professionalism and a "watchdog" media, and many accounts of these systems are quite negative in tone (e.g., Padovani and Calabrese 1996; Hibberd 2001), just as, in general, Southern Europe has often been judged as deficient in relation to the norm of Western development. It therefore seems inevitable to confront some of the normative questions about the role of the media in the democratic process in Southern Europe in closing this chapter. The point here is not to make any sort of final judgment about whether Mediterranean systems are ultimately better or worse then the systems of North America or the rest of Western Europe. It is not clear that it makes sense to judge media systems by any kind of standard abstracted from the historical conditions in which they function, and in any case, the kind of comparative research that would be needed to make real judgments about media performance across systems has been done only to a very limited extent. So our purpose here is only to clarify some of the similarities and differences in their democratic functions that might be relevant to making such judgments.

In the first place, it should be kept in mind that all of the countries of Southern Europe are in important ways success stories in the late twentieth century: all emerged from very difficult circumstances politically and economically to consolidate democratic political systems and to narrow dramatically the economic gap that separated them from the rest of Western Europe earlier in the century. There are certainly many aspects of their media systems that seem problematic and are felt as problematic by journalists, citizens, and scholars within these countries. These include the narrow readership of the print press and the large gender gap in that readership; certain remnants of authoritarian culture that are reflected in restricted access to public information and official pressures against critical reporting; and the tendency toward instrumentalization of the media, both by political elites and by commercial owners (who are often, of course, the same people). Some elements seem much more positive, including the pluralism of the media, which unquestionably represent a wide range of views – though how one measures that pluralism and how one could compare it across systems, remains a problem scholars have not really confronted. In many ways, the media of the Mediterranean countries seem close to Curran's (1991) model of the "radical democratic" public sphere, in which the media function as a "battleground between contending social forces" (29).

Other elements are more difficult to judge. One of those is the heavy focus of the media on political affairs – in Italy the space dedicated to political coverage by print press more than doubled between 1976 and 1996 (Mancini 2002) – which might be seen either as a healthy alternative to the commercial depoliticization that is more advanced in other media systems or as a manifestation of the hegemony of party elites over the media. Political parties unquestionably have great importance in all of the Mediterranean countries. This results both from the history of political conflict and from the strong role of the state and historically weaker development of civil society. It takes different forms in different countries. It is probably somewhat less true of France because of the strength of the presidency and the bureaucracy. In Spain and Portugal, as mentioned earlier, the parties do not have the kind of penetration into the mass public that they do – or did – especially in Italy. Nevertheless, the parties play an extremely important social role, having to a significant degree managed the transition to democracy (Colomer 1996). Therefore it is not surprising either that parties would have considerable influence on the media, or that the media should focus to a significant degree on their activities.

The relation of the media to the parties is related both to their strengths and to their weaknesses – it has encouraged the development of a pluralistic media system that would cover politics in a serious way. At the same time it has contributed to the elitism of journalism, the unevenness of its readership (manifested, e.g., in gender differences), its tendency often to be a collaborator with political power, and a tendency for the media to concentrate rather narrowly on the activities of party elites. A common concern of media critics in Liberal systems has been the prevalence of the strategic or game frames in political reporting, which focus on the strategies of political elites and their success or failure in playing the political game, at the expense of the policy concerns that motivate ordinary citizens. The media in Mediterranean systems show this tendency even more strongly. Our comparative content analysis of political reporting in French and U.S. papers showed 10.8 percent of *New York Times* stories emphasizing a "political game" frame, as against 21.7 percent in *Le Monde* and 23.6 percent in *Le Figaro*. Italian media similarly emphasize the political game over policy issues, giving enormous attention to the negotiations among the parties, the rise and fall of particular leaders and factions, and the like. (Mancini 1996; Marletti 1985). We should keep in mind, of course, that Italian political coalitions are typically fragile and are constantly being remade.

Does the close relation of the media to political institutions – and particularly to party elites – in the Polarized Pluralist system mean that the public sphere is less open? Little research is available that bears on this question, but what there is suggests that the answer is probably "no" – that there is no general tendency for the public sphere in Polarized Pluralist systems to be less open. Sampedro (1997), for example, examined coverage in the Spanish media of the movement against compulsory military service, which reached its peak with extensive civil disobedience in the late 1980s and early 1990s. Because social movements involve the attempt of groups outside the political establishment to put an issue on the political agenda, media coverage of social movements is an important test of the democratic performance of a media system. Sampedro's study was not comparative, but easily lends itself to comparison with similar studies in the Liberal countries. Certain elements of what he found were clearly different from what one would find particularly in North America, most notably the fact that partisan differences among newspapers were strongly reflected in the news agenda, the use of sources, and other elements of coverage. *ABC*, for instance, had privileged access to sources in the Defense Ministry, while *El País* had such access to Justice Ministry sources. The conscientious objectors' movement had difficulty for quite some time penetrating the news agenda. Once it reached a certain threshold – in part by disrupting social order through civil disobedience, and in part because it provoked divisions within the political elite – it garnered extensive and quite pluralistic coverage for a period of time, again tied in part to the existence of "a diversity of communication media, which, according to their editorial lines, played conflicting roles and promoted conflicting interests (291)." Later, elites succeeded in regaining control of the news agenda. Aside from the importance of media partisanship and diversity – which would not play a significant role in the United States – what Sampedro found was very similar to the findings of research in the Liberal countries on media and social movements, and certainly suggest no less openness in the Spanish media.

Benson (2000) studied the reporting of immigration politics in the French and U.S. media from the 1970s to 1990s. He again found many differences rooted in different journalistic cultures and different relations of the media to political institutions. The French media, like the Spanish, were more distinct politically, represented a wider range of ideological positions, included more commentary and analysis but fewer feature stories, and tended to focus more on both political party sources and on organized civil society groups,[20] while American news focused more on neutral, apolitical sources like judges. He did not find any clear tendency for either system to be more open to vigorous debate, criticism of official policy or full information than the other. These are particular studies, of course, focusing on particular kinds of issues. It seems a reasonable hypothesis, however, that broader comparative research would show a pattern of differences in the political role of the media far too complex to be understood in simply terms of a "backward" Mediterranean media.

[20] Padioleau (1985: 307–8) argues that French journalism tends to prefer the role of "subject" dependent on the state to that of the active citizen, while the American media prefers the active citizen role. This conflicts with Benson's research (he also notes that French media gave the kind of "mobilizing information" that some scholars have suggested tends to be absent in American media, e.g., advance information about political demonstrations or legislative debates), as well as our own, which suggests that American media are often wary of organized citizen activism (Hallin and Mancini 1994).

# SIX

# The North/Central European or Democratic Corporatist Model

What we call the Democratic Corporatist Model developed Northern and Central Europe – in Scandinavia, the low countries, Germany, Austria and Switzerland. Like the Mediterranean countries, those we discuss in this chapter are geographically proximate, and like each of our three groups of countries they have a history of frequent and intense social contacts, in this case often marked by strife. In terms of language they are diverse, though they include three countries with large German-speaking populations, and Dutch, Norwegian, Danish, and Swedish are closely related to German, which, along with English in a later period, has served as *lingua franca* in the region.

The exchange of experiences and the mutual influence of cultural and political models has been particularly strong within certain groups of countries – among Austria, Switzerland, and Germany, among the Scandinavian countries, and between Belgium and the Netherlands;[1] but a strongly intertwined historical evolution has affected the communication system across the whole region. The interaction of these countries has often been conflictual in character. But conflict too is a social relationship, and has often meant exportation or mutual influence of cultural models. As we shall see, the "colossal war of religious propaganda" (Anderson 1983) that was started by Luther's challenge to the Church played a particularly important role in creating a common culture and a common public sphere in Northern and Central Europe: it shaped not only religious beliefs but political structures and media practices, including the fact that, across the region, the emerging print media

---

[1] The Scandinavian democracies still share many political decisions: beyond being part of the European Union (except Norway), in 1952 a Nordic Council was established whose goal was that of integrating policies in these countries.

became vehicles for expression of deeply rooted, conflicting political and religious subcultures.

Germany apart, all the countries discussed in this chapter have rather small populations: the name we give to this model, Democratic Corporatist, is strongly influenced by the analysis of Peter Katzenstein's (1985) *Small States in World Markets*. As Katzenstein points out, the small countries of Northern and West-Central Europe adopted political models in the early twentieth century that involved compromise and power sharing among the major organized interests of society and an expansion of the welfare state, with Germany, as well as Austria, adopting much of this model after World War II. (When we speak of Central Europe in this chapter we are thinking of Austria, Switzerland, and Germany; countries such as Poland, Hungary, and the Czech Republic share much of the history with the Democratic Corporatist countries, but the experience of communism obviously separates their political and media history from that of the countries discussed here.) Katzenstein traces the historical origins of this political model, as we shall see in the last section of his chapter, to a pattern of historical development in which the conservative forces of the Catholic Church and land-owning aristocracy were much weaker than in the Southern European countries where the Polarized Pluralist Model developed. We shall see that this history is associated with a distinct pattern of evolution of the media system as well.

The common history of the countries of this region and the intensity of their interaction both in peace and in war, has meant that, despite many differences among them, their media systems share important common characteristics. These characteristics can be summarized in terms of three "coexistences" that we will identify as distinctive to the Democratic Corporatist countries – three sets of media system elements that in other systems do not appear together (or only at different historical moments), and that we might assume (particularly if we take the Liberal Model as "normal") to be incompatible, but which have been simultaneously present in the Democratic Corporatist countries throughout the twentieth century.

In the first place, a high degree of political parallelism, a strong tendency for media to express partisan and other social divisions, has coexisted in the Democratic Corporatist countries with a strongly developed mass-circulation press. The first of these two elements, political partisanship, has clearly weakened substantially over the last generation. Nevertheless we believe that the experience of a strong advocacy press not only characterizes the history of the media in Northern and Central

Europe, but in important ways still affects journalism, media structures, and the way these interact with other social forces. At the same time strong commercial media markets developed in all these countries, and the Democratic Corporatist countries remain distinctive for their high levels of newspaper circulation, as can be seen in the data presented in Table 2.1. Norway, Finland, and Sweden have the highest circulation rates in the world, along with Japan. A little lower down are Denmark, Germany, the Netherlands, and Austria. Only Belgium among this group of countries is further down the list. As we shall see in this and in a number of other ways, Belgium lies partway between the Democratic Corporatist and Polarized Pluralist models.

The second "coexistence," which seems to us distinctive to the Democratic Corporatist Model, is closely related to the first: a high level of political parallelism in the media has coexisted with a high level of journalistic professionalization in the sense we outlined in Chapter 2, including a high degree of consensus on professional standards of conduct, a notion of commitment to a common public interest, and a high level of autonomy from other social powers. Again, the former characteristic has weakened in relation to the latter; the decline of political parallelism across Europe will be explored in detail in Chapter 8. Nevertheless, we believe the historical coexistence of political parallelism and journalistic professionalism in the Democratic Corporatist countries is both an important historical fact that needs explanation and something that continues to be important to understanding their media systems. The presence of these "coexistences" means that the Democratic Corporatist countries share certain characteristics with the Polarized Pluralist Model (a relatively high degree of political parallelism, advocacy, and external pluralism in the press) and certain characteristics with the Liberal Model (strong development of media markets and professionalism).

The third "coexistence" has to do with the role of the state. In the Democratic Corporatist countries traditions of self-government go back, in certain forms, to early historical periods and – except in Austria and Germany – liberal institutions were consolidated early. In this sense there is a strong tradition of limits on state power – one of the most important manifestations of which is the early development of press freedom. On the other hand, strong welfare state policies and other forms of active state intervention developed in the Democratic Corporatist countries in the twentieth century, and these tendencies are manifested in important forms of public-sector involvement in the media sphere that distinguish the Democratic Corporatist from the Liberal countries.

## THE EARLY ROOTS OF THE PRINT PRESS

The countries of Northern Europe – both on the continent and in Britain – pioneered the development of press freedom. The principles of publicity that characterize both parliamentary democracy (Humphreys 1996) and the press as a social institution developed early and strongly. In some cases the development of the first newspapers was linked to merchant capitalism while in other cases it was linked to political or religious struggles. As we shall see more fully in a later section of this chapter, the strong development of the press in Northern Europe is related to the weakness of the *ancien régime* relative to rising forces of liberalism. The exact historical pattern varied from country to country, but in one way or another the development of print media tied to a growing literate middle class is central to the media history of all the Democratic Corporatist countries.

In Germany and in the Austro-Hungarian Empire, out of which Austria was formed, both the aristocracy and the absolutist state remained strong much longer than in the smaller countries. In these countries, as in the Polarized Pluralist countries, the transition to a liberal order was longer and more conflictual. Nevertheless, the development of a commercial and industrial middle class was sufficient to support many of the institutions of the new social order, including a strong mass-circulation press.

In the Netherlands, Switzerland, and Belgium, merchants – whose widespread commercial interests made them the first consumers of newspapers – dominated society from a very early period. In Scandinavia industrialism did not develop strongly until the late nineteenth century. Nevertheless, feudal institutions were not as strong as in other parts of Europe, and the emerging urban middle class, often in alliance, as we shall see, with an independent peasantry, rose to power relatively early – and played a key role in the development of the press. As Gustafsson and Hadenius point out, referring to what is often considered Sweden's first modern paper, established in 1830: "mine owners, merchants and intellectuals – pillars of pre-industrial society – constituted the *Aftonbladet* readership. They needed an efficient means of communication and the paper provided it" (Gustafsson and Hadenius 1976: 32). *Aftonbladet* not only carried advertising and political and commercial information useful in the emerging market society, but expressed the desire of the new middle class for liberal political and economic reforms (Hadenius and Weibull 1999). "Conservative forces,"

Hadenius and Weibull note (132), "were not strong enough to stop the paper."

Sweden was the first country in the world to establish the principles of publicity and press freedom. Its constitution of 1766 recognized both the right of access to official documents and the freedom of the press. Setbacks would take place in certain periods, but over the long run Sweden moved toward a legal system that favored the right of citizens to participate in political life and valued the free flow of information as essential to this end – clearly favorable conditions for the development of the press. Other Northern European countries also were relatively early to establish freedom of the press: Norway did so in 1814 (Wolland 1993), the Netherlands in 1815 (van Lenthe and Boerefijn 1993), Denmark in 1848 (Søllinge 1999). Belgium recognized freedom of the press in its constitution of 1831 and abolished the so-called taxes on knowledge in 1848 (Van Gomple 1998), a few years before Britain. Press freedom came later in Austria (1867) and Germany, where conflicts between the press and state censors were common until 1874 when, under Bismarck, a *Reichspressegesetz* (Imperial Press Law) eliminated prior censorship and made possible the birth of national newspapers (Sandford 1976; Humphreys 1994).

These legislative milestones clearly accelerated the growth of the press, but they also reflected the fact that newspaper circulations already had grown considerably as market institutions, civil society, and the nation state had gradually developed. The first "corantos," the forerunners of the modern newspaper, came out in the urban centers – Amsterdam, where the first coranto was probably issued as early as 1607,[2] Cologne, Frankfurt, and Antwerp. These cities were situated along Europe's main commercial routes and demand was strong not only for economic and commercial news but also for political news that might affect commerce. Habermas (1989: 16) stresses this point in his account of the origin of the public sphere:

> With the expansion of trade, merchants' market-oriented calculations required more frequent and more exact information about distant events. . . . The great trade cities became at the same time centers for the traffic in news; the organization of this traffic on a continuous basis became imperative to the degree to which the exchange of commodities and securities became continuous.

[2] The first newsletters in English were printed in Amsterdam and exported to England in 1620 (Clark 1994: 6).

LIVERPOOL JOHN MOORES UNIVERSITY
LEARNING SERVICES

This took the form initially of newsletters circulated more or less privately among merchants. In Habermas's account the circulation of news began to take a truly public form (subject of course to the qualification that "the public" was still a small part of the population in this era) and the press in the modern sense to develop, as a modern administrative state was created to regulate the emerging market. The development of the press, in other words, was connected with the emergence of rational-legal authority, whose significance in the Democratic Corporatist countries we will take up later in this chapter.

In Germany the first periodicals or *Messrelationen*, containing summaries of the most important events, started to appear as early as the sixteenth century, though the first to appear regularly date from 1609 with *Aviso* in Wolfenbuttel and *Relation* in Strasbourg. The first daily in Germany, *Einkommende Zeitungen*, was founded in Leipzig in 1650. In the German-speaking part of Switzerland, meanwhile, an early daily *Ordinari Wochenzeitung* started publication in 1610, and what may be the first prototype of the modern quality paper, the *Neue Zürcher Zeitung*, appeared in 1780, eight years before *The Times* of London. In 1798 the bookseller Johann Friedrich Cotta founded his *Allgemeine Zeitung*, which was a leading paper through the first half of the nineteenth century. This early establishment of the press in Northern and Central Europe was followed in the nineteenth century by a dramatic expansion of circulation that would end with the Democratic Corporatist countries leading the world in newspaper readership.

The birth of a mass market of the press was based on several structural elements that distinguish these countries from others. One key factor was clearly the early growth of mass literacy. Historians of literacy note that prior to 1800 Europe could be divided into three groups of countries in terms of the diffusion of literacy. The first group included Sweden, Denmark, Finland, Iceland, Scotland, Geneva, the Netherlands, part of France, England, and Germany, which had already reached a sort of mass literacy. Another group of countries, geographically proximate to these, had lower, but still relatively high literacy rates, while the lowest rates were found in Southern and Eastern Europe. The early development of literacy in Northern Europe was closely connected to the Protestant Reformation, which stressed the principle that every person should "learn to read and see with their own eyes what God bids and commands in his Holy Word," in the words of a Swedish Church Law of 1686 (Johansson 1981: 156–7). Organized literacy campaigns were common in much of Northern Europe during this period, generally supported both by the Church and the State.[3] Some parts of Germany had compulsory education in the seventeenth century. Figure 3.1 shows the literacy rates at the end of nineteenth century: with the exceptions of Austria and Belgium, the Democratic Corporatist countries had rates in excess of 90 percent by that time and led the world in this respect.[4]

The development of mass literacy was closely connected with the beginning of industrialization and the growth of market institutions, both of which contributed in a variety of ways to the growth of the mass-circulation press. As we have seen they increased the demand for information, as well as the political motivation for establishing newspapers as a voice of the emerging bourgeoisie. They also provided the economic and cultural context within which newspapers could be established as business enterprises, funded by advertising and circulation revenue, and motivated to innovate both in terms of technology and of content in an effort to expand the newspaper market. The stages of growth of the press in the Democratic Corporatist countries are closely parallel to those in the Liberal countries or, up to a certain point, France, which also saw the growth of a mass-circulation press by the late nineteenth century (though in the French case that development was partially reversed). Hadenius and Weibull (1999) note that Swedish media entrepreneurs imitated both British and French models. In the Swedish case, *Aftonbladet* was founded by the liberal Stockholm industrialist Lars Johan Hierta in 1830 – just as the penny papers were beginning in the United States. Like the latter it innovated with a wider range of content than earlier papers – "political commentary, columns, personal notices, news from Parliament and foreign affairs (132)." *Dagens Nyheter* further expanded circulations from 1864, and the first true mass-circulation paper, *Stockholms-Tidningen*, was founded in 1889.

Søllinge (1999) points to "local patriotism" as another possible reason for the high newspaper circulation of the Nordic countries: even in

---

[3] The Swedish Church, for instance, conducted examinations to certify the ability of parishioners to read, in some areas as early as the 1620s, and during the century following the Church Law of 1686 a systematic reading campaign produced a massive shift to mass literacy. Certification of literacy was necessary for confirmation in the church, which in turn was necessary to obtain permission to marry (Johansson 1981). This was important particularly in the countryside. As noted in the following text Scandinavian countries are characterized by only modest historical differences in urban and rural literacy rates.

[4] Postal flows also tended to be high in the Democratic Corporatist system (Vincent 2000). Habermas stresses the creation initially by merchants of private postal systems as an important early step in the origin of the public sphere.

the smallest towns, citizens wanted to have their own local newspapers. High circulation of the local press remains a characteristic feature of all the Scandinavian countries, and to some extent of other Democratic Corporatist countries as well (e.g., Germany and Switzerland). "Local patriotism" in this sense – a high level of civic involvement in local communities – is tied historically to the fact that liberal institutions developed strongly in rural areas of Northern Europe as well as in urban areas: the kind of split between the liberal cities and a countryside where traditional hierarchical relations or their clientelist successors prevailed, as they characteristically did in the Mediterranean countries, did not exist in the same way in the Democratic Corporatist countries, nor did strong urban-rural differences in literacy rates. We will examine the roots and consequences of this difference more systematically later in this chapter.

## BETWEEN MARKET AND PARTISANSHIP

Along with trade, the growth of early newspapers was rooted in the religious conflicts that followed the Protestant Reformation and the political conflicts that accompanied the birth of the nation-state. Here we see in its early form the duality so strongly characteristic of the newspaper in Northern and Central Europe, as an institution simultaneously of the market and of political conflict, a source of information for merchants, and a means of shaping and mobilizing opinion. In Sweden, for example, the first regularly appearing newspaper, *Ordinari Post Tijdender*, came out in 1645, preceded by *Hernes Gothicus* in 1624. Both emerged in the context of the Thirty Years War (1618–48). *Ordinari Post Tijdender* was "founded at a time when Chancellor Axel Oxensterna, who ruled the land under Queen Christina's minority, found it necessary to intensify nationalistic propaganda. Sweden had suffered setbacks in the Thirty Years War, and morale was low" (Hadenius and Weibull 1999: 129). Salokangas similarly notes that when the Finnish-language press expanded, in this case quite a bit later in the second half of the nineteenth century, it was closely connected with the Finnish nationalist movement.

The coexistence of media partisanship and mass circulation that characterizes the history of Northern and Central Europe clearly had its origin in Protestantism and Calvinism. "Protestants and printers," as Elisabeth Eisenstein (1979: 406) observes, "had more in common than Catholics and printers did." "Protestantism was the first movement of any kind, religious or secular, to use the new presses for overt propaganda and agitation against an established institution. By pamphleteering directed at arousing popular support and aimed at readers who were unversed in Latin, the reformers unwittingly pioneered as revolutionaries and rabble rousers" (Eisenstein 1979: 304; see also Edwards 1994). Protestantism not only, as we have seen, contributed to the spread of literacy, and thus to the development of mass-circulation media, but also pioneered the tradition of using print as a tool for religious and, by extension, political and social advocacy. This tradition eventually spread to Catholics, and beyond the religious into other arenas of social life. Eisenstein also points out that Protestantism had, in some of its forms at least, a close affinity to the rationality of the Enlightenment, with its emphasis on debate and critical reasoning. Not much research has been done on this subject, as far as we are aware, but there is probably a story to be told about the Protestant ethic and the spirit of journalism, just as there was about the Protestant ethic and the spirit of capitalism: habits of discourse were transferred from religion to the secular public sphere, producing a cultural model that favored reading, reasoning, diffusing, and defending one's own ideas, that encouraged the the lay public "to compare the two sides, think for themselves, and choose between alternatives instead of doing as they were told (Briggs and Burke 2002: 81).[5]

The Protestant Reformation and the political conflicts it spawned also left many of the countries of Northern and Central Europe permanently divided between adherents of different faiths, and these religious differences were often entangled with political and economic divisions. These cleavages, in some cases combined with ethnic and linguistic divisions and in all cases combined after the late nineteenth century with class divisions, continued to shape media systems – as they did the rest of social and political life – through most of the twentieth century. One of the most important characteristic of the Democratic Corporatist countries is their strong division into political and cultural subcommunities, a pattern often referred to as segmented pluralism. Media institutions, like political parties, tended to be rooted in these communities, a fact that increased the strength of media institutions (as it did of political parties also) and preserved the tradition of an ideologically plural press with strong advocacy functions.

The most obvious example of segmented pluralism is the pillarization ("*verzuiling*") of Dutch society described in Lijphart's (1968) well-known

---

[5] Perhaps another literate culture also prevalent in Central Europe – the Jewish – contributed to this cultural environment, as well.

analysis. Brants and McQuail (1997: 154) write: "Dutch society between the beginning of the twentieth century and the mid-1960s (and notably the first twenty years after the Second World War) was a principal example of 'segmented pluralism,' with social movements, educational and communications systems, voluntary associations and political parties organized vertically (and often cross cutting through social strata) along the lines of religious and ideological cleavages." The concept of "segmented pluralism" was originally introduced by Lorwin (1971) to indicate the clear, consolidated religious and ideological cleavages that he observed not just in the Netherlands but in other small European countries such as Austria, Switzerland, and Belgium. In the Dutch case, the principal pillars were the Protestant, Catholic, and Socialist subcultures, which organized late in the nineteenth century to preserve their autonomy from the then (and now once again) dominant conservative liberal culture.

One of the main characteristics of segmented pluralism is that the subcommunities have their own channels of socialization and communication (Lijphart 1968; Brants and McQuail 1992; Nieuwenhuis 1992; Van der Eijk 2000).

> Catholics and Protestants not only founded their own schools, political parties, trade unions, employers' organizations and hospitals but also their own welfare organizations, travel organizations, sporting associations, etc. The religious affiliation of a citizen decided the community he lived in from cradle to grave. A Catholic, for example, learned arithmetic from a Catholic school, learned chess from a Catholic youth club, played football in a Catholic team, learned typing at a Catholic course, went on holiday with a Catholic group and sometimes even preferred to do his shopping with a Catholic shopkeeper. . . . Seeking shelter within the group was seen as a pre-condition of emancipation. . . . The main communication medium, the printing press, was the principal tool of this process of pillarization. It kept the group together and gave it, literally, a voice. There were Catholic, Protestant and Socialist dailies and weeklies and each group also had its own illustrated press (Wigbold 1979: 193).

This function of the press has clearly contributed to the high circulation rates in Northern and Central Europe, and to the central role the press has played in social life. The depth of the roots of religious, ethnic, and ideological groups, the intensity of the clashes among them, and the strength of the institutions they built encouraged the development of a press that would reach an almost capillary diffusion among group members, for whom reading the paper was essential to being part of their religious, political, and/or ethnic community. As Hadenius and Weibull (1999: 135) write for the Swedish case, "Links between papers and political parties also meant that newspaper reading spread among most social groupings. For example, trade unions urged their members to read party-affiliated papers, thus establishing regular reading habits among the working class." In Sweden voluntary associations for newspaper development were established by parties and other social and religious organizations at the end of the nineteenth century.

The extent and the forms of "segmented pluralism" vary considerably among the Democratic Corporatist countries. But in all of them organized social groups have played a central role in the structuring of social, political, and cultural life, and important parts of the media system have been closely connected to them: the press has developed as an instrument of identification and organization within social groups, and of discussion, comparison, and conflict among them. In Finland, for example, the first paper *Åbo Tidningar*, founded in 1771, represented the Swedish elite in Turku, which at that time ruled Finland. Five years later the first Finnish-language paper appeared, also in Turku; and the press of the nationalist Finnish movement of the beginning of the following century became an organizational tool to free the country from Swedish occupation. In reaction to this attempt the Swedish community further developed its own press (Salokangas 1999).

In Belgium, partisanship has simultaneously involved ethnic-linguistic, religious, and ideological divisions. Not only did a Flemish press and a French press exist, but within these there were distinctions based on political affiliation: Catholic, socialist, and liberal papers with strong ties to political parties existed into the 1990s (Burgelman 1989). In Switzerland, of course, the press has always been linked to the different linguistic groups, though the level of intergroup conflict has not been as sharp as in other countries with linguistic divisions.

In Sweden and the other Scandinavian countries, where religious or ethnic divisions have historically been less important, political partisanship rooted in social class and ideology is central, and newspapers have been tied to parties and unions. "It was clearly quite impossible for a party to exist without the support of a press in the form of news coverage and concurring editorial opinion," as Gustafsson and Hadenius

(1976: 35) put it. "Papers were also necessary both to communication within the parties and to the dialogue between them."[6] The first to appear were the liberal papers, beginning with *Aftonbladet* in 1830. Social Democratic, Conservative, and Agrarian papers were organized later in the nineteenth century or near the beginning of the twentieth century. The socialist papers were often organized on a regional basis and supported by voluntary contributions of party members (Hadenius 1983). The fact that the socialist papers were born out of the local party organizations is a good illustration of the nature of the "local patriotism" mentioned by Søllinge and no doubt helps to account for the still-high circulation of the regional press in Sweden.

As late as 1977 two Norwegian researchers would still write, "political journalism in Scandinavia is firmly anchored in political parties. In Denmark the share of party dailies represents 92 percent (1968) of the total press, in Finland 45 percent (1972), in Sweden 97 percent (1974), and in Norway 87 percent" (1973) (Høyer and Lorentzen 1977). Denmark's "four-paper system" is particularly revealing of the "party-press-parallelism" of mid-twentieth-century Scandinavia: in every middle-size town each of the four major parties had its own newspaper (Cheesman and Kyhn 1991). In Copenhagen other smaller cultural and political groups established their own "national" papers, sometimes with supplements for some of the other major cities (Søllinge 1999).

For the Norwegian case Østbye (1991) writes that, even if the links between parties and newspapers had lost importance since the 1920s and 1930s, most of the newspapers declared their party affiliation openly in the 1970s. Similarly in Finland, the earlier ethnic-based papers were followed by the "grand era" of party press from 1905 through the early 1930s, with the Communist press developing in the 1940s. In 1910 only 20 of 117 newspapers had no clear party affiliation and in 1925 only 11 out of 109 (Salokangas 1999).

---

[6] Gustafsson (1980) lists four functions of the press as a social institution outlined by a Swedish government committee in the 1970s. The importance of functions connected to organized groups is notable:

- To give information to citizens so that they can form views on social questions
- To comment on events in society either independently or as a representative for organized social groups
- As a representative of the public to scrutinize the activities exercised by those holding power in society
- To promote communication within and between political groups, trade unions, and other voluntary groups in society

In Germany and Austria, as in Scandinavia, partisanship was linked primarily to ideology and social class, more than to religion or ethnicity. Liberal and radical papers (including the *Neue Rheinische Zeitung*, one of whose founders was Karl Marx) emerged with the revolution of 1848, and Social Democratic papers were founded starting in the 1860s, *Vorwärts*, founded in 1876, being the most important. The German journalist in this period was a "publicist," one who propagated ideas, more than a reporter. The most important flourishing of the party press occurred during the Weimar Republic, when about a third of the press was linked to political parties – the rest being accounted for by the commercial *Generalanzeiger* press and the relatively apolitical local papers – the *Heimatzeitungen*. Catholic-connected political parties had more than 400 papers, the Social Democrats around 200, and the Communists around 50 (Humphreys 1994, 1996). This was a period of considerable innovation in the forms of political journalism – for example with the development of illustrated periodicals such as the *Arbeiter-Illustrierte Zeitung* (Hardt 1996). It was also in this context that Weber (1946: 99) described a journalist as a "type of professional politician." The sharp political polarization of the Weimar period and its aftermath also saw the creation of the highly politicized commercial media empire of Alfred Hugenberg, a supporter of the Nazis and a leading member of the extreme right-wing German National People's Party (DNVP), who created Europe's first multimedia conglomerate, involving mass-circulation newspapers, a news agency, an advertising agency, and cinema production. Hugenberg's papers dominated both the party press and the traditional quality commercial papers during this period, and clearly served both political and commercial ends. The instrumentalization of the German press by the industrialist Hugenberg is clearly similar in important ways to the pattern of the Polarized Pluralist Model – the Weimar republic is considered one of the classic examples of polarized pluralism – though with the difference that these were commercially successful papers with far higher levels of circulation than could be found anywhere in the Mediterranean region. With the Nazi seizure of power, control of the press as an instrument of political propaganda was of course instituted in a particularly pure form and included the seizure of Hugenberg's own empire.

The extreme form of polarized pluralism that prevailed in Germany during the Weimar period would not recur after World War II. But in certain ways the partisan character of the German press was then reestablished. The allies' policy toward the reconstruction of the German press was twofold. On one hand the United States – in part to promote the market position of its own wire services and media industries – tried to export the U.S. model of a neutral commercial press (Blanchard 1986). On the other hand, in an effort to promote "denazification," the allies initially licensed newspapers linked to individuals or organizations that took a clear position against the ideology of the defeated Nazi regime. The first paper to be licensed in the American zone was the *Frankfurter Rundschau*, founded by a group of three Communists, three Social Democrats, and a left-wing Catholic (Sandford 1976; Humphreys 1994). The *Frankfurter Rundschau* still exists and still tends toward the political left. The British occupying forces, meanwhile, were particularly explicit in supporting the idea of the so-called *Parteirichtungszeitungen*, a plural press organized along diverse ideological orientations.

The Austrian experience is historically similar to the German in the sense that a strong party press developed in the period of political polarization early in the twentieth century and was revived to some extent following World War II. During the occupation each of the three major political parties was granted a third of the newsprint allocation. The party press persisted longer in corporatist Austria – similar to the pattern in Scandinavia – than in more liberal Germany, however. Some analysts described the party press in Austria in the 1970s as the strongest in Europe: about half of Austrian papers were then linked to parties, including Socialist and Christian Democratic tabloids, and the Socialist Party's *Arbeiter Zeitung*, founded in 1889, was fourth in circulation. By the end of the 1990s it survived as an independent paper with 3.7 percent of the newspaper market, and three true party papers also survived, the largest with a circulation of about 65,000.

Party-press parallelism or political parallelism more generally, as we saw in Chapter 2, has a number of dimensions: It can be manifested in the ownership of news media; in the affiliations of journalists, owners and managers; in readership patterns; and in media content. On each of these dimensions it has been strong historically in the Democratic Corporatist countries. In terms of ownership, newspapers directly linked to parties, trade unions, churches, and other social organizations have been an important part of the media system of all the Democratic Corporatist countries. This tends to be especially true on the political left, where socialist parties and trade unions have traditionally supported their own media – sometimes directly and sometimes through cooperative associations of party members – and expected "their newspapers to reflect their organizational structure" (Hadenius and Weibull 1999: 134). Conservative

Table 6.1 *Political Activity among Norwegian Journalists, 1970s*

| | Party Commitment of Paper | Editors-in-Chief | Managing Editors | Journalists |
|---|---|---|---|---|
| Member of Municipal | Socialist | 40% | 32% | 12% |
| Council | Bourgeois | 26 | 6 | 9 |
| Office in Political | Socialist | 83 | 82 | 51 |
| Party | Bourgeois | 59 | 32 | 28 |
| Member of Political | Socialist | 92 | 95 | 75 |
| Party | Bourgeois | 74 | 54 | 46 |

*Source:* Høyer and Lorentzen (1977: 99).

and especially liberal groups did have directly owned newspapers as well, but tended more often to rely on support from papers owned by private entrepreneurs who mixed economic and political goals (Gustafsson and Hadenius 1976; Picard 1988; Weibull and Anshelm 1991). "Behind each of the nonsocialist papers founded during the 1800s," Hadenius writes (1983: 290), "stood people with dual objectives: to influence opinion and to make money. In some cases, the commercial objective was clearly the dominant one, but in most cases the political and commercial motives were equally heavy." Both owners and journalists typically had political affiliations, and often were actively involved in politics. Table 6.1, based on a survey of Norwegian journalists in the early 1970s by Høyer and Lorentzen (1977), shows the percent of Norwegian journalists who belonged to a political party, held party office, and held local political office.

Newspaper readership has traditionally been divided along partisan lines, with this tendency again particularly strong among socialists and within religious communities in "pillarized" societies. In 1983 Weibull found that in Sweden reading "one's own press," that is the press of the party to which each reader belongs, was common among supporters of all parties, and especially for Social Democrats, whose papers depended on their readers' support.[7] This habit often persisted even after organizational links between parties and papers had atrophied, and has played

[7] Hadenius (1983) makes a distinction between newspapers that were "intradistributed," that is diffused essentially among the party's members, as was true especially of Social Democratic papers, and those that were "extradistributed," that is diffused outside as well as inside the community of a party's members, the latter being more characteristic of conservative papers.

an important role in both journalistic and political culture, strengthening the bonds between citizens and parties and promoting a view that newspapers naturally have points of view that are important to their own bonds with their target readerships. Finally, political parallelism has been manifested in the content of the press, and is connected with a journalistic culture in which the role of opinionated editor and commentator (Donsbach and Klett 1993) has an important place.

Simultaneously with the rise of party and group-affiliated newspapers, a strong commercial mass-circulation press was developing in Northern and Central Europe. This happened a bit later than in the Liberal countries, in general, in part because of later industrialization and the barriers segmented pluralism posed to the formation of a mass market. In the German case, a government monopoly on advertising held back the development of commercial newspapers until later in the nineteenth century (Donsbach and Klett 1993). After the abolition of the state monopoly on advertising, however, and after newspapers began the new practice of selling by subscription, commercial media markets developed rapidly. As Sandford (1976) notes, the German press developed a highly complex structure, composed many sectors and layers; the same is true in all the Democratic Corporatist countries. One was the independent quality press, whose main representative was the *Allgemeine Zeitung* of Johan Friedrich Cotta, followed later by the *Frankfurter Zeitung*, established in 1856, and *Berliner Tageblatt* in 1871. A second sector was composed of the party press, initiated in 1810 by the conservatives with the *Berliner Abendblätter* and later followed by the liberal and socialist press. The third sector was the mass-circulation press, which began around the 1870s and 1880s, and expanded at the beginning of the early twentieth century with the coming of the *Boulevardzeitungen*, newspapers sold in the streets, whose innovations included extensive sports coverage. *Boulevardzeitungen* developed both in Germany and in Austria. Finally, a strong regional and local press developed.

In Sweden the greatest boom in the independent/commercial press occurred in the 1920s and was followed by the introduction of afternoon tabloids in the 1940s (Hadenius and Weibull 1999). "Tabloids," in the sense of "popular" mass-circulation newspapers often sold on the street, with a much greater human interest and entertainment-oriented content than the "quality" press, exist in most of the Democratic Corporatist countries and are significant in many. In Austria, for example, the *Neue Kronenzeitung* has a 40 percent share of the market. British "red-tops" are often taken as the paradigm case of the tabloid press; but the British case is actually rather unusual, and tabloids or popular papers in the Democratic Corporatist countries generally have a different place in the media system than those in Britain. They are not as central to the newspaper market: in most countries the aggregate circulation of quality and local papers is higher. There is also not the same sharp class segmentation of the newspaper market. Tabloids have more middle class readers than in Britain. In some cases, as for example with the Norwegian tabloid *Dagbladet*, which has substantial cultural coverage, they actually have a higher educational level than newspapers readers in general (Høst 1999: 114). It is also common for people in the Democratic Corporatist countries to read both a quality paper and a tabloid. Tabloids in the Democratic Corporatist countries are often not as sensationalist as those in Britain, though Germany's *Bild*, with its more than four million circulation, and the *Neue Kronenzeitung* are close equivalents.

The expansion of "omnibus" commercial papers is one of the most important developments in the media of the Democratic Corporatist countries in the twentieth century: the political press, which was dominant in the beginning of the century, had by its end been marginalized by the commercial press. In Denmark, as Søllinge (1999) notes, newspaper penetration had reached essentially 100 percent of households by the beginning of the twentieth century. This was achieved under the politically oriented four-party paper system, and is impressive testimony to the ability of the political press to expand the newspaper audience. It also meant that newspapers could no longer expand by recruiting new readers – those who did not read any paper – but only by appealing to readers of other papers, who could be convinced either to switch or to read a second paper. This competition, Søllinge argues, had to be pursued through other means than by appeal to political affiliation, and the result was to encourage the growth of "omnibus" newspapers and the diversification of newspaper content, diminishing the place of political commentary. The pioneer in this process was *Politiken*, a Copenhagen daily that in 1905 abandoned its format as a traditional political paper and repositioned itself as an "omnibus" paper. As for the local press, Salokangas (1999) notes that in the Finnish case, there were at least two newspapers in each local market at the beginning of the twentieth century. In most cases, one of these developed into an omnibus paper and become the market leader, while the paper in the weaker market position generally strengthened its political affiliation to hold on to its remaining market share, thus institutionalizing the coexistence of the political and commercial press.

Eventually, as we shall see, the balance shifted decisively against the political press, and today in the Democratic Corporatist countries commercial newspapers clearly dominate. Nevertheless, we shall argue in a later section of this chapter that the history of a strong political press still shapes the media systems of Northern and Central Europe in important ways.

## THE STATE AND THE MEDIA

In our view the state has a responsibility for the mass media. Firstly, it has the responsibility to ensure that freedom of expression and freedom of the press are formally and in reality guaranteed by legislation. Journalists must be guaranteed the right to seek information and to disseminate their knowledge. However, the state's responsibility is wider than this. In the service of democracy and its citizens the state has a responsibility to create and maintain an information and press system that will accommodate many and diverse voices (Gustafsson 1980: 104).

As we have seen, liberalism triumphed early in Northern Europe, and most of the Democratic Corporatist countries have been characterized since the early nineteenth century by limited state power. In the media sphere, this has been manifested in strong protections for press freedom and strong provisions on public access to government information.

The development of democratic corporatism in the early twentieth century, however, modified the liberal tradition in important ways. Democratic corporatism, as we shall see in greater detail in the last section of this chapter, was formed out of a process of bargaining among social interests, including most prominently capital, labor, and agrarian interests. A key part of that bargain involved the expansion of the welfare state, and a strong welfare state is among the distinctive characteristics of the countries of Northern and Central Europe. This is one of the most important differences in political structure and culture between the Democratic Corporatist and the Liberal countries. It is also something they share with France and Italy among the Mediterranean countries; less so with Greece, Spain, and Portugal, where the state has played an important social role, but the ideology of social democracy has been much weaker. There are differences among the Democratic Corporatist countries in this respect. Katzenstein (1985) distinguishes between what he calls social corporatism, which prevails in Austria, Norway, and Denmark, and liberal corporatism, exemplified by Belgium, the Netherlands, and especially Switzerland.[8] Germany is also close to the model of liberal corporatism. In the media sphere, a desire to limit state power in order to avoid the recurrence of totalitarianism has influenced the development of a relatively liberal system in Germany. Despite these distinctions, the Democratic Corporatist countries in general are characterized by relatively high levels of social spending as well as other forms of active state intervention in economic and social life, including an active industrial policy. The political culture of the Democratic Corporatist countries tends to emphasize the duty of the state to provide conditions for full participation of all citizens and all groups in social life. The view expressed by Gustafsson in the quotation that begins this chapter – Gustafsson took it from an article by a Liberal party politician and cites it as evidence for the strong consensus in 1970s Sweden on the social role of the press – reflects this philosophy as applied to the media, which tend to be seen in the Democratic Corporatist countries not simply as a private commercial enterprise but as a social institution for which the state has an important responsibility. This tradition is manifested in media policy in several ways: in the system of press subsidies, in stronger regulation of media industries than is found in the Liberal countries, and in strong institutions of public broadcasting.

All the Democratic Corporatist countries except Switzerland and Germany have direct state subsidies for the press. Denmark (which here deviates from Katzenstein's categorization of social and liberal corporatist countries) is a marginal case, with a Finance Institute of the Press that provides security for low-interest loans.[9] Denmark, however, also has a system of subsidies for local noncommercial radio (Peterson and Siune 1997). All also have indirect subsidies, usually in the form of tax exemptions and reduced postal and sometimes telecommunications rates. These subsidy systems had their origins in the 1960s, when growing press concentration threatened the pluralism that had characterized the press in Northern Europe throughout the early twentieth century. The evolution of media markets particularly threatened politically affiliated

---

[8] Katzenstein places Sweden between these two groups. He does not discuss Finland. Social corporatism, in Katzenstein's analysis, arises where social democratic parties are dominant and is characterized by particularly strong welfare states. Liberal corporatism arises where bourgeois parties are dominant and involves more market-oriented policies. In both cases, however, policies are strongly shaped by bargains reached across class and other lines of social division.

[9] Some sources, for example Petersen and Siune (1992) and Humphreys (1996: 106), describe the Danish financing as a direct subsidy system and some (Søllinge 1999) as a system without direct subsidies.

newspapers that were the second or third papers in their respective markets: it threatened plurality both in the sense that the sheer number of competing newspapers was dropping rapidly and in the sense that the existence of diverse editorial voices and the function of the press as a forum for debate among social groups seemed in peril. In Sweden, for example, Social Democratic and Center (formerly Agrarian) party papers were particularly threatened, and these parties were the primary supporters of press subsidies, as the most successful commercial papers were more likely to be Liberal or Conservative in their politics (Gustafsson 1980; Cheesman and Kyhn 1991; Østbye 1991).

Some countries have subsidy systems directed indiscriminately at all newspapers, some have systems targeted at economically weak newspapers or those with a "special character" – in most cases those that represent political parties or other kinds of social groups (including, for example, newspapers that serve the Sami population in Norway) – and many have a combination of these systems (Humphreys 1996: 105; Murschetz 1998). Subsidies usually represent a small proportion of the turnover of large commercial papers, but can be quite significant for economically weaker ones. Hadenius and Weibull (1999) estimate that in Sweden they represent between 5 and 35 percent of revenue for second papers in metropolitan areas.

Subsidy systems have not been able to reverse the powerful trends in newspaper markets that motivated them, either the trend toward concentration or the trend toward displacement of politically distinct by "omnibus" newspapers. There is evidence, however, that they have slowed that trend in many of the Democratic Corporatist countries, and preserved in a limited way some of the pluralism of an earlier era. In Norway, for example, the number of local markets with more than one paper declined from 20 to 10 between 1972 and 1999, though Høst (1999) estimates that without subsidies all ten remaining second papers would die. He also argues that the subsidy system has been responsible for an expansion of local weekly newspapers, often with distinct political points of view, which have to some extent replaced the politically oriented dailies of an earlier era. Subsidy systems may also have contributed modestly to the continuing high circulation of newspapers in Northern Europe. Høst estimates that in 1997 the newspaper circulation in Norway would have been 514 per thousand without subsidies, in contrast to the actual 589 per thousand. The debate over subsidy systems always included the issue of whether subsidies would make newspapers subject to pressure from the state and less willing to play a "watchdog" role, but there does not seem to be evidence that this has occurred in the Democratic Corporatist countries. Actually the media were more deferential to political elites in the 1950s, before these subsidy systems were put in place, than in the 1970s: the growth of "critical professionalism" in journalism in Northern Europe came, as we shall see in the following text, in the period when subsidies were highest. The subsidies are granted according to clearly established criteria – consistent with the strong role of rational-legal authority in the Democratic Corporatist countries. This, along with the process of bargaining and compromise characteristic of democratic corporatism, makes political manipulation of the subsidies for purposes of pressuring newspapers unlikely. Newspaper subsidies have been reduced in most countries over the past decades, as the welfare state in general has been cut back. But they remain an important feature of the media systems of most of the Democratic Corporatist countries.

The Democratic Corporatist countries also tend to combine strong protection for press freedom with a significant level of regulation – again reflecting the assumption that media are a social institution and not simply a private business. Most countries have hate-speech laws banning media content that denigrates specific social groups. Many – for example, Germany, Austria, and the Netherlands – also have specific bans on dissemination of Nazi propaganda, holocaust denial, and the like. Norwegian law bans advertising that "conflicts with the inherent parity between the sexes" (Wolland 1993: 128); Sweden bans advertising directed at children. Regulation of commercial broadcasting generally involves limits on the total amount of advertising, the frequency of commercial interruptions, and mixing of advertising and program content, as well as requirements for political pluralism. Paid political advertising on television is banned or narrowly restricted in Belgium, Denmark, Sweden, and Switzerland.[10] Access of parties to electronic media during election campaigns is regulated in Austria, Denmark, Finland, Germany, and Sweden (Farrel and Webb 2000: 107). All countries, following a variety of different policies, give free television time for party election broadcasts. According to Danziger (1986) right-of-reply laws exist in Austria, Belgium, Denmark, Finland, Germany, Norway, and Switzerland. The strong press councils that exist in most Democratic Corporatist countries also reflect the tendency in these countries to treat the media as a social institution and consequently to place limits, at least in principle, on the

---

[10] Farrell and Webb also list Finland; Salonkangas (personal communication) tells us that paid political advertising is not banned in Finland but is not much used.

logic of commercial competition. These institutions are not generally connected to the state, however.[11] In this sense they reflect another side of the political culture of democratic corporatism: the strength of civil society and a tendency to devolve to institutions of civil society functions that otherwise might be exercised by the state. Strong press councils in the Democratic Corporatist countries in some ways makes state intervention less important than it might otherwise be: libel laws, for example, may be less important than in the Liberal or Polarized Pluralist systems. We will discuss press councils more fully in the following text, in relation to the professionalization of journalism.

Broadcasting in the Democratic Corporatist countries constitutes a particularly strong example of the logic of the welfare state as applied to the media. In the case of the print media, the state intervenes to modify market mechanisms, but the system is predominantly a liberal one, based on private ownership and the market. In the case of broadcasting, on the other hand, the role of the state was absolutely dominant until the 1980s or 1990s, and is still very important. Broadcasting has been treated as part of the *res publica*, as an institution whose influence on society is too great to be left under the control of private interests and that must be run under the authority of the state as a representative of the general interest. The Democratic Corporatist countries generally introduced commercial broadcasting relatively late. Their public broadcasting systems have been well-funded and relatively "pure" in the sense that advertising revenue has constituted a small part of their funding. They placed relatively strong emphasis on public service as opposed to entertainment functions, reflecting what Bastiansen and Syvertsen (1996: 141) call, in the Norwegian case, a "social democratic enlightenment ethos." They also have been organized in a way that reflects a strong concern to assure that they serve a wide range of social interests. Looking back at Table 2.4, which shows the strength and "purity" of public broadcasting systems according to a number of measures, it is clear that the Democratic Corporatist countries are distinguished by their strong commitment to that institution. Denmark and Austria head the list in terms of audience share. Denmark and Switzerland (with an expensive system because it must broadcast in so many languages) is the highest, along with Britain, in per capita funding. Norway is the only country without

---

[11] In Denmark the Press Council is established by law and in some countries the equivalent of the press council for broadcasting is linked to the state, for example the Radio Council in Sweden.

any commercial revenue for public broadcasting, while Sweden also has minimal commercial revenue.

## GOVERNANCE OF PUBLIC BROADCASTING

The intent to establish public broadcasting systems that would serve the general interest obviously raises the question of how these systems will be governed. There is a fair amount of variation among the Democratic Corporatist countries in this regard. In terms of the four models of public broadcast governance introduced in Chapter 2 – the government, parliamentary, professional, and civic models – the Democratic Corporatist countries show various combinations of the last three. Given the strong emphasis on consensus among diverse political groups that characterizes democratic corporatism, it is not surprising that all have moved away from the government model that remains strong in many of the Polarized Pluralist countries – all, that is, have developed mechanisms to insulate public broadcasting from control by the political majority. All give broadcasting professionals fairly high levels of autonomy, and in this sense are similar to the professional model, whose classic case is the BBC. But compared with the Liberal systems, Democratic Corporatist countries often give a greater role in the governance of public broadcasting to organized political forces, either in the form of political parties (this is what defines the parliamentary model) or in the form of "socially relevant groups" other than political parties (the civic model).

The Dutch system is a particularly strong and unusual case of a system based on the representation of organized social groups. Dutch broadcasting was organized originally following the same "pillarized" structure that prevailed in the print press. Time on the publicly owned radio channels was divided among broadcasting organizations linked to the existing social pillars: the Catholic KRO, the Protestant NCRV, the Socialist VARA, and AVRO, a "neutral" organization that was supported by the liberal subculture. Funding and broadcast time was divided among these organizations originally according to political criteria, and from the 1960s according to their memberships, as reflected in subscriptions to their program guides. Television was organized along the same lines. In 1967 a common umbrella organization, the Dutch Broadcasting Foundation (NOS), was established. NOS produced the main daily news program as well as sports programming. It represented the beginning of a process of standardization and secularization that would later accelerate with commercialization, as we shall see in detail in Chapter 8 (Brants and McQuail 1997). In 1976 – as pillarization in Dutch society continued to weaken – new legislation allowed the creation of more neutral/liberal broadcast organizations, TROS and Veronica (the latter a commercially oriented organization that originally started as a pirate station), as well as EO, linked to the Evangelical church (Nieuwenhuis 1992). The separate broadcasting organizations that originated in pillarization do still exist, though the differences among them are dramatically less significant than they were a generation earlier.

The Dutch system has been based on a form of "external pluralism" (Hoffman Riem 1996), with separate broadcasting companies representing different social groups. In other Democratic Corporatist countries internal pluralism in broadcasting is preferred: An attempt is made to represent the different organized voices of the society within a single organization (or, in the case of linguistically plural societies such as Switzerland and Belgium, within systems organized by language). Internal pluralism, in the sense Hoffmann-Riem employs here, involves both the content of broadcasting – which is required to reflect the diversity of perspectives within society – and the structure of broadcast organizations, which often incorporate representatives of the different social, political, and cultural groups. In this latter characteristic, the broadcasting systems of the Democratic Corporatist countries differ from those of the Liberal countries. The "professional model" exemplified by the BBC is based on the separation of broadcasting both from the government and from parties and other organized social forces. Pluralism is, in theory, achieved by keeping politics *out* of the governance of broadcasting, leaving it to neutral broadcasting professionals to represent the diversity of society. The Democratic Corporatist countries, in contrast, tend toward a model in which pluralism is guaranteed by making sure that a diversity of political and social forces is included *in* the governance of broadcasting. As Porter and Hasselbach (1991: 5–6) say of the German system:

This interpretation of pluralism modifies the liberal model, widely accepted in Anglo Saxon thinking, in several respects. In the Federal Republic, the political parties are permanent institutions of public life and are constitutionally assigned the strongest pluralist role. . . . [They] are seen as the political voice of a majority of citizens cutting across particular interests. The classic idea of liberalism, that of social groups defending civil liberties against an absolute ruler, has thus been replaced by the concept of the all-embracing democratic state, the social and legal state [*sozialer Rechtsstaat*], which gains its legitimacy through political representation of its citizens in parliament. This strong reliance upon political parties naturally means that factional politics permeate every aspect of West German life, including its broadcasting system. The Constitutional Court regarded not only political parties, but also other associations of interests, as "intermediary forces" which precede parliamentary decision-making and are necessary for the democratic formation of public will. Therefore, non-partisan interests have also been hierarchised in order to carry out a number of state regulatory duties, such as the allocation of public funds to charities, collective bargaining and public insurance. Last but not least, they have a mandate to participate in the regulation of broadcasting.

This pattern, which Kelly (1983) called a "politics in broadcasting system," is most strongly manifested in Germany, Austria, and in a different way in Belgium, while the Nordic countries could probably be said to tend more in the direction of the professional model discussed in Chapter 2.

The German system is complex, in part because Germany is a federal system, and broadcasting falls under the authority of the Länder governments, and is organized a bit differently in each of the Länder. The federal structure of German broadcasting, which grew out of the reorganization of the German media system by the Western Allies immediately after the defeat of the Nazi regime, was intended as part of a series of guarantees of pluralism, as a barrier to the monopolization of political power by any single force. In a sense it introduces a degree of external pluralism into the German system, as the different Länder are governed by different political majorities, and these political differences are reflected to a degree in the different public broadcasting organizations. This also carries over into private broadcasting: RTL, owned by Bertelsmann and licensed in Nord-Rhein-Westphalia, which is governed by the Social Democrats and Greens, is commonly regarded as a bit to the left of the other main commercial broadcaster Sat 1, which is licensed in conservative Bavaria (Patterson and Donsbach 1993; see Figure 6.1).

Public broadcasting organizations based in each of the Länder are governed by boards that are independent of the state and that typically include representatives both of political parties, appointed by proportional representation, and of "socially relevant groups" including trade unions, churches, industrial and professional associations, and a variety of others. Proportional representation penetrates down through the organization, as considerations of political balance affect the appointments of journalists and other key personnel. The boards that regulate private broadcasting are organized along similar lines, and in certain of the Länder commercial broadcasters have been required to or have voluntarily set up programming boards with similar representation, though these boards are only advisory in character. The German system is thus, along with the very different Dutch one, the classic example of a "civic" broadcasting system based on representation not just of political parties but of organized civil society. There are, to be sure, critiques of this system. One is that the parties dominate it in the end, in part because the representatives of the "socially relevant groups" often have party alignments. In this sense the German system would collapse into the "parliamentary" model of broadcast governance. Another critique is that the German system fails to represent social interests that are not formally organized and not incorporated into the structure of corporatist representation.

One other characteristic of the German system should be mentioned. The Federal Constitutional Court plays an extremely important role in the supervision of broadcasting in Germany. This is probably due both to the strength of the tradition of rational-legal authority in Germany – which will be discussed later in this chapter – and to the federal character of broadcast regulation, which often leaves it to the court to set central broadcasting policy. The Constitutional Court has played an important role on a number of occasions in protecting the independence of the broadcasting when either the federal or Länder governments have tried to bring it under stronger government control (Humphreys 1994: 161–2).

Austria also has a broadcasting system based strongly on a philosophy of political representation. Originally it was based on the parliamentary model, with a board of directors appointed by party proportional representation. In 1967, in an effort to make it more independent, the board was enlarged to include nine members appointed by the federal government, six by Parliament according to proportional representation, one each by each Länder government, six by a Council of Viewers and Listeners, and five by the employees, and the position of the director was strengthened. As in Germany, however, most directors have party links; political parties are strong in Austria, and the "*Proporz*" principle still affects appointments at many levels, in broadcasting as in many aspects of Austrian life.

Belgium originally had a system based on external pluralism, similar to the Dutch system. After World War II, however, it moved toward a unitary system and then in the 1960s toward two systems, French and Flemish, each based on internal pluralism, with directors appointed by proportional representation. "The composition of the board of public service broadcasting changed every time a new general election was held," according to Burgelman (1989: 179–80)... "[M]embers of the board of directors define themselves . . . explicitly as being 'mandatories' of the political parties. . . . [T]he board explicitly used the argument that only a physical representation of the political parties could guarantee an objective news bulletin." Of all the Democratic Corporatist countries Belgium is closest to the Polarized Pluralist model in the party-political character of its broadcasting system, as it is in other respects.[12]

The Nordic countries tend more toward the "professional" model, that is toward a system in which broadcasting is conceived as a nonpolitical institution serving society as a whole, though the degree of political insulation does vary. In Sweden, the logic of the civic/corporatist model is reflected in the fact that ownership of the Swedish Broadcasting Corporation has been divided since the 1960s between "popular movements" such as trade unions, consumers' organizations, and churches, the other 40 percent being divided between the press and business (Weibull and Anshelm 1992; Gustafsson 1996; and Hulten 1997). The Swedish system is generally seen, however, as very close to the BBC in the sense that it has a relatively high degree of autonomy from political influence (Humphreys 1996: 156–7). As Weibull and Djerf-Pierre (2000) stress, professionalization strengthened in the 1960s. Swedish public broadcasting shifted toward a stance that it had a responsibility to scrutinize the political system and its influence in political life increased. The Danish and Norwegian systems probably shade more toward the parliamentary

---

[12] The party-politicized character of Belgian public broadcasting is consistent with the generally party-political character of public administration in Belgium (Keman 1996: 240) and is one of the characteristics Belgium shares with the Polarized Pluralist countries. Belgium has not had a particularly high level of ideological polarization, though this may in part be due to the religious and linguistic character of social cleavages. Polarization may also have increased in recent years as anti-immigrant right-wing parties have grown in strength. Belgium does share with the classic Polarized Pluralist Model a high degree of fragmentation of the party system and a low level of government stability: thirty-eight governments in the period 1945–96, a number very close to that of Italy (Keman 1996).

model, though still with a relatively high level of autonomy. In Denmark a form of external pluralism has emerged in the fact that the head of Danmarks Radio (DR) has generally come from the political left, while the head of the newer TV2, a public broadcaster with advertising, has come from the right.

Even though broadcasting in the Democratic Corporatist countries reflects the importance of organized social and political forces in society, it is important to note that the level of partisanship in broadcasting has consistently been less than in the print press. Public ownership and internal pluralism – the coexistence of representatives from different social groups within the same organization – restrain the clear expression of the partisan points of view: the different groups check each others' power and there is also a feeling of working for an organization that is the common property of all of them, with a responsibility to represent all of them fairly. In most cases, moreover, there were only one or two channels for many years, and the law required their programming to be balanced politically and ideologically, particularly in the case of main news broadcasts. The BBC model of a independent and "neutral" broadcasting system was influential everywhere, even if its implementation was often substantially modified by the strong role of parties and social groups in Northern and Central Europe. In this sense television may have contributed to the "secularization" of society in Northern and Central Europe (a theme we will take up in greater detail in Chapter 8) among other things by introducing a model of nonpartisan journalism that eventually influenced the professional culture of the news media – to which we will next turn our attention.

## PROFESSIONALIZATION

The media in the Democratic Corporatist countries have historically had strong associations with organized political forces. It might be assumed that such associations would hold back the professionalization of journalism. In fact, however, the Democratic Corporatist countries are characterized by an early and strong development of journalistic professionalism. As Høyer and Lorentzen (1977) explain for the Scandinavian case, the high circulation of newspapers enabled news organizations to accumulate substantial economic resources and therefore to offer the journalists decent salaries that made it unnecessary for them to seek other sources of income. Increasingly those employed in the print press were thus full-time journalists – a very different picture from the one

Chalaby gives regarding early French journalism, in which journalists were employed in many different activities, often in fields of art, literature, and politics, and a distinct professional identity was slow to develop (Chalaby 1996). At the same time, despite the ideological, religious, and political divisions that existed within the world of journalism, many opportunities opened up for social contact among those working as full-time journalists. Høyer and Lorentzen note that the first association of Norwegian journalists was formed in 1883, a year before the introduction of the parliament, and "a year of unbridgeable political cleavages" (1977: 102). "The confluence of these events does not appear altogether logical," they note. "A period of bitter political conflicts in the press is followed immediately by efforts to unite journalists, why not before or after?" They go on to explain that "the party conflicts brought editors and political reporters from the whole nation together. It was of secondary importance that Parliament served as their meeting place, more important was the concurrent situation where common interests could be discovered and discussed" (102).

The first unions of journalists were founded in Scandinavia and other parts of Northern Europe, and such organizations are very strong today compared with their counterparts in the Liberal or Polarized Pluralist countries. The formation of the first professional association in Norway in 1883 preceded the Institute of Journalists in Britain by seven years. In the Netherlands the first journalists' union (NJK) was established in 1894; other unions followed later, established on the basis of religious and political affiliation.[13] In Germany a central journalists organization, the Verband deutscher Journalisten- und Schriftstellervereine was formed in 1895. In Sweden a Publicists' Club was established in 1874, uniting journalists and publishers and centrally concerned with ethical issues in journalism (Weibull and Börjesson 1992); the Union of Journalists was founded in 1901 (Høyer & Lorentzen 1977). The Finnish journalists' union was founded in 1921. Often these unions did suffer from political divisions in their first decades, but by the 1930s–40s, as democratic corporatism was becoming fully consolidated, they usually developed into strong, unified organizations.[14] The oldest press club, "Presseclub

[13] With the depillarization process the different unions underwent a process of integration and in 1965 the three main journalist organizations formed one single union: the Nederlandse Vereniging van Journalisten (NVJ).

[14] Høyer and Lorentzen describe the development of professionalism in Scandinavia as being delayed by the political connections and divisions of the press. But in comparative context, that development actually occurred early and strongly.

Concordia" was established in Austria in 1859 bringing together leading Austrian journalists and foreign correspondents. Organizations also exist that establish rules for coverage of particular "beats"; in the German case the most important is the Bundespressekonferenz – similar to the Westminster Lobby in Britain or Japanese Press Clubs – that organizes press conferences and establishes rules for much of the most important political and parliamentary reporting. Very often these organizations also have the power to decide penalties (mostly of a symbolic nature) for journalists who do not respect the established rules.

Similar to other "peak associations" in Democratic Corporatist countries, the journalists' unions today are usually unitary – without sectarian or political divisions (though clubs that bring together journalists with similar political or religious orientations sometimes also exist) – with high rates of membership, ranging from near-universal membership to levels around 50–60 percent (e.g., in Germany [Schoenbach, Stuerzebecher, and Schneider 1998: 221] and in the Netherlands [van Lenthe and Boerefijn 1993]), still quite high in comparative perspective. These organizations have been active in the discussion of issues of ethics and press freedom as well as purely economic issues. Heinonen (1998: 175) notes that almost all Finnish journalists report reading the union's twice-monthly newspaper regularly, and Humphreys (1994) notes that the German journalists' union has the character more of an "association of practicing journalists and editors than of trade union." Often, again similar to other "peak organizations" in Democratic Corporatist countries, journalists' unions have a formal voice in discussions of media policy, as do press owners' associations.

The Democratic Corporatist countries also tend to have relatively strong, formalized systems of self-regulation of the press. Every country except Belgium has a press council. The strongest of these is the well-known Swedish Press Council, whose origins go back to an honorary court of justice set up by the Publicists' Club in 1916 (Weibull and Börjesson 1992). Several elements make it particularly strong: it has the power to levy fines against newspapers as well as to require them to publish its decisions; it is headed by a judge, and representatives of the media industry make up a minority of its members; and it is supplemented by a Press Ombudsman who helps to investigate complaints, taking part of the burden of preparing a case off of members of the public who wish to bring complaints. It also has a high level of legitimacy among Swedish journalists and publishers – probably more important in the end than the power to levy fines. As Weibull and Börjesson (1992) observe, the reporting of the investigation of the 1986 assassination of Swedish Prime Minister Olof Palme is an excellent illustration of the strength of self-regulation in the Swedish media: over two years of investigation, the suspect was never named in the Swedish press, something impossible to imagine in Britain, for example, or in Italy. The Norwegian Press Council goes back to 1936 and also includes representatives of the public (as does the Dutch) and provides assistance to members of the public wishing to file complaints, though it has no legal sanctions. Heinonen (1998: 181) notes that decisions of the Finnish Press Council are published in the journalists' union magazine, and that 40 percent of journalists report reading them carefully and 96 percent at least occasionally. The German Press Council has only journalists' and publishers' representatives, and in that sense is probably somewhat weaker, as is the Austrian, whose decisions are often ignored by the dominant tabloid the *Neue Kronenzeitung* (Humphreys 1996: 61–2).

Press councils in the Democratic Corporatist countries were established either by journalists or by publishers' organizations or by the two jointly, rather than established by the state, though in some cases concern about state regulation was an important motivating factor. Their operation is based on codes of ethics that, again, have been adopted by journalists or publishers' organizations (Laitila 1995), and that usually have high levels of acceptance among journalists and publishers (e.g., Heinonen 1998: 180). Only Denmark deviates somewhat from this pattern: its press council was established by a 1992 Media Liability Act, which also incorporated into law a code of ethics that had been adopted twenty-five years earlier by the publishers. The journalists' union had refused to endorse it, taking the view that particular journalists and newspapers should make their own ethical judgments (Kruuse n.d.). The ethical culture of Danish journalism is not, however, dramatically different from that of other Scandinavian countries. Following Humphreys and others (Article XIX 1993; Humphreys 1996) press councils in Sweden, the Netherlands, and Norway are judged to be the most effective.

Formal education in journalism also often serves to promote a distinct professional identity, though this has for the most part come later than the development of journalists' organizations and systems of self-regulation in the Democratic Corporatist countries. In Finland it started in the 1920s, following the civil war, when a centralized university system was created and journalism education was established along with education in other professions. As in most of the Democratic Corporatist countries, however, it remained small-scale until the 1960s. In Sweden the first university course in journalism was started in 1930 in Göteborg, and the first full degree programs introduced in 1960. In Norway formal journalism education dates from 1951. In the Netherlands journalism education was conducted within the "pillars" until the first nonaffiliated program was established in Utrecht in 1966.

The level of journalistic autonomy is also relatively high in the Democratic Corporatist countries. Donsbach and Patterson's (1992) survey of journalists in Britain, Germany, Italy, and the United States found that German journalists were the least likely to report that pressures from senior managers and editors were an important limitation on their work with 7 percent of German journalists reporting such influence from senior editors, compared with 14 percent in the United States, 22 percent in Britain, and 35 percent in Italy. They – along with Swedish journalists (Donsbach 1995) – were also the least likely to report that the news they prepared was changed by another person in the newsroom: "the news they prepare is usually printed or broadcast without interference." This finding is consistent with Esser's (1998) research on British and German newsrooms, which showed that German newsrooms lacked the hierarchical structure of British ones, and that German journalists tended to work as individuals with minimal supervision.[15] The culture of German journalism is strongly shaped by the experience of totalitarianism and the value placed on autonomy is in part related to that legacy. German journalists also have strong job security, as is true in general of workers in the Democratic Corporatist countries, and this probably increases their autonomy, though newspapers, as *tendenz* or "ideological" enterprises, are exempted from laws on worker participation in management that apply to other industries (a good illustration of the assumption in German culture that it is the function of a newspaper to exercise "ideological

---

[15] In his comparative study of the newsroom organization in Great Britain and Germany Esser finds two very different sets of routines. The main difference lies in a much clearer division of roles in Great Britain than in Germany: in Germany there is not a precise division between the roles of reporter, editor, and commentator. Even if German newspapers distinguish in their layout between news stories and commentaries, in terms of organizational structure the separation of these functions is not strong. Esser relates this to different professional cultures, German professional culture being more inclined historically to commentary and evaluation. Moreover, most of the press in Great Britain has been set on the model of the main national papers that have functioned as models both in content and in organizational procedures. Because of their large resources, national newspapers have been able to provide a segmented organization with professionals performing very specified roles. In contrast the prevalence of the regional press in Germany has meant a smaller and more flexible organization with less division of labor.

guidance with respect to information and the expression of opinions").[16] Germany had debates on *innere Pressefreiheit,* or internal press freedom – the freedom of journalists within the news organization – in the 1970s. There were efforts at this time to roll back the protection of the owner's prerogative provided by the *tendenz* exception and to give journalists stronger rights of participation in decision making within media organizations. A few newspapers and the magazine *Stern* established editorial statutes that gave journalists some such rights (the strongest surviving today is at the left-wing daily *Taz*); but legislation to establish such a right in law was beaten back by media owners (Humphreys 1994: 108–10; Holtz-Bacha 2002), and the movement faded after the 1970s. In the 1980s, when private broadcasting was introduced, some of the Länder required broadcasting organizations to negotiate editorial statutes protecting journalistic autonomy, as a means of promoting pluralism in media content and preventing instrumentalization of private broadcasting.

In the Netherlands journalists were successful in the 1960s and 1970s in winning editorial statutes (*redactienstatuten*) that protected their independence. In the view of van der Eijk these statutes help explain why the "depillarization" discussed in the next section did not "leave the field open for the establishment of an all-out commercial or tabloid press" (316). State economic subsidies are granted in the Netherlands and in Norway only if journalists have complete editorial autonomy (Humphreys 1996). In Norway, the Redaktørplakaten or Editor's Code as well as the Norwegian Press Association Code of Ethics give the editor-in-chief sole power to decide what to publish, excluding the publisher from any right to control content; this right has come to be recognized by the Norwegian courts. Interventions by owners have on occasion produced mass resignations of journalists from Norwegian papers and led to the death of the paper *Midhordaland* in 1987 (Wolland 1993: 120–1).

The high level of professionalization in the Democratic Corporatist countries means that the issue of instrumentalization of the media,

---

[16] The phrase about "ideological guidance" comes from the European Union Directive on the worker participation in business enterprises, which gave countries the option of excepting "ideological enterprises." Three of the Democratic Corporatist countries, Germany, Austria, and Sweden, elected to exclude news media according to this provision (Holtz-Bacha 2002). As we shall see in the following text there is a tendency for German journalists to work for newspapers whose politics are similar to their own. It is possible that this is one reason for the low level of editorial intervention – that political coordination is already partly achieved in the hiring process.

which, as we saw in Chapter 5 is a strong concern in the Polarized Plural-ist countries, is not nearly as central a focus either of media scholarship or of public debates over the media in Northern and Central Europe. Probably there is even less focus on this issue in the Democratic Corpo-ratist than in the Liberal countries. The greatest exception can be found in Germany, where Axel Springer, owner of the right-wing *Bild* and *Welt*, was the subject of considerable controversy, particularly in the 1960s and 1970s (Humphreys 1994: 92ff).[17] In general, though, debates over the political implications of media ownership usually are more structural than instrumental in character: they concern the decline of diversity with media concentration and the tendency for "bourgeois" papers of the center and right to drive out papers of the left through commercial competition, more than the role of individual media owners as political actors.

The development of this level of journalistic autonomy, and at the structural level a strong differentiation of news media as an indepen-dent social institution, has a fairly complex historical evolution. In the early twentieth century, even if professional ethics and solidarity were already significantly developed, the political content of journalism was largely controlled by owners or in the case of party papers by the party hierarchy. "The editorial board controlled with an iron grip who among journalists could speak about politics" (Olsson 2002: 61). By the 1950s – in Olsson's account of the Swedish press – the editorialist, who was the journalistic figure most closely tied to the political world, was becoming less important and the "socially responsible news reporter" more so. The latter was generally deferential toward the leaders of parties and social organizations, but did play the role of being an "active proponent of modernization and progress." "News journalism now [had] the right to engage in the politics of the day – with the proviso that it remain non-controversial (165)." By the 1960s in Sweden (Hadenius 1983; Djerf-Pierre 2000; Olsson 2002) as in other countries (e.g., Wigbold 1979; van der Eijk 2000) the proviso that journalism remain noncon-troversial was being challenged. A culture of critical professionalism was emerging and journalists were asserting the right to criticize political and social elites and to focus attention on social problems, often with an activist orientation: "journalists . . . had the ambition to scrutinize

---

[17] The politics of the Springer press is a prominent theme in the popular novel *The Lost Honor of Katherina Blum* (Böll 1975).

the actions of policy-makers and to influence both public debate on social and political issues and the policies made by public institutions" (Djerf-Pierre 2000: 254). The activist orientation – which was also manifested in the push for "internal press freedom" – has faded since the 1970s and journalists are less likely to see themselves as mobilizers of an active citizenry. But a critical orientation toward established institutions remains, along with an insistence that journalists should actively set the news agenda.

The shift to "critical professionalism" took place both in print media and in broadcasting – at this time strictly public – and both in the commercial and in the party press. Hadenius (1983: 300) observed of the Swedish party press in the wake of this shift:

> It used to be well-nigh unthinkable for a newspaper to expose or criticize its own party. Today it is the general rule that one's own party members be subjected to the same critical journalism as that to which an opposition party is subjected. . . . Today's journalists make entirely different demands than previously. They do not take orders from either politicians or organizations. They require that the news columns of a newspaper not be administered according to political principles. It is noteworthy, however, that it is still possible to discover the political color of a newspaper in the news columns.

Hadenius goes on to explain that at party papers, like commercial ones, journalists were hired on a professional basis and could shift from one news organization to another: they were clearly part of a professional culture that transcended political affiliation. In economic terms, meanwhile, party papers competed with commercial ones and like commercial papers did not want to be seen by readers as "party rags." In Hadenius's discussion we can see very strongly the coexistence of political parallelism and professionalization that is one of the distinctive features of the Democratic Corporatist model and that was particularly strong in the period Hadenius was describing.[18] The journalist is a professional who respects rules and routines agreed upon by the profession as a

---

[18] Høyer and Lorentzen (1977: 109) talk about "ambivalence towards politicians... partly as fellow conspirators and partly as adversaries" and the "double sidedness in the professional culture," and cite surveys showing, for example, 74 percent of Norwegian journalists agreeing, in the early seventies, that journalists must be independent of parties, and 62 percent that they must be loyal to the (party) policy of their paper.

whole and who insists on the autonomy of journalistic practice from political interference.[19] At the same time he or she maintains a political/ideological identity, both as an individual and as part of a news organization, and in many cases aspires actively to intervene in the political world.

## THE DECLINE – AND PERSISTENCE – OF POLITICAL PARALLELISM

The evolution Hadenius saw in the 1980s, with party papers distancing themselves from the strong political identifications of the past, has clearly continued. Weibull and Anshelm (1991: 38), writing a decade later, saw a much more fundamental change than Hadenius:

> the press is by tradition affiliated to political parties: almost all newspapers officially declare a partisan orientation – 4/5 with a non socialist and 1/5 with a socialist outlook – on their editorial page. Until the mid-1970s the partisan orientation was also visible in the news presentation, but the latest decades have meant a breakthrough for a modern professional journalism, predominantly of the Anglo-Saxon type.

The true party press, still significant in many of the Democratic Corporatist countries in the 1970s, hardly exists at all today; and the level of political parallelism of the whole media system has decreased quite significantly. Depoliticization of newspapers has occurred together with a process of more general secularization of society, which we will examine in greater detail in Chapter 8. The traditional mass parties have declined in their membership base and have lost much of their symbolic and representative functions in face of the increasing role of other socialization agencies, increased fragmentation of society and the disappearance of structured social cleavages (Dalton 1988; Panebianco 1988). This process of "secularization," which was well under way in the 1960s and 1970s, was accentuated in the following decade by the "commercial deluge" that transformed broadcasting – and that continued to accelerate in print media as well. This process has clearly weakened the ties between media and national political systems. There is clearly a strong

---

[19] Holtz-Bacha (2002) also notes that the strongest editorial statutes in Germany were at papers owned by the Social Democratic party.

Table 6.2 *Political Affiliations of Danish Newspapers*

|  | 1960 | 1970 | 1980 | 1990 | 1995 | 2000 | 2002 |
|---|---|---|---|---|---|---|---|
| Social Democrat | 14 | 7 | 7 | 7 | 1 | 1 | 0 |
| Social Liberal | 7 | 4 | 3 | 2 | 2 | 2 | 2 |
| Independent Social Liberal | 2 | 2 | 2 | 2 | 1 | 1 | 1 |
| Conservative | 16 | 8 | 4 | 1 | 1 | 1 | 1 |
| Independent Conservative | 2 | 1 | 2 | 2 | 2 | 0 | 0 |
| Liberal | 36 | 27 | 14 | 13 | 6 | 5 | 5 |
| Independent Liberal | 2 | 2 | 7 | 7 | 9 | 9 | 9 |
| Communist/Socialist | 1 | 2 | 2 | 1 | 0 | 0 | 0 |
| Other Independent | 8 | 9 | 12 | 16 | 15 | 14 | 14 |
| Total | 88 | 62 | 49 | 47 | 37 | 33 | 32 |

*Source:* Søllinge (1999: 57), and personal communication.
The group "Other Independent" covers a range of cross-party positions. Not all changes in the table are due to newspaper closures; some stem from papers changing their political position. Three new free daily newspapers are not included in the table, as they are not dailies in the conventional sense. All are politically independent.

trend toward "catchall" or "omnibus" media, rooted much more in the market than in the world of politics, for which "viewers and . . . readers are no longer seen as followers of a particular social and religious sector but essentially as individual consumers" (Nieuwenhuis 1992: 207).

The decline of political parallelism in the Democratic Corporatist countries is manifest in many ways. Table 6.2 shows figures on party affiliation of newspapers in Denmark, as reported by Søllinge (1999). The sharp increase in the number of "independent" papers relative to politically affiliated ones is related to concentration of the newspaper market: the total number of papers declined from 88 to 37 between 1960 and 1995 and many of those that remained were local monopoly newspapers, which toned down their politics as they sought to recruit readers from dying papers of other political persuasions. The last Social Democratic paper, *Aktuelt*, which had lasted for 130 years and was funded by the Confederation of Trade Unions, closed in 2001. Salokangas (1999) reports similar data for Finland. Hadenius and Weibull (1999) report that while 75 percent of Swedish papers, representing 80 percent of circulation, did still declare a political affiliation, professional norms had weakened the effect of affiliation on content. They also report figures on the percent of the population reading a paper that corresponded with their own political affiliation – which declined from 1979 through 1997 among Conservatives and Social Democrats (in the latter case most substantially, from 32 to 15 percent) – as liberal papers increasingly became dominant. Schoenbach, Stuerzebecher, and Schneider (1998: 225) report that between 1980–2 and 1992 survey data on journalists showed that "'expressive' elements of the profession – to be able to pass on one's own opinion to other people and to have a political impact – retreated in favor of intrinsic rewards, which manifested themselves more in everyday work routines.... Also, a service orientation increased. More journalists were ready to offer something to the audience, and fewer wanted to stir it up, train it or educate it." What their data show, above all, is an increase in the proportion of journalists saying that it is their role to entertain the public or to "mirror what the public thinks" – a finding consistent with Djerf-Pierre's (2000) analysis of the content of Swedish TV news, which showed an increasingly "conformist" attitude toward the news audience.

As significant as these trends are, however, an important degree of political parallelism does persist in the Democratic Corporatist countries. Pfetsch (2001: 64) observes that the relationship between politicians and journalists is marked by "a more media-oriented style of interaction in the United States, a more politically motivated interaction style in Germany." Her analysis suggests some similarity to the pattern noted in the Italian case in Chapter 5, in which journalists are involved in the process of bargaining among political forces and to a significant extent participate in and play by the rules of that political process. In the German case, there has been something of a polemic about the degree of politicization of journalists. Some scholars, for example, Köcher (1986), Donsbach (1995), and Donsbach and Klett (1993) have argued that German journalists tend to have, in Köcher's words, a "missionary" orientation, a concern with expressing ideas and shaping opinions. Donsbach's data show German, along with Italian journalists, more likely to say that "championing particular values and ideas" as important to their work as a journalist (71 percent and 74 percent respectively) compared with British (45 percent), Swedish (36 percent), and United States (21 percent) journalists, and also more likely to say that advocacy is typical of their work. His data also show that German journalists are more likely to combine the roles of reporter or editor and of commentator, which was less common among Italian and British and still less common among Swedish and U.S. journalists.[20] In Belgium, too, the roles of reporter and commentator tend to be fused.[21] The contrast with Sweden suggests that in this sense Germany (like Belgium) shades toward the Polarized Pluralist Model, something that would be consistent with the historical pattern of polarized pluralism in Germany and with the continuing centrality of political parties there. Schoenbach, Stuerzebecher, and Schneider (1998) and Weischenberg, Löffelholz, and Scholl (1998), on the other hand, reject this view, the latter maintaining that "for economic, technological and educational reasons, there has been a convergence in journalism in the Western Democratic countries" (251).

In terms of content, Kindelman (1994) found in a study of the reporting of the 1990 German Bundestag election that the major German newspapers did have clearly identifiable slants in their coverage of the parties and candidates, and Schulz (1996) discussing Kindelman's results, points out that German television news broadcasts, though less clearly, also had distinguishable political slants (see also Kepplinger, Brosius, and Staab 1991; Hagen 1993). German papers, it might be added, do not openly campaign for political parties during election campaigns. Even the *Bild* differs from the British popular press in this respect, though it is recognized as clearly a paper of the political right and has the most explicit value judgments on political candidates of any German paper (Semetko and Schoenbach 1994: 53), it does not openly proclaim its sympathies (its banner proclaims that it is "*Unabhängig – Überparteilich*" – "Independent – Non-Partisan").

The existence of a significant degree of external pluralism in the German media – and also in the Swedish, despite apparently strong professional values of separation of news and commentary – is suggested in research by Patterson and Donsbach (1993; also Donsbach, Wolling, and von Blomberg 1996) in which journalists were asked to place both parties and news organizations on the political spectrum from left to right. The results for Germany and Sweden are shown in Figure 6.1. In both of these countries, as also in Italy and Britain, they placed the news media across a wide spectrum, with television broadcasters grouped relatively close to the center, reflecting requirements of internal pluralism, while newspapers varied widely in their political tendencies. United States journalists, by contrast, placed all the news organizations

---

[20] This is consistent with Esser's findings.
[21] Els de Bens, personal communication.

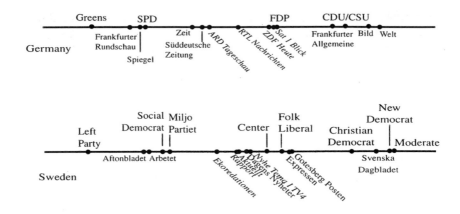

Parties above the line, media below. Television news programs in italics.
*Source*: Patterson and Donsbach (1993).

*Figure 6.1* Left-Right Positions of German and Swedish Media.

mentioned in the survey between the Republican and Democratic parties. This fact of external pluralism in the press remains significant across the region, at least among national papers. Local papers are much more likely to be catchall papers avoiding clear political tendencies. Distinct political tendencies coexist with a new emphasis on internal pluralism – each paper, that is, will report the views of the full range of major parties. Political tendencies are also more amorphous ideologically than in the past, and rarely take the form of narrow identification with single parties. But ideological tendencies do still exist. Van der Eijk (2000: 312, 319), for instance, writes about the Netherlands:

> As a direct result of their loss of *zuil* [pillar] identity [newspapers] gradually redefined their substantive profiles, a process that in some instances resulted in substantive distinctiveness and in others in indistinct "catchallism." Most national papers opted for distinctiveness order to appeal to audiences differentiated along left-right and lifestyle lines. . . . *Trouw*, for example, is clearly progressive Christian in character and makes much of its sympathy for Third World causes, environmental protection and progressive theology. *De Telegraaf,* by contrast, is socially and politically more conservative in tone, even evincing a certain dislike for all political parties and their strategic and tactical maneuvering. Of the national dailies, the *Volkskrant* is most strongly oriented toward postmaterial values

such as education, multiculturalism and socioeconomic equality, in addition to having a positive fascination with the political world that it shares with the more conservative and academically-oriented *NRC-Handelsblad.*

Van der Eijk notes that content analysis has shown that these orientations are manifested in news content in a variety of ways, including the fact that "newspapers are still more critical of parties the more the political views of these parties, as expressed in left-right terms, are different from their own" (329).

Distinct political orientations in the press of the Democratic Corporatist countries persist despite the fact that journalists have, to varying degrees in different countries, accepted the principle of separation of commentary and reporting (the same reporter may write both, but not at the same time, in the same article, as in an Italian *pastone*) and adopted more "objective" styles of writing. In this sense, the form of external pluralism that exists today in the Democratic Corporatist countries is different from what exists in the Polarized Pluralist ones, where commentary and information are mixed much more promiscuously. Political orientations are manifested more in patterns of selection and emphasis in news reporting than in explicit commentary. Table 6.3 shows the opening paragraphs of front-page stories from two of the principal Danish newspapers, *Jyllands Posten*, a conservative paper, and *Politiken*, a liberal one, on a government report dealing with the issue of immigration, which, as in other parts of Europe, has become increasingly important in Danish politics. Both articles are written in an "objective" style: neither contain explicit commentary. But the different politics of the papers are strongly evident in the articles, *Jyllands Posten* presenting immigrants as an economic burden to Danish society, while *Politiken* includes the views of critics of the report (which do not appear at all in the *Jyllands Posten* story) and focuses on the debate about whether only migrants or also ethnic Danes should be expected to adapt culturally.

## POLITICAL HISTORY, STRUCTURE, AND CULTURE

Katzenstein (1985) argues that systems of democratic corporatism developed in Scandinavia, the low countries, and Switzerland in the 1930s out of a series of political compromises, as these countries struggled to

## Table 6.3 *Contrasting Stories on Immigration in the Danish Press*

| Jyllands Posten, August 16, 2001<br>**Integration unsuccessful** | Politiken, August 17, 2001<br>**New bid on Danishness** |
|---|---|
| Migrants and their descendents will be a serious economic burden for A/OUR welfare society, if it does not succeed SOON to get them jobs. That is the prediction by the so-called Think Tank under interior minister Karen Jespersen (S) [Social Democrat]. Ex-wiseman [economic consultant for the government] Nina Smith has resigned in protest. | Ministerial Think Tank risks its skin and gives a new definition of Danishness. In a report Danish values that foreigners are supposed to adopt in order to get on here are drawn up. The proposal is criticized because only foreigners have to adapt. |
| **Migration**<br>By Orla Borg and Ulla Østergaard | By Christian Hüttemeier and Rikke Egelund |
| There is a need for much more heavy-handed methods to get migrants into the workforce. For there is still a long road before one can talk about a successful integration of refugees, migrants and their descendents in Denmark. This is the main conclusion by the so-called Think Tank that will publish its first report on integration in Denmark tomorrow. | Foreigners have to adopt a minimum of Danish norms and values in order to function in Danish society, maintains the ministerial think tank that was set up last fall by the interior minister Karen Jespersen to come up with new ideas on the problems with integration of foreigners. |
| The Think Tank was set up last year by the interior minister Karen Jespersen to come up with a proposal on integration policy in Denmark. | The think tank takes a risk – and draws up a number of concrete values that foreigners have to "live by and subscribe to," if they are going to take part in the working world and social life on an equal footing. |
| The Think Tank suggested measures on seven concrete areas for what a successful integration is. And on all seven areas things are not too good, the report maintains. | According to the think thank these are values such as respect for constitutional rights, such as freedom of faith and speech and individual freedom. . . . [F]oreigners are also supposed to acknowledge that inhabitants in Denmark have a voice in important decisions in their own life – for instance marriage. |
| This concerns among others their participation in the job market, where the measure for success is that migrants and their descendents | Finally they are supposed to respect equality between the sexes, and they have to show tolerance for other people's values. |

gain equal status as Danes. But in the real world more than half of the migrants of working age are outside the labor market. And it has worsened the last decade. In 1985, 48 percent of migrants from non-Western countries were outside the labor market. Today the figure is 59 percent.

The Think Tank maintains also that it is strongly worried that many migrants cannot provide for themselves. All in all 38 percent of all welfare expenses by society goes to the five percent of the population who come from non-Western countries.

These two points make the Think Tank conclude that they will become a serious burden on the welfare society if it does not succeed in getting migrants into the job market so that they can maintain themselves at a much higher level than today, according to JP's sources.

"An acceptance of fundamental Danish attitudes and values is necessary if integration is going to succeed. . . . I am not saying that all Danes live up to these norms, but we have drawn up a number of requirements that also apply for the Danes," says the chairman of the think thank. . . .

But according to Jørgen Bæk Simonsen, lecturer, dr. phil. at the University of Copenhagen who is an expert in Islam and the Arabic world, the list of criteria for Danishness will hardly encourage integration:

"This is an odd understanding of integration, when it is in fact all about how foreigners have to submit to Danish society. There is nothing in this relation that indicates that Danes also have to make a move."

Muharrem Aydas, the chairman of the POEM, the umbrella organization for ethnic minorities, calls the list "an arrogant forefinger."

confront the economic crisis of the Great Depression and to avoid the polarization and collapse of democracy that occurred in neighboring Germany and Austria, as it did in Spain and Italy to the south. These compromises involved industrial peace agreements, cross-class agreements on plans for economic and political stabilization, and in many cases broad political coalitions incorporating both left and right, many of which continued to work together as governments in exile during the Nazi occupation. The system that resulted, according to Katzenstein "is distinguished by three traits: an ideology of social partnership expressed at the national level; a relatively centralized and concentrated system of interest groups; and voluntary and informal coordination of conflicting objectives through continuous political bargaining between interest groups, state bureaucracies and political parties" (32). Austria and Germany adopted much of this model after World War II, though in the German case, in Katzenstein's analysis, modified by the dominant role of political parties and some other differences. The corporatist bargain of the 1930s was preceded, in most countries, by an agreement to adopt proportional representation, usually at the beginning of the twentieth century. The Democratic Corporatist countries tend to have large numbers of political parties and consensus, rather than majoritarian politics, in Lijphart's (1999) terms: they tend to have broad coalitions in which no single party has a majority and to practice power sharing, both among parties and among interest groups and cultural communities. Switzerland and Belgium are pure consensus systems and the other countries covered here are mixed systems, most tending toward consensus politics. They also tend toward moderate rather than polarized pluralism (Sartori 1976) – with Germany and Austria, again, moving in that direction after World War II.[22]

Democratic corporatism was able to develop in Northern Europe, according to Katzenstein, because the political right was relatively weak and divided – in contrast both to larger countries such as Germany and France and to the countries of Southern Europe – and therefore unable to block accommodation with the left. Feudalism was not strongly developed in the low countries, in Scandinavia, or in Switzerland. Urban interests were stronger relative to the landed aristocracy, as was the independent peasantry. Economic activity frequently was carried out by "individual producers residing in communities," rather than by large landholders and landless peasants, and political authority was often "concentrated in the hands of producer-merchants" (157). In Switzerland, the Netherlands, Belgium, and Denmark merchants engaged in long-distance trade had strong influence, while in Scandinavia the independent peasantry was particularly important. The existence of this independent peasantry – in Denmark, for instance, peasants were freed in the 1780s and a land reform was passed in the early nineteenth century – meant that, while in Southern Europe and other areas where feudalism had been strong, the aristocracy controlled the votes of the rural population, in Scandinavia and other smaller countries independent agrarian parties were often available for alliances with liberal or socialist forces. In Scandinavia, moreover, the economically weak aristocracy often turned to commerce in order to survive, making its interests less distinct from those of the urban bourgeoisie. This social structure provided the context for the early triumph of liberal institutions that was manifested in an early development of a free press.

---

[22] Data on polarization and numbers of parties appear in Table 3.2.

*THE CENTRALITY OF ORGANIZED SOCIAL GROUPS.* One of the most important characteristics of the Democratic Corporatist system is the central role played by organized social groups, including political parties, trade unions and employer associations, religious communities, and many other sorts of "socially relevant groups," in the German phrase. The corporatist system is based on the existence of strong, unified "peak organizations" that can represent the interests of their members in bargaining with other groups. Such groups are formally integrated into the policy-making process in corporatist systems and in many cases have the status of public institutions, exercising what in other systems would be state functions – running welfare systems, for instance, or in the Dutch case, public broadcasting. The corporatist bargain of the 1930s institutionalized the place of organized social interests in the Democratic Corporatist countries, but a history of strong social self-organization goes back many centuries earlier. The pattern of strong civic life that Putnam (1993) describes in northern Italy was evident very early as well in much of Northern Europe, Germany, and Switzerland. Local communities with significant rights of self-governance were an important part of the history of these countries, including trading cities of the Netherlands and Germany, and Swiss cantons. Merchants formed joint-stock companies and other forms of association; artisans formed guilds; in many cases independent agricultural producers formed cooperatives; the Protestant tradition of self-governing church congregations also played a role in the development of this organizational culture. The strength of this kind of civil society no doubt is an important factor in the growth of newspaper readership in Northern and Central Europe, as civic organization depends on a flow of publicly available information. And as we saw earlier in this chapter, conflicts among these groups were fought out from early on through the print press. It is worth underscoring here the fact that traditions of civic organization were not confined to the cities but existed in the countryside as well. The strong urban-rural split that characterized the Mediterranean countries – and held back the growth of newspapers in Southern Europe – did not exist to nearly the same degree in the north. The strongest urban-rural split in newspaper readership today, among the Democratic Corporatist countries, is in Austria – which as a part of the Austro-Hungarian empire has a feudal history more similar to that of Southern Europe.

In the nineteenth century, strong mass political parties emerged in the Democratic Corporatist countries, usually first in the form of social democratic parties, with mass conservative and agrarian parties organized later.[23] These parties built strong structures that penetrated to the base of society, with networks of institutions that served to link them with their members. They had strong links in many cases to other kinds of social organizations, including trade unions, business associations, and religious communities. They were closely tied to the major divisions of interest and cultural identity in society – class, religion, language, and others – and members often had strong allegiances to them. Their constituencies were in important ways separate subcultures in society – in keeping with the pattern Lorwin (1971) called *segmented pluralism*.

The centrality of organized social groups and political parties is reflected in the media systems in a number of ways. It can be seen clearly, of course, in the role that political parties and "socially relevant groups" often play in the organization of public broadcasting and media regulation systems. It is also manifested in the strength of journalists' unions and associations, which in their high membership levels and strong organization are similar to other peak associations in Democratic Corporatist countries, and like these organizations often are incorporated into the process of forming media policy, as well as being represented on broadcasting councils and similar bodies. Most importantly, the centrality of social organizations in Democratic Corporatist countries is related to the high degree of political parallelism that has persisted through most of the twentieth century. Newspapers, in particular, have played important roles both internal to political subcommunities, linking the party or the leadership of a "pillar" with its members, and external to them, as newspapers have expressed the views of the various political forces in the public sphere and participated in the process of bargaining among parties and social groups that is so central to democratic corporatism and to consensus government. A traditionally high prevalence of debate, commentary, and interpretation is connected with a political culture based on negotiation and discussion. Note here that the press has traditionally played a role both in expressing the differences among parties and groups and mobilizing their constituents around their separate identities, and in facilitating the bargaining process through which the governing process works. Concluding her comparative research on the relationship between mass media and politics in Germany and the United States, Pfetsch (2001: 64; see also Keman 1996) states: "political

---

[23] The oldest Socialist Party is the German (established in the 1860s). The Danish followed in 1871. The Finnish is the youngest. As for the conservative parties the oldest is the Finnish (established in 1907); but most appeared at the end of World War I.

opportunity in Germany is still characterized by the traditionally strong and constitutionally entrenched role of the political parties. The success of political programmes is the result of complex negotiation processes and compromises in the parliamentary groups and party organizations, which are accompanied by efforts to generate support in the media only in the course of negotiation."

As we noted in Chapter 5, this kind of communication process, in which parties and other organized social groups are central – something that the Democratic Corporatist countries share to a degree with the Mediterranean countries, particularly Italy – is close to what James Curran calls the "radical democratic" public sphere. Curran (1991: 30) identifies the "radical democratic" public sphere with the countries of Northern Europe covered in this chapter, defining it in terms of the view that:

> a democratic media system should represent all significant inter-
> ests in society. It should facilitate their participation in the public
> domain, enable them to contribute to public debate and have an
> impact in the framing of public policy. The media should also fa-
> cilitate the functioning of representative organizations and expose
> their internal processes to public scrutiny and the play of public
> opinion. In short a central role of the media should be defined
> as assisting the equitable negotiation or articulation of competing
> interests through democratic processes.

Curran goes on to contrast this with the liberal system, in which "the media are conceived as vertical channels of communication between private citizens and government": in the "radical democratic" conception, Curran argues, "media are viewed as a more complex articulation of vertical, horizontal and diagonal channels of communication between individuals, groups and power structures. This takes account of the fact individual interests are safeguarded and advanced in modern liberal democracies partly through collective organizations like political parties and pressure groups, and at a strategic level through the construction and recomposition of alliances and coalitions (31)." Curran's conception describes an important element of the media systems of the Democratic Corporatist countries, where media institutions have long been among the "consociational devices" (Lijphart 1977; Colomer 1996) through which intergroup relations are managed. In practice, of course, as Curran recognizes, a public sphere organized in this way is not necessarily "radical," nor necessarily as democratic as the ideal he puts forward: the ties between media and social organizations have produced pluralism and have guaranteed the representation of a substantial range of interests in the Democratic Corporatist countries, to be sure, but also they often have limited pluralism within established organizational forms. Like other systems explored in this book, the Democratic Corporatist system must be seen simultaneously as a system of democratic communication and as a system of social and political power.

THE ROLE OF THE STATE. There are two sides to the role of the state in the Democratic Corporatist countries. On the one hand, traditions of local liberties and the early triumph of liberal institutions mean that there is a strong philosophy of limits on state power. This is manifested both in the early development of press freedom and in the strength of laws on public access to government information. This tradition was reinforced by the emphasis in democratic corporatism on the role of social organizations, which often assume responsibilities that would otherwise fall to the state. In the media field, this is evident both in Dutch public broadcasting, where responsibility for broadcasting was delegated to the "pillars" through their broadcasting organizations, and in the system of self-regulation of the press, which is shared by almost all the Democratic Corporatist countries. On the other hand, democratic corporatism involves a partnership between social organizations and the state, and the social agreement that emerged along with the corporatist system involved a major expansion of the role of the state in society, through an expanded welfare state, active industrial policy, and other forms of intervention. The Swedish concept of the *folkhem* or the "peoples' home," based originally on conservative concepts of national unity and adapted and popularized by Social Democratic leader Per Albin Hansson in 1928, as the Democratic Corporatist system was beginning to emerge in Sweden (Åsard and Bennett 1997), was based on the idea that the state had a responsibility to intervene in the economy and in many spheres of life to ensure progress and equality. The strength and the forms of the welfare state and other forms of state intervention have varied from country to country, and the welfare state has been cut back since the 1980s, but in general the Democratic Corporatist countries are marked by an active state. In the 1990s Sweden was first among European countries in expenditures for general government as a percent of GDP, followed by Denmark and the Netherlands (Lane and Ersson 1991: 328). As we have seen, this general characteristic of Democratic Corporatist societies is manifested in strong public broadcasting and press subsidy systems, as well as in a general attitude that the media are social institutions for which the state has a responsibility, and not purely private businesses. This is a principal difference between the Democratic Corporatist Model and Liberal Model where the state, both as funder or regulator, plays a much weaker role.

JOURNALISTIC PROFESSIONALISM, THE "IDEOLOGY OF SOCIAL PARTNERSHIP," AND RATIONAL-LEGAL AUTHORITY. One of the distinctive characteristics of the Democratic Corporatist media system, we have argued, is the coexistence of political parallelism and journalistic professionalism. Political parallelism, of course, is closely related to the strength of parties and social organizations. Journalistic professionalism is related to the "ideology of social partnership" that Katzenstein describes as one of the central characteristics of democratic corporatism, to the moderate pluralism that develops out of the ideology and practice of social partnership, and also, we believe, to a tradition of rational-legal authority that predates democratic corporatism. "Although it may seem paradoxical to outsiders," Katzenstein notes (1985: 88), "pragmatic cooperation and ideological conflict are not incompatible." Democratic corporatism involves a process of bargaining through which parties and groups with distinct ideologies and social interests strive to reach consensus. This is how governing coalitions are formed, how policy is made, and how labor-management relations and other conflicts of social and economic interest are managed. Despite wide political diversity, this process of continuous bargaining has produced a culture and procedures of accommodation and cooperation. It has also produced a shift in the Democratic Corporatist countries toward moderate rather than polarized pluralism, as the various segments of society have maintained separate identities but moderated their demands and come to have a stake in the basic rules of the game.[24] Democratic corporatism thus "incorporates a continuous reaffirmation of political differences with political cooperation" (Katzenstein 1985: 88).

The coexistence of political parallelism and journalistic professionalism thus mirrors the nature of democratic corporatism generally: political diversity coexists with a common journalistic culture manifested in a relatively high level of consensus on standards of practice and

---

[24] This is also reflected in relatively high levels of trust in political institutions. Eurobarometer 55, for example, shows all the Democratic Corporatist countries above the EU average in trust in government institutions. See also Borre 1995 and Listhaug and Wiberg 1995. Almond and Verba (1963) also noted the greater trust in institutions in Germany, Britain, and the United States, compared with Italy.

cooperation in institutions such as journalists' unions, press councils, and the *Bundespressekonferenz*. In Chapter 2 we proposed as one of the defining characteristics of journalistic professionalism a notion of journalism as a public trust, a conception, that is, that journalism in some sense serves a public interest that transcends particular social interests. This ideology, we believe, is connected with the two other defining characteristics of journalistic professionalism, the development of a distinct common culture of journalism, and the achievement by journalists of relative autonomy in relation to other social actors. One of the principal differences between the Polarized Pluralist system – where journalistic professionalism is less developed – and the Democratic Corporatist and Liberal systems, where it is more so, is that the general political culture in the Polarized Pluralist system offers less support to the idea of a general interest transcending particular groups and ideologies. The political culture of democratic corporatism, by contrast, clearly includes a strong notion that common general interest does in fact exist. This is manifested in the Swedish concept of the "*folkhem*" that represented a rejection of both liberal individualism and the Marxist concept of class struggle, and rested on the idea that a spirit of cooperation among social interests could produce a society in which all citizens would share fully in social life. This became the consensus ideology of Swedish society until neoliberalism began to challenge it in the 1970s (since that time democratic corporatism has clearly weakened, though not disappeared). The culture of Swedish journalism, which, despite the persistence of political parallelism, rested on a shared notion of the responsible journalist serving the ends of social progress, is clearly rooted in this ideological consensus. Sweden may be a particularly clear case, but similar developments also took place in other Democratic Corporatist countries.

In explaining the "paradox" of ideological diversity and social partnership in democratic corporatism, Katzenstein emphasizes the prominent role of technical experts, who "provide a common framework and acceptable data" (88) that serve as a basis for the bargaining process. This reflects the strong development of rational-legal authority in the Democratic Corporatist countries, something that predates democratic corporatism, and is also important to understanding the strength of journalistic professionalism in this system. The concept of rational-legal authority, of course, was developed most fully by Max Weber. The underlying idea of a system of rule based on a universalistic legal framework, goes back to Hegel's *Philosophy of Right* and has deep roots in German history. One of the key elements of a system of rational-legal authority is the development of an administrative corps selected by qualifications rather than by patronage, governed by established rules, relatively autonomous from outside control, and in theory serving the nation as a whole. Such a system was established by the Hohenzollerns in Brandenburg-Prussia in the eighteenth century, in an effort to balance the power of the landed aristocracy, and strengthened after the Napoleonic invasion (Shefter 1977: 423ff). In Scandinavia, "centralized, powerful, relatively independent bureaucracy came to play a central role" (Esping-Anderson 1985: 48) beginning as early as the seventeenth century, and was generally well consolidated by the early nineteenth century. In Denmark, for instance, "The Danish Law of 1685 standardized the payment of service dues, replacing a decentralized and personalistic system organized around the landed aristocracy with a centralized and bureaucratic one run by the state" (Katzenstein 1985: 159). Lægried and Olsen (1984: 210) write of Norwegian civil servants, who dominated the state from the early nineteenth century:

> Their ideology came close to what Weber later labeled an ideal bureaucracy based on rational-legal authority. The main task of civil servants was seen as the implementation of enacted rules – to find the proper solution and guard the public interest, unhampered by arbitrary outside pressure. The role model was the objective and impartial judge, and their primary loyalty was toward an impersonal system of laws.

Clientelism, meanwhile, never took strong root in most of the Democratic Corporatist countries (with Austria and Belgium often considered as partial exceptions).[25]

A strong tradition of rational-legal authority affects the media systems of Democratic Corporatist countries in several ways. First, as we note in Chapter 3, the expansion of the newspaper is connected with the development of rational-legal authority, as it is with the expansion of the market and parliamentary democracy. Second, the relative autonomy of public service broadcasting systems in Democratic Corporatist countries is consistent with the independent character of public institutions

---

[25] On the absence of clientelism in Northern Europe see Papakostas (2002) and Randeraad and Wolffram (2002).

generally. Third, legal institutions often have an important influence on the media systems in the Democratic Corporatist countries. This is probably most important in Germany, where the Federal Constitutional Court has played an important role in protecting the independence of the public broadcasting system when the politicians at either the federal or Länder level have tried to assert greater control (Humphreys 1994: 161ff). Fourth, a pattern of rational-legal authority makes the kind of instrumentalization of media that frequently characterizes the Polarized Pluralist systems less likely. Because resources are allocated and decisions taken on the basis of transparent rules, particularistic pressures and alliances are less crucial to success in business or other social endeavors. Media owners thus have less incentive to use their media properties as means of pressure and particularistic bargaining, and other business interests have less incentive to enter the media field for that purpose. We will elaborate on this argument in the following chapter, as this is a characteristic the Democratic Corporatist countries share with the Liberal ones. In the Democratic Corporatist system, the existence of formally neutral legal and administrative institutions combines with the highly institutionalized representative process by which policy decisions are made to decrease the importance of media as a means of applying political pressure outside this system. Business and other social interests are formally represented by their peak associations in a highly organized bargaining and consultation process, and cannot, for example, be excluded from the process or systematically discriminated against if they lack ties to the particular politicians or factions in power. It should be added that the economics of the newspaper industry in Democratic Corporatist countries also works against instrumentalization: newspapers have been either profitable commercial enterprises or have been supported by representative institutions such as parties, churches, and trade unions, and thus are less susceptible to falling under the control of particular patrons.

Finally, a high level of journalistic professionalism is more likely to develop in societies with a tradition of rational-legal authority. In part, this is a matter of homology among social institutions, of cultural resonance and mutual influence: in a society where the idea of professional communities with special qualifications, rules of practice, social functions, systems of ethics, and claims to autonomy flowing from these is widely diffused, it is more likely that journalists, too will seek to adapt to this model. In Germany the idea of journalism as a profession developed in the late nineteenth century as other occupations were also redefining themselves as professions.[26] Karl Bücher, for example, who had an important influence on journalism education in Germany, argued that journalists were similar to civil servants in their social functions and that systematic journalism education should for that reason be supported by the state (Hardt 1979). Weber, who wrote extensively for the *Frankfurter Zeitung*, describes journalism in "Politics as a Vocation" as part of the world of politics. At the same time he writes that "the responsibility of the journalist is far greater . . . than that of the scholar . . . as the war has shown. This is because, in the very nature of the case, irresponsible journalistic accomplishments and their often terrible effects are remembered." Political involvement, an ethics of public service and a notion of common standards of conduct coexist in Weber's interpretation of journalism.

The association between rational-legal authority and journalistic professionalism is also connected, more specifically, with the interaction between journalism and the administrative and legal state: the existence of administrative and legal procedures and authorities that serve as a common reference and framework facilitates the development of common standards of journalistic practice and an ideology of public service in journalism. These procedures and authorities provide common sources for journalists and common criteria of newsworthiness; and commitment to the rules of the game they establish provides a common normative framework and makes concrete the idea of a "public interest" transcending particular interests. As we shall see in the following chapter, a similar connection can be found in the Liberal countries.

## CONCLUSION

The countries of Northern and Central Europe are distinguished by a set of characteristics that we have called "the three coexistences," which both set them apart from the Liberal and Polarized Pluralist Models and give them similarities to each of these. These "coexistences" include the simultaneous development of strong mass-circulation commercial media and of media tied to political and civil groups; the coexistence of political parallelism and journalistic professionalism; and the coexistence

---

[26] The development of professionalism in Germany followed a different path than in Britain and the United States, in the sense that professionals worked with the state to establish educational and regulative institutions. But it occurred early and relatively strongly; German models of professional education were often imitated elsewhere (McClelland 1990).

of liberal traditions of press freedom and a tradition of strong state intervention in the media, which are seen as a social institution and not as purely private enterprises.

The early development of the market, a culture of entrepreneurial capitalism, and liberal political institutions, together with the push toward literacy that followed from the Protestant Reformation combined to produce an early and strong development of newspaper markets in Northern and Central Europe, and these countries retain extremely high rates of newspaper readership and strong commercial newspaper industries. Simultaneously, religious confrontations, together with ethnic-linguistic and political clashes encouraged the use of the press as an instrument for diffusing ideas and organizing civil society. A strong political press tied to interests and perspectives of distinct social groups thus came to coexist with the commercial press. The system of democratic corporatism that developed in these countries in the early twentieth century institutionalized the crucial role that organized social groups (parties, unions, interest groups, and cultural and religious groups) play in these systems, and the centrality of the process of bargaining and power sharing among them. A strong form of political parallelism developed in this context, in which the mass media served as instruments of public discussion, representing the different social, political, and economic interests that through them debate important issues, struggle for consent, and build the symbolic ground that makes agreement possible. Despite the process of homogenization that has led to a shift in the balance between the commercial and political press and the diffusion of the model of "neutral" professionalism, a significant degree of political parallelism still characterizes the Democratic Corporatist countries.

As Katzenstein points out, democratic corporatism is characterized simultaneously by the presence of a wide range of parties and organized groups with distinct interests and ideologies rooted in historic divisions of society and by widely shared agreement on the rules of the game by which these groups share power, resolve their differences, and come to collective decisions about the "common good." The media are characterized historically by a similar duality, which we have referred to as the coexistence of political parallelism and professionalism: they have traditionally reflected the divisions and diversity of society, yet have functioned as members of a profession with strong institutional coherence, consensus on its own rules of conduct, and substantial autonomy from other social institutions. The experience of the Democratic Corporatist countries, we believe, supports the argument we made in Chapter 2, that political parallelism and journalistic professionalism should not be collapsed into a single conceptual dimension, that high levels of both can in fact coexist; or to put it a bit differently, the experience of the Democratic Corporatist countries suggests that other forms of journalistic professionalism can exist, apart from the Liberal Model of neutral professionalism.

The Democratic Corporatist countries, finally, are characterized by early and strong development of liberal institutions and strong development of civil society. State power has historically been limited, and this fact has been reflected in early development of press freedom and other elements of an open public sphere, including strong rights of access to government information. At the same time, the democratic corporatist bargain institutionalized a strong welfare state; and the Democratic Corporatist countries tend to be "social states" characterized by an ideology of collective responsibility for the welfare and participation of all groups and citizens. This is reflected in the media field by a strong consensus that the state must play a positive role as the guarantor of equal opportunities of communication for all the organized social voices in pursuit of the "common good."

# SEVEN

# The North Atlantic or Liberal Model

The Liberal or as it is often called the Anglo-American model of the mass media is in some sense the only model that has really been analyzed in media studies as such, as a coherent model. Indeed, while other media systems have rarely been conceptualized as coherent wholes, it could be said that the "Anglo-American" model has been treated as far more coherent and unitary than it actually is. There are in fact substantial differences between the United States – which is a purer example of a liberal system – and Britain, where statist conservatism, liberal corporatism, and social democracy have been stronger than in the United States. Canada and Ireland, the other two examples of liberal media systems that will be discussed here – are also quite distinct in certain ways. In both countries, for example, issues of national identity result in substantial modifications of the Liberal Model. All of these countries, moreover, have substantial internal differences. This is probably most obvious in the case of Britain, with its sharp distinction between the quality and the mass press and striking – though diminishing – differences between the regimes governing print and broadcast media.

Nevertheless, there are important common features of the media systems in the four countries covered in this chapter, countries whose media histories are obviously bound together by strong political and cultural ties. In each, commercial newspapers developed relatively early, expanded with relatively little state involvement, and became overwhelmingly dominant, marginalizing party, trade union, religious, and other kinds of noncommercial media. In each, an informational style of journalism has become dominant and traditions of political neutrality tend to be strong – though with a very important exception in the British press. In all four countries journalistic professionalism is relatively strongly developed. In three of the four – Ireland being the exception – commercial broadcasting played a larger role than in most of continental Europe, though here there is a marked difference between the United States, where public service broadcasting has always been marginal, and the three other countries, where it has played a central role in media history. All four have traditions of political insulation of public broadcasters and regulatory authorities.

## LIBERALISM AND THE DEVELOPMENT OF A COMMERCIAL MASS-CIRCULATION PRESS

J. S. Mill once wrote that the British character was shaped by two primary influences, "commercial money-getting business and religious Puritanism" (cited in Altick 1957: 24). These, along with the political conflicts that led to the development of parliamentary democracy and the opening of the public sphere, were clearly the primary forces behind the strong early development of the press in Britain. As in the Democratic Corporatist countries, Protestantism played an important role in the early expansion of literacy, even if religious groups were often ambivalent about the extension of reading from religious to secular content. In the United States, where Protestantism was particularly strong in the early years, literacy was nearly universal in the white population, male and female, by early in the nineteenth century (illiteracy would remain high among blacks until well into the twentieth century). As in the Democratic Corporatist countries, too, the expansion of the market and of the social classes connected with it was central to the development of the press. "It was the milieu of the City – the Royal Exchange, the coffee houses, the docks, the crowded and filthy streets, the guild halls and the shops – that spawned the London newspaper" (Clark 1994: 35). The English revolution, moreover, was the first of the great revolutions that produced the modern political world, and the development of the "fourth estate" was part of this political transformation.

The first newsletters were circulated in England beginning in 1620, among the growing community of merchants. Publication of home news was forbidden, however, until 1641, when conflict between the Crown and the Long Parliament had erupted. In 1642 the English civil war began, arising out of religious conflicts similar to those that fueled the Thirty Years War on the continent and out of the conflict between landed interests and the moneyed interests centered in the City of London, which were increasingly central to the British economy. A huge volume of political tracts and pamphlets was produced to fight the propaganda war, giving a powerful boost to the practice of reading secular literature. By the early eighteenth century the English political system had been fundamentally changed. The king or queen could rule only through a majority in Parliament, which controlled public finance – previously inseparable from the royal household; approved the appointment of ministers; and had the exclusive right to remove judges. Extensive royal control of the economy and traditional guild privileges had given way to *laissez faire* economic policy. Religious toleration had advanced substantially. And with the expiration of the Licensing Act in 1695, a major step had been taken toward the development of press freedom. In terms of political culture, as Hill (1961: 3) puts it, "politics had become a rational inquiry, discussed in terms of utility, experience, common sense, no longer in terms of Divine Right, texts, antiquarian research." The development during this period of political parties and of the division between government and opposition in Parliament had particularly important consequences for media history. "From Queen Anne's reign, politicians excluded from power consistently used the press to mobilize public opinion and put pressure on successive administrations. This in turn provoked a barrage of counter-propaganda, and money raised by subscription or extracted from public funds was injected into the London press from both sides" (Harris 1978: 95). The first daily, the *Daily Courant*, was financed by the government as part of this pattern of political competition.

The expiration of the Licensing Act in 1695 resulted in a proliferation of newspapers, twenty in London in the following decade and some in the provinces as well. Political elites were uncomfortable with unchecked expansion of the press, however, and after a number of failed attempts by the government to reinstitute licensing, the Stamp Act of 1712 imposed taxes on newspapers, pamphlets, advertisements, and paper, resulting in an immediate drop in the number of newspapers in circulation. The stamp duties were raised and tightened in 1789, in 1797 – following a great upsurge in radical political activity that saw massive increases in the circulation of political literature – and again in 1815 and 1819. The same transformation of English society that led to emergence of parliamentary rule also included the enclosure movement, the elimination of old economic controls and privileges, and the expansion of industrial capitalism, and produced growing economic inequality and an expansion of the urban and rural poor. Both the "taxes on knowledge" and other controls on the press – prosecutions for seditious libel, for example – were motivated to a large extent by fear of the propertied classes that expansion of the press would lead to political rebellion by the poor. These repressive measures did not, in fact, prevent the development of a substantial radical press. Prosecutions for seditious libel or other press crimes often boosted the circulation of radical publications, and radical unstamped newspapers and pamphlets – the most celebrated being Cobbett's *Political Register* – reached impressive levels of circulation during the early nineteenth century (Curran 1979; Chalaby 1998). These restrictions did, however, delay the development of the commercial mass-circulation press in Britain until the 1850s.

British press institutions – both journalistic practices and the legal framework – were exported in most of their essentials to the colonies in North America, as well as to Ireland (where London newspapers accounted for much of newspaper circulation before independence). With the American revolution, however, the United States moved further in the direction of press freedom. Stamp duties had been extended to the American colonies by the British parliament in 1765 (some colonies had earlier instituted their own "taxes on knowledge"), but this became one of the principal points of conflict between Britain and the colonies, and the stamp duties were repealed even before the American Declaration of Independence. The First Amendment to the United States Constitution subsequently made press freedom a fundamental legal principle, though press freedom in the modern sense did not emerge immediately. In earliest years of the American republic there was considerable ambiguity about the meaning of the First Amendment. It was often interpreted narrowly, either as leaving the regulation of the press to the states rather than the federal government (it reads, "*Congress* shall make no law . . . abridging the freedom of speech or of the press"), or as referring to the traditional English principle of press freedom, which forbade "prior restraint" in the form of licensing or censorship, but did not exclude the punishment of publishers for such crimes as seditious libel or insulting government officials (Levy 1985). A broader "libertarian" interpretation emerged during the controversy over the Sedition Act of 1798, which made it a crime to publish anything that would "bring into disrepute" the federal government. The Sedition Act was allowed to lapse after the opposition won the election of 1800: the libertarian theory emerged along with the development of competing political parties, a political structure not intended by those who wrote the constitution. There would be many subsequent conflicts over the meaning and limits of freedom of the press. During World War I, for example, radical publications were banned from the mails and foreign-language publications were required to submit English translations to the government. In 1925 the state of Minnesota passed a law allowing suppression of "malicious" publications, leading to a key Supreme Court ruling (*Near* v. *Minnesota*) affirming the application of the First Amendment to the states. But the basic principle that the press had a right to criticize government was the prevailing view after 1800.

The most distinctive characteristic of the media history of the North Atlantic countries is the early and strong development of commercial newspapers, which would dominate the press by the end of the nineteenth century, marginalizing other forms of media organization. The development of the commercial press began earliest in the United States, with the penny press of the 1830s (Schudson 1978; Schiller 1981). In Britain, where the liberal political tradition was not yet as fully hegemonic as it was in the United States, the "taxes on knowledge" held back the development of commercial newspapers until their repeal in the 1850s. In Canada imitators of the American penny press began to appear in the 1830s, though most accounts place the real flourishing of the commercial press a bit later, in the 1880s to 1890s. In Ireland, similarly, the first penny paper appeared in 1859, and the first modern newspaper emerged in 1905, when new ownership transformed *The Irish Independent* into a financially successful paper appealing to the business community across religious and political lines. The development of the commercial press was slower in Ireland, however for reasons we will explore presently.

Though it began as early as the 1830s, the height of the commercial revolution occurred roughly in the 1870s to 1890s, as a large-scale newspaper industry developed in conjunction with the full development of industrial capitalism, with "large-scale factory production, an urban work force, strategic centers of investment capital, and extensive marketing of standardized products" (Baldasty 1992: 52). The development of newspapers such as Pulitzer's *World*, beginning in 1883, and the *Daily Mail* in 1896 produced true mass readerships reaching all classes of society. Newspaper circulations fell from their peak in the Liberal countries following the introduction of television, and are not as high today as some countries of continental Europe and East Asia, but remain relatively strong, as can be seen in Table 2.1. Britain is the highest of the Liberal countries at about 400 newspapers sold per thousand population, comparable to many of the Democratic Corporatist countries, while the United States, Canada, and Ireland range from 263 to 191 per thousand, circulation rates below those of the Democratic Corporatist but above those of the Polarized Pluralist countries.

Commercialization not only expanded circulations but transformed newspapers from small-scale enterprises, most of which lost money and required subsidies from wealthy individuals, communities of readers, political parties or the state, into highly capitalized and highly profitable businesses. By the 1870s the big newspaper companies were among the largest manufacturing companies in the United States. This in turn transformed the political role of the press. The nature of this transformation and its implications for democracy has been the subject of one of the most important debates in media scholarship in the Liberal countries, a debate posed most explicitly in Britain, though it is present in some form in all four countries.[1] The traditional interpretation, dominant in media scholarship for many years as well as in public discourse about the Liberal media system that has been diffused around the world, is the view that "the increasing value of newspapers as advertising mediums allow[ed] them gradually to shake off government or party control and to become independent voices of public sentiment" (Altick 1957: 322). This view was challenged by a revisionist scholarship that began to develop in the 1970s, which saw the commercialization of the press as undermining their role in democratic life, first by concentrating media power in the hands of particular social interests – those of business, especially – and second, by shifting the purpose of the press from the expression of political viewpoints to the promotion of consumerism. This debate is closely connected with the issue of differentiation discussed in Chapter 4 – with the question of whether commercialization meant the differentiation of the media system from politics or the colonization of the public sphere by business.

Certainly it is correct that commercialization freed the newspaper in the Liberal countries from dependence on subsidies from politicians and from the state, which were standard means of financing the press prior to the mid–nineteenth century. Commercialization did not mean that the press lost all ties to political parties, nor that it ceased to play a political role; instead it meant that the press, its editors, and its owners became independent political players as time went on. Featherling (1990: 96) writes of the Canadian case:

> The 1890s saw the rise of what was called independent journalism: that is of large, even sometimes monolithic papers that were independent of the political parties themselves without necessarily

[1] In the U.S. case, for example, the revisionist view is expressed in Schiller (1981), Steele (1990), and Baker (1994).

being in the least non-partisan. Put another way, independent journalism marked the rise of the editor as a full-fledged player in the
political game, instead of a politicians' tool.

In the United States, the rise of newspaper circulations came just after
the extension of the franchise at the end of the 1920s to essentially all
white males, without regard to property. This was the period when mass
political parties developed most strongly and newspapers continued to
be intimately involved with them, though partisanship would begin to
fade late in the nineteenth century. The first generations of commercial
newspapers in all four countries had partisan identities and commitments, though occasionally shifting ones, and their owners were often
deeply involved in party politics. Hearst, who sought the Democratic
nomination for president, and Lord Beaverbrook, who told the 1948
Royal Commission on the Press – not entirely honestly – that he ran
his newspapers "purely for the purpose of making propaganda" are representative of this era. At the same time, the logic of the marketplace
clearly modified and limited the political involvement of the press and
its owners, encouraging them to play down open partisanship – more,
as we shall see, in the United States and Canada than on the other side
of the Atlantic – forcing them to respond to public sentiment and to
the views of advertisers[2] and making political opinion less central to the
content of the paper than it had been in the early nineteenth century.

It is also clearly true that the commercialization of the newspaper in
the Liberal countries drove out of the media system a variety of forms
of noncommercial media. Tocqueville wrote in *Democracy in America*
(1969: 519) that "A newspaper can survive only if it gives publicity to
feelings or principles common to a large number of men. A newspaper
therefore always represents an association whose members are its regular
readers." He was presumably thinking here both of the party press and
of newspapers connected with a variety of other kinds of social groups.
The 1830s and 1840s, when the expansion of newspaper circulation began in the United States, was a period of reform movements (the most
important being the abolitionist movement) and many newspapers were
connected with them (Nord 2001). In Britain, as we have seen, the radical,
unstamped press, much of which was connected to working-class movements, flourished while the taxes on knowledge were in effect; like the
American papers Tocqueville described, they died once the commercial

---

[2] Baldasty (1992: 75ff) discusses the influence of advertisers on the political content of
nineteenth-century American newspapers.

press was able to flourish (Curran 1978; Chalaby 1998). The connections between newspapers and associations so central in Tocqueville's analysis, however, and so central in the other media system models we have explored, largely disappeared once commercial mass-circulation papers began to expand.

The Liberal countries thus do not have the diversity of different kinds of newspapers that characterizes the Democratic Corporatist system – all but the commercial press became marginal by the twentieth century. They never did have party papers of the sort that developed in continental Europe in the late nineteenth century – papers directly connected to political party organizations – the main exception being the Communist *Daily Worker* (later *Morning Star*) in Britain that had a circulation of 115,000 in 1950. Ireland is a bit of a different story, as we shall see in more detail. It is, of course, a newer political system and party papers have continued through the late twentieth century. They have been mainly marginal, though the magazine of Sinn Fein, *An Phoblacht/Republican News*, has had important influence (Horgan 2001: 148). Party papers also existed in Québec, the last dying in 1962 (Gagnon 1981: 27). Neither have religious papers played a very significant role, though a few have existed, for example in Ireland.[3] Britain did have a significant labor press, despite the death of the radical unstamped papers. Its most important representative in the twentieth century, the *Daily Herald*, was owned by the Trades Union Congress (TUC) from 1922 to 1929, and the TUC retained editorial control until 1961, when the paper was absorbed by the Mirror group (later to be sold to Murdoch and transformed into *The Sun*). The demise of the labor press despite high circulations – which was due in large part to the fact that advertisers not only disliked its politics but had little interest in its overwhelmingly working-class readership – is a key point in the argument of the revisionist school in British media studies against the idea that commercialization produces a free fourth estate unaffected by power. In the United States and Canada, the commercial press developed before the labor movement had emerged in a significant way and labor papers remained very marginal. The largest in the United States was the weekly *Appeal to Reason*, which reached a

---

[3] In the United States there is *The Christian Science Monitor* and the Church of Jesus Christ of Latter-day Saints owns many media outlets in the state of Utah. *The Washington Times* is also bankrolled by the Unification Church. Religious broadcasting goes back to the early days of radio, but expanded considerably with the growth of cable television in the 1970s (Hoover 1988), and can be seen as the beginning of a shift toward greater external pluralism in electronic media.

peak circulation of 760,000 in 1912. Foreign language and ethnic papers have also always been part of the United States and Canadian media landscape, most of them hybrids in the sense that they survived on the market, and sometimes even made money, but have seen themselves as representatives of a particular social group more than as pure businesses. The groups they served were often excluded by the mainstream media in a racially stratified society, and political advocacy was often central to their role.[4] The most important black papers, the *Chicago Defender* and the *Pittsburgh Courier,* reached circulations of 200,000–300,000 in the first half of the twentieth century. Today the largest ethnic media are Spanish-language media. These, however, increasingly follow the standard commercial and professional models, even if their content reflects the distinct concerns of the Latino community (Rodriguez 1999).

Though early development of mass-circulation commercial papers is common to all the Liberal countries, the market structure of the contemporary press has developed in quite different ways. Britain has a class-stratified newspaper market, characterized by a sharp separation between "quality" papers with mainly middle- to upper-class readerships and the sensationalist tabloids, which are further differentiated into "middle market" and "mass market" papers. In the United States and Canada, by contrast, local newspapers with cross-class readerships predominate; only the New York City market, where circulation is dominated by the *Post* and the *Daily News,* is really comparable to the British newspaper market. (Some other large cities in North America – Chicago and Toronto, for example – do have tabloids, but they do not dominate circulation as the British tabloids do.) The main reason for this probably lies in the simple fact that Britain has a national newspaper market, which can support multiple newspapers (thirteen national daily newspapers in 1998) directed toward distinct market segments. The United States and Canada are so large that national daily newspapers were not technologically feasible until advances in telecommunication made it possible to send large amounts of data cheaply around the country (*USA Today* was founded in 1982 and *The New York Times* also introduced its national edition in the 1980s; the *National Post* in Canada was founded in 2000). Both are also federal systems. Newspaper markets are essentially local and, as in most of the world, the economics of advertising-supported local newspaper markets pushes strongly toward a single monopoly newspaper

---

[4] See, for example, Bekken (1997). Many, of course, imported journalistic cultures similar to those of the Polarized Pluralist or Democratic Corporatist Models from their countries of origin.

with a catchall audience. In the case of Ireland, a tabloid market does exist, but it is mostly dominated by British imports, which account for about 20 percent of daily and 26 percent of Sunday circulation. The British newspaper market is essentially unique in the sharp separation that exists between quality and mass papers and the market dominance of the latter – in 1994, mass-market tabloids accounted for 54 percent of the circulation of national dailies and midmarket tabloids accounted for an additional 27 percent. Germany is perhaps the closest comparison, but the strength of the local press in Germany diminishes the significance of the *Bild*, which overwhelmingly dominates the market for "street papers."

## POLITICAL PARALLELISM

The commercial press that developed so strongly in North America and in Britain played a pioneering role in developing what Chalaby (1996) calls a "fact-centered discourse." Commercial papers emphasized news at the expense of the political rhetoric and commentary that had dominated earlier papers. They were innovators in the development of organizational infrastructure to gather news rapidly and accurately, as well as in the development of the cultural forms of factual reporting. In his comparison between French and Anglo-American papers early in the twentieth century, Chalaby notes that the British and American papers had more information, more accurately and more recently reported; more wide-ranging in its focus, as British and American papers had networks of correspondents around the world; and, finally, more "factually presented," without the strong mixture of facts and personal opinion that characterized French journalism. Journalists in the Liberal countries remain more oriented toward informational and narrative styles of writing compared with continental journalists, who give greater emphasis to commentary, though the differences have diminished.

Often it is assumed that this kind of "fact-centered discourse" goes naturally with a stance of political neutrality and that a strong commercial press inevitably means a low level of political parallelism.

> ... [F]rom the 1850s onwards, Anglo-American journalists began to make the typically journalistic claim to be neutral and objective. ... [E]ven though what they wrote was politically arbitrary, they generally did not admit any political allegiance or even preference. In any case, the emphasis on news and information did not give much space to Anglo-American journalists to express their opinions (Chalaby 1996: 311).

In fact, there are significant differences among Liberal countries in the extent to which political neutrality or partisanship prevails. In the United States, Canada, and Ireland, political neutrality has come to be the typical stance of newspapers. Broadcasting in all four countries is also characterized by neutrality, though with some important signs of change as channels proliferate and the broadcasting industries are deregulated. The British press, on the other hand, is still characterized by external pluralism. It is no coincidence that the concept of "party-press parallelism" was developed in Britain, where despite their commercial character and despite the importance of the fact-centered discourse stressed by Chalaby, the press has always mirrored the divisions of party politics fairly closely.

It would make little sense to characterize American newspapers as Europeans commonly do theirs, by assigning them distinct locations on the political spectrum or distinct partisan sympathies. As noted in Chapter 6, Patterson and Donsbach (1993) found that, while journalists they surveyed in Britain, Sweden, Germany, and Italy placed the major national newspapers across a wide political spectrum, their American counterparts located all the major news organizations in a small range between the Democratic and Republican parties. On their editorial pages, to be sure, many American newspapers have relatively consistent political orientations. But these carry over only to a limited extent to news reporting.[5] *The San Diego Union-Tribune*, for example, is a strongly Republican paper on its editorial page. It is a relatively recent convert to political neutrality – in the 1970s it was one of the last surviving papers with a clear party orientation – and still has a stronger identity on the editorial page than many American papers. Nevertheless, in the sharpest partisan conflict in recent history – the controversy over the outcome of the 2000 presidential election – a good deal of its coverage was taken from *The New York Times* news service. *The New York Times* had the opposite editorial stance on the controversy – but there is a strong assumption in American journalism that this is irrelevant to news reporting. There are exceptions – occasions when reporters feel (or assume) pressures from management to follow the editorial line of the paper (there are also occasions – much more frequently – when reporters feel pressure not to depart from the centrist views shared by the many papers; more on this in the following text). There are also particular papers that have less

[5] Some empirical research on the U.S. media has shown correlations between editorial stance and news coverage, for example, Nacos (1990), who found that newspapers tended to use more sources consistent with their editorial policy. These differences are all in all relatively subtle, however.

separation between editorial position and news coverage; and there is the special case of *The Washington Times,* which was set up in the 1980s with funding from the Reverend Sun Myung Moon's Unification Church to be a conservative alternative to the mainstream press. Regional variations in political culture are also reflected in differences among newspapers, almost all of which are locally based. The *San Francisco Chronicle* covers a gay pride march differently than a paper in the Bible Belt. For the most part, however, American newspapers are not significantly differentiated in their political orientations. The principle of neutrality is particularly strong in American journalism today exactly where newspapers in the nineteenth century, or those in some other countries, would display their political colors most strongly – in election campaigns, where American newspapers typically take great care to balance the coverage of the two major parties, putting the story about one party on top one day, for example, and reversing them the next.

The story is essentially similar for Canadian papers; only the *National Post* is generally seen as having a clear ideological orientation, toward the right. Most accounts of the Canadian media also make the point that the culture of the Francophone journalism in Quebec is somewhat different (Gagnon 1981; Saint-Jean 1998; Hazel 2001), with a greater emphasis placed on commentary (similar to the French press) and more of a tradition of political involvement on the part of journalists, many of whom entered politics during the 1960s and 1970s (e.g., René Lévesque). This does not, however, mean that strong external pluralism has developed in the Quebec press and according to many accounts there has been a shift toward professional norms of neutrality more recently (Pritchard and Savageau 1998; Saint-Jean 1998).

In Ireland the shift toward a neutral press took place later. The development of the commercial press was slowed by Ireland's relative poverty and by competition from British imports. The political situation was also distinct: Ireland was under colonial rule into the early twentieth century and went through a revolution followed by a civil war. The party system was only consolidated in the 1920s and 1930s. Under those circumstances, "A newspaper is almost forced to take sides in the controversies, burning topics and struggles of its day" (Brown 1991 [1937]: 53). Or, to put it more positively, politicized newspapers had an extremely important role to play in the political mobilizations that formed the Irish democratic system, as they had earlier in the United States, Britain, and Canada (Carty 1981; Curran 1996) – and indeed in all the countries covered in this study. The three major newspapers thus reflected distinct political traditions and affinities relatively late, the *Irish Times*, the original penny paper, being originally Unionist in orientation and then shifting toward neutrality, the *Irish Independent* supporting the Fine Gael party until 1979, and *The Irish Press* close to the Fianna Fail party, whose leader, Eamon DeValera, founded the paper in 1931 and ran it for much of its history. Today, however, the party affinities and ideological orientations of the two surviving papers – the *Irish Press* went out of business in the 1990s – are not greatly different (Kelly and Treutzschler 1992).

Of course, the fact that the major papers of the United States, Canada, and Ireland are not differentiated in their political orientations does not necessarily mean that they have none. They all have essentially the *same* orientation – a centrist one (as suggested by Patterson and Donsbach's survey, in which all the major media were located between the Republicans and Democrats), as well as one oriented toward the views of the white middle-class readers who are the preferred target of advertisers. An orientation toward the center and toward the political "mainstream," is still a political orientation. As noted in Chapter 2, the use of the term *neutral* to refer to the "Anglo-American" style of journalism is not meant to imply that it is literally "value free" or without a point of view; scholarship in the Liberal countries debunked this notion long ago. The point is that these media position themselves as "catchall" media cutting across the principal lines of division between the established political forces in society.

The British press is a very different story. As in other countries, the party affiliations of British newspapers have become weaker over the postwar period, a trend we will explore further in Chapter 8. "Between 1945 and 1995," as Seymour-Ure (1996: 214) puts it, "the press became less predictable and manageable for the parties." Newspapers became less consistent in their support for one party or another, less inclined to follow the agenda set by party leaders, and less focused on the rhetoric of party politics. There have been ups and downs in this trend. Seymour-Ure argues that partisanship increased somewhat in the 1980s, when Margaret Thatcher challenged much of the prevailing consensus in British politics, only to fade again as the popularity of the Conservative party waned, and papers on the right began to distance themselves from it.

Despite this general trend toward diminishing political parallelism, however, the political orientations of British newspapers today are as distinct as anywhere in Europe, with the possible exceptions of Italy and Greece. The spectrum of political views is surely not as wide – Britain is characterized by moderate pluralism, and its politics have a strong orientation toward the center. Nevertheless, within the limits of the British political spectrum, strong, distinct political orientations are clearly manifested in news content.

Strong political orientations are especially characteristic of the tabloid press. It is part of the style of tabloid or popular journalism in most of the world to reject the constraints of objective reporting, and to present the newspaper as speaking for the common citizen and "common sense," often mobilizing a tone of outrage. In Britain as in Germany, this most commonly takes the form of a right-wing populist stance, emphasizing nationalism, anticommunism, traditional views on gender and on many social issues, and hostility to politicians. British tabloids often market themselves by launching campaigns around causes they expect to be popular (Harcup and O'Neill 2001). Beyond this populist stance, however, the British tabloids are also intensely partisan. In election periods, particularly, partisanship is more often than not both prominent and explicit, more so than the German *Bild*, which has a right-wing ideological orientation but does not openly campaign for a political party. In the period immediately preceding the 1997 election campaign, for example, *The Mirror* – in most years (though not 1997) the only pro-Labour tabloid – carried the slogan "Loyal to Labour, Loyal to You" on its banner, and on most days devoted the first six or so pages mainly to election propaganda: "MUTINY: 59 top doctors break silence to tell Mirror the NHS [National Health Service] will die if the Tories win this week"; "Tony Blair Answers Your Questions."[6] Even the page three girl was mobilized in the campaign effort: each day a different "Blair Babe" appeared to say why she was voting Labour. Five years earlier Rupert Murdoch's *Sun* had claimed credit for the Conservative victory in its famous headline, "IT'S THE SUN WOT WON IT!" (April 11, 1992). Whether the boast was true or not, it represents a strikingly different attitude from North American papers, which deny any influence on the outcome of elections (British papers of course go back and forth, and are often more coy about their political role).

The quality papers are more subtle in their style. But the British broadsheets do employ a more interpretive style of writing than is typical in North American papers.[7] Recent surveys showed 83 percent of British

---

[6] *The Mirror*, April 28, 1997.
[7] This, at least, is our strong impression from reading British papers. We don't have the kind of content analysis data we do for U.S. and French papers and do not know of

journalists saying that it was "very or extremely important" for a journalist to "provide analysis and interpretation of complex problems," while 48 percent of American journalists felt the same (Henningham and Delano 1998: 153). A headline like "Whitehall forgot our debt of honor" (*The Independent*, February 27, 1997, on a story about illnesses of Gulf War veterans), would be much too opinionated to appear on the lead story of a U.S. newspaper of comparable stature, in a story on domestic politics. So would "Brown's claim to be tough backfires" (the same day, on a report on the reaction of financial markets to statements by the Labour shadow Chancellor of the Exchequer).

The British quality papers also have distinct political identities. This can be seen in the political affinities of their readers. As Table 7.1 shows, the readerships of British national papers – both tabloid and broadsheet – are differentiated politically very much like those of newspapers in the Polarized Pluralist or Democratic Corporatist countries. In 1997, for instance, 57 percent of *Daily Telegraph* and 42 percent of *Times* readers supported the conservatives, as compared with 16 percent of *Independent* and 8 percent of *Guardian* readers. A good example of differing political orientation – outside election campaigns – is provided by the release in 2000 of the Parekh Commission's report on race in Britain – which provoked tremendous controversy in the press – that focused on an argument in the report that the historic concept of Britain was associated with racial exclusion.[8] None of the major papers supported the report wholeheartedly: as we have seen, the British press shares with other Liberal countries a strong centrist bias, and this report, largely the work of academics, strayed too far from the center for even Labour papers to support. But contrasting interpretations clearly showed the different political orientations in the British press. Table 7.2 contrasts the first few paragraphs of the stories in the *Telegraph* and *Guardian*, October 12, 2000. The *Daily Telegraph* tries to tie the Labour

comparable empirical studies. Semetko et al. (1991: 159–60) found in a comparative study of election coverage that British papers were about twice as likely as American to include journalists' contextualizing remarks, though the remarks by American journalists were more likely to be directional – usually disparaging toward whatever politician was involved. This is not quite a comparable measure to the one we use in Chapter 5 in comparing French and U.S. media, however.

[8] The conservative midmarket tabloid *Daily Mail* (October 11, 2000) printed on the top of the paper, using the background of the British flag, this attack on the Labor government, a summary of a comment that appeared inside the paper: "The flashy vacuity of the Dome, the trashy icons of Cool Britannia . . . and now the idea that to be British is racist. This is a government that knows nothing of our history and cares about it even less."

Table 7.1 *Party-Press Parallelism in British Newspaper Readership*

| | | Party Supported by Readers | | |
|---|---|---|---|---|
| | | Conservative | Labour | Liberal Democrat |
| **Tabloid** | | | | |
| *Sun* | 1997 | 30% | 52% | 12% |
| | 1992 | 45 | 36 | 14 |
| *Mirror* | 1997 | 14 | 72 | 11 |
| | 1992 | 20 | 64 | 14 |
| *Daily Mail* | 1997 | 49 | 29 | 14 |
| | 1992 | 65 | 15 | 18 |
| *Express* | 1997 | 49 | 29 | 16 |
| | 1992 | 67 | 15 | 14 |
| **Broadsheet** | | | | |
| *The Daily Telegraph* | 1997 | 57 | 20 | 17 |
| | 1992 | 72 | 11 | 16 |
| *The Times* | 1997 | 42 | 28 | 25 |
| | 1992 | 64 | 16 | 19 |
| *The Guardian* | 1997 | 8 | 67 | 22 |
| | 1992 | 15 | 55 | 24 |
| *The Independent* | 1997 | 16 | 47 | 30 |
| | 1992 | 25 | 37 | 34 |

*Source:* Scammell and Harrop (1997: 161). Papers are listed in order of circulation.

government as closely as possible to the report, presenting Home Secretary Jack Straw as backing down because the newspaper forced him to (it shows a picture of its own headline from the previous day – "Straw wants to rewrite our history"). Inside the paper, near the continuation of the story on Straw's comments, is another story with the headline, "More whites become victims of racially motivated crime." The *Guardian* by contrast takes at face value Straw's effort to distance himself from the report and does not suggest that that effort constitutes a "retreat." It puts the onus for the controversy on the far left rather than the Labour party.

The Liberal Model thus encompasses cases unusually high (Britain) and unusually low (the United States, Canada, and Ireland) in political parallelism in the press sector. Certainly, this suggests that the development of commercial media markets does not automatically eliminate

Table 7.2 *Contrasting Stories on Immigration in the British Press*

| The Daily Telegraph | The Guardian |
| --- | --- |
| **Straw beats a very British retreat over race report** | **Be proud to be British, Straw tells left** |
| JACK STRAW yesterday distanced the Government from a report on "multiculturalism" that provoked a furious row over what it means to be British. | **Do not leave patriotism to the far right, urges home secretary** |
| | Jack Straw, the home secretary, yesterday blamed lack of patriotism of the political left for allowing modern British identity to be seen as "narrow, exclusionary and conservative." |
| The Home Secretary was forced to repudiate key findings of the Commission on the Future of Multi-Ethnic Britain, which he launched almost three years ago. | Mr. Straw declared himself to be proud to be British and insisted he did not accept the arguments of some on the liberal left or the nationalist right that the idea of Britain as a cohesive nation was dead. The existence of people happy to be known as "black British or Chinese British" demonstrated that "Britishness" had a future. |
| Although the commission is not a Government body, the Home Office had welcomed its 400-page report as "a timely contribution" to the debate on race relations. | |
| But as controversy deepened over its portrayal of Britishness as "racist" and its call for a "reworking" of British history – as disclosed in *The Daily Telegraph* on Tuesday – both Mr. Straw and Downing Street dissociated themselves from its conclusions. | The modern challenge now, said Mr. Straw, was to meld the enormous range of races, accents and attitudes in the country into a single shared identity. "This is made even more difficult by the way those on the left turned their backs on the concept of patriotism and left the field to those on the far right," the home secretary said. |

political parallelism. Why such great differences between the British and North American press? We will look at possible explanations that lie in the realm of political culture later in the chapter. But the differences in market structure already mentioned provide one possible explanation. Just as the competitive national media market in Britain permits segmentation of the market by class, it may also permit segmentation of the market by political affinity, in a way that the local monopoly markets of North America (or the much smaller national media market of Ireland) do not.

Two final points should be made about political parallelism in the British press. The fact that the newspaper market has reflected political divisions does not mean that it has *accurately* reflected them: since the rise of the Labor Party there has been a strong partisan imbalance, with most of the press – with only the exceptions of the *Mirror, Guardian,* and *Independent* – clearly on the political right (Negrine 1994; Curran and Seaton 1997). It may be that this is changing, with the shift of Labour to the right and the shift of some right-wing papers to more "pragmatic" orientations: it may be, in other words, that the partisan dealignment that began in the 1970s and was temporarily reversed, has resumed and will result in the disappearance of political parallelism, though it is too early at this point to draw such a conclusion. The dominance of right-wing papers in Britain is one of the reasons a strong revisionist current arose to contest the view that commercial press means a free fourth estate expressing public sentiment.

The closeness of the press to the political system in Britain is also manifested in more substantial and more party-centered reporting of politics. Semetko et al. (1991) in a comparative study of election coverage in the two countries in the late 1980s, describe British election coverage as "more ample, more varied, more substantive, more party-oriented, less free with unidirectional comment and more respectful" than American coverage (142).[9] These differences they attribute in large part to differences in political culture, which lead British journalists to take a "sacerdotal" attitude toward election coverage, a view that an election is inherently important and journalists have a responsibility to convey what the parties are saying: "the more structured character of the British party system, the clearer ideological character of these parties and the consequent higher degree of politicization of British society as a whole," they argue, "might place political activity in a relatively higher position in the public's esteem (5)."[10] The strength of the British party system,

---

[9] The finding that "unidirectional" comments are more common in the United States than the British press might seem strange given the partisan character of the British press, confirmed by their study. Semetko et al. don't fully explain this; presumably partisan bias is expressed in many ways that don't show up in the count of "unidirectional comments," in headlines, for instance, and in the selection of news and quotations. In the U.S. case, unidirectional comments are not generally partisan in character but reflect the journalists' attitude of cynicism about politics in general. The general differences they observe between election coverage in the two countries are probably due not only to the strong, more ideological party system but to the strength of public broadcasting in Britain and also, as they note, the fact that professionalized political marketing has developed more slowly there.

[10] Though it might be noted that some surveys show relatively low levels of confidence in political institutions in Britain today, compared with other European countries. See Eurobarometer 55: 7.

and the closeness of the media to that system, is manifested, in other words, not only in external pluralism but also in the fact that news coverage centers more on the parties and their views – Semetko et al. found that the agenda of election coverage followed more closely the parties' own agendas in Britain – and in a generally greater attention to politics. There is some evidence that this "sacerdotal" and party-oriented attitude toward the political world has declined in recent years, in favor of a more American-style coverage driven by journalists' market-oriented judgments of what makes a good story (Franklin and Richardson 2002).

In broadcasting, in contrast to the press, all four countries have strong traditions of political neutrality. To a large extent, this has been a matter of public policy. In Britain, both the BBC and the Independent Television (ITV) companies are bound by requirements for impartiality and balance in news and public affairs. The actual practice of balanced reporting of government and opposition dates from World War II, when Labour was integrated into the government, eventually coming to power on its own in 1945. In the early days of radio Britain was a one-party dominant system and coverage of the Labour opposition was limited (Seaton and Pimlott 1987, ch. 7). During election campaigns, both the BBC and ITV have regarded the formula according to which the free broadcast time was allocated to the parties (e.g., 5:5:4 for Conservatives, Labour and Alliance in 1983) as a guide for election coverage (Semetko et al. 1991: 42–3). British broadcasting also has strongly manifested the "sacerdotal" attitude toward elections, with BBC news expanding the broadcast during election periods, as is the case with public broadcasting in most of Europe.

In the United States, when the initial debates took place over the regulation of radio broadcasting, commercial broadcasters were successful in arguing that they should control the airwaves because they served the public as a whole, while nonprofit stations that institutions such as trade unions, churches, and universities were trying to establish, were characterized as "propaganda" stations, serving particular, sectarian interests (McChesney 1994). Until the mid-1990s the Fairness Doctrine required U.S. broadcasters to provide "balanced" coverage of controversial issues, though the kinds of set political formulas that often govern the allocation of coverage in European systems – especially during elections – did not exist, and journalists exercised more discretion in judging the "newsworthiness" of political events. Market forces have also pushed toward neutrality in U.S. broadcasting just as they did in the press, as we shall see in the following section of this chapter. The broadcasting market was national and at the same time highly oligopolistic, with three networks competing for the same mass audience. Just as the networks sought the "least objectionable programming" in the realm of entertainment, so in news they had a strong interest in bridging political and ideological differences. They even had to bridge the regional differences that account for much of the modest variation in the political orientations of American newspapers. This stance of political neutrality was generally successful in all four countries in giving the broadcasters a level of prestige and credibility not enjoyed during some periods by newspapers. Frank Capra's classic *Mr. Smith Goes to Washington*, produced in the 1930s when newspapers in the United States were still often highly partisan, portrays newspaper owners as political villains, manipulating information to thwart the will of the people. Radio, on the other hand, is portrayed as a source of objective information.

There are signs of change in broadcasting today, connected with the shift toward neoliberalism in broadcast policy and the shift toward a multichannel environment. The Fairness Doctrine, which required "balanced" coverage of controversial public issues and which free-market advocates saw as unwarranted government interference with broadcast content, was abolished in 1987 and highly ideological radio programs, mostly on the right, have proliferated. In television, Rupert Murdoch's Fox network has established a news division that also seems to be adopting a distinctive, rightward tilt. During the 2003 war against Iraq, both Fox and the radio giant Clear Channel sought to differentiate themselves from market rivals by taking a particularly explicit "patriotic" stance. Republicans and conservatives are overrepresented among Fox News viewers, in contrast to the three traditional networks and CNN, whose viewers are not significantly differentiated politically from the general population (Pew Research Center 2003: 13).

## PROFESSIONALIZATION

Journalistic professionalism is relatively strongly developed in the Liberal countries. Certainly journalism has developed into a distinct occupational community and social activity, with a value system and standards of practice of its own, rooted in an ideology of public service, and with significant autonomy. At the same time, many contradictions in the nature and significance of professionalization emerge when we look at journalism in Liberal systems.

The professionalization of journalism began, in some sense, when the emerging commercial newspapers began to hire full-time paid reporters. In the earliest years, these reporters were for the most part poorly paid and low in status, and had little in the way of job security or autonomy. There were exceptions; from fairly early on, there were star reporters whose public reputations gave them bargaining power vis-à-vis newspaper owners. Henry Villiard, for example, agreed to work for James Gordon Bennett's *Herald* during the Civil War on the condition that he would not be required to follow the paper's anti-Lincoln politics (Kluger 1986: 99–100). But this was not typical. Ethical standards were low. Low pay meant that reporters were tempted into corruption, and piece rates – payment by the column inch, for example – tempted them into sensation, embellishment, and fabrication (Smythe 1980).

By the 1880s – a period when the notion of professionalism had growing prestige in the wider culture – there was considerable discussion in the United States of the need to professionalize journalism (Dicken-Garcia 1989; Marzolf 1991) and the perspective Siebert, Peterson, and Schramm would later call the Social Responsibility Theory was articulated. This took place against the background of intensified competition in the newspaper industry – this was the era of sensationalist "yellow journalism" – and led to numerous proposals for reform, including proposals for endowed, noncommercial newspapers and for licensing of journalists. The first trade publications were started in the 1880s – *The Journalist, Newspaperdom, Fourth Estate,* and *Editor and Publisher.* The Columbia School of Journalism was endowed in 1903 and opened in 1912, by which time there were three professional schools of journalism and about a dozen colleges and universities with journalism courses. In 1910 the Kansas State Press Association (state press associations began in the 1850s, originally as social institutions) adopted the first code of ethics. The American Society of Newspaper Editors was founded in 1923 and soon passed the first national code of ethics. At the same time, specialist reporters were beginning to establish professional communities, including most importantly the Washington press corps. As Kernell (1986) shows, political correspondents gradually came to see Washington reporting as a long-term career. Many increased the stability of their careers by working for multiple papers – thus becoming less dependent on particular employers. Their level of expertise increased, as did their orientation to their peers and sources, rather than to their employers. Educational levels of reporters gradually increased, as did the use of bylines identifying individual reporters, which was standard by the mid-twentieth century.

In North America, the professionalization of journalism was closely associated with the shift toward politically neutral monopoly newspapers and the dominant form of professional practice came to be centered around the notion of "objectivity" – that is, fundamentally, the idea that news could and should be separated from opinion, including both the opinions of journalists and those of owners. It also involved a shift of organizational structure, with owners increasingly withdrawing from day-to-day management of newspapers, turning that task over to professional journalists. With these developments, instrumentalization of the media declined. There were always some exceptions: there remained media owners who continued to see their media properties as a means of shaping public opinion and to assert control on a regular basis over the news as well as the editorial page. In the United States, the most important of these owners in the mid-twentieth century were Colonel Robert McCormick, owner of the *Chicago Tribune* and New York *Daily News*, and Henry Luce, owner of Time-Life (McCormick died in 1955 but his designated successors carried on his policies for another couple of decades; Luce died in 1967). Other owners certainly continued to intervene at times when they felt vital interests, political or economic, were at stake, and subtle pressures to conform to "policy" have always flowed downward within news organizations (Breed 1955). As a general pattern, however, instrumentalization of the press declined very substantially in North America during the twentieth century.

The early and strong development of this form of professionalization, centered around the principle of objectivity and connected with a sharp decline in party-press parallelism, is clearly one of the distinctive characteristics of North American media history and its origins deserve some discussion here. Two principal explanations have been offered and both are probably important. The first is economic. This argument has been developed most systematically by Baker (1994). The shift toward politically neutral newspapers, according to Baker, was a product of the shift from a reader-supported to an advertising-supported press and of the related trend toward concentration of media markets. With the growth of department stores and brand-name marketing beginning in the late nineteenth century, the percent of newspaper and periodical revenues derived from advertising increased from 44.0 percent in 1879 to 70.9 percent in 1929 (15). Advertisers often expressed a clear preference for newspaper content that focused on the "bright side of life" and avoided political controversies that could offend readers and decrease the effectiveness of advertisements (see also Baldasty 1992: 78).

Table 7.3 *Percent of U.S. Cities with*
*Competing Daily Newspapers*

| | |
|---|---|
| 1880 | 61.4 |
| 1910 | 57.1 |
| 1920 | 42.6 |
| 1930 | 20.6 |
| 1940 | 12.7 |
| 1954 | 6.0 |
| 1960 | 4.2 |
| 1986 | 1.9 |

Advertising, moreover, increased the incentive for newspapers to maximize circulation, even if many of their core readers would have preferred a newspaper with a distinct political orientation. Advertising thus combined with the economies of scale that characterize the newspaper industry – the fact that most costs are first-copy costs, and that large newspapers therefore have strong cost advantages – to produce a strong trend toward concentration of newspaper markets. Table 7.3 shows the percent of U.S. cities with competing dailies (the U.S. newspaper market is almost entirely local). The trend toward monopoly was particularly steep around 1910–50 – exactly the period when the professional norm of objectivity was taking root in American journalism. Baker interprets the development of that norm as a means of routinizing the exclusion of offensive material that might limit the expansion of newspaper circulation.

Schudson (1978; 2001), on the other hand, stresses changes in American political culture that took place in the late nineteenth and early twentieth centuries, involving a decline in the importance of partisan politics and a growing emphasis on neutral expertise. This argument we will take up more fully in the second half of this chapter, where we discuss the development of rational-legal authority and the influence of the Progressive Movement on American journalism. Here it is useful, however, to note something about the political context of the period when neutral professionalism was becoming dominant in the American press. This was a period when there was considerable controversy over the political role of the "press barons," expressed, for example, in Upton Sinclair's (1919) book *The Brass Check*. With the political realignment of 1932, moreover, a long period began in which the Democratic party dominated American politics and newspaper owners were in a delicate position politically. This was the first period in U.S. history in which political divisions reflected class differences primarily, at least outside the South: the working class favored the Democrats and the business supported the Republicans. In earlier eras party divisions had been defined more by regional differences. This was also the first period in which there was a significant partisan imbalance in the press – whose owners were by definition upper class and tended to support the Republican party; about two thirds of U.S. newspapers opposed Roosevelt editorially. Newspaper owners were thus out of step with public opinion and had a bad image in popular culture. As mentioned previously, the villain of Capra's *Mr. Smith Goes to Washington* is a newspaper baron who uses his papers to prevent the hero from communicating with the people. There were also tensions within news organizations, as the Newspaper Guild was being organized, and journalists often differed politically from owners over Roosevelt's New Deal, the role of trade unions, and many other issues. *Mr. Smith Goes to Washington* not only portrays media owners as antidemocratic manipulators of public opinion, but also incites journalists to set aside the constraints of "objective" reporting and denounce corrupt enemies of the people explicitly. There was, finally, some discussion of the possibility of regulation of the press – the Hutchins Commission, whose 1947 report articulated the idea of the press as a social trust and called for professionalization, also suggested that if professionalization were not successful some kind of public regulation might be necessary. In this context, media owners had not only economic but also political incentives to accept professionalization, which limited their ability to use the press as an instrument of political intervention, but which also minimized political tensions that might disrupt business and, through the objectivity norm, provided an alternative mechanism of control over journalists.

In Britain, as we have seen, political parallelism remained much stronger. Instrumentalization of the press by owners did diminish during the twentieth century, though probably not as strongly as in North America. Rupert Murdoch, who entered the British newspaper market in 1969, has brought a partial reversal of the shift, insisting on control of the political content of his media and using them to intervene in politics (Shawcross 1992). (Murdoch's role in the United States has been more limited, as his newspaper holdings have been relatively marginal and Fox television did not have a news operation until the late 1990s.) In Canada, Conrad Black has similarly asserted his right to control his papers politically (Taras 1999: 212–14), particularly *The National*

*Post*, and had strongly hostile relations with Liberal Prime Minister Jean Chretien. Black, who also owns the *Daily Telegraph* in Britain, renounced his Canadian citizenship and sold his Canadian papers in 2001 to Canada's dominant media conglomerate, Can West, whose owners support the Liberal party.[11] There has been some controversy since the sale over Can West's imposition of a policy that requires all its local newspapers to follow particular positions on the editorial page. Can West has said that this does not affect news coverage, though some journalists have claimed Can West is undermining professional autonomy (Brown 2002).

As the partisanship of the British press and the prevalence of interventionist owners suggest, professionalization may be less fully developed, or at least less consistently so, in the British than the North American press (broadcast journalism is a different story, as we shall see in the following text). In Britain as in all the Liberal countries journalism is strongly professionalized in the sense that journalists have their own set of criteria for the selection and presentation of news. This is closely related to the strong development of the press as an industry in Britain, and in this way Britain is very different from, say, Italy, where the standards of journalistic practice are less separated from those of politics. With the development of the press as an industry, as Chalaby (1998: 107) puts it, "journalists began to report politics according to their own needs and interests, covering the topic from their own perspective and professional values." On the other hand, specialized professional education developed later in Britain than in North America (Henningham and Delano 1998) and until the 1980s relatively few British journalists had college degrees. Journalism in this sense remained a white collar, semiprofessional occupation relatively late (Tunstall 1971: 59–60). Surveys have also suggested that British journalists are less fussy about information-gathering methods than their counterparts in the United States (Henningham and Delano 1998). This is presumably related to the highly competitive nature of the British press, and it could be said that in this sense ethical self-regulation and the notion of journalism as a public service are weaker in the British press.

As far as journalistic autonomy is concerned, the picture is mixed. As we shall see later in this chapter, broadcast journalists in Britain are probably more autonomous than their counterparts in the commercial

---

[11] It was also Conrad Black whose purchase of the *Jerusalem Post* and imposition on that paper of a more conservative line provoked the resignation of editor Erwin Frenkel, whose comments on journalistic autonomy are quoted in Chapter 2.

media of the United States or Canada. Journalists at *The Times* were protected, in the 1960s and 1970s, when the paper was owned by the Canadian publisher Thompson, by the appointment of four independent national directors whose sole function was to ensure editorial independence. The *Guardian* is also controlled by a trust whose statutes separate editorial and business control. No such formal protection of editorial autonomy has ever existed in the United States. The 1960s and 1970s are often described by British media scholars as a high point of journalistic autonomy, with a trend toward more centralized editorial control developing since that time (Curran and Leys 2000: 232). In the case of *The Times*, a new agreement on editorial autonomy was reached when Murdoch bought the paper in 1979, but it proved ineffective (Shawcros 1992). In general, journalistic autonomy is probably more limited in the British than the North American press, particularly at the tabloid papers. Donsbach (1995) reports that British journalists were second, after Italians, in the percentage reporting that their stories were changed "to give a political slant," 6 percent saying that this happened at least occasionally, as compared with 8 percent in Italy, 2 percent in the United States and Germany, and 1 percent in Sweden (a lower percent of the news in Britain concerns politics, compared with Italy, it might be noted). Another survey showed 44 percent of British journalists saying they had suffered "improper editorial interference" with a story (Henningham and Delano 1998: 154).

Formal organization of the profession of journalism is not developed particularly strongly in the Liberal countries, at least compared with Democratic Corporatist systems. Professional self-regulation takes place mainly informally, within particular news organizations and in the wider peer culture of journalism. In the United States, in the 1980s, only 17 percent of journalists in one survey belonged to the Society of Professional Journalists, the largest national professional association, and a similar percentage to a trade union, usually either The Newspaper Guild or the American Federation of Television and Radio Artists (Weaver and Wiloit 1991: 106–7). The American Society of Newspaper Editors (ASNE) also has played a significant role in developing ethical standards and a common journalistic culture. In Britain a professional association, the Institute of Journalists, was formed in 1890. It was eclipsed in the twentieth century, however, by the development of the National Union of Journalists (NUJ), which eventually became a strong trade union to which virtually all journalists belonged. In this sense Britain, with its strong trade union movement, has had a stronger collective organization of journalism, though in the context of a union rather than a professional association. The NUJ was badly damaged by the attack on trade unions during the Thatcher government, though by the end of the 1990s it had recovered somewhat and 62 percent of British journalists were members (Henningham and Delano 1998). A branch of the NUJ represents Irish journalists. Union membership in Canada, as well as membership in the Canadian Association of Journalists, is spotty, as in the United States; except in Quebec, where virtually all journalists belong to the Syndicat des Journalistes. Quebec also has an unusual history of militant contestation by journalists over newsroom power, mainly during the 1960s and 1970s, with efforts to negotiate "professional clauses" protecting journalists' autonomy within the news organization (Clift 1981; Saint-Jean 1998).

Formal institutions of self-regulation of the media are similarly less developed in the Liberal than in Democratic Corporatist countries, though more so than in the Mediterranean region. Ireland has no news council or press complaints commission. Neither does the United States, where news organizations have been extremely reluctant to submit to any outside interference, with the exception of the Minnesota Press Council, established in 1970 (perhaps in part a reflection of the Scandinavian influence on Minnesota's political culture?).[12] At the other end of the spectrum is Quebec, which has a relatively strong press council, without policing powers but with some public financing and with a policy of taking complaints about all newspapers, whether they have voluntarily joined the council or not (Clift 1981). Other Canadian provinces have relatively weak voluntary press councils funded by the newspaper industry. Britain moved in 1991 from a very weak press council to the Press Complaints Commission (PCC), a move intended to avoid continental-style privacy and right-of-reply legislation. The British tabloids, especially, have a heavy emphasis on sex scandals, about both public and private figures. The PCC is clearly stronger than its predecessor, and its presence is a characteristic the British system now shares with the Democratic Corporatist countries, though it is still essentially run by the newspaper industry, "illustrative of the enduring British commitment to 'hands-off' self-regulation" (Humphreys 1996: 61).

Journalistic self-regulation in Liberal countries is organized primarily in an informal way, within individual news organizations. Its evolution

---

[12] An organization called the National News Council existed from 1973–83. It was supported by a private foundation and one of its functions was to take complaints on media ethics, but cooperation of news organizations was always limited.

began in the late nineteenth and early twentieth centuries. Pulitzer's New York *World*, for instance, established an internal Bureau of Accuracy and Fairness in 1913, mainly to cut down on the number of libel suits (Marzolf 1991: 66–8). Eventually, this function would become integrated into the general organization of the editing process. News organizations in the Liberal countries are characterized by extensive editorial hierarchies with many "checks and balances" on the work of individual journalists, in contrast to many continental newspapers where journalists work separately, with little editorial supervision (Donsbach 1995; Esser 1998).

As this last point about editorial control suggests, the professionalization that developed in Liberal societies actually has two sides as far as journalistic autonomy is concerned. It constrains owners and often has served to increase journalistic autonomy and limit instrumentalization of the media. But it also constrains journalists, who are expected to renounce any ambition of using their position as a platform for expressing their own political views, and to submit to the discipline of professional routines and editorial hierarchies.[13] As noted previously, the development of journalists' unions in the 1920s and 1930s is probably one reason owners considered it in their interest to move toward professionalization. The balance between the constraints on journalists and the constraints on owners varies over time and also from one paper to another. At times, the balance leans toward the owners enough that professionalization actually facilitates instrumentalization of the press. Thus Smith (1975: 35), discussing the campaign of the *Express*, then the largest British paper, against the Labour party during the 1945 election, quotes the editor as saying, "Even the Socialists on the staff – and there were plenty – carried out their briefs with professional gusto. It was all-in wrestling, hand-to-hand fighting, commando stuff, and we were, we thought, very good at it." Here professionalization takes a narrower form: a "professional" is a journalist who has mastered the routines of creating political news in the tabloid style, with heroes and villains that

---

[13] One of the more interesting illustrations of the significance of these constraints is the case of A. Kent MacDougall, a reporter for *The Wall Street Journal* who wrote an article after he retired revealing that he was a Marxist, and telling fellow radicals that they could make a difference working in the mainstream press. This created a furor about "hidden radical influence" in the press, but analyses of MacDougall's reporting made it clear that most of the time it was not distinguishable from that of other journalists (Reese 1990). Köcher (1986) found British journalists less likely than German journalists to endorse a "missionary" orientation toward expressing opinions and shaping public opinion. The political slants of British newspapers, of course, are not necessarily those of the individual journalists.

will appeal to popular sentiments. Journalists take collective pride in doing this well, apart from their own political opinions. The development of this form of professionalism is critical to understanding how it is possible that a strong majority of British journalists have historically been on the left politically, while most of the newspapers are on the right.

The dominant form of professionalism in North America is different in that it is tied to the notion of objectivity. But it also imposes constraints on journalistic autonomy. The American author of this book spent a lot of time in the 1980s interviewing journalists covering the conflict in Central America. American and European journalists among the world press corps often criticized one another's professionalism. The Americans would say that the European journalists were "unprofessional" because they were too politicized, and were always injecting their own opinions into their reporting. The Europeans would say that the Americans were "unprofessional" because they were so constrained by the routines of balance and "objectivity" that they didn't exercise independent judgment. So, for example, they might travel to the countryside to report from the scene of what strongly appeared to be a government massacre of unarmed peasants, but in writing the story they would have to balance the accounts of the local population with denials from the army and the U.S. embassy, and write the story in a way that suggested they had no opinion of their own about which account was right (cf. Pedelty 1995). To the Europeans, they were not "honest witnesses" in the sense expressed by Frenkel, who was quoted in our discussion of continental European notions of professionalism in Chapter 2. Much of the media research of Liberal societies has been devoted to showing how professional routines can lead to subservience of the news media not to the particular political commitments of individual owners, but to a broader dominant view among political elites. The notion of professional routines is worth underscoring here. Because of the relatively strong professionalization of journalism in Liberal systems, media scholarship in these countries has developed a distinctive focus on this notion, and the politics of news is normally explained primarily by the cultural assumptions and structural limits built into these routines, rather than in terms of the personal views or political connections of journalists, instrumental control by owners, or political pressures from outside of news organizations (Sigal 1973; Tuchman 1978; Gans 1979; Gitlin 1980; Hallin 1986; Ericson, Baranek, and Chan 1987; Schlesinger 1987).

The relation of professionalization to commercial constraints on journalists is similarly ambivalent. The early drive toward professionalization late in the nineteenth century was at least as much a response to the effects of commercial competition as to concerns about political manipulation of the media, a reaction to the "pervading spirit . . . of vulgarity, indecency and reckless sensationalism" that characterized the "yellow" press of that era, as E.L. Godkin put it in *The Nation* (quoted in Marzolf 1991: 27). The "separation of church and state" that became a key metaphor of American journalistic professionalism had a double meaning. It meant a separation between the opinions of the newspaper as expressed on the editorial page, opinions that reflected the view of the owner, and the news pages, which were the product of professional journalists. It also meant a separation between the business departments of the news organization and the newsroom. Nevertheless, professionalism did develop primarily in the context of market-based media and incorporated much of this context within it. The professional routines of journalism in Liberal societies incorporate a strong emphasis on accessibility and audience interest that is rooted in the market. And the multileveled editing process previously mentioned always has had as one of its primary functions the production of market-friendly news. Thus Donsbach (1995) found 36 percent of American and 28 percent of British journalists reporting that stories were changed "to enhance audience interest," as opposed to 18 percent of Swedish, 14 percent of Italian, and 7 percent of German journalists.

In significant ways professionalism, as we have defined it here, has declined over the past twenty years or so. In Britain, as mentioned, many scholars argue that journalistic autonomy has eroded from a high point in about the 1960s. In the United States, the "separation of church and state" has been eroded over recent years as owners have moved to reduce the barrier between the business and editorial operations of news organizations, and considerable tension has arisen with journalists who feel professional integrity has been undermined (Squires 1993; Underwood, 1993; Hallin 2000). "MONEY LUST: How Pressure for Profit is Perverting Journalism," reads the cover of the *Columbia Journalism Review* for July/August 1998. In the press this shift has resulted from declining circulations and the fact that newspaper companies shifted toward corporate ownership in the 1970s and 1980s, two developments that combined to produce intense pressure for news organizations to pay attention to circulation figures and to the bottom line. In the electronic media, deregulation of broadcasting and increasing competition have produced a similar, indeed even stronger result.

## THE ROLE OF THE STATE

The Liberal countries are, by definition, those in which the social role of the state is relatively limited and the role of the market and private sector relatively large. Britain was the birthplace of industrial capitalism and the United States the center of its twentieth-century growth. Market institutions and liberal ideology developed strongly in both countries – in general, and specifically in the media field, where they are manifested in the early development of commercial media industries and of the liberal theory of a free press rooted in civil society and the market. State subsidies to the press have been minimal in all four Liberal countries through most of the twentieth century. Commercial broadcasting has always been the dominant form in the United States and to a lesser degree in Canada, and was introduced in Britain a generation before most of continental Europe; Ireland resisted its introduction much longer.

The state has always played a significant role in the development of capitalist society, however, and its role in the development of the media is important even in the most distinctively liberal societies. There is also considerable variation among the four countries covered here in the role of the state. Even in the United States, clearly the purest case of the Liberal Model, the role of the state cannot be ignored. The state built the initial communication infrastructure – the postal system – that made possible the development of the press, as well as underwriting the development of what could be called the human infrastructure of the press through public education. As party newspapers developed, moreover, the political class clearly looked upon the press not merely as a business, but as a crucial public institution, and supported it accordingly (Cook 1998). Subsidized postal rates, including the right for publishers to exchange copies of newspapers between themselves without charge, were extremely important to the survival of early newspapers, as were government printing contracts and patronage jobs for editors (Smith 1977). These forms of sponsorship began to fade in importance after 1860, with the establishment of the Government Printing Office, the initiation of civil service reform, and the development of newspaper-owned distribution networks, which diminished the importance of subsidized postal rates (though the latter remain in effect). The postal service did acquire a new regulatory role in 1912 when newspapers were required to file sworn statements of circulation and ownership, which facilitated the development of a transparent advertising market (Lawson 1993). Journalists have also been granted certain legal rights that imply a continued recognition by the state that the press is an important social institution, for example the right to protect the confidentiality of sources, which is provided by "shield" laws in many states (such a law also exists in Britain, but not in Canada).

If the role of the state cannot be dismissed, it is nevertheless true that United States media history is characterized by important limitations on the state's role. Very important here is the legal tradition connected with the First Amendment, which clearly distinguishes the United States media system from most European ones. European constitutions always have guarantees of press freedom, but this is generally one legal principle among others, to be balanced against principles of privacy, social welfare, political pluralism, public order etc. Both legal doctrine and political culture in the United States tend to treat the First Amendment in a more absolutist way, and this means that many kinds of media regulation that are common in Europe – privacy rules, regulations on political advertising, free time requirements for political communication, and right-of-reply laws (one such law passed in Florida was struck down by the courts) – are politically and legally untenable in the United States. One area where the state in the United States has at certain moments played a very important role is in the regulation of media concentration. Two of these moments are the separation of NBC's "white" and "blue" networks by the Federal Communication Commission (FCC) in 1945, and the Paramount Decrees of 1948 separating the Hollywood studios from movie theater ownership. The antitrust conviction of Microsoft looked at one time as if it might prove another example of this tradition, but the Bush administration took a softer line and the case ended without dramatic results. It could probably be argued that the U.S. state historically has intervened as actively against media concentration as most European states. Of course, antitrust intervention is not incompatible with the prevailing liberal ideology in the United States, and is also particularly persuasive given the size of United States media markets.

The United States was the only industrialized country of any size to develop a privately owned telephone and telegraph system, and then a predominantly commercial broadcasting system. The public broadcasting system (PBS) was established only in 1967 and has remained weak by comparative standards. Less than 50 percent of its funding now comes from government sources (in 1990 16 percent came from the federal government and 30 percent came from state and local governments, with the rest coming from viewers, corporate donations, and commercial sources) and total expenditure has been about $1 per capita – compared with $38 per capita for British public broadcasting (Twentieth Century Fund 1993; Hoynes 1994).

The regulation of commercial broadcasting in the United States has been described as "regulation by raised eyebrow," in the sense that the FCC has stayed away from issuing specific directives on broadcast programming. Nevertheless, state regulation has shaped the commercial broadcast sector in the United States in important ways. From the 1930s to the 1980s broadcast licenses had to be renewed by the FCC every three years, and this renewal process, coupled with the Fairness Doctrine and the requirement that licenseholders serve the "public convenience and necessity," had many important effects. It protected the markets of the established broadcasters; encouraged the early development of a neutral, internally pluralist style of news with significant insulation from commercial pressures; provided a mechanism for groups in civil society to challenge broadcasting practices – as civil-rights groups did in important cases in the 1960s (Horwitz 1997); and no doubt, for better or for worse, inhibited the development of much potentially controversial programming. By the 1990s the license renewal process had become a formality, the Fairness Doctrine had been repealed, and the United States had shifted considerably toward a pure market model of broadcasting. Even today, however, the convergence of media industries and the formation of multimedia conglomerates with interests spanning telecommunication, the traditional audiovisual industries and the new Internet industries, has meant that the companies involved in broadcasting continue to have a strong stake in maintaining good relations with the state, which will continue to play a central role one way or another in establishing the ground rules for these industries. That stake is well illustrated by the large sums of money media industries donate to politicians and political parties (Lewis 2000).

In Britain, a strong liberal tradition is modified both by a legacy of conservative statism and by a strong labor movement, whose integration into the system of power in the 1940s shifted Britain in the direction of a kind of liberal corporatism similar in many ways to the democratic corporatism we examined in Chapter 6 (Curran 2000). Britain, moreover, has no written constitution, and the doctrine of parliamentary sovereignty is central to its legal framework, so freedom of the press remains an important cultural tradition but not the privileged legal principle it is in the United States The press sector remains essentially liberal in character, with neither subsidies nor significant regulatory intervention, though the threat of such intervention did induce the formation of the

PCC – and regulation continues to be discussed, as many argue that the PCC is ineffective. Important manifestation of Britain's strong state tradition include the D-notice system, which restricts reporting of information that affects "national security," and the Official Secrets Act, under which both journalists and public officials can be punished for "leaks" of privileged information. American journalists were bemused in 1996 when the *Mirror* was leaked a copy of the government's budget, the day before it was to be presented to Parliament, and returned it to the government. Prosecutions under the Official Secrets Act are rare, but it is a part of a wider political culture, partly connected with the strength of party discipline in the Westminster system, in which inside political information is not so freely leaked as in the more fragmented American political system. Libel law is also less favorable to the press in Britain than in the United States.

It is in the sphere of broadcasting, however, that the differences between the United States and Britain have been most marked, with Britain building a strong public service broadcasting system. The BBC was based on an ideology that rejected "both market forces and politics in favor of efficiency and planned growth controlled by experts" (Curran and Seaton 1997: 114), to which its first director, John Reith, added a Calvinist form of paternalism in the early years. In 1954 Britain became the first major European country to introduce commercial broadcasting; even then, however, its broadcasting system retained a strong public-service orientation. The BBC and ITV competed for audiences but not for revenue, with the BBC relying on the license fee and ITV on advertising. And the Independent Broadcasting Authority (IBA), which regulated commercial broadcasting until the Broadcasting Act of 1990, was a far different, far stronger institution than the FCC. It was not a mere regulatory agency, but held the license for commercial broadcasting, contracting with the ITV companies to provide programming and retaining ultimate authority over programming decisions. For this reason it has been common to refer to the BBC and ITV together as the "public service system" in British broadcasting. Channel 4 exemplified this unusual structure particularly well, as a part of the commercial broadcasting system charged with the public service missions of providing minority programming and supporting the independent production sector. The Independent Television Commission (ITC), which replaced the IBA in the 1990s, no longer holds the broadcast licenses itself, nor is it required to approve program schedules or advertising, though it still has more influence over these than the FCC. Like the rest of Europe, British broadcasting, including the BBC, is increasingly affected by market logic, though the public service system remains stronger in Britain than in much of Europe.

In Canada and Ireland concerns about national culture have modified the logic of the Liberal Model. Both are small countries proximate to much larger countries with the same dominant language, and both have feared with some justification that purely market-based media would inevitably be dominated by U.S. or British media industries. In Canada, the philosophy that it was "either the state or the United States" had a particularly important influence on broadcasting policy. Canada has always had a dual, commercial and public broadcasting system. But the public Canadian Broadcasting Corporation (CBC) dominated broadcasting through its early history (it was both public broadcaster and regulatory authority for commercial broadcasting until 1958), and remains stronger than U.S. public broadcasting (with a 9 percent audience share in 1997, for instance, in contrast to the 2 percent share of PBS). Canada has protected its domestic print media through legislation that made advertising expenses tax deductible only when placed in Canadian-owned publications, and that restricted the import of "split-run" editions of U.S. magazines with advertising directed at the Canadian market. The World Trade Organization (WTO) ruled against this policy recently, and Canada has been trying to revise it. American magazines account for about 80 percent of the Canadian market. Canada has also had more debate than the United States about regulation of press ethics and press concentration, but without in the end enacting such regulation. It does have an Official Secrets Act similar to that of Britain, and more restrictive libel laws than those of the United States.

Ireland is a postcolonial state. Its political culture combines a tradition of liberalism with a strong official ideology of nationalism. It also has a history of economic dependency and weak development of domestic capital, which like other postcolonial societies – Greece, for example – has resulted in a postindependence tradition of an interventionist state (Bell 1985). Public broadcasting has therefore been strongly dominant in Ireland, with free-to-air commercial television introduced only in 1998, although Irish public broadcasting has a high level of commercial funding, 66 percent in 1998 (see Table 2.4).[14] Unlike Canada, Ireland has not protected its print industry, although at one time censorship of publications considered by the Catholic Church to be immoral served

---

[14] The late introduction of commercial television was also due to the small size of the Irish market, particularly given the fact of competition with British television.

in part to restrict imported publications (Horgan 2001: 12–13). About 20 percent of daily newspaper circulation today represents British titles. The Censorship of Publications Act, which lasted until 1967, resulted from the political conflicts of the civil war of the 1920s, and Ireland, like Britain, has restrictions on media related to the conflict in Northern Ireland.

The relation between the state and the media is not solely a matter of regulation, subsidy, and state ownership. It also involves the flow of information – including images, symbols, and interpretive frames. And in this sphere, it is not at all clear that the media and the state are more separate in Liberal countries than in the other two systems studied here: though the rhetoric of the Liberal countries tends to stress an adversary relation between the media and the state, and though the state's formal role as regulator, funder, and owner is more limited than in other systems, it is important to stress that this does not necessarily mean the state has less influence on the news-making process. Here there is clearly a need for more extensive comparative research.

An adversary attitude toward state officials is certainly part of the culture of journalism in the Anglo-American countries. It is manifest among other things in the strong development of techniques of investigative reporting and the strong emphasis on scandal (not always the same thing) that have been legendary since Watergate, particularly in the U.S. where access to government information is relatively easy. At the same time, the notion of the state as the "primary definer" – the idea that the production of news is structured around information and interpretation provided by state officials – originated in Anglo-American media studies (Hall et al. 1978), and there are large bodies of research showing the strongly institutionalized relationship in Liberal systems between journalists and government officials, perhaps most clearly exemplified by the Westminster Lobby system in Britain. Mutual dependence between state and media institutions means that the structure of each reflects its relation with the other: news organizations are structured to a large extent around the "beat" system that connects reporters to their sources in the state, and state agencies are organized to a large extent around the needs of the media. According to some estimates, more than half the personnel in the White House are involved in public relations activities, a large proportion of which involve dealing with the media (Grossman and Kumar 1981: 83–4). In the Liberal system (and to some degree also in the Democratic Corporatist system, in recent years) both state officials and journalists claim a kind of neutral authority as representatives of the public standing apart from partisan and sectarian interests, and this would seem to provide the basis for a relationship just as strong – despite a very different form – as the kind of relationship that results from common party ties between journalists and politicians in Southern Europe. As a result of these relationships, news content is powerfully shaped by information, agendas, and interpretive frameworks originating within the institutions of the state.[15]

It should be noted finally that the closeness of this relationship between the news media and the state has been strongly influenced by the development of the "national security state." Both the United States and Britain are world powers with nuclear weapons and considerable involvement in international conflict. Both have histories of wartime cooperation – even interpenetration – between the media and that state: in World War II neither the United States nor Britain had formal press censorship, but in both media cooperation with the state was extensive. This kind of cooperation has been more limited in the post–World War II period, though it has not disappeared (in the aftermath of the September 11 terrorist attacks, for instance, Hollywood executives asked to meet with government officials to discuss how they could contribute, as they had in World War II, to the "war effort"). The "national security culture" has contributed substantially to the cultural assumption that journalists and government officials both in some sense represent a common public interest, and to the institutionalized relations of trust and mutual dependence that have developed between them. At times, of course, there have been tensions between the media and the state over "national security" reporting – in Britain, for example, over the Suez Crisis and later Northern Ireland; in the United States, over Vietnam or Central America. And the state has responded with a variety of restrictions and pressures on the media and the flow of information; we have already mentioned the British D-notice system as an example. Newton and Artingstall (1994) in a comparative study of censorship in nine western democracies, found that it was most frequent in Britain, the United States, and France – the three nuclear powers.[16] Britain they

---

[15] The literature on this point is vast. A few key works include Sigal (1973), Gans (1979), Hallin (1986), Herman and Chomsky (1988), and Bennett (1990).

[16] Their study is based on incidents reported in the Index on Censorship, for the period 1972–90. The other six countries, in order, are Canada, West Germany, Italy, Australia, Denmark, and Sweden (Democratic Corporatist countries thus tend to be lowest in the incidence of government censorship). Because incidence of censorship was not correlated with population size, Newton and Artingstall simply ordered countries by the raw numbers of censorship incidents.

noted, was far higher than other countries, probably a reflection of the fact that it shares with the United States the status of a world power, but has a more centralized state and lacks the constitutional limits on government censorship present in the United States. Clearly the fact that the Liberal countries also are often world powers requires important qualifications to the notion that the state plays a limited role in these systems, as well as to the notion of the press as an independent "fourth estate."

## GOVERNANCE OF BROADCASTING

In contrast to continental European systems in which political pluralism is assumed to require the "physical presence" of the parties in broadcasting, the assumption in the Liberal system is that in order for the broadcasting system to serve a pluralistic society, it must be separated from party politics and managed by neutral professionals without party ties. The BBC is the classic case of what we called in Chapter 2 the professional model of broadcast governance. In its formal structure, it is really no different from government-controlled or parliamentary systems: The director general and board of governors are appointed by the queen in council – in effect by the prime minister, and by convention with the consent of the opposition. A strong cultural norm has developed, however, that the governors should be "remarkable men and women . . . of the highest calibre," chosen not as representatives of political parties but of society as a whole, willing to uphold the independence of British broadcasting against political pressure. Journalists, producers, and other creative personnel are similarly chosen without regard to party ties, and have considerable autonomy; as Jeremy Tunstall (1993) has argued, the BBC has historically been a "producer-driven" enterprise.

Political pressures do certainly affect the BBC (Etzioni-Halevy 1987; Curran and Seaton 1997). They were particularly marked during the 1980s, when Margaret Thatcher frequently clashed with the BBC, as she did with local governments and other institutions that remained outside of ministerial control. The sharpest conflict was the *Real Lives* affair in 1985, in which the home secretary asked the BBC governors to cancel a documentary on Northern Ireland that included an interview with a Sinn Fein leader. The BBC governors cancelled the scheduled broadcast of the program, a decision that provoked a twenty-four-hour strike by BBC journalists; the program was later broadcast in modified form. Tensions reemerged in 2003 as Tony Blair's government attacked

BBC coverage of its handling of intelligence on Iraq. In comparative perspective, however, professionals at the BBC, and indeed at ITV as well, enjoy a high level of autonomy, and the most important political limits on broadcasting are to be found not in political intervention from outside, but within the community of broadcasting professionals, in their commitment a centrist, consensualist view of "responsible" professional broadcasting.

The Canadian and Irish public broadcasting systems are essentially modeled after the BBC, though in the Irish case broadcasting was under the control of a government department until 1961, and was "essentially a government mouthpiece" (Horgan 2001: 70) from about 1932 to 1948. Public broadcasting in the United States has a complicated structure because of its decentralized character and its reliance on private donations as well as public funding. But the main national body, the Corporation for Public Broadcasting, is similar in its institutional form to the British, Canadian, or Irish systems – an independent public corporation, with directors appointed by the president, and a norm that they should be politically independent. Nobody has studied American public broadcasting in comparative perspective, but it has probably been more subject to pressures from politicians (see e.g., Twentieth Century Fund 1993: 36) than the BBC, as it is a much more marginal institution without comparable prestige or a dedicated source of funding such as the license fee (various proposals to give it a source of funding apart from general tax revenues have been rejected). It is also subject to pressure from its other funders, including both local and state governments and corporate donors (Hoynes 1994).

In the United States, of course, most broadcasting is commercial. But the American commercial networks are ultimately not dramatically different in their relation to the political system than the public broadcasting of Britain, Ireland, or Canada. They of course have autonomy from political control, but they are not completely free from political pressures.[17] The latter result in part from the fact that broadcasting – like the related telecommunication businesses in which the broadcast networks are increasingly involved – is government regulated and the network owners

---

[17] Many examples of such pressures can be given over the years. Some are recounted for the Nixon period in Porter (1976) and for the Reagan period in Herstgaard (1988). Recently the networks went along with pressures from the Bush administration not to show videotapes released by Osama bin Laden. The BBC rebuffed similar pressures and said it would make its own decision on the newsworthiness of bin Laden videotapes.

have a strong interest in smooth relations with political authority. At the same time – and again like their public broadcasting counterparts in Britain, Ireland, or Canada – the legitimacy of commercial broadcasters in the United States depends on an ethic of neutral professionalism. They do differ in the fact that commercial pressures are much stronger. In this sense it might be said that the level of professional autonomy is higher at the BBC than at the American networks, where creative professionals, including journalists – especially since the 1980s – are more subject to control by business managers.

The institutions that regulate commercial broadcasting in the Liberal countries are organized as independent regulatory agencies with substantial political autonomy, similar to – probably not quite as strongly as – a central bank. The commissioners of the FCC, for example, are nominated by the president and ratified by Congress. These appointments are often relatively politicized: the party affiliations of the commissioners certainly matter, and Congress does intervene when it is unhappy with the direction of the FCC. But the agency is not subject to presidential control and must operate according to procedures of administrative law that strongly limit the direct influence of party politics.

## POLITICAL HISTORY, STRUCTURE, AND CULTURE

The bourgeois revolution occurred first in Britain. As we have seen, the early development of parliamentarism and the market, coupled with the high literacy rates associated with Protestantism, led to an early development of the press and of press freedom. The liberal institutions of Britain, including press freedom, were transferred in large part to Ireland and the North American colonies. The United States, as Tocqueville observed, was a liberal society from the very beginning. Its social structure was relatively egalitarian in the early nineteenth century (aside, of course, from the plantation system of the South) with large numbers of small producers – artisans and "yeoman" farmers (the United States never had a true peasant class) – and virtually all of them literate. The franchise was extended to all white males in the late 1820s, and both mass politics and mass circulation newspapers developed quickly thereafter. We have already explored the most fundamental connections between this social and political history and the development of the media, most particularly the early development of press freedom and the strength of commercial media industries. In the remainder of this section we would like to explore some more specific elements of the political structure and culture of the Liberal countries, as well as some of the less obvious connections between liberalism and the media system, including, for example, the question of how to account for professionalization of journalism.

## MODERATE PLURALISM

In the case of continental Europe, we have argued that the distinction between polarized and moderate pluralism has important implications for the media. Polarized pluralism tends to be associated with commentary-oriented journalism, higher levels of political parallelism, and interpenetration of the political and media systems, while moderate pluralism is more conducive to the development of catchall commercial media and neutral professionalism. The countries of Southern Europe tend toward polarized pluralism, while the Democratic Corporatist countries tend more in the direction of moderate pluralism, and the Liberal countries even more so, though, as with the other groups of countries, there are important variations among them. These differences are connected, as we noted in Chapter 4, with political history: Polarized Pluralism tends to occur where the *ancien régime* was strong and conflict over the introduction of liberal institutions was protracted. Moderate pluralism is more characteristic of countries where – as in the four covered here – liberalism triumphed early. Variations in political polarization, we believe, are extremely important to understanding both the differences between the Liberal countries and those of continental Europe, and among the Liberal countries themselves, particularly in the degree of political parallelism in the press.

It is useful here to recall the argument of Louis Hartz's *The Liberal Tradition in America* (1955). Taking off from Tocqueville's observation about the lack of a feudal past in American history, Hartz argues that American politics lacks the ideological divisions that characterize European politics. Liberalism never had to contend with an opposing conservative ideology rooted in feudalism and by the time the industrial working class came along the dominance of liberalism was strong enough that a socialist movement could not emerge. "Socialism," Hartz argues, "arises not only to fight capitalism but the remnants of feudalism itself" (9); and its ideology of class struggle does not arise directly out of the objective reality of economic inequality, but against the background of political conflict between the bourgeoisie and the landed aristocracy. There is also a way in which socialist ideology actually draws on the conservatism associated with the old regime: both tend to oppose the individualist ideology of liberalism with a collectivist ideology based on a more organic view of social order.

The fact that it lacks ideological differences does not, of course, mean that the United States lacks political conflict. The American Civil War was the bloodiest war anywhere in the world in the nineteenth century. American labor history is much more violent than the labor history of many European countries. Recent history is no different: forty-three people were killed in the Detroit riot of 1967, while four people died in the 1968 uprising in France, and two people were killed in the Portuguese revolution of 1975. These political conflicts are rooted in underlying conflicts of interest connected to divisions of race, class, region, etcetera. Economic inequality is in general greater in the United States than in European countries with strong welfare states. Social divisions have not, however, been expressed in distinct political ideologies, or in a political party system organized around such ideologies. The American political party system is organized around two catchall, centrist parties, both committed to a liberal political culture that is essentially taken for granted. "[T]his fixed, dogmatic liberalism" – strongly hegemonic, in Gramsci's terms,

> is the secret root from which has sprung many of the most puzzling of American cultural phenomena. Take the unusual power of the Supreme Court and the cult of constitution worship on which it rests. Federal factors apart, judicial review as it has worked in America would be inconceivable without the national acceptance of the Lockian creed, ultimately enshrined in the Constitution, since the removal of high policy to the realm of adjudication implies a prior recognition of the principles to be legally interpreted (Hartz 1957: 9).

The same logic would seem to apply to the institution of neutral professionalism in the mass media: the latter would be inconceivable without a large ground of shared values and assumptions whose inclusion in the news is not seen as politically partial.[18] Journalism can never simply

---

[18] Thus Gans (1979) identifies a set of "enduring values" that American journalists assume as a common sense that stands outside political controversy.

"report the facts"; it must give meaning to events, and this can be done with "due impartiality," to use the British phrase, only when the major political actors in society do not have sharply divergent world views.

Britain, by contrast, did have both feudalism and a strong socialist movement. Its political parties are traditionally more unified and more ideologically coherent than American parties. The Labour party was clearly identified with the social interests of the working class and, until the shift to New Labour in the 1990s, remained officially socialist in ideology. According to Lane and Ersson's (1991: 185) index of ideological polarization, Britain was close to the European average for the whole of the 1955–85 period, though higher in the 1950s than later. This greater ideological diversity, or greater "thematization" of ideology, to use Luhmann's term, is no doubt part of the reason that political parallelism is traditionally higher in the British press, though it should be noted that difference is overdetermined: The fact that the British newspaper market is national and competitive rather than local and monopolistic also may encourage external pluralism in the press. At the same time, compared with many continental European countries, Britain is characterized by moderate pluralism: antisystem parties are marginal and the degree of common ground among the major parties and other political actors – on parliamentary democracy, a market economy combined with a relatively strong welfare state, British nationalism, and so on – is very extensive. The political independence of British broadcasting is clearly rooted in this common ground. And the British press, though it is characterized by partisan differentiation, does tend to present itself as representing "the people" in general.

Canada would seem to lie between the United States and Britain, with greater ideological diversity than the United States. It clearly did have a tradition of Tory conservatism and socialism has been stronger in Canada than in the United States, though less than Britain (Horwitz 1966). In Ireland a strong liberal tradition combines with the central role of nationalism to produce a consensual political culture: The divisions between Irish political parties have their origins in the split over the Treaty with Britain in 1922 and are more symbolic than substantive in character. Lane and Ersson's polarization index is lower for Ireland than for any other European country (indeed it approaches zero). These moderate-to-low levels of political polarization, again, combine with media market conditions (perhaps particularly decisive in the case of Canada) to encourage a journalistic tradition of political neutrality.

## Individualized Pluralism

Political representation in the Liberal systems tends to be seen more in terms of the accountability of government to individual citizens than in terms of the involvement of organized social groups – parties and "peak associations" – in the political process. Again, the United States is the extreme case, of what we called in Chapter 2 *individualized pluralism*, with Britain tending a bit more toward continental European patterns and Canada and Ireland probably somewhere between those two. The United States does, of course, have many organized interest groups, and they play an important role in the political process. But they do not have strong legitimacy as political actors – they are referred to derisively as "special interests" – and they are not formally integrated into the political process in the way they often are especially in the Democratic Corporatist societies. Britain has a stronger tradition of corporatism as well as a stronger tradition of party government. At the same time, however, its interest groups are less unified and less integrated into the formal political process than in continental forms of democratic corporatism – like the United States it tends toward "free-for-all" pluralism in which "a multiplicity of interest groups . . . exert pressure on government in an uncoordinated and competitive manner" (Lijphart 1999: 16). British political culture also emphasizes the notion of the member of Parliament serving the public as a whole. This is consistent with the fact that media in the Liberal societies have presented themselves not as mouthpieces of social groups, but as providers of information for individual citizens, or as the voice of the "common man or woman." Like Parliament itself, the fourth estate is seen as standing "above" particular social interests.

Individualized pluralism is also consistent with the professional model of broadcast governance, which seeks to exclude organized social groups from the governance of public broadcasting. John Reith's views on the BBC's relation to organized social groups is a good illustration of the contrast between British political culture and those of Democratic Corporatist systems:

> If the TUC [Trade Unions Congress] was a proud exponent of collectivism, the BBC was an equally determined upholder of liberal individualism. . . . Reith . . . saw his own resistance to TUC "pressure" as part of a personal crusade against organizational pressures in general. The ethic of hostility to organizations pervaded his staff as well. In broad cultural terms, the BBC was far from

conservative.... [T]he list of pre-war broadcasters included many of the most fertile and imaginative speakers of the day.... Party or organization politics, on the other hand, were another matter. The BBC would only countenance reform in terms of which it approved: "non-partisan," advocated by speakers talking in an individual capacity... (Seaton and Pimlott 1987: 137).

In Chapter 4 we noted an interesting illustration of this difference between the Liberal and Democratic Corporatist countries: The fact that when local radio was introduced in the 1980s, Britain banned political parties and churches from holding licenses, while Scandinavian countries specifically encouraged such ownership (De Bens and Petersen 1992).

## MAJORITARIANISM

All four Liberal systems tend toward majoritarian politics. The British Westminster system, which Ireland and Canada essentially share, is of course the classic case of a majoritarian system. All except Ireland have single-member districts and "first-past the post" electoral systems, rather than proportional representation, all have relatively small numbers of political parties, and each system is dominated by two broad, catchall parties. In the United States, majoritarianism is modified by federalism (as it is in Canada as well) and by separation of powers, but these countries can still be described as predominantly majoritarian, at least on Lijphart's Executives/Parties Dimension. As with other aspects of the Liberal systems, majoritarianism implies the existence of a unitary public interest that in some sense stands above particular interests: parties compete not for a larger or smaller *share* of power, but to represent the nation as a whole.

In the specific case of broadcast regulation and governance, we argued in Chapter 4 that majoritarianism tends to result in movement toward the professional model, which is indeed the pattern we find in the Liberal countries. In a majoritarian system, power sharing is not an option: Public broadcasting must either be controlled outright by the majority or separated from political control. As we have seen in the case of Mediterranean countries that have essentially government-controlled systems, these lead to diminished credibility with audiences and sharp conflict between government and opposition, and such systems seem unlikely to survive the alternation of government and opposition beyond a short period of time. The alternative in a majoritarian system is professionalization, and this is the pattern that has developed in the long-standing democracies covered here, though it developed later in the younger Irish system, where separation from government control took place in 1961.

More generally, the experience of the Liberal countries suggests that the conception of politics inherent in majoritarianism reinforces the notion that media, like other political institutions, represent a unitary general interest of society, and in this sense majoritarianism tends to be associated with professionalization, separation of media from particular social groups, and the norm of objectivity.

## RATIONAL-LEGAL AUTHORITY

Party politics in both Britain and the United States was based on pervasive patronage systems through the middle of the nineteenth century. In each case, however, there was a strong movement by a "rationalizing bourgeoisie" (Shefter 1977) that resulted in a shift toward neutral, professionalized administration. These movements were motivated, in part, by a concern that a complex national market system could not operate without a predictable, rule-governed political and legal structure and an efficient administrative apparatus capable of providing a widely available infrastructure that would permit broad economic growth and dealing with the externalities of industrialization. Civil service reform dates from 1870 in Britain and a bit later in the United States. Both now have strong systems of neutral administration based on meritocratic recruitment and promotion and separation of the civil service from party politics (Heclo 1984; Rose 1984). Clientelist politics did survive in many city governments in the United States well into the twentieth century, but mostly faded at the national level. Ireland has long had a kind of clientelist system in the relation of politicians with their local constituencies (Carty 1981),[19] though it also has a civil service and judicial system very similar to those of Britain.

An autonomous legal system with considerable power is also an important part of rational-legal authority in Liberal countries. Autonomy of the legal system is in part built into the decentralized nature of common-law systems, which assign an important role both to juries and to law made through judicial precedent rather than legislation (the jury system always made it difficult for the state in Britain and its former colonies

---

[19] Carty notes that Ireland – similar to the Mediterranean countries – is a Catholic country that industrialized late and where a rural peasant culture survived well into the twentieth century.

to enforce controls on the press). In the United States, constitutionalism also contributes to the strength of the legal system, which, as Wiebe (1967) argues, was expanded in the same period of rationalization that produced civil service reform, as the judiciary stepped in, often with the consent of other branches of government, to provide the kind of broad national policy framework a particularistic party system could not provide. In the United States these developments were also accompanied by other reforms intended to reduce party-political control of public administration, including the phenomenon of the nonpartisan election – a bizarre notion to most Europeans – that is common in many local governments particularly in Western states and that leaves American voters poring through piles of campaign flyers trying to figure out the party affiliations of candidates for local office (Ireland also has nonpartisan elections in some localities).

The development of rational-legal authority has a number of consequences for the media system. First, it establishes a cultural context in which the notion of neutral professionalism is seen as both plausible and desirable. Journalistic professionalism began to develop more or less simultaneously with the professionalization of public administration and the growing authority of the courts. In the United States, journalists and newspaper owners were often deeply involved in the Progressive Movement that championed neutral public administration over party politics (Nord 2001) and the professional culture of American journalism is often seen as having its roots in Progressivism (Gans 1979).[20] As noted in the preceding text, Schudson (1978) attributes the rise of the objectivity norm in American journalism to this cultural context.

Second, it provides authoritative sources of information that can be considered as politically neutral and that provide the basis of the informational model of journalism that prevails most strongly in the United States. In the 1870s, for example, charges of electoral fraud – a common news story in postelection periods – were fought out in the political arena by the parties. No neutral sources of information existed; newspapers participated in the partisan battle, championing one side or the other. By the end of the century, most such disputes were moving from the political arena into the courts and newspapers were increasingly reporting in "objective" fashion the

---

[20] Ryfe (forthcoming) discusses in some detail the ambivalent relationship between journalistic professionalism and political culture of Progressivism.

arguments of the lawyers on both sides and the decisions of the courts. One of the differences Benson (2000: 438) found in his comparative study of U.S. and French coverage of immigration was a considerably greater prevalence of politically neutral sources (bureaucrats, judicial sources, and unaffiliated individuals) in U.S. news as opposed to French news.

Third, a strong regime of rational-legal authority reduces the tendency for media owners to form partisan alliances, and thus reduces the importance of the kind of "instrumentalization" that is particularly prevalent in the Mediterranean countries. As we have seen, one important initial effect of civil service reform was to cut off the kinds of patronage that connected newspaper owners and editors to partisan clientelist networks in the nineteenth century. More generally, because the Weberian state is based on universalistic rules that treat similarly situated actors equivalently, there is less incentive for business in general – including media owners – to be directly involved in party politics. This does not mean that business has no stake in political outcomes or does not try to influence them. Indeed, the legal and administrative rules in liberal societies often serve precisely to institutionalize the influence of business over public policy, though at times they may open avenues for other social groups to have an influence. Most analysts of the FCC, for example, have described it as generally protective of established broadcasting interests, though in the 1960s, when the courts expanded "standing rights" to intervene in regulatory decisions to a wider range of social groups, the process became more pluralistic (as it did in the 1980s, in a different way, when a greater range of business interests began to have a stake in telecommunication policy) (Horwitz 1989). The American state is considered to be highly penetrable by social interests, partly because of federalism and division of powers. Business is active in attempting to influence political decisions that affect its interests, mainly through lobbying and campaign contributions, and media corporations are no exception. In 1998, for example, media firms spent $28.5 million on lobbying, a bit more than securities and investment firms, though less than airlines, electric utilities, or defense contractors (Lewis 2000). The relationships between media companies and politicians generally cut across party lines, however, rather than taking the form of stable partisan alliances or clientelist networks. The FCC favored the broadcast networks in general, at least until the deregulation in the 1980s, not one network under Republicans and a different network under Democrats. The rules of administrative law by which an American regulatory agency operates would make it very difficult for such a pattern to emerge. It is thus not surprising that media owners in the United States are rarely active politicians. In Britain it has historically been a bit more common – Robert Maxwell, owner of the *Mirror*, was a member of Parliament – though much less so than in Mediterranean countries.

Finally, as the point about administrative law and the FCC suggests, rational-legal authority specifically underpins the professional model of broadcast governance and regulation. Thus broadcasting professionals at the BBC have a similar status as civil servants; like higher civil servants they are a self-regulating corps of professionals whose process of promotion and evaluation is insulated from political intervention and like civil servants they are restricted from outside political activities.

## CONCLUSION

The early consolidation of liberal institutions in Britain and its former colonies, together with a cluster of social and political characteristics related to this history – early industrialization, limited government, strong rational-legal authority, moderate and individualized pluralism and majoritarianism – are connected with a distinctive pattern of media-system characteristics. These include the strong development of a commercial press and its dominance over other forms of press organization, early development of commercial broadcasting, relatively strong professionalization of journalism, the development of a strong tradition of "fact-centered" reporting, and the strength of the objectivity norm. Media have been institutionally separate from political parties and other organized social groups, for the most part, since the late nineteenth century. And state intervention in the media sector has been limited by comparison with the Democratic Corporatist or Polarized Pluralist systems.

We have also seen that there are important differences among the four countries, enough that we should be careful about throwing around the notion of an "Anglo-American" media model too easily. The British and to a lesser extent the Irish and Canadian systems share important characteristics in common with continental European systems – particularly those of the Democratic Corporatist countries – both in their political institutions and cultures and in their media systems. This is manifested most obviously in the strength of public broadcasting and in the persistence of party-press parallelism in the British press. The latter also suggests that the common assumption that commercialization automatically leads to the development of politically neutral media is incorrect. There are, finally, many tensions or contradictions in the Liberal media systems: There is a tension between the fact of private ownership and the expectation that the media will serve the public good and a closely related tension between the ethics of journalistic professionalism and the pressures of commercialism. There is also a tension between the liberal tradition of press freedom and the pressures of government control in societies where the "national security state" is strong.

As we noted in the introduction to this volume, the Liberal Model is commonly taken around the world as the normative ideal. In some ways this is ironic, as the media in the Liberal countries have often and not altogether unjustly been subject to intense criticism within them. Only 15 percent of the British public, for example, say that they trust the press, the lowest level of trust by far in the European Union; the next lowest country is Greece, where, in 2001, 43 percent of the public trusted the print press. Britain was also last in the European Union in respect for journalists (European Commission 2001: B7, B81). In many ways global focus on the Liberal Model as an ideal is understandable. The Liberal countries have long and strong traditions of press freedom. They also have extremely successful cultural industries. The BBC can certainly be said to deserve its reputation as a model public broadcasting system, with both relatively strong political independence and a good balance of responsiveness to public taste and a public service orientation. And in the field of journalism, the Liberal countries clearly have been leaders in the development of a powerful form of information-based journalism. The big American news organizations remain in some ways particularly impressive as news-gathering institutions.

Other characteristics of the Liberal systems are clearly less attractive, however. They are not leaders in newspaper circulation, falling lower than most of the Democratic Corporatist countries. The British press is characterized by partisan imbalance and a fairly high degree of instrumentalization and the U.S. press by a lack of diversity. Both the British press and American television are characterized by high degrees of commercialization that strain journalistic ethics and raise questions about how well the public interest is served. And for all the attractiveness of the First Amendment tradition, one can certainly question whether the weakness of privacy protection, for instance, or the absence of regulation of campaign communication are ideals to be followed. The Liberal Model, as we shall see in the following chapter, is indeed the wave of the future, in the sense that most media systems are moving in important ways in its direction. It is also, however, a system that has developed within very specific social and political contexts, with tensions and contradictions like any other system we have examined, and the field of media studies would be best off abandoning the notion that it is the natural measure of all media systems.

# PART III

# The Future of the Three Models

# EIGHT

# The Forces and Limits of Homogenization

The preceding chapters have described three distinct media system models, and many variations among individual countries. It is clear, however, that the differences among these models, and in general the degree of variation among nation states, has diminished substantially over time. In 1970 the differences among the three groups of countries characterized by our three models were quite dramatic; a generation later, by the beginning of the twenty-first century, the differences have eroded to the point that it is reasonable to ask whether a single, global media model is displacing the national variation of the past, at least among the advanced capitalist democracies discussed in this book. Increasingly, as McQuail (1994) put it, an "international media culture" has become common to all the countries we studied. In this chapter we will focus on this process of convergence or homogenization, first summarizing the changes in European media systems that tend in this direction, then moving on to the questions of how the change can be explained, its limits and countertrends, and its implications for media theory, particularly focusing on the debate about "differentiation" raised in Chapter 4.

## THE TRIUMPH OF THE LIBERAL MODEL

The Liberal Model has clearly become increasingly dominant across Europe as well as North America – as it has, no doubt, across much of the world – its structures, practices, and values displacing, to a substantial degree, those of the other media systems we have explored in the previous chapters. Important qualifications need to be added to this claim; as we shall see later on, there are significant countertendencies that limit the spread of the Liberal Model in many countries or even transform that model itself. But in general, it is reasonable to summarize the changes in European media systems as a shift toward the Liberal Model that prevails in its purest form in North America.

Party newspapers and other media connected to organized social groups – media whose primary purposes were to mobilize collective action and to intervene in the public sphere and that once played a central role in both the Democratic Corporatist and Polarized Pluralist systems – have declined in favor of commercial papers whose purpose is to make a profit by delivering information and entertainment to individual consumers and the attention of consumers to advertisers. In Finland, to take one typical example from the Democratic Corporatist system, the market share of politically aligned papers declined from 70 percent in 1950 to a bit more than 50 percent in 1970, and less than 15 percent in 1995 (Salokangas 1999: 98). Polemical styles of writing have declined in favor of "Anglo-Saxon" practices of separation of news and commentary and emphasis on information, narrative, sensation, and entertainment, rather than ideas. A model of journalistic professionalism based on the principles of "objectivity" and political neutrality is increasingly dominant.

In the field of broadcasting, the "commercial deluge" of the 1980s–90s has displaced the public service monopolies of an earlier era in favor of mixed systems in which commercial media are increasingly dominant. Broadcasting has been transformed from a political and cultural institution in which market forces played a minimal role into an industry in which they are central, even for the remaining public broadcasters who must fight to maintain audience share. Styles of broadcast journalism have shifted from informational forms centered around the political party system toward the dramatized, personalized, and popularized style pioneered in the United States (Brants 1985, 1998). Telecommunications industries have similarly been liberalized.

Patterns of political communication have also been transformed, away from party-centered patterns rooted in the same organized social groups as the old newspaper system, toward media-centered patterns that involve marketing parties and their leaders to a mass of individual consumers. Political parties, like newspapers, tend to blur their ideological identities and connections to particular social groups and interests in order to appeal to as broad an electorate as possible – they tend to become "catchall" parties. Politics is increasingly "personalized" or "presidentialized," as individual party leaders become more central to a party's image and appeal. Politics is also "professionalized," as parties and campaigns are increasingly run not by rank-and-file party members and activists – who are decreasing in number – but by specialists in political marketing often drawn from the media world. Berlusconi's Forza Italia is the purest example of this pattern – a party originally built without members, in which political and media professionals play a key managing role, and that exists solely as a marketing vehicle for the individual leader; but the tendency is general, also illustrated by Tony Blair's New Labour, for example, or Gerhard Schröeder's Social Democrats. Politics, finally, is more media centered, as the mass media become more independent as agenda setters, and as the "retail" politics of rallies, activist campaigning, and, in some countries, patronage give way, above all, to television-centered campaigning directed at a mass audience. What is true of elections is also generally true of the communication involved in the governing process.

These changes could be summarized by saying that European media systems, which in both the Democratic Corporatist and Polarized Pluralist Models are closely connected with the political system, have become increasingly separated from political institutions. This "differentiation" of the media system from the political system – to use the language of structural-functionalist theory – is one of the principal characteristics of the Liberal Model and generally occurred in the North Atlantic countries much earlier than in continental Europe. "Differentiation" of the media from the political system does not mean that media lose all relationship with the political world. Indeed it is commonly argued that media have come to play an increasingly central role in the political process, as they have become more independent of parties and other political actors, and as the latter have lost much of their ability to shape the formation of culture and opinion. Differentiation means, instead, that the media system increasingly operates according to a distinctive logic of its own, displacing to a significant extent the logic of party politics and bargaining among organized social interests, to which it was once connected. As Mazzoleni (1987) has put it, a distinctive "media logic" has increasingly come to prevail over the "political logic" subordinated to the needs of parties and political leaders, that once strongly dominated the communication process in Europe.

There are important difficulties with the concept of differentiation as a means of understanding change in European media systems. These have to do, first of all, with an important ambiguity about the notion of a distinctive "media logic," an ambiguity about whether this is essentially a *professional* or a *commercial* logic. And, as we shall see at the end of this chapter, there are difficulties – endemic to the structural-functionalist perspective from which the notion of differentiation is taken – about how to account for social and political *power*. Nevertheless, the idea that media systems in Europe have become increasingly differentiated from the political system, and in this respect have come to resemble the Liberal Model, is a good way to begin the discussion of the process of convergence.

What forces propel the homogenization of media systems, or their convergence toward the Liberal Model? Most accounts focus on "Americanization" and modernization, which in turn are closely connected with globalization and commercialization (Negrine and Papathanassopoulos 1996; Swanson and Mancini 1996; Blumler and Gurevitch 2001). We will attempt to clarify how these four processes – along with a fifth related process we will call secularization – have affected European media systems and how they are related to one another. We will begin with Americanization, and, more generally, with an examination of exogenous forces of homogenization, that is, forces outside of European societies that have pushed in the direction of convergence with the Liberal Model. We will then turn to endogenous factors, including the "secularization" of European society and politics and the commercialization of European media. The last two sections of this chapter will focus on limits and countertendencies to the process of homogenization and on the concepts of modernization and differentiation.

## EXOGENOUS FORCES OF HOMOGENIZATION: AMERICANIZATION AND THE DEVELOPMENT OF A GLOBAL CULTURE OF JOURNALISM

The notion of "Americanization" has been a popular starting point for analysis of media system change in Europe since the end of the 1960s, when the cultural imperialism perspective focused attention on the cultural power of the United States and its impact on media systems around the world (Schiller 1969, 1973, 1976; Boyd-Barrett 1977; Tunstall 1977). It clearly captures an important part of the process. Not only have European media and communication processes come to resemble American patterns in important ways, but there is clear evidence of direct American influence, starting at least from the late nineteenth century, when American forms of journalism were widely imitated. This pattern continued in the interwar period with the growing strength of Hollywood and of U.S. news agencies, accelerated after World War II as the United States became the world's political, economic, and cultural hegemon (Schou 1992), and in some ways accelerated further still with the global shift to

neoliberalism in the 1980s. We generally associate Americanization today with the conservative influence of neoliberalism, but as a number of
scholars have pointed out (e.g., Gundle 2000) leftist culture in Europe
was also strongly affected by the "American dream."

The process described by the theory of cultural imperialism is essentially one of *outside* influence, involving the displacement of one culture
by another imported culture. We will argue that, in fact, the changes
in European media systems are driven above all by processes of change
*internal* to European society, though certainly connected with the integration of European countries into a global economy. Outside influences
are clearly an important part of the story, however, and we will begin
with a fuller discussion of American influence and the wider process
by which a global culture of journalism has developed – including the
influence of technology – before going on to the internal processes of
change that are commonly referred to as "modernization."

As we have seen in the preceding chapters, international influences
have been a part of media history from the beginning: Southern European
media were deeply influenced by the French, and intense interaction
among Northern European countries was central to the formation
of their media culture. The influence has moved in many directions.
German journalism, for example, has had significant influences on the
American media. Josef Pulitzer worked in the large German-language
press in the United States before starting his English-language newspaper industry, and German photojournalists moving to the United States
during the 1930s had important influences on American photojour-
nalism (as did European filmmakers in Hollywood at the same time).
American influence on European media, as we have noted, goes back
at least to the late nineteenth century. We saw in Chapter 5, for example, that the emerging French mass press was clearly influenced by the
American, with one of the most important papers, *Le Matin*, owned by
an American who said it would be a "unique newspaper . . . that will not
have any political opinions . . . a paper of worldwide and accurate telegraphic news" (Thogmartin 1998: 93–4). Schudson (1995) shows that
the practice of interviewing was spread to Europe by American reporters.

American influence clearly intensified following World War II, as
the United States became the dominant political and economic power.
It was not something that simply happened. As Blanchard (1986) has
shown it was in part the result of an organized effort led by the American
Society of Newspaper Editors (ASNE) and the U.S. Department of
State to promote the U.S. conception of press freedom and journalistic

professionalism around the world. The principal aim of the "free press crusade" was to reestablish democracy in European countries that had experienced fascism and to further the policy of containment against the political model of the Soviet bloc. One important manifestation was the influence exercised by the allies on the media systems of Germany, Austria, and Italy during the occupation. At the same time, the crusade reinforced the sphere of influence and market of American news agencies and mass media generally. The crusade Blanchard describes largely focused on international agencies – the United Nations and UNESCO – and in formal terms enjoyed limited success, in the sense that American proposals were often rejected. Nevertheless it contributed to the dissemination of liberal media principles that were indeed becoming increasingly hegemonic.

If the "free press crusade" of the 1940s and 1950s was connected with the political goals of the struggle against fascism and then the Cold War, other initiatives and associations were the result of the growing globalization of media industries. Markets had to be penetrated and expanded and there was a need for information on those markets, coordination of initiatives to develop them, and promotion of the conditions, including political and cultural conditions, suitable for their development. One association that pursued these ends was the World Association of Newspapers (WAN), which was founded in 1948 and now includes seventy-one national newspaper associations as members, and describes its goals as:

1. Defending and promoting press freedom and the economic independence of newspapers as an essential condition for that freedom.
2. Contributing to the development of newspaper publishing by fostering communications and contacts between newspaper executives from different regions and cultures.
3. Promoting cooperation between its member organizations, whether national, regional, or worldwide.

WAN pursues these objectives through training programs, conferences, publications, and lobbying with international organizations and governments. Its "Code of Newspaper Practices" approved in 1981 clearly reflects the influence of the Liberal conception of press freedom and professionalism, Point 1 reaffirming the basic principle of press freedom; Point 2 the need for impartiality; Point 3 the separation of news from commentary; down to Point 11 that reaffirms independence of the press from every outside pressure "whether by government, political parties, commercial interests or private individuals." The symbiosis between politics and journalism, which at one time represented constitutive characteristics of the Democratic Corporatist and Polarized Pluralist Models, is thus clearly rejected by the global commercial newspaper industry, in favor of an emerging liberal "common sense" of media freedom; to a large extent this is the "international media culture" described by McQuail (1994).

The role of WAN is a good illustration of Tunstall's (1977) argument that American influence on world media cultures resulted in part from the key role the United States played in the "production of knowledge." Formal journalism education and the academic study of communication were relatively strongly developed in the United States by the end of World War II. These institutions generated a coherent, readily exportable body of doctrine focusing around the liberal conception of press freedom and the idea of neutral professionalism that eventually had profound influence on media cultures in Europe and around the world.[1] The influence of *Four Theories of the Press* on media scholarship and education worldwide – an influence that, as we argue in Chapter 1, hindered even the theoretical conceptualization of other media systems – is a good illustration of Tunstall's point. Barnhurst and Nerone (2001: 276) in an analysis of the Americanization of newspaper design, similarly found that "U.S. consultants spread their design sensibility by touting modernist form as an efficient conveyor of local journalism and advertising. To bolster their argument, they could claim the ostensibly neutral support of legibility research and psychological principles." (Barnhurst and Nerone further argue that U.S. design techniques embodied a particular, liberal ideology about the role of the newspaper as an institution of the market more than of the political world.)

There is not a lot of systematic research, particularly of a comparative nature, on journalism education. But it does seem likely that American models of journalistic education have played an important role in changing cultures of journalism worldwide. There is a significant trend in the direction of a greater role for formal training in journalism. This is significant in itself – even apart from the content of that education – in the sense that the development of a distinct education track for journalists almost inevitably would seem to promote the development of a culture of journalism distinct from, among other things, party politics.

---

[1] Drake and Nicolaidis (1992) similarly show how the transformation of international telecommunications regimes in the 1980s resulted from the production by experts in western countries of new ways of understanding telecommunication.

We think it is likely, moreover, that the content of journalism education stresses exactly the conception of the media's role emphasized by WAN.[2] Splichal and Sparks (1994) seem to share this opinion, concluding their research on journalism education in twenty-two countries by stressing that, with some qualifications, journalism is moving from craft to profession thanks to the diffusion of common educational practices. Weaver (1998), in another work based on surveys of journalists, also stresses the importance of formal education in creating a global journalistic culture.

The example of WAN – which was heavily influenced by American newspaper publishers in its early years, but became very much an international institution – also illustrates another significant force in the development of a global media culture, one that by now has become much broader than "Americanization," namely the intensity of interaction among journalists worldwide. This takes place in many contexts. WAN, which is based in Paris, organizes international gatherings of journalists and other media personnel, and many other organizations play a similar role, including the European Journalism Training Association established by many European schools and institutes of journalism. Journalists also interact intensively in covering world events or international institutions (Hallin and Mancini 1994). This kind of interaction does not produce homogenization automatically; research on journalists covering EU institutions in Brussels has stressed the extent to which their reporting remains dominated by national political agendas.[3] But it does lead to diffusion of techniques, practices, and values, in the same way that national journalistic cultures began to develop as journalists assembled to cover emerging national political institutions. This interaction also takes place in a more mediated way through the global flow of information. Journalists are heavy consumers of global media, many of them based in the United States and Britain, both because these represent large powerful media organizations and because they are in English – the international *Herald-Tribune*,[4] the *Financial Times* and other representatives

---

[2] When we presented an early version of our research at the journalism school at the University of Dortmund, our host, Professor Gerd Kopper, stressed that the liberal conception of neutral professionalism was exactly what the students there were taught.

[3] Much of this research is summarized in Schlesinger (1999). Schlesinger notes that Europeanized news coverage is produced mainly for a highly elite audience, while the media that address the mass public follow national political agendas.

[4] Rieffel (1984: 114) notes the influence of the *Herald-Tribune* on French journalists. An interesting recent example of U.S. influence is the fact the *Le Monde* has begun providing its readers a version of *The New York Times* as a supplement.

of the global business press,[5] CNN, and the BBC World Service, both radio and TV. Journalists also make heavy use of international news agencies, including wire services and global TV agencies such as Reuters TV and Worldwide Television News. The global sharing of news tends to increase both with technology, as new information technology makes it increasingly easy for journalists to access information from across the world at the touch of a button, and with commercialization, as priority is placed on low-cost news gathering. All of this tends to promote common conceptions of the journalist's role – the influence of Watergate mythology on journalism worldwide is a perfect example – and common styles of news presentation.

We have focused here on journalism, but similar processes have been at work in other areas of media and communication practice. Blumler and Gurevitch (2001: 400; see also Plasser 2000), for example, note that in the 1996 and 1997 election campaigns "experts of the British Labour Party and the Clinton team observed each other in action and shared their tactical expertise. . . ."

## THE ROLE OF TECHNOLOGY

Technology can be said to be another "outside" force toward homogenization. In one of the most interesting chapters of *The Printing Revolution in Early Modern Europe*, Elizabeth Eisenstein (1983), building on an idea originally stressed by McLuhan, points out how the invention of the printing press produced a process of standardization, which over the next few centuries affected many aspects of culture and society. Writing styles and typefaces, as well as many social practices that were addressed in the content of books (Eisenstein uses fashion as an

---

[5] The business press is the most global sector of the media. This is not surprising because capital is globalized in a way government or other spheres of social life covered by the news media are not. The world business press is also clearly dominated by the style of journalism that prevails in the liberal countries. This is in part because so many key players are based in the liberal countries – the *Financial Times*, Dow Jones, Reuters, Bloomberg. It is probably also connected with the fact that business journalism has always been largely informational in character, going back to the earliest days of the press. This is to a large extent the function of the press for market participants, to provide the information they need to make decisions. Business papers do also, of course, serve to advance ideas – promoting neoliberalism, for example – and as a forum for debate over political issues. But because the business community – like the countries of the Liberal Model – is characterized by a high degree of consensus on basic ideological assumptions, it is easy for "objective" styles of presentation to become dominant.

example) tended to spread to every country where the printing industry was diffused. Eisenstein's analysis reminds us that every technological innovation eventually leads to wide-ranging adaptations by individuals and social institutions. People tend to assume the behavior, forms, structures, and, in this case, communication procedures that are associated with the new technology, and this influence often produces common cultures of practice across different social contexts. Golding (1977: 304), in an analysis of the spread of western practices of journalistic professionalism to the developing world, made a similar point: "the transfer of professionalism runs parallel to the transfer of technology which can be alternatively understood as the problem of technological dependence."

The influence of technology cannot be separated from the social context in which technologies are adopted and implemented, of course, and we should not exaggerate the standardizing effects of technologies of mass communication. The printing press, for example, certainly diffused many communication practices. But as we have seen, quite different forms of print media developed in the different political contexts we have studied here, and their disappearance clearly owes much more to economic and sociopolitical forces than to any change in print media technology. Nevertheless, there is no doubt that the process of homogenization is also connected with technological innovation. Changes in television technology, for one thing, clearly played an important role in disrupting the existing media structure by facilitating cross-national broadcasting and the multiplication of channels, developments whose significance we will explore further in subsequent pages. In many ways technology has increased the ease by which media content can be shared across national boundaries, with journalists around the world having access on their computer screens to the same sets of words and images. News agencies, of course, have played this role for some time, providing news written in a single style, produced to a single set of news-gathering practices. The dominant news agencies of the twentieth century have been the British ones, and they have played an extremely important role in spreading the Liberal Model of journalism. Another more recent example would be a service similar to Evelina produced by European Broadcasting Union (EBU) that provides images, filmed according to a common standard and supplied to every European user. CNN is obviously another powerful instrument for the spreading of common procedures and skills, as is the Internet.

It is likely that the growth of professional education in journalism also is connected with technological change. As the written word is increasingly displaced by multimedia forms of presentation, the boundaries between production and journalistic labor become blurred, and technology comes to play an increasingly central role in journalistic practice. In this context it matters less what a journalist has to say about politics than whether she or he can create a compelling television narrative or an appealing visual display on a computer screen. This creates a need for specialized training of journalists, and probably tends to create a global culture of technical expertise that is relatively separate from national political cultures. Similar processes also take place in other areas of political communication, as, for example, the use of computers in political campaigning similarly produces a need for standardized technical expertise. The homogenization produced by technological innovation mainly involves younger professionals who are more exposed to innovations and more likely to have received specialized training focused on their use. This may be one reason generation gaps often exist between older journalists whose professional concerns revolve more around the political lines of their news organizations, and younger ones more concerned with "strictly professional" characteristics of their jobs (e.g., Ortega and Humanos 2000: 158).

## ENDOGENOUS FORCES OF CHANGE: "MODERNIZATION," SECULARIZATION, AND COMMERCIALIZATION

External influences on European media systems clearly have played an important role. As we have tried to show in the preceding chapters, however, the media systems that evolved in Europe – quite different in many ways from North American media systems – were deeply rooted in particular political histories, structures, and cultures. It is not plausible that they would have been transformed without significant changes in politics and society. European media professionals did not immediately or directly adopt American forms. To some extent, in fact, the *ideology* of the Liberal media system spread without actually changing journalistic or other media *practices*. We have always been struck by how common it is, in Southern Europe particularly, for journalists to express allegiance to the global notion of "objectivity," while they practice journalism in a way that is very much at odds with U.S. or British notions of political neutrality. Papathanassopoulos's (2001) analysis of the transformation of Greek journalism is consistent with this observation. The deeper penetration of liberal media practices has only occurred as structural transformation of European media and political systems has made these practices increasingly relevant and appropriate, and must be understood in the context of these deeper changes. We turn now, therefore, to the fundamental processes of internal change at work in European media systems.

One of the most common ways to understand these deeper processes of change is in terms of "modernization." In the 1963 classic *Communications and Political Development*, Pye wrote:

> in any society only a small fraction of political communication originates from the political actors themselves, and this proportion tends to decrease with modernization as increasing numbers of participants without power join the communications process. In a fundamental sense modernization involves the emergence of a professional class of communicators.... The emergence of professionalized communicators is . . . related to the development of an objective, analytical and non-partisan view of politics (78; see also Fagen 1966).

Pye's view is connected with structural-functionalism, which argues that societies tend to evolve toward greater functional specialization among social institutions, and greater differentiation of those institutions from one another, in terms of their norms, practices, and symbolic identities. For Parsons and other structural-functionalists, professionalization is central to this process. The notion of differentiation clearly does capture an important part of the change in European media systems. And if modernity involves, as Giddens (1990: 21) puts it, the "disembedding" or "'lifting out' of social relations from local contexts of interaction and their restructuring across indefinite spans of time-space," it makes some sense to say that media systems in Europe have become increasingly "modernized." At the same time, the concept of modernization as it is commonly understood is problematic in many ways: not only does it carry dubious normative assumptions about the universal superiority of a particular model, there are also real problems with describing change in media systems in the countries covered here in terms of a unilinear shift toward greater differentiation, problems that we will explore in detail in the final sections of this chapter. We propose therefore to start with the more neutral and specific concepts of secularization and commercialization.

## MASS MEDIA AND SECULARIZATION

The notion of secularization has been fundamental to understanding modernity since Marx, Weber, and Durkheim. What we mean by it here is the separation of citizens from attachments to religious and ideological "faiths," and the decline of institutions based on these faiths that once structured wide parts of European social life. Just as the Church is no longer able to control the socialization or behavior of populations now attracted to values and institutions outside the field of faith, so parties, trade unions, and other institutions that structured the political order Lipset and Rokkan (1967) once described as essentially "frozen," can no longer hegemonize the citizen's community life. The European political order was once organized around social institutions rooted in ideological commitments based on broad social divisions, especially those of social class and religion. The ties of individuals to these groups was central both to their identity and to their material well-being. These institutions also had broad functions in structuring the public sphere, creating and circulating cultural and political symbols, and organizing the participation of citizens in the life of the community. By secularization we mean the decline of a political and social order based on these institutions, and its replacement by a more fragmented and individualized society. With the general decline of parties, trade unions, churches, and similar institutions, the mass media, along with many other socialization agencies, become more autonomous of them, and begin to take over many of the functions they once performed.

The "depillarization" of Dutch society is perhaps the classic example of this change. Pillarization, as we saw in Chapter 6, was the separation of the population into organized subcommunities based on religious or political persuasion. The Dutch pillars maintained a wide variety of institutions – schools, hospitals, social clubs, welfare organizations, and mass media – and carried out a wide range of social functions, including the production of symbolic meaning, the "aggregation of interests" and organization of political decision making, the organization of leisure time, the provision of social welfare, and more (Lijphart 1968, 1977, 1999; Lorwin 1971; Nieuwenhuis 1992). In the field of communication, an individual could spend his or her entire life within a flow of representations structured by the institutions of a single pillar. By the 1970s, this structure had broken down, and "the average Dutch citizen had become primarily an individual consumer rather than a follower of a particular religious or political sector" (Nieuwenhuis 1992: 207).

A similar process has taken place in Italy, where two main political subcultures, the Catholic and the Communist, based on deeply rooted religious and political faiths, simultaneously represented the main instruments of political power and the most important socialization agencies in the country. The Catholic subculture was essentially, though not exclusively, linked to the structures of the Catholic Church, its charity organizations, and interpersonal networks. The Christian Democratic party was its political arm. The Communist subculture was built out of the first trade unions and workers' solidarity organizations. Associated with the Communist Party were many other organizations active in different fields: social solidarity, sport, culture, leisure, education, media, and so on. (Galli 1968; Sani 1980; Trigilia 1981; Mannheimer and Sani 1987). In Italy as in the Netherlands – though more recently – these two subcultures and their organizations have declined in importance. The birth and the victory of Berlusconi's Forza Italia, relying almost completely on mass media for its connections with the electorate, is an excellent illustration of this decline – and of the tendency for media correspondingly to expand their social role.

In Scandinavia agrarian, conservative, liberal, and socialist parties, together with trade unions, once pervaded many fields of society, but have substantially declined. One interesting illustration of the shift "from a collectivist to an individualist political culture," and its effect on journalism, can be found in a content analysis of Swedish news media from 1925 to 1987 (Ekecrantz 1997: 408), which found the use of the term *we* was more frequent than the use of the term *I* in news discourse in earlier decades, with the relationship reversed by the 1980s. Similar stories can be told, with many local variations, about most of the countries covered in this book.

The decline of political parties is closely related to this process of "secularization," and is particularly important to understanding change in media systems. There is a large literature on the "decline of party," and some debate about whether, or in what sense, it has actually taken place. Some argue that parties have not so much declined as "modernized" and narrowed in their functions, that they are actually more effective in mobilizing voters at election time now that they have been professionalized and separated from their connections with institutions such as trade unions. Some argue that rather than speaking of "party decline" in general we need to look specifically at the decline of the traditional "mass parties" that were powerful in Europe through much of the twentieth century, as well as in the United States in an earlier form and an earlier period (Panebianco 1988; Mair 1990; Katz and Mair 1994). Mass parties served as central instruments for the representation and defense of social and economic interests, for "aggregating interests" and forming consensus, and served as important structures of communication through the interpersonal networks on which their organizations were built. Mass parties, among their other functions, were responsible for the production of social representations and imagery. In the service of this function they owned and controlled newspapers, and journalists working within these newspapers had the duty of spreading and defending the ideas of the party. Journalists' practices of information gathering, writing, and interacting with readers were rooted to a significant degree in the ideological framework and party-centered social network to which they belonged. Being at the same time both journalists and political figures, they acted according to models of practice shaped by specific political cultures that varied from country to country – hence the substantial differences we have found among national media systems.

The decline of the mass party, ideologically identified and rooted in distinct social groups, and its replacement by the "catchall" or "electoral-professional party" oriented not primarily toward the representation of groups or ideologies but toward the conquest of electoral market share, has been widely documented in political science (Kirchheimer 1966; Panebianco 1988). The stable psychological and sociological bonds that once existed between parties and citizens have been weakened in this transformation. Party membership has declined (as have church and trade union membership). So has party loyalty, measured either by identification with political parties or by partisan consistency in electoral behavior, at least in many cases. Voting turnout has declined in many countries. "When partisanship was closely tied to class and religion, the conjoint of social and political identifications provided a very strong incentive for party identifiers to turn out. These linkages, however, have withered in recent years . . ." (Dalton and Wattenberg 2000: 66). The "grassroots" political organizations that once tied parties to citizens have atrophied, while professional staffs concerned with media and marketing have grown. Individual leaders have become increasingly important to the appeal of parties, while ideology and group loyalties have become less so.

The weakening of mass political parties is in turn connected with a wider process of social change, which involves the weakening or fragmentation of the social and economic cleavages on which mass parties were built (Panebianco 1988). The clear lines of social division stressed originally in Marxist theory and later in the comparative politics literature of the post–World War II period have declined, some argue, to the vanishing point, with the result that mass parties have lost their social basis. A proliferation of social groups with specific economic needs has grown in importance, making the distinctions between owners and workers, landowners and peasants, less relevant. One important factor in this change is the fact that the manufacturing industries in which traditional working-class organizations were rooted have declined, displaced by the growing service sector. Perhaps most fundamentally, European economies have expanded and it seems likely that increased affluence and the growth of the consumer society resulted in an increasing emphasis on individual economic success rather than political defense of group interests. A different, though not necessarily incompatible interpretation of the effect of economic growth is Ingelhart's (1977) argument that affluence and the stabilization of liberal democracy led to the rise of "post-materialist values." This change in political culture is seen as undercutting the ideological divisions on which the old party system was based and making individuals increasingly unwilling to defer to the leadership of traditional organizations. It may in turn be related to the rise of new social movements raising issues that cut across traditional party lines.

These same factors cited by Ingelhart – affluence and the consolidation of parliamentary democracy within the context of a capitalist economy – may also be responsible for a marked decline in ideological polarization. There is evidence that the ideological differences between political parties has decreased (Mair 1997), though we will see later that there also may be countertrends, and it cannot necessarily be assumed that such differences will continue decreasing indefinitely. This is connected with the acceptance of the broad outlines of the welfare state by conservative parties and of capitalism and liberal democracy by the parties of the left. An important symbol of the shift would be the "historic compromise" that incorporated the Communist Party into the division of political power in Italy in the 1970s. The literature on "plural" societies such as the Netherlands, where the various subcultures had separate institutions at the grassroots level, often notes that the leaderships of these communities became accustomed to cooperation and compromise at the level of national state institutions.

Some accounts of change in European political systems also point to increased education, which might result in voters seeking information independently rather than relying on the leadership of political parties.

In some accounts this is connected with a shift from voting based on party and group loyalty to issue-based voting. Some also mention that patronage systems have declined, in part because of economic integration, particularly with the formation of the European Monetary Union, and the pressures it puts on government budgets, undercutting the ability of parties to provide material incentives to their active supporters (Kitschelt 2000; Papathanassopoulos 2000). The rise of new demographic groups as a result of immigration may also have weakened the old order, both because the new populations are not integrated into traditional group-based structures and because tensions over immigration lead to the defection of traditional adherents.

Finally, many have argued that globalization and economic integration have weakened political parties by shifting the locus of decision making away from the national political spheres that the parties dominated. As Beck (2000) puts it, the nation state was the "container" for policy decisions as well as other social processes that affected citizens across most areas of life. The nation state has progressively lost this role of "container," and many of the decisions affecting its citizens are now taken at a supranational level, removing power from the state and therefore from political parties, organizations, and interest groups that represent the interests of the citizens. The constraints of the emerging global economic regime tend to force parties to abandon distinct policy positions that once defined their identities, and also hinders their ability to deliver benefits to their constituents. These constraints also specifically force the harmonization of media policy in many cases, often disrupting the previously existing relations between the state, political parties, and the media. Thus Canada feels pressure to abandon protection of national cultural industries and Scandinavia feels pressure to liberalize regulations on advertising. Clientelist patterns of political alliance in Spain, meanwhile, are disrupted by the fact that companies can appeal to Brussels to overturn regulatory decisions made in Madrid.

## MEDIA SYSTEM CHANGE: CAUSE OR EFFECT

The changes in European media systems outlined at the beginning of this chapter – particularly the shift toward catchall media, models of journalistic professionalism based on political neutrality, and a shift toward media-oriented forms of political communication – are surely related to this process of secularization. But which is the tail and which is the dog? Is media system change simply one result of these changes in society and politics, or might it play some independent role? To a large extent, media system change is certainly a result of the deeply rooted processes summarized previously, which have undercut the social basis of mass parties and of group solidarity and of a media system connected with them. It is clearly also true, however, that processes of change internal to the media system have been at work and it is quite plausible that changes in European media systems have contributed to the process of secularization. It is common in the literature on decline of political parties in Europe to point to the media system as one key source of change:

> ... [N]ew technologies and ... changes in the mass media ... have enabled party leaders to appeal directly to voters and thereby undermined the need for organizational networks ... (Mair 1997: 39).

> Increasingly ... media have taken over [information and oversight functions] because they are considered unbiased providers of information and because electronic media have created more convenient and pervasive delivery systems.... The growing availability of political information through the media has reduced the costs of making informed decisions (Flanagan and Dalton 1990: 240–2).

> The mass media are assuming many of the information functions that political parties once controlled. Instead of learning about an election at a campaign rally or from party canvassers, the mass media have become the primary source of campaign information. Furthermore, the political parties have apparently changed their behavior in response to the expansion of mass media. There has been a tendency for political parties to decrease their investments in neighborhood canvassing, rallies, and other direct contact activities, and devote more attention to campaigning through the media (Dalton and Wattenberg 2000: 11–12).

The element that emerges most strongly in these accounts is the rise of electronic media, which is considered to have undercut the role of political parties, and presumably also would have undercut the role of churches, trade unions, and other institutions of socialization. As we have seen in the preceding chapters, however, the electronic media were organized originally in Europe under political authority, and in most systems political parties had considerable influence on broadcasting, as did "socially relevant groups" in some systems, most notably the German.

One might, therefore, have expected electronic media to *reinforce* rather than to undercut the traditional role of political parties and organized social groups. Why did this not occur?

One account of the impact of television is provided by Wigbold (1979), focusing on the particularly interesting Dutch case. Broadcasting was organized in the Netherlands following the pillarized model that applied to the press, education, and other cultural institutions. Each of the different communities of Dutch society had a separate broadcasting organization, just as they had traditionally had separate schools and newspapers. One might have thought that by extending their reach to a powerful new medium, the pillars would have become even more entrenched in Dutch society. Nevertheless, depillarization clearly did coincide historically with the rise of television. Wigbold makes the argument that Dutch television "destroyed its own foundations, rooted as they were in the society [it] helped to change" (230).

His argument has three parts. First, he argues that despite the existence of separate broadcasting organizations, television broke down the separateness of the pillars:

Television was bound to have a tremendous influence in a country where not only the doors of the living room were closed to strangers but also the doors of schoolrooms, union meetings, youth hostels, football grounds and dancing schools. . . . It confronted the masses with views, ideas and opinions from which they had been isolated. . . . [T]here was no way out, no hiding place, except by the difficult expedient of switching the set off. Television viewers could not even switch to a second channel, because there wasn't one. . . . Catholics discovered that Socialists were not the dangerous atheists they had been warned about, Liberals had to conclude that orthodox Protestants were not the bigots they were supposed to be (201).

Second, he argues that television journalists shifted substantially in the early 1960s toward a more independent and critical relationship with the leaders of established institutions, to whom they had previously deferred.

Third, a new broadcasting organization (TROS), which was the broadcasting equivalent of the catchall party, was founded at the end of the 1960s: originating from a pirate broadcaster, it provided light entertainment and "was the very negation of the broadcasting system based . . . on giving broadcast time to groups that had something to say" (225).[6] TROS acted as a strong force toward homogenization.

The Dutch case is unique in many ways, of course. Still, it seems likely that each of these factors had close parallels across most of Europe: the role of *television as a common ground*, the development of *critical journalism*, and *commercialization*. These tendencies not only are common to broadcasting across Europe, but are closely related to changes in the print press, changes that to some degree reflect the impact of television on the latter. We shall discuss in this section the first two topics: television as a common ground and the journalist as a "critical expert," and take up in the following section the crucial and complex topic of commercialization.

### TELEVISION AS COMMON GROUND

Across Europe, broadcasting was organized under political authority and often incorporated principles of proportional representation drawn from the political world. Nevertheless, it is quite plausible that it served as a social and political common ground and had some role in weakening separate ideological subcultures. It was highly centralized, with one to three channels (of television and of radio) in most of the post–World War II period. Most programming was aimed at the entire public, regardless of group boundaries. The production of news was generally bound by the principles of political neutrality and internal pluralism, which separated broadcast journalism from traditions of partisan commentary common in the print press (in the Dutch case, while the pillarized broadcasting organizations produced public affairs broadcasts, news, like sports, was produced by the umbrella organization NOS). Television entertainment, meanwhile, provided a common set of cultural references, whose impact on political culture would be very difficult to document, but certainly might have been quite significant.

Even aside from the content of broadcast programming, the fact that broadcast media developed as "catchall" media, capable of delivering messages across ideological and group boundaries, may have had important political effects, as some of the accounts of the decline of party quoted in the preceding text suggest: it made it possible for political parties to appeal to citizens outside their established social base in a

---

[6] Rules on the allocation of broadcast slots had also been changed in 1965 to emphasize the number of dues-paying members each broadcast organization had, increasing the importance of building an audience and decreasing the importance of pillar affiliation (Van der Eijk 2000: 311).

very efficient manner, and thus may have encouraged both the growth of catchall parties and the atrophy of traditional means of communication that were tied to social networks in particular subcommunities. It should also be kept in mind that television was not the only "catchall" medium to expand in this period, particularly in the Democratic Corporatist and Liberal countries. Catchall commercial newspapers were also increasingly central to the communication process. It could be said that in general, the development of the media in the twentieth century led to an increased flow of culture and information across group boundaries, reducing the dependence of citizens on exclusive sources within their particular subcommunities.

## "CRITICAL EXPERTISE" IN JOURNALISM

The diffusion of television also coincided with the development of a new journalistic culture that Padioleau (1985), in a comparative study of *Le Monde* and *The Washington Post*, termed a culture of "critical expertise." In both Western Europe and North America (Hallin 1992), there was a significant shift in the 1960s and 1970s from a form of journalism that was relatively deferential toward established elites and institutions, toward a relatively more active, independent form of journalism This shift took place both in electronic and in print media. In the case of Swedish television, for example, Djerf-Pierre (2000; see also Ekecrantz 1997; Olsson 2002) writes:

> The journalist culture of 1965–1985 embraced a new ideal of news journalism, that of critical scrutiny. The dominant approach was now oriented toward exerting influence, both *vis-à-vis* institutions and the public at large. . . . [J]ournalists sought to bridge information gaps in society and to equip their audiences for active citizenship and democratic participation. . . . Journalists also had the ambition to scrutinize the actions of policy makers and to influence both public debate on social and political issues and the policies made by public institutions (254).

This shift varied in form and extent, but seems to have been quite generalized across national boundaries in the countries of all of our three models. It involved the creation of a journalistic discourse that was distinct from the discourse of parties and politicians, a conception of the media as a collective watchdog of public power (Djerf-Pierre and Weibull 2000) and a conception of the journalist as representative of a generalized public opinion that cuts across the lines of political parties and social groups. Critical professionals, as Neveu (2002) puts it, "[S]pot blunders in strategy, mistakes in governing, from an in-depth knowledge of issues. They question politicians in the name of public opinion and its requests – identified 'objectively' by the polls – or in the name of suprapolitical values such as morality, modernity or the European spirit."

Why did this change take place? Surely it was to a significant extent rooted in the broader social and political changes discussed previously. If, for example, affluence, political stability, and increasing educational levels led to a general cultural shift toward "postmaterialist" value of participation and free expression, the rise of critical expertise in journalism might be seen as one effect of this deeper social change. It might be noted that this change was not reflected only in journalism, but also in popular culture more generally. It is reflected, for example, in the growth of political satire on television, in the form of shows such as *That Was the Week that Was* and *Monty Python's Flying Circus* in Britain and *The Smothers Brothers Show* in the United States, comedy programs that relied heavily on political humor. If catchall parties were already being formed in the 1950s – Kirchheimer noted their rise in 1966 – the discourse of a general public opinion made up of individualized voters committed to "suprapolitical" values, which would be crucial to the perspective of critical professionalism in journalism, may predate the latter.[7]

Even if the rise of critical professionalism in the media was in part an effect or reflection of other social forces, however, it seems likely that at some point it began to accelerate and amplify them. It is also possible that a number of factors internal to the media system contributed to the shift in the political role of journalism, and thus in turn to the secularization of European society and to the diminution of differences among political systems. These internal factors include:

1. Increased educational levels of journalists, leading to more sophisticated forms of analysis, in part by the incorporation into journalism of critical perspectives from the social sciences and humanities.
2. Increased size of news organizations, leading to greater specialization and greater resources for news gathering and news processing.

---

[7] Marchetti (2000: 31) notes in a discussion of the rise of "investigative reporting" in France: "... the depoliticization of the stakes of the political field induced by the 'neoliberal alignment,' particularly of the socialist party ... contributed to modifying the conditions of political struggle. The weakening of traditional left/right oppositions, the important fact of homogenization of political personnel trained by the schools of power, has shifted the stakes of political struggle toward more strictly moral stakes. ..."

3. Internal development of the growing professional community of journalism, which increasingly develops its own standards of practice.

4. Development of new technologies of information processing that increase the power of journalists as information producers. This includes the visual techniques of television as well as many developments in printing and in information technology. One interesting example would be polling: Neveu (2002) argues that opinion polling gave journalists increased authority to question public officials, whose claims to represent the public they could independently assess.

5. Increased prestige of journalists, related to all these factors, to the central position large media organizations came to occupy in the general process of social communication, and probably also to the image of catchall media as representative of the public as a whole. Thus Papathanassopoulos (2001: 512) argues for the Greek case (a bit different, to be sure, because, as we shall see, partisan attachments do survive more strongly in Greece, as in much of Southern Europe):

> One can say that the commercialization and the rapid development of the Greek media market have increased the social and professional status of Greek journalists. In fact, television journalists and especially television news anchorpersons have become public figures. They have adopted the role of authorities, i.e. they present their views and interpret social and political reality. They do this by presenting themselves both as professionals with the right to make judgements and as representatives of the people. By taking on both these roles, they increase their public profile and authority.

## COMMERCIALIZATION

The most powerful force for homogenization of media systems, we believe, is commercialization that has transformed both print and electronic media in Europe. In this section we will describe the process and outline the principle causes of commercialization of European media, and in the following section we will examine its consequences for the social and political role of the media. In the case of print media the later part of the twentieth century is characterized by a decline of the party press (in some countries this was already under way by the 1950s, in others, Italy and France most clearly, the party press revived after World War II, then began to decline), an increasing dominance of "omnibus" commercial newspapers, and, in consequence, a separation of newspapers from their earlier rooting in the world of politics. To some degree, this shift was no doubt a result of the broader process of secularization, as readers became less committed politically and less inclined to choose a newspaper on the basis of its political orientation. But it is also clear that the internal development of newspaper markets pushed strongly in this direction. Indeed market forces were beginning to put pressure on the party press early in the twentieth century, when party allegiance was still strongly entrenched in the political culture. The number of newspapers in Sweden, for example, peaked in 1920 (Picard 1988: 18). From that point on, just as in the North American case we explored in Chapter 7, there was a trend toward concentration in newspaper markets, with the result that newspapers increasingly attempted to expand their markets by appealing across traditional group and ideological boundaries. Highly capitalized, advertising-funded commercial papers tended to drive less wealthy, politically oriented papers out of the market, eventually leading to an almost complete eclipse of the party press that dominated the media in these countries for most of the twentieth century.

Even more dramatic than the changes in the print press, however, is the transformation of European broadcasting from an almost purely public service system in 1970 to a system in which commercial broadcasting is increasingly dominant. The "commercial deluge," as it is commonly called, began in Italy, following a 1976 decision of the Italian Supreme Court that invalidated the legal monopoly of public broadcasting allowing private stations to broadcast within local areas. (Even earlier, TROS and Veronica, the latter originating from a pirate radio station and oriented toward the youth culture, had begun operating in the Netherlands, within the public service structure but by a very different logic.) By 1990, most of the rest of Europe had introduced commercial broadcasting and by the end of the century only Austria, Ireland, and Switzerland had no significant commercial television.[8] In most countries (see Table 2.4) commercial broadcasting had a majority of the audience and competition for audience had significantly transformed public broadcasting

---

[8] All are small countries next to large countries with the same language. Foreign television has a large audience in all of them – a majority of the audience in the Swiss case – and the market has generally been considered too small, given this competition, to sustain domestic commercial broadcasters at the national level.

as well, forcing it to adopt much of the logic of the commercial system.

Beyond the changes in the social structure that we have already outlined, many forces combined to produce this change in the European broadcasting system. In the first place, competing forms of broadcasting emerged, and these siphoned audiences away from the public broadcasters, undercut their legitimacy, and contributed to a change in the perception of media programming, which with the multiplication of channels – by one count a shift from 35 channels in 1975 to 150 in 1994 (Weymouth and Lamizet 1996: 24) – came to seem less like a social institution, a public good provided for and shared by everyone in society, and more like a commodity that could be chosen by individual consumers. The development of the VCR no doubt also contributed to this change of consciousness. The earliest alternative forms of broadcasting were pirate radio stations, the first of which began broadcasting from ships off the coast of Scandinavia in the late 1950s. These were advertising funded and to some degree their popularity was fueled by the growth of a distinct – and globalized – youth culture. In both these characteristics they are clearly connected with the larger cultural trend toward global consumer culture. Pirate radio proliferated substantially in many countries during the 1970s, when it was often connected not only with youth culture but also with the new social movements of that era. The efforts of public broadcasting to suppress pirate radio undercut their image as a champion of political pluralism. Private radio and television stations based in Luxembourg that started broadcasting to neighboring countries in French, German, Italian, and Dutch also undercut public service monopolies, as did Radio Monte Carlo and Radio Capodistria (based in Croatia), which revolutionized Italian radio in the 1970s. The phenomenon of transborder broadcasting, with its tendency to undercut the connection between broadcasting institutions and national political systems, expanded in the 1980s with the growth of cable and direct broadcast satellite TV.

Another important factor was the growth of strong lobbies pressing for change in media policy. The most important of these was the advertising lobby, which pushed hard in many countries for access to electronic media (Humphreys 1996: 172–3). Pilati (1987) stresses that Italian private television stations were born when various commercial and manufacturing companies were making enough money to invest in advertising and public broadcasting was not able to meet this new demand for air time. In many cases advertising interests were joined in the push for commercial broadcasting by media companies hungry to expand into electronic media. To some extent laws limiting concentration in print media encouraged this desire, as many companies could not expand their print empires without running afoul of these limits. Another, very different kind of force that in many cases pushed toward private broadcasting came from social movements (student movements, unions, etc.) that were looking for new opportunities and means to express their voice outside of the established circuits of communication, often turning to pirate broadcasting to obtain that voice.

Also significant was the fact that funding for public broadcasting became increasingly problematic as the market for color television sets became saturated, and natural growth in license fee revenue therefore leveled off. From that point forward, additional license fee revenue could only be obtained by raising the fee, which was of course politically unpopular. This meant that expansion of television beyond the limited number of channels then in operation seemed to depend on the introduction of private broadcasting.

Finally, economic globalization, both in general and in media industries specifically, played an important and many-sided role. As early as 1974, the European Court of Justice ruled that broadcasting was covered as a form of trade under the Treaty of Rome. This decision was reaffirmed on a number of occasions in the early 1980s, in the context of strong shift globally toward liberalizing trade in services – the General Agreement on Trade in Services was ratified in 1994 – and toward defining broadcasting in these terms, rather than as a national social and cultural institution. When the European Commission turned its attention to broadcasting policy in the 1980s – producing the Television without Frontiers Directive in 1989 – it stressed the goal of creating a common European audiovisual market that would facilitate the development of transnational media companies capable of competing with American media conglomerates. Individual European governments, as well, increasingly saw media policy in terms of global competition in the cutting-edge information industries. These policies facilitated the transnationalization of media industries, in which ownership is increasingly internationalized (e.g., the Spanish television channel Tele5 was owned, in 1998, by Berlusconi [25 percent], by the German firm Kirch [25 percent], and by the Bank of Luxembourg [13 percent], with some participation from Bertelsmann), coproduction is often necessary to compete in global markets, and in general the forces of the global market tend to displace the national political forces that once shaped the media.

## THE CONSEQUENCES OF COMMERCIALIZATION

A broad range of consequences flow from the commercialization of media. Commercialization, in the first place, is clearly shifting European media systems away from the world of politics and toward the world of commerce. This changes the social function of journalism, as the journalist's main objective is no longer to disseminate ideas and create social consensus around them, but to produce entertainment and information that can be sold to individual consumers. And it clearly contributes to homogenization, undercutting the plurality of media systems rooted in particular political and cultural systems of individual nation states that characterized Europe through most of the twentieth century, and encouraging its replacement by a common global set of media practices. Public broadcasting systems, especially, always placed strong emphasis on the goal of giving voice to the social groups and cultural patterns that defined national identity, "sustaining and renewing the society's characteristic cultural capital and cement" (Blumler 1992: 11; Avery 1993; Tracey 1998). Increasingly even public broadcasting systems must follow the logic of global cultural industries.

Commercialization of media has no doubt played some significant role in the "secularization" of European society. As we have seen, secularization has deep roots, and was already well advanced by the time the most dramatic change – the commercialization of broadcasting – occurred. As the case of TROS in the Netherlands suggests, however, commercial forces were beginning to make themselves felt in a variety of ways before the commercial deluge of 1980s: in the shift toward commercial newspapers, through import of American media content and imitation of American practices, through advertising in some European systems, through pirate and transborder broadcasting, and with the breakdown of the public service monopoly in Italy at the end of the 1970s. It is certainly plausible that if Europe was becoming more of an individualist consumer society in the 1960s the growth of television and radio and the commercialization of the press contributed to that trend; and it seems certain that they have intensified the process since the 1980s.

Commercialization also has important implications for the process of political communication. Commercial media create powerful new techniques of representation and of audience creation, which parties and politicians must adopt in order to prevail in the new communication environment. Two of the most important of these techniques – closely related to one another – are personalization and the tendency to privilege the point of view of the "ordinary citizen." In Italian public broadcasting in the 1980s, for example – at a time when commercial television still was not allowed to broadcast news – spokesmen from each significant party appeared to comment on any major political story (Hallin and Mancini 1984). They appeared as representatives of their parties, not as individual characters in a dramatic portrayal of politics: political logic dominated the presentation of news, and the personal characteristics of these politicians were generally as irrelevant as those of the news readers, who were rotated each night and had none of the significance for the news audience of American anchors. By the 1990s Berlusconi could dominate the news because he was a good story, and the narrative logic of commercial news was increasingly dominant in the Italian media scene. In the era of commercial media politicians increasingly become "media stars" who act well beyond the borders of politics: they appear in sport broadcasts, talk shows, and entertainment programs (Mancini 2000). Personalization, it might be noted, is not exclusively a characteristic of television, but of popular commercial media generally: nowhere is it stronger than in the sensationalist press of Britain, Germany, or Austria; and it has increasing importance in print media everywhere.

Another important manifestation of the new logic of commercial media is the tendency to focus on the experience and perspective of the "common citizen." Earlier traditions of European journalism were heavily focused on the perspectives of official representatives of parties, organized groups, and the state (e.g., Hallin and Mancini 1984), while with the shift toward commercial media the perspective of the individual citizens is increasingly privileged (Neveu 1999; see also Blumler and Gurevitch 2001). This results both from changes in news coverage and the development of new forms of infotainment in which public issues are discussed, such as the talk show, where politicians, if they appear at all, are typically relegated to a secondary role, and "common sense," as Leurdijk (1997) puts it, is privileged over political discourse. As many analysts have noted, these changes very likely have contributed to the erosion of the influence of the traditional mass party and the social organizations connected to it.

Commercialization contributes to a shift in the balance of power between the media and political institutions, with the media themselves becoming increasingly central in setting the agenda of political communication. One important manifestation of this tendency is the increased frequency of political scandals, which can be found across both Europe and North America. In the case of Greece:

> . . . media have begun to fight with the politicians for control of the political agenda and have started to make themselves heard in the process of political communication with a constant stream of criticism of politicians and the actions of parties. . . . The rise of commercial media may have precipitated this trend and created a situation where, today, Greek citizens can watch an endless stream of stories about political scandals, rivalry and self-interest. And, as with the media in other liberal democratic countries, Greek media have tried to create stories about political conflict by giving particular attention to politicians who hold controversial views or who oppose the actions of the government (Papathanassopoulos 2000: 58).

These tendencies are not produced solely by commercialization. They are also connected with the rise of critical professionalism, which in many countries took place before the full flowering of commercialization (Djerf-Pierre 2000). Scandals are often driven simultaneously by the desire of journalists to build professional prestige and assert their independence vis-à-vis political actors, and by the desire of media organizations to compete for audience. The rise of scandal politics is also connected with changes in the political system, including the judiciary, which, as we saw in Chapter 5, has become more independent and assertive particularly in Southern Europe. As Waisbord (2000) has pointed out, scandals almost always require the participation of political sources and cannot therefore be explained strictly in terms of the media system. Nevertheless, commercialization tends to give the media both the independent power base and the incentive to assert their own agenda, often at the expense of politicians.

One of the more difficult questions to sort out is whether commercialization has increased or decreased the flow of political information and discussion. European media have traditionally given central attention to politics; in the case of public broadcasting, a "sense of some responsibility for the health of the political process and for the quality of public discussion generated within it" (Blumler 1992: 36) was always a central value, and news and public affairs programming were significantly privileged. Though it is difficult to compare levels of political knowledge across populations, there is some evidence that Europeans know more than Americans about world affairs, even in countries where newspaper readership is low (Dimock and Popkin 1997). One of the central fears expressed by European commentators about "Americanization" of the media is that political information and discussion would be marginalized in a commercial system. Public broadcasting systems have traditionally broadcast the news in the heart of prime time, and in an era when nothing else was on television, news broadcasts had enormous audiences. In a commercial environment this practice is clearly threatened, as manifested in the decision of Britain's regulated commercial broadcaster, ITV, to cancel the country's most popular news program, *News at Ten* and follow the American practice of broadcasting the news in early fringe time at 6:30 P.M.

At the same time, it is a common assumption that there has been an explosion of information with the expansion of media. One of the arguments of the political scientists quoted in the preceding text about the role of the media in the decline of parties is that "growing availability of political information through the media has reduced the costs of making informed decisions" (Flanagan and Dalton: 242). In some sense it is surely true that there is more information available, at least if we compare across the post–World War II era. Not only have television channels proliferated, but news organizations in general are larger. Newspapers are generally physically larger than in the past; in 1967 *Il Corriere della Sera* had sixteen to twenty-eight pages, while today it has forty to fifty. On the other hand, it seems unlikely that increasingly commercialized media will consistently give the emphasis to public affairs that either the politically connected newspapers of the past or public broadcasting monopolies did.[9]

The existing empirical evidence is fragmentary and not entirely consistent, however, and the patterns are likely to be complex (e.g., Brants and Siune 1998). Rooney (2000), for example, finds a decrease in public affairs content in the *Sun* and *Mirror* in Britain from 33 and 23 percent of news content, respectively, in 1968, to 9 percent in 1998 – consistent with a common view in British media research that commercialization has driven political content out of the British popular press, a development symbolized by the demise of the trade-union supported *Daily Herald* and its replacement by the sensationalist *Sun*. McLaughlan and Golding

---

[9] The question of how much political information is produced, is also different from the question of how much is consumed. Prior (2002) argues that multiplication of television channels makes it easier for citizens to avoid political information, and is therefore likely to increase inequality in political knowledge, even if more information is available overall.

(2000), however, using a narrower definition of political coverage, find no consistent trend in the content of either the tabloid or broadsheet press in Britain, and point out that "the very essence of tabloid provision continues to be suffused with the political, or if you like, the ideological" (87). Franklin (1997) reports a decline in reporting of Parliament in British broadsheets in the 1990s. Negrine (1998) also reports a decline in parliamentary coverage (British broadsheets had dedicated pages for parliamentary coverage until the 1990s). He also reports declines in political reporting in French and German TV news. Pfetsch (1996) found a decline in reporting of political institutions – government, Parliament, parties – in German TV news, though not a decline in political coverage overall, in part because coverage of political violence increased. Winston (2002) shows that the percent of news items devoted to politics declined from 21.5 percent on the main news bulletin of the BBC1 in 1975 to 9.6 percent in 2001, while the percent of items devoted to crime grew from 4.5 to 19.1. ITN showed similar – slightly larger – shifts. Brants (1998: 322) found that "in most countries commercial television has not marginalized political news. In eight West European countries, almost six out of an average of 13.3 items per newscast in the early 1990s were about politics." Italian newspapers, finally, though they have become more market oriented, have not decreased their political coverage: samples of thirty issues of Italian newspapers in each year showed 80 political stories in 1966, 647 in 1976, 560 in 1986, and 1257 in 1996 (Mancini 2002). Of course, politics is treated differently than in the past, through discourse genres that increase the possibility of dramatization (Bionda et al. 1998; Mancini 2002). In television too the prevalence of current affairs programs has increased, as these programs seem to be popular with Italian viewers (Menduni 1998).

The question of whether political content will decrease with commercialization thus clearly remains open.

Closely related to the question of whether political content will be marginalized in an increasingly commercialized media system is the question of whether commercialization is likely to lead to an alienation of the mass public from political life. Again there are conflicting views. Many have argued that focus of commercial media on private life, the deemphasis of collective political actors, the emphasis on scandal, and the often negative portrayal of political life will tend to undermine the involvement of the public in the political process (e.g., Patterson 1993). Changes in campaign style connected with the rise of commercial media are also often seen as having this effect. Papathanassopoulos (2000: 56) argues that "in adopting television-centered-campaigning the parties have moved away from the traditional emphases on public rallies and personal contacts with party workers, thus lessening opportunities for citizens to participate directly in campaigns and further distancing the parties from voters." Others (e.g., Brants 1998) have argued that the dramatization of politics and the migration of political discussion into "infotainment" venues in which the voice of the ordinary citizen has a greater role is likely to increase popular involvement in politics.

The difficulty of sorting out the effects of commercialization arises partly from the fact that it arose in the context of a complex set of changes in Western societies and interacts with those changes. This is well illustrated by the phenomenon of pirate radio, which was pushed forward by the advertising industry and simultaneously by new social movements with a desire for a greater voice in the public sphere. Much of pirate radio was pervaded by a youth culture that represented both a cultural challenge to an established system of power and a manifestation of the growing global consumer society. It is similarly evident in the way contemporary journalistic practices were influenced both by the rise of critical expertise and by commercialization. We will also argue, in the following section, that commercialization is not necessarily incompatible with a degree of political parallelism and under certain circumstances might even increase partisanship in the media. Despite these complexities it can be said that commercialization has in general weakened the ties between the media and the world of organized political actors that distinguished the Democratic Corporatist and Polarized Pluralist from the Liberal system, and has encouraged the development of a globalized media culture that substantially diminishes national differences in media systems.

## LIMITS AND COUNTERTENDENCIES OF THE
## HOMOGENIZATION PROCESS

There is no question that the forces of homogenization are strong, and that considerable convergence has taken place, primarily in the direction of the Liberal Model. It is very reasonable to assume that this trend will continue in the future, as, for example, younger journalists socialized to different conceptions of the media's role replace earlier generations, and as the consequences of commercialization of broadcasting – still relatively new in many European countries – continue to work themselves out. If this trend were to continue unchanged into the future, it is possible to imagine a complete convergence of media systems in the United States and Western Europe toward something close to the Liberal Model. History does not usually move in straight lines, however, and there are many reasons to doubt whether it makes sense to project the trend toward homogenization of the past couple of decades indefinitely into the future.

There are, for one thing, important variations in the political systems of the countries considered here that seem likely to persist despite the changes in political institutions and culture that have clearly taken place. It is common to say that European politics has been to some degree "presidentialized." But parliamentary systems remain different from presidential ones. As Blumler, Kavanaugh, and Nossiter (1996: 59) observe:

> separation of powers in the U.S. government has imposed a continual pressure on the President to court mass opinion through the mass media in order to keep the heat of popular support for his measures. . . . In Britain's parliamentary system, however, the Prime Minister and his or her Cabinet can count on party discipline to ensure passage of almost all proposed legislation. . . .

Proportional representation also remains different from a first-past-the-post electoral system and produces a different kind of party system. Constitutional changes could of course lead to homogenization here too – Italy, in particular has been debating such changes. But in most of Europe there is no sign that any such changes are in the offing. The structure of the political systems does not, of course, affect the media system as deeply as it once did, because the mass media have become more differentiated from it. But the news media still interact intensively with the political system. The flow of information and structural organization of news sources seems inevitably different in contrasting systems, and so too the narrative conventions of reporting politics. It seems unlikely that media systems could entirely converge while party and electoral systems remain sharply different.

Legal systems also remain different in important ways. There is no reason to assume, in particular, the "first amendment absolutism" that characterizes the U.S. legal system would ever spread to Europe. And this difference seems likely to have continuing consequences for media systems. It seems likely, for example, that electoral communication will continue to be more regulated in Europe, with much television time allocated according to political criteria and paid advertising restricted (Belgium, Denmark, France, Norway, Portugal, Spain, Sweden, Switzerland, and the United Kingdom currently ban paid political advertising on television) (Farrell and Webb 2000: 107).[10] Stronger regulation of broadcast media in general may well also survive the "commercial deluge." (It is possible, in fact that certain aspects of European regulatory regimes will increasingly affect U.S. regulation, as well as the other way around, as the European market becomes increasingly important for U.S. companies. It may be, for example, that stronger EU regulations on privacy will eventually affect U.S. regulation of the information industry.) The European welfare state has clearly been rolled back as a consequence of the global shift to neoliberalism. But here again many scholars doubt that complete homogenization is a likely outcome of this process. Moses, Geyer, and Ingebritsen (2000: 18), for example, conclude that "the Scandinavian model remains a potent indicator of the limitations of the powers of globalization/Europeanization, the capabilities of individual nations to pursue distinct policy strategies, the capacity of the Left to oppose and successfully counter international market forces, and the ability of social democratic parties to adapt to the demand of a changing international order." The same logic may certainly apply to Scandinavian media systems. Similarly, Blumler and Gurevitch (2001) found that, although there were important signs of convergence between U.S. and British styles of election coverage, the differences between the United States in the amount of campaign coverage actually grew between the 1980s and 1990s, as commercialization intensified in the United States and the culture of public service broadcasting persisted in Britain.

It is also possible that some of the trends that have led to the convergence of media systems would not only slow or stop but even reverse, either in general or in particular countries. There is, for example, some evidence that the decline of political polarization and of ideological differences among parties that has taken place in most if not all of the countries considered here, and which seems clearly to undercut political parallelism in media systems, has been affected by countertendencies in recent years. In the United States, for example, according to Jabobson (2001), partisan consistency in voting and political attitudes declined

---

[10] "In Britain, advertising is a lower-status occupation compared to the higher status that politicians have traditionally enjoyed, and a legal ban on all political advertising and radio remains in force despite the recent exposure of British broadcasting to market forces in many respects" (Blumler, Kavanaugh, and Nossiter 1996: 59).

from the 1950s to 1970s, but has subsequently strengthened. In Europe, Communist and in some cases Fascist parties have declined, as have differences between traditional parties of the left and right. But new extremist parties have arisen on the right in many countries, motivated by opposition to immigration, multiculturalism, and European integration, while Green parties have grown on the left and there are some signs that other parts of the left may persist or even grow. In France in the first round of the 2002 presidential election the right-wing National Front beat out the centrist Socialists, getting 17 percent of the vote, while the Greens and Trotskyists did well on the left.

Homogenization is usually taken to mean a shift toward the neutral journalistic professionalism, of the sort that has been particularly strong in the United States. This, as we have seen, is clearly the prediction of modernization/differentiation theory, which sees media institutions built around the idea of neutral professionalism as the most developed. And indeed there has been a significant trend in this direction. But here there are quite important limitations and countertrends that need to be stressed. Not only do forms of advocacy journalism persist in European countries where they have always been strong, but new forms are also beginning to proliferate, and this is occurring in the Liberal at least as much as in other systems. If there is convergence here, it is not proceeding only in one direction.

In Chapter 5, we saw that advocacy forms of journalism have persisted in the Polarized Pluralist countries, particularly in Italy, Spain, and Greece. In Italy, though the press has become more market oriented since the 1970s, the papers that have led this shift, for example *La Repubblica* and *Il Giornale*, have strong political identities, and attempts to establish neutral papers have failed. In Spain most of the media, print and broadcast alike, became divided during the 1980s and 1990s into two opposing political camps. In Greece, Papathanassopoulos (2001) argues that increasingly popular, market-oriented forms of journalism have not eliminated the pattern of political instrumentalization of the news media, but have shifted the balance of power away from politicians and toward the media owners, who have increasingly powerful tools of political pressure. Deregulation and commercialization have produced sensationalism but not neutrality, according to Papathanassopoulos, who quotes Zaharopoulos and Paraschos's (1993: 96) comment that "the vast majority of Greek media are unabashedly partisan, sensational, and political." The same pattern prevails in Italy (Bechelloni 1995; Mancini 2000; Roidi 2001).

In Chapter 6 we saw that in the Democratic Corporatist countries, though there has been an important trend toward neutrality as a journalistic norm and market strategy, political parallelism in the national press persists, and shows no sign of vanishing in the immediate future. In Liberal systems, meanwhile, new forms of advocacy journalism are proliferating. In the United States, politicized talk programs on both radio and cable TV have become increasingly common, and Fox News has differentiated itself from other broadcast networks with a clear political profile, evident in both content and the political preferences of its audience.

The evidence suggests that there is no necessary connection between commercialization of media and neutral professionalism. The shift toward commercialization is likely to create new forms of advocacy journalism and political parallelism, even as it undercuts old ones. Commercialization can, without question, increase pressures toward "catchallism" and therefore toward neutral professionalism. This seems to happen under specific market conditions, however – most strongly in highly concentrated local newspaper markets. Indeed, neutral professionalism seems to flourish best where competitive pressures are *not* particularly intense (Hallin 2000) – in monopoly local newspapers (in the U.S. case especially when competition from other media was less intense and when newspaper companies were not listed on the stock exchange); in public service broadcasting, where the latter has political independence; or, again in the U.S. case, in the government-regulated oligopoly broadcasting that prevailed before deregulation in the 1980s. In other cases commercial pressures can encourage media to differentiate themselves politically and to stress the color and drama of opinion over the gray utility of information. Thus in Chapter 7 we saw that the competitive British press – especially the tabloid press – is much more politicized than the monopoly American press. Under the right political and economic conditions, opinion sells. This is obvious not only in the tabloid press, particularly in Britain, Germany, and Austria, but also in Spanish radio, where the hosts of "tertulias" – political discussion programs – build their popularity on the strong expression of opinions and command princely salaries as a result (Barrera 1995), or in American cable TV, where opinions are also central to the popularity of talk show hosts and increasingly journalists as well (e.g., Rutenberg 2002). The "commercial deluge" of the past twenty years is also accompanied by a dramatic expansion in the number of channels of electronic media, and seems likely for this reason to produce new forms of political parallelism, as the fragmentation of the audience makes catchall strategies less viable, at least for many channels.

Finally, it is important to keep in mind that, as we saw in discussing professionalization in the Liberal systems in Chapter 7, neutral professionalism in the news media was based in part on a separation of journalism from the commercial logic of media industries. As commercialization undercuts this separation, often reducing the autonomy of journalists within media organizations and disrupting the boundaries between news and entertainment, neutral professionalism is likely, not to disappear, but to find itself reduced to one genre among many. This is evident in the growth of "infotainment" genres, sometimes referred to as the "new news" (Taylor 1992), which often depart from the traditional professional ideal of objectivity.

## DIFFERENTIATION AND DE-DIFFERENTIATION

In the final section of this chapter we return to the question posed in our discussion of differentiation theory in Chapter 4 and in a slightly different way at the beginning of this chapter: Does it make sense to understand change in media systems in Western Europe and North America as a process of "modernization" in the sense of structural-functionalism – as a move toward increased differentiation of the media from other social institutions? Clearly in many ways this theoretical perspective seems to fit. The process of secularization is certainly consistent with differentiation theory. In the early twentieth century many European societies – including those belonging to both our Democratic Corporatist and Polarized Pluralist Models – were characterized by a strong fusion of institutions and identities: ideological, social class, and religious identities were fused in important ways, as were institutions of party, church, trade union, and mass media. In the last decades of the century these connections were substantially dissolved, and the relations of media to political parties as well as to individuals and social groups became much more fluid, much less bound by stable loyalties or organizational connections. As we saw in Chapter 4, Alexander argued that three major forces propelled the process of differentiation of the media: demands for more universalistic information put forward by new social groups against forms of advocacy journalism linked to the preexisting social order; the growth of professional norms and self-regulation, leading toward the development of journalistic autonomy; and, finally, the degree of universalism in national civil cultures, which is connected with rational-legal authority. Our analysis of historical development of the media in the three groups of countries confirm these connections, though the differentiation of media from political groups was also driven by economic factors, whose role in Alexander's theory, as we shall see, is more ambiguous and problematic.

Also consistent with differentiation theory, the media became increasingly central to political and much of social life, which according to differentiation theory is a necessary outcome of the differentiation process. As political parties, for example, become separated from churches, trade unions, and other social groups – as well as from portions of the state they may once have controlled (an increasingly professionalized judiciary, for example) – they increasingly must depend on the media to establish ties with individual voters and other social actors. In general, a differentiated society relies on media to connect actors and institutions no longer connected by more direct ties, according to differentiation theory. These processes took place in all of the countries studied here, but earliest in the Liberal and later in the Democratic Corporatist and Polarized Pluralist systems.

At the same time, there are real problems with differentiation theory and the concept of modernization connected with it as a way of understanding media system change. In Chapter 4 we considered two alternative perspectives to differentiation theory, associated with Habermas and with Bourdieu, both of whom have argued that media history can in some ways be seen as a process of de-differentiation. Our analysis suggests that in important ways they are correct.

## DIFFERENTIATION AND THE MARKET

One of the central arguments of Habermas and Bourdieu is that the media have lost autonomy in relation to the market and economic system. And indeed, when we turn from the first of the two principal processes of change discussed in this chapter – secularization – to the second – commercialization – the modernization hypothesis of a unilinear shift toward greater differentiation begins to seem increasingly simplistic. As we saw in Chapter 2, Alexander (1981) argues that modernization of the media requires that "there must be differentiation from structures in the economic dimension, particularly social classes." The main meaning he gives to the differentiation of media from "economic structures" has to do with ties of media to class-linked parties and organizations: he argues that trade union–linked papers are historically a hindrance to professionalization and differentiation, though he also mentions highly partisan bourgeois papers in nineteenth-century Germany. He does not address the role of the market in detail, nor that of private media owners. He makes only one comment about media economics, in discussing U.S. media history: "This transition in content [away from partisanship] coincided with the birth of journalistic professionalization and the emergence of newspapers as big business. By the turn of the twentieth century, the notion of the news media as a 'public institution' was, then, beginning to be institutionalized (31)." Clearly this implies that commercialization contributed to or at least was in harmony with differentiation and professionalization.

In important ways this is correct: the development of strong media markets frees media institutions from the kind of dependence on patrons that leads to the pattern of instrumentalization we identified particularly in the history of Polarized Pluralist systems, and size of media organizations is likely connected with the growth of a journalism as a distinct occupational category. Competition for readers and for advertisers, meanwhile, often encourages media to seek audiences across subcultural boundaries, as well as leading to a process of concentration that disrupts older patterns of association between media and social groups, and enhances the power and independence of the large surviving media organizations. Of course, professionalization and differentiation did also occur within other institutional structures, as we have seen in preceding chapters: it occurred strongly in public broadcasting systems in both the Democratic Corporatist and the Liberal countries, and occurred to a substantial degree in party and trade union–linked papers in the Democratic Corporatist countries, in a later stage of their development. Commercialization is not *necessary* to the development of autonomous institutions or professions; obviously the professionalization and autonomy of the judiciary or administrative corps does not depend on their commercialization.

Professionalization in the news media, moreover, though it has developed in a commercial context in many cases, has by no means developed in total harmony with commercialization. It involves a form of differentiation that often takes place within news organizations themselves, as journalists assert the integrity of journalistic criteria *against* purely commercial ones, and their own autonomy against the intervention of owners, marketers, and advertising sales staff. We have seen this form of differentiation in the "separation of church and state" that was institutionalized in U.S. newspapers in the mid–twentieth century, in the journalistic autonomy achieved in much of the French elite press in the post–World War II period, or in the editorial statutes that can be found in some of the Democratic Corporatist systems, as well as in systems of journalistic self-regulation such as press councils, which are intended to uphold professional values to a large extent against the pressures of economic self-interest.

In the U.S. case, there is certainly strong evidence that this form of differentiation has declined – reducing journalistic autonomy and bringing into question the "notion of the news media as a 'public institution,'" which is no longer taken for granted today as it was from about the 1950s through the 1970s (Hallin 2000). Though the U.S. media were always primarily commercial in character, commercial pressures have intensified with deregulation of broadcasting and changes in ownership patterns that have brought newspapers under the influence of Wall Street. Similar changes are clearly under way to varying degrees throughout Europe, most dramatically in the sphere of broadcasting.

Here it is worth going back to the distinction Mazzoleni makes between media logic and political logic. As many have observed, the changes in European media systems have meant that "media logic" has become differentiated from "political logic," and in many ways has become increasingly dominant over the latter. Story selection, for example, is increasingly determined not by political criteria – such as principles of proportional representation – but by journalistic or media-based criteria of what is a "good story." It is important to recognize, however, that this "media logic" that has emerged in the late twentieth century is a hybrid logic: as we have seen, it is rooted in two developments that overlapped historically, and were intertwined in important ways, but are also distinct:

1. the growth of critical professionalism, which was particularly important in the 1960s and 1970s (and even later in some European countries) and probably has slowed down or even been reversed to a degree since that time; and
2. commercialization, which was beginning in the 1960s and 1970s but accelerated in the 1980s and 1990s.

The former fits the story told by differentiation theory much better than the latter. The growth of infotainment as a hybrid form of programming is a good illustration. Luhmann argues that the differentiation of mass media content into three genres – news and current affairs, advertising, and entertainment – each with distinct social functions, is "the most important internal structure of the system of mass media" (2000: 24). But clearly commercialization undercuts this form of differentiation, not only by blurring the boundaries between news and entertainment, in fact, but also those between advertising and the other two, as product placement, for example, increases in entertainment and as news is used to cross-promote other products of media conglomerates.

It is, in sum, quite plausible to argue that the media are becoming less differentiated in relation to the economic system, even as they are becoming more differentiated in relation to the political system. Many would argue that this is part of a general tendency toward de-differentiation in contemporary society: that with the shift toward neoliberalism market logic tends to dominate wide swaths of society – including politics, which increasingly resembles marketing, education, leisure, social services, etc. If an increasingly commercialized media are growing more central to social life they may be an important agent of this broader process of de-differentiation. This is clearly Bourdieu's argument.

## DIFFERENTIATION AND THE STATE

We have focused here on the tendency for media to become de-differentiated in relation to the economic system. It is worth adding a few words, however, about the relation of media to the state. The media, as we have seen, have become increasingly differentiated over the course of the twentieth century from organized social and political groups such as parties, trade unions, and churches. Has their relation to the state followed the same course? If we look at the past twenty years, we would clearly say they have become more differentiated from the state as well. Liberalization and deregulation have diminished the role of the state as an owner, funder, and regulator of the media, and journalists have become more assertive in relation to state elites. If we look over a longer historical period, however, the picture is more complicated, and the direction of change looks a lot less linear. In the early days of the newspaper the state played an important role everywhere, printing official gazettes and often taxing, subsidizing, and censoring the media. During the nineteenth century, as we have seen, there was a general shift toward press freedom, which took place at different rates in different countries: the media became separated from the state in important ways, especially in the Liberal and Democratic Corporatist countries, and became rooted either in the market or in civil society, where they were supported by parties and social organizations. With the growth of corporatism and of the welfare state in the mid–twentieth century, which integrated into the state the social groups of civil society on which much of the media depended, it could be said that the media differentiation from the state lessened in important ways. As Ekecrantz (1997: 400) says about Sweden, "strong labor organizations, a regulatory framework negotiated by the state, journalist training within state universities, heavy subsidies to the press as well as tax redemption belong to the picture of journalism as a public institution in Sweden." Obviously Ekecrantz could add public broadcasting. It was in this context, moreover, that the role of the state as the "primary definer" of news content developed. In the Liberal countries corporatism was weaker, but the rise of the national security state during World War II and the Cold War led to the partial integration of the media into the growing state apparatus. In many countries, finally – though most strongly in the Polarized Pluralist countries, where it also continues especially strongly – media owners continued to be important political actors, often with a share of state power, either formally or informally. Here too, then, we should be careful about assuming that a unilinear trend toward differentiation is the "natural" course of media development.

## DIFFERENTIATION AND POWER

It is also worth focusing, finally, on the issue Alexander raises about the differentiation of media from social class, which brings us back to the broad issue of power raised at the end of Chapter 4. For Alexander, the fact that media in the modern, liberal system become part of "big business" does not prevent their differentiation from social class. Much European scholarship, on the other hand, has historically referred to the commercial press as the "bourgeois" press. This is typical in the Scandinavian literature, for example. The displacement of party papers and public broadcasting by commercial media could thus be seen as reinforcing the power of a particular social class over the media system as a whole. As we have seen, the argument that commercial media reflect a class bias in the sense that they tilt toward the political right has also been made strongly by scholars in the Liberal countries (e.g., Murdock and Golding 1977; Westergaard 1977; Curran 1979). Britain's commercial press has always had a particularly strong slant toward the political right. It is also supported by the comparative research of Patterson and Donsbach (1993: 13), who observe that:

> Historically, conservative parties have been overrepresented by news organizations. The press receives an indirect subsidy from business in the form of advertising, which has worked to the benefit of right-wing parties in the past. The data presented in this paper suggest that these parties are still advantaged; as perceived by journalists, there is a closer parallelism between news organizations and conservative parties than liberal ones.

It could be added that this tendency is particularly marked if we set aside public broadcasting and focus on the most commercially viable news organizations. To the extent that this is correct, the commercialization of media currently under way could be expected to strengthen 'bourgeois" dominance of political communication. This is one of the arguments of Herman and McChesney (1997) and others writing within the critical political economy tradition.

How is it that Alexander sees trade-union papers as tied to a particular social class, but commercial papers not? We might interpret this as a sort of inversion of Georg Lukacs's conception of the working class as the universal class, as a claim that the bourgeoisie is the universal class whose interests are identical to those of society as a whole. In fact, Alexander's claim is really about professionalization and about the development by the media of a network of connections with a variety of parties, social groups, and sectors of society – not organizational connections, which tend to die out as the media become commercialized, but relations of influence and exchange of information. Clearly it is true that commercial papers in general have tended to distance themselves from earlier narrow connections to conservative parties and to broaden and blur their political identities, as they have sought to capture readers from the party press of the left – and in some cases have even merged with papers that previously had other political orientations.

Whether this tendency has been strong enough to counterbalance the decline of noncommercial papers with diverse political orientations, in the representation of different social classes – or of different social interests more generally – is difficult to say. For much of the twentieth century, the support parties, trade unions, churches, and the like, gave to their own papers partly counterbalanced the support business gave to "conservative liberal" papers through advertising. As the last Social Democratic papers disappear in Northern Europe, what does this mean: Are they no longer needed, because the existing commercial media adequately represent all the major interests in society? Or does this development increase what Lindblom (1977) called "the privileged position of business" in Western societies? This of course is a general issue raised by the global trend toward neoliberalism, of which the specific case of media commercialization is one important facet.

Here again, the relation between commercialization and professionalization is an important issue. Donsbach and Patterson (1993), for example, after noting that news organizations – and they could add particularly commercial ones – tend to support the political right, at least in their editorial positions, go on to argue that this is counterbalanced by the fact that journalists in most countries shade somewhat to the left. Their influence, then, might provide through other means some of the balance lost through the decline of the political press. It is probably true that the rise of "critical professionalism" in the 1960s and 1970s to an important degree counterbalanced the effect of media concentration and the diminution in the political diversity of news organizations that accompanied it, producing greater degrees of internal pluralism to replace declining external pluralism. If, however, commercialization has the effect of eroding journalistic professionalism over the long run, the issue of diversity and political balance will presumably become more pressing.

We cannot, unfortunately, resolve this issue here: as we noted in Chapter 4, research that systematically addresses issues of media and power in a comparative way is almost totally lacking.

## CONCLUSION

The differences among national media systems described in the preceding chapters of this book are clearly diminishing. A global media culture is emerging, one that closely resembles the Liberal Model we explored in Chapter 7. The homogenization of media systems involves, most centrally, the separation of media institutions from the strong ties to the political world that distinguished both the Democratic Corporatist and Polarized Pluralist from the Liberal Model. This transformation has many causes. We have stressed a distinction between forces external to European society, including direct influence from the United States and the impact of technological innovation, and forces that are essentially internal to European society, though certainly linked to the process of globalization. The most important of these internal forces, we have argued, are "secularization" – that is, the decline of the political faiths connected to organized social groups that once structured much of European politics and culture, and the shift from a collectivist to a more individualist political culture – and commercialization. Although we have made the case that changes in European media systems are driven by deeper processes of social change, we have also argued that media system change has played an independent causal role, as the rise of television, the development of "critical professionalism," and the growth of media markets have transformed the relations between political parties and organized social groups and the individual citizens who once relied upon them.

We have also noted that there are important factors that limit, and in some ways might even reverse, the process of convergence toward the Liberal Model. Differences among national political systems remain substantial and are likely to prevent complete homogenization of media systems for the foreseeable future. And changes in media markets have created countertendencies that can be seen even in the Liberal countries, as, for example, the multiplication of television channels reintroduces external pluralism into the American media system.

We have, finally, posed the question of whether this process of change in the relation between media institutions and the social and political system can be understood in terms of differentiation theory – which is often implicit in the use of the term *modernization*. Differentiation theory fits well in one very important way: The "secularization" of European society involves the decline of social institutions – mass parties and religious and class-based communities – that at one time fused many different social functions, from political representation to the organization of leisure time to socialization and communication; and the mass media have emerged as specialized institutions of communication independent of these groups. Commercialization, on the other hand, is much harder to integrate into the perspective of differentiation theory: commercialization seems clearly to involve significant de-differentiation of the media system in relation to the market, an erosion of the professional autonomy journalists gained in the later part of the twentieth century, and also, possibly, a subordination of the media to the political interests of business that could diminish political balance in the representation of social interests.

# NINE

# Conclusion

At the beginning of this book we raised the question of whether stable connections could be identified between media systems and political systems. We believe we have shown that indeed, such connections can be identified. We have proposed a set of four principal dimensions for comparing media systems: the structure of media markets, including, particularly, the degree of development of the mass circulation press; the degree and form of political parallelism; the development of journalistic professionalism; and the degree and form of state intervention in the media system. And we have argued that there are important connections between the patterns of development of media systems, based on these dimensions, and certain key characteristics of the political system: the role of the state in society; the majoritarian or consensus character of the political system; the pattern of interest group organization, including the distinction between more fragmented liberal and more corporatist systems; the distinction between moderate and polarized pluralism; and the development of rational-legal authority in contrast to clientelist forms of social organization. A set of hypotheses about the connections between these variables is presented in Chapter 3 and we need not repeat them in detail here.

At times, political system characteristics are manifested more or less directly in media structures, as for example majoritarian or consensus patterns of government are reflected in the organization of public broadcasting institutions. Usually, however, the connections between media system and political system variables cannot be interpreted as a mechanistic, one-to-one correspondence. Elements of political structure interact, for one thing, with other kinds of factors, including technological and economic factors, some general to the society as a whole – characteristics of industrial structure and the culture of consumption, for example – and some specific to media industries, such as newspaper market structures. Nor do these connections arise from one-way causal relationships. Media systems have their own effects on the political system in many cases; and the process we are describing is really one of co-evolution of media and political institutions within particular historical contexts.

We conceive the political variables discussed here as simultaneously characteristics of political structure and of political culture. They are structural factors in the sense that they involve sets of institutions and procedures, patterns of resource allocation, and so on. These institutional structures shape the development of the media by creating constraints and opportunities to which media organizations and actors respond. Thus in systems where political parties have powerful control over decision making – this is most characteristic of the Polarized Pluralist Model – media owners and even individual journalists have incentives to form alliances with party actors. In systems where organized social groups have strong followings and important influence, media organizations are likely to develop ties with them, and journalists are likely to form their own such organizations. Where the market is particularly dominant, commercial media are likely to prevail over media tied to political and social organizations. At the same time, the political variables we have discussed involve characteristic patterns of political culture – characteristic political values and beliefs, and ways of thinking about and representing the political world. These may not be "reflected" directly in the culture of journalism and the media, but they clearly affect journalists' conceptions of their own role in society, their professional values and representational practices, and so on.

We have argued that it is possible to identify in the eighteen countries covered in our study three distinct media system "models," which we have called the Polarized Pluralist, the Democratic Corporatist, and the Liberal Models. The similarities among the three groups of countries we associate with these models are based both on historical connections among these groups of countries and on historically rooted similarities in their political structures and cultures. As we have seen, the media systems of individual countries fit the ideal types that our models represent only roughly, and many media systems must be understood as mixed cases. Nevertheless, we think that the models are useful both for understanding patterns of relationship among media and political system characteristics and as points of reference for comparing the media systems of individual countries.

We have summarized the characteristics of these three models at a number of points in this book, most comprehensively in each of the three chapters of Part II. Here is one more version of a summary, with the emphasis, in this case, on the connections between political culture and media culture.

The Polarized Pluralist Model is characterized by a high level of politicization, with the state and political parties intervening strongly in many areas of social life, and with much of the population holding strong loyalties to widely varying political ideologies. Loyalty to these ideologies goes along with widespread skepticism about any conception of a "common good" that would transcend them, and a relative absence of commonly agreed rules and norms. Polarized Pluralist systems, finally are characterized by unequal consumption of public information, with a fairly sharp division between the politically active population that heavily consumes political commentary in the press, and a politically inactive population that consumes little political information. The news media are similarly characterized by a high degree of external pluralism, in which media are seen as champions of diverse political ideologies, and commitment to these ideologies tends to outweigh commitment to a common professional culture. Ties between journalists and political actors are close, the state intervenes actively in the media sector, and newspapers emphasize sophisticated commentary directed at a readership of political activists.

The Democratic Corporatist Model is characterized by a strong emphasis on the role of organized social groups in society, but simultaneously by a strong sense of commitment to the "common good" and to rules and norms accepted across social divisions. A strong value is placed on the free flow of information, and at the same time the state is seen as having a positive obligation to promote that flow. There is, finally, a culture of heavy consumption of information about public affairs. The media culture is characterized by a surviving advocacy tradition that sees the media as vehicles for expression of social groups and diverse ideologies, and at the same time by a high level of commitment to common norms and procedures. State intervention in the media is extensive, but a high value is placed on media autonomy. Political information is relatively highly valued and is produced for dissemination to a mass audience.

The Liberal Model is characterized by a more individualistic conception of representation, in which the role of organized social groups is emphasized less than in the other two systems and is often seen in

Table 9.1 *Pattern of Variation in Four Media System Dimensions*

|  | Polarized Pluralist | Democratic Corporatist | Liberal |
|---|---|---|---|
| Development of Mass Press | Low | High | High |
| Political Parallelism | High | High | Low |
| Professionalization | Low | High | High |
| State Intervention | High | High | Low |

negative terms, as elevating "special interests" over the "common good." The latter tends to be emphasized over ideological loyalty or consistency. The role of the state tends to be seen in negative terms and the free flow of information is understood as requiring the limitation of state involvement. An emphasis on consumption of public information as essential to citizenship is modified by the individualism and antipolitical elements of the culture, which tend to privilege private over public life. The role of the media tends to be seen less in terms of representation of social groups and ideological diversity than in terms of providing information to citizen-consumers and in terms of the notion of the press as a "watchdog" of government. A common professional culture of journalism is relatively strongly developed, though not formally institutionalized as in the Democratic Corporatist Model. Strong emphasis is placed on limiting government intervention in the media sphere. The media tend to target a wide mass audience and also to emphasize public affairs less than in the other models.

One issue we raised in introducing our four principal dimensions for comparing media systems was the question of whether these were independent of one another. We have argued that they should be treated as independent, though it is impossible to demonstrate through this study that they are: we have four variables, and in some sense only three empirical cases, given the interrelations among the countries we have assigned to our three models. Nevertheless it may be useful to look at a simplified representation of the patterns of variation on these dimensions that we found in our three models, which appears in Table 9.1. The table obviously oversimplifies our argument in many ways, and we hope that readers will not substitute it for the more complex analysis we have presented in the preceding pages. It reduces our four dimensions to quantitative terms, when we have argued that they involve qualitative differences as well – the state plays a large role in both the Polarzed

Pluralist and Democratic Corporatist models, for example, but it does so in very different ways. The table also dichotomizes the four dimensions, and it abstracts from single-country variations, as well as change over time (it is meant to represent the three models in a period when they were maximally distinct, say the 1950s to 1970s).

With all those qualifications, this schematic representation may nevertheless be worth considering for a moment. One thing it shows is that two pair of media system variables show the same pattern of differences across models: the development of the mass press and professionalization, and political parallelism and the role of the state. It does seem plausible that there are connections between these dimensions. Professionalization may tend to develop where the mass circulation press is strong, in part because both result from strong development of capitalism, mass democracy, and the middle class, and in part because professionalization tends to develop in large-scale, economically self-supporting media organizations, where the relation of journalists to their readerships is crucial to the success of the enterprise. And it seems plausible as well that there may be a connection between political parallelism and state intervention. Where the state plays a large role in society, parties are likely to have deep social roots and strong influence, and to some extent it may work the other way around as well: where parties are strong, collective action through the state may be a favored means of solving social problems. It makes sense that where politics is central to social life, and parties play a central role in the community decision-making process, the influence of the political field, in Bourdieu's terms, on the media should be strong and political parallelism high. We would not propose collapsing our four dimensions into two, but we would suggest the hypothesis that the two pair of variables identified here may be interrelated in important ways.

We also have placed considerable emphasis in this book on history: we believe that it is essential to go back both to the origins of the press and to those of the political system, and to trace the development of both historically to understand how media systems function today. In one of the classic works of comparative politics of the 1960s, Lipset and Rokkan (1967: 2) wrote, "As soon we move into comparative analysis we have to add an historical dimension. We simply cannot make sense of variations in current alignments without detailed data on differences in the sequences of party formation . . . before and after the extension of suffrage." They go on to trace the origins of party systems to transition from feudal or patrimonial to liberal institutions, and explain variations in party systems in terms of the particular patterns of conflict that transition involved in different countries. Media systems, no less than the party systems to which they were in most cases closely connected, were strongly shaped by the same social conflicts and by the institutions and cultural patterns that emerged out of them. This does not mean that the past entirely determines the present, or certainly that change does not take place. But there are clear relationships between patterns of historical evolution going back to the beginnings of modernity and the media system patterns that prevail today.

We have also seen that changes in economic and political structure, together with the influence of technology and commercialization of media systems, particularly since the 1980s, has produced a process of homogenization that is substantially eroding the variations among national media systems that prevailed through most of the twentieth century. This process of homogenization involves, most notably, a weakening of the connections that historically tied the media in the Polarized Pluralist and Democratic Corporatist systems to political parties and organized social groups, and a shift toward the commercial structures and practices of neutral professionalism that are characteristic of the Liberal system. There is, in this sense, a clear tendency of convergence toward the Liberal system. At the same time, we have noted that important differences among systems do persist and have identified limits and countertendencies that suggest that we should be cautious about projecting the "end of history" in the development of media systems, in the form of a complete triumph of the Liberal Model.

We have also explored the utility of differentiation theory as a framework for understanding the development of media systems. The assumptions of differentiation theory, as we have noted, are often implicit in the comparative study of the media, particularly in the view that the Liberal Model, because it involves a high degree of differentiation of the media from the political system, is the most advanced model, and that media systems should be compared essentially as evolutionary stages toward that model. We have argued that differentiation theory is indeed useful in important ways for the comparative analysis of media systems. The degree of differentiation of the media from other social and political structures is a centrally important variable, and the changes we have grouped under the label of homogenization can certainly be interpreted in the light of differentiation theory: political parties and social and political groups that once took on multiple social functions, including that of organizing much of the process of social communication, have ceded many of these functions to other institutions, including a mass media system increasingly autonomous from them. Nevertheless we have argued that, consistent with the views of such theorists as Habermas and Bourdieu, important processes of de-differentiation are also at work. Most important here, the process of commercialization, though it may accelerate the differentiation of the media from political institutions, tends to subordinate them to the logic of the market and of the corporate struggle for market share, often diminishing the autonomy of journalists and other communication professionals. In this sense the media become less differentiated from economic institutions as they become more differentiated from political institutions. This shift, as we noted, also raises important questions about power and democracy that we cannot answer adequately here: does the shift toward the Liberal Model make the flow of communication more open and equal, as entrenched political groups lose their control of the media system, or less so, as media fall more exclusively under the control of business, and as consumers', investors', and advertisers' dollars rather than citizens' votes come to underlie the development of media structure?

Also we hope we have illustrated here the potential of comparative analysis as a methodological approach in communication and the need for much more extensive comparative research in the field. This may seem like a commonplace, as the ambition for comparative communication research, as we argued in the introduction, has been around since *Four Theories of the Press*. But in writing this book – if we can switch to Italian for a moment – *abbiamo sperimentato sulla nostra pelle*, we have "experienced on our skin" the value of comparative research to address theoretical questions about the relation between media systems and their social and political contexts, to understand change over time in media systems, and to deepen our understandings of particular national media institutions. As Bendix (1963: 537) says, comparative analysis has the capacity to "increase the 'visibility' of one structure by contrasting it with another." Analysts deeply steeped in one media system will often miss important characteristics of their own system, characteristics that are too familiar to stand out to them against the background. Obviously they will be even less able to address any kind of question that involves explaining *why* these particular system characteristics developed rather than some other set of characteristics. Comparative analysis is essential if we want to move beyond these limitations.

The analysis presented here is a very tentative, exploratory one, hampered in many ways by the limits of existing research and the database it has produced, as well as by the sheer difficulty of generalizing across so many complex cases. We hope other scholars will follow up on many of the ideas proposed here. We also fully expect that when they do not all of what we have argued will prove to be correct or sufficiently developed.

We do have a number of suggestions about specific kinds of comparative research that seem to us to be potentially fruitful. There is a need, for one thing, for comparative data on media content that would show differences or similarities in news selection criteria, conventions of presentation, and the representation of different social groups and interests (we use the example here of news coverage but comparative analysis of other forms of media content would also be quite useful, e.g., looking at representation of different social groups or issues in entertainment television). Comparative content data is rare, partly because of language barriers, and much of what there is is descriptive and conceptually thin, often focused on coverage of some particular event, and not addressed to theoretical issues connected to differences between media systems. Comparative analysis of media content, moreover, need not be only quantitative in character. Very often qualitative, interpretive analyses carried out in a systematic way can be of great value, for example to show differences in characteristic genres of news presentation.

There is also a shortage of "ethnographic" studies of the media, both on single countries and, certainly, genuinely comparative ethnographic studies. Here we are thinking of studies, based on field observation and extensive interviewing, of the operation of media organizations and/or their interactions with other social actors and institutions.[1] In the study of the news media survey research has often been used to ask journalists in a number of countries comparable questions about their role conceptions, values, and so on. There are plenty of challenges in carrying out such surveys, but this is easier than many other kinds of research to standardize and replicate in many countries. It is also useful up to a point; but our research suggests that the differences in how journalists actually do their work are larger than the differences in their survey responses, which are heavily shaped by cross-national normative expectations and aspirations. (Of course, the influence of these cross-national expectations could be studied through this kind of ethnographic research. We found in looking at the literature on "Americanization" that there was relatively little work done tracing how this process happens concretely – what

[1] Examples include Tuchman (1978), Gans (1979), Gitlin (1980), Padioleau (1985), Schlesinger (1987), Semetko et al. (1991), Pedelty (1995), and Esser (1998).

kinds of changes in journalism education take place, what interactions there are among journalists from different countries, what consultants are brought in, and what seminars held, and so on.) What really matters is how journalists or other media personnel function in *practice* – how they make decisions, process information, negotiate constraints, coordinate their activities – and this can only be studied to a very limited extent through survey research. Detailed field research is difficult, though not impossible to do in a comparative way. But even single case studies can be useful to comparative analysis, if they are done with awareness of other cases and with reference to a conceptual framework that is rooted in comparative analysis.

There is a need for comparative historical research in communication. We were struck, just to take one example, at how little was available – at least in the English-language literature and in other literatures we could read in the original – on the history of the party press, which was important to our work given the fact that the story conventionally told about media history focuses on the commercial press. We argued in our discussion of the Democratic Corporatist countries that the available literature suggested that common professional standards developed across both commercial and party papers, with the result that political parallelism coexisted with a high degree of journalistic professionalism, but there is probably much more that could be done to explore exactly how and why this happened in these particular countries, while in others it did not.

There is a need, finally, for more case studies of the interaction of the media with other social actors in the coverage of particular kinds of events or issues. Such studies could again be genuinely comparative, or simply individual case studies designed to be comparable to similar studies carried out in other countries. This kind of study could focus on elections (the most common focus in existing research), on social movements, on media events (which have the advantage of being a common focus for coverage in different countries), or on particular types of issues or events – immigration, strikes, scandals. This kind of study is particularly important for exploring issues of power that, we have argued, are very much underexplored given their significance to many of the normative questions that communication researchers often return to in the end: This kind of study would make it possible to explore which points of view are able to enter the public sphere, which actors and institutions are able to shape the process of debate, and how these processes are affected by the structural characteristics of media systems.

All of the forms of analysis suggested here can of course be combined in a variety of ways: so for example a case study of the interaction of the media with a social movement could make use of content analysis or ethnographic field research. It could also be historical in character, looking, for instance, at coverage in a period when party papers were still strong and in a period when commercial media were overwhelmingly dominant.

We would like to close with a few words about the applicability of the analysis presented here to media systems outside of Western Europe and North America. We have deliberately focused here on a limited range of different media systems. We have rejected the kind of universalistic approach that characterized *Four Theories of the Press*, and hope that our work will not be used as *Four Theories* was, as a set of categories to be imposed on systems that developed in very different contexts, in a way that would actually prevent us from analyzing other systems on their own terms and understanding their distinctive logics. At the same time, we hope that our work will be useful to those working on other media systems as a general example of how to think about the relation of media and political systems, and as a set of models against which others can be constructed.

We do have some very tentative ideas about how our three models might relate to other systems. The Liberal Model, of course, will be relevant to the study of most others in part because its global influence has been so great and because neoliberalism and globalization continue to diffuse liberal media structures and ideas. It is probably particularly relevant to understanding Latin American systems, which have been strongly influenced by the North American model, and perhaps many Asian systems, given the strongly capitalist character of their recent development. In both cases, of course, the Liberal principles are modified in important ways, among other things by a strong role of the state. The Democratic Corporatist Model, we suspect, will have particularly strong relevance for the analysis of those parts of Eastern and Central Europe that share much of the same historical development, like Poland, Hungary, the Czech Republic, and the Baltic states. It may also be relevant in some ways to the analysis of Asian systems, which share with the Democratic Corporatist countries a relatively collectivist political culture.[2]

---

[2] German media law, for example, seems to have significant influence on media law in some Asian countries (e.g., Youm 1993); no doubt there are similarities between Hegelian and Confucian conceptions of the state.

Even though the Liberal Model has dominated media studies and has served as the principal normative model against which other media systems have traditionally been measured, it is probably the Polarized Pluralist Model, more than the other two we outline here, that is most widely applicable to other systems as an empirical model of the relation between media and political systems. We suspect that scholars working on many parts of the world – Eastern Europe and the former Soviet Union, Latin America, the Middle East and all of the Mediterranean region, Africa, and most of Asia will find much that is relevant in our analysis of Southern Europe, including the role of clientelism,[3] the strong role of the state, the role of media as an instrument of political struggle, the limited development the mass circulation press, and the relative weakness of common professional norms.

In all of these cases, however, we think it is likely that substantial modifications would need to be made to our models to apply them, and indeed that they would be useful primarily as inspiration for creating new models based on detailed research into specific political and media systems.

[3] The comparison between Southern Europe and Latin America on this point is developed in Hallin and Papathanassopoulos (2002).

# Bibliography

Agee, Warren K. and Nelson Traquina (1984). "A Frustrated Fourth Estate: Portugal's Post-Revolutionary Media." *Journalism Monographs* no. 87, February.

Albert, Pierre (1983). *La presse française.* Paris: La Documentation française.

Alexander, Jeffrey C. (1981). "The Mass News Media in Systemic, Historical and Comparative Perspective." In E. Katz and T. Szecskö, eds., *Mass Media and Social Change,* pp. 17–51. Beverly Hills: Sage.

Almond, Gabriel and Sidney Verba (1989). *The Civic Culture.* Newbury Park: Sage.

Alsop, Joseph and Stuart Alsop (1958). *The Reporter's Trade.* New York: Renal and Company.

Altick, Richard D. (1957). *The English Common Reader: A Social History of the Mass Reading Public, 1800–1900.* Columbus: Ohio State University Press.

Altschull, J. Herbert (1995). *Agents of Power: The Media and Public Policy.* White Plains, NY: Longman.

Alvarez, Jesús Timoteo (1981). *Restauracion y Prensa de Masas: Los Engranajes de un Sistema (1875–1883).* Pamplona: Ediciones Universidad de Navarra.

Anderson, Benedict (1983). *Imagined Communities.* London: Verso.

Article XIX (1993). *Press Law and Practice.* London: Article XIX.

Åsard, Erik and W. Lance Bennett (1997). *Democracy and the Marketplace of Ideas: Communication and Government in Sweden and the United States.* Cambridge: Cambridge University Press.

Avery, Robert (1993). *Public Service Broadcasting in a Multichannel Environment.* New York and London: Longman.

Bagnasco, Arnaldo (1977). *Tre Italie.* Bologna: Il Mulino.

Baker, C. Edwin (1994). *Advertising and a Democratic Press.* Princeton: Princeton University Press.

Baldasty, Gerald J. (1992). *The Commercialization of News in the Nineteenth Century.* Madison: University of Wisconsin Press.

Barbrook, Richard (1995). *Media Freedom: The Contradictions of Communication in the Age of Modernity.* London: Pluto Press.

Barnhurst, Kevin and John Nerone (2001). *The Form of News: A History.* New York: Guilford Press.

Barrera, Carlos (1995). *Sin Mordaza: Veinte Años de Prensa en Democracia.* Madrid: Temas de Hoy.

Bastiansen, Henrik and Trine Syvertsen (1996). "Towards a Norwegian Television History." In Ib Bondebjerg and Francesco Bono, eds., *Television in Scandinavia: History, Politics, Aesthetics.* Luton: University of Luton Press.

Bechelloni, Giovanni (1980). "The Journalist as Political Client in Italy." In A. Smith, ed., *Newspapers and Democracy.* Cambridge, MA: MIT Press.

———— (1995). *Giornalismo o postgiornalismo?* Napoli: Liguori.

Beck, Ulrich (2000). *What is Globalization?* Cambridge: Polity Press.

Bekken, Jon (1997). "The Chicago Newspaper Scene: An Ecological Perspective." *Journalism and Mass Communication Quarterly.*

Bell, Desmond (1985). "Proclaiming the Republic: Broadcasting Policy and the Corporate State in Ireland." *West European Politics* 8(2): 26–49.

Bellah, Robert (1974). "Le cinque religioni dell'Italia moderna." In F. Cavazza and S. Graubard, eds., *Il caso italiano.* Milano: Graznati.

Bendix, Reinhard (1963). "Concepts and Generalizations in Comparative Sociological Studies." *American Sociological Review* 28(4): 532–9.

Bennett, W. Lance (1990). "Toward a Theory of Press-State Relations." *Journal of Communication* 40: 103–25.

Benson, Rodney D. (1998). "Field Theory in Comparative Context: A New Paradigm for Media Studies." *Theory and Society* 28: 463–98.

———— (2000). *Shaping the Public Sphere: Journalistic Fields and Immigration Debates in the United States and France, 1973–1994.* Ph.D. diss., University of California, Berkeley.

Berka, Walter (1993). "Press Law in Austria." In Article XIX, *Press Law and Practice.* London: Article XIX.

Bettetini, Gianfranco (1985). "Un fare italiano nella televisione." In Fondazione Giovanni Agnelli, ed., *Televisione: la provvisoria identità nazionale.* Torino: Fondazione Giovanni Agnelli.

Bionda, M. L., A. Bourlot, V. Cobianchi and M. Villa (1998). *Lo spettacolo della politica.* Roma: Eri.

Bird, Karen L. (1999). "Racist Speech or Free Speech? A Comparison of the Law in France and the United States." *Comparative Politics* 32:1: 399–418.

Blanchard, Margaret A. (1986). *Exporting the First Amendment: The Press-Government Crusade of 1945–1952.* New York: Longman.

Block, Fred (1987). *Revising State Theory: Essays in Politics and Postindustrialism.* Philadelphia: Temple University Press.

Blumler, Jay G. (1992). *Television and the Public Interest.* London: Sage.

Blumler, Jay G. and Michael Gurevitch (1995). "Towards a Comparative Framework for Political Communication Research." In Blumler and Gurevitch, eds., *The Crisis of Public Communication,* pp. 59–72 [first published 1975]. London: Routledge.

———— (2001). "'Americanization' Reconsidered: U.K.-U.S. Campaign Communication Comparisons Across Time." In Lance Bennett and Robert M. Entman, eds., *Mediated Politics: Communication in the Future of Democracy.* New York: Cambridge University Press.

Blumler, Jay, Dennis Kavanaugh, and T. J. Nossiter (1996). "Communication versus Politics in Britain." In D. Swanson and P. Mancini, eds., *Politics, Media and Modern*

*Democracy: An International Study of Innovations in Electoral Campaigning and Their Consequences.* Westport, CT: Praeger.

Blumler, Jay, Jack M. McLeod, and Karl Erik Rosengren, eds. (1992). *Comparatively Speaking: Communication and Culture Across Space and Time.* Newbury Park: Sage.

Böll, Heinrich (1975). *The Lost Honor of Katharina Blum: How Violence Develops and Where it Can Lead.* New York: McGraw-Hill.

Borre, Ole (1995). "Scope-of-Government Beliefs and Political Support." In O. Borre and E. Scarbrough, eds., *The Scope of Government*, pp. 343–66. Oxford: Oxford University Press.

Bourdieu, Pierre (1998). *On Television.* New York: The New Press.

Boyd-Barrett, Oliver (1977). "Media Imperialism: Towards an International Framework for the Analysis of Media Systems." In J. Curran, M. Gurevitch, and J. Woolacott, eds., *Mass Communication and Society*, pp. 116–35. London: Arnold.

Brants, Kess (1985). "Broadcasting and Politics in the Netherlands: From Pillar to Post." In R. Kuhn, ed., *Broadcasting and Politics in Western Europe.* London: Cass.

——— (1998). "Who's Afraid of Infotainment?" *European Journal of Communication* 13: 315–35.

Brants, Kees and Denis McQuail (1997). "The Netherlands." In Euromedia Research Group, ed., *The Media in Western Europe.* London: Sage.

Brants, Kees and Karen Siune (1998). "Politicization in Decline?" In D. McQuail and K. Siune, eds., *Media Policy: Convergence, Concentration and Commerce*, pp. 128–43. London: Sage.

Breed, Warren (1955). "Social Control in the Newsroom." *Social Forces* 33: 326–35.

Briggs, Asa and Peter Burke (2002). *A Social History of the Media: From Gutenberg to the Internet.* Cambridge: Polity.

Brown, DeNeen (2002). "Canadian Publisher Raises Hackles." *The Washington Post*, January 27: A25.

Brown, Stephen J. (1991). *The Press in Ireland: A Survey and Guide* [first published 1937]. New York: Lemma Publishing.

Budge, Ian (1996). "Great Britain and Ireland." In J. Colomer, ed., *Political Institutions in Europe*, pp. 18–61. London: Routledge.

Burgelman, Jean-Claude (1989). "Political Parties and Their Impact on Public Service Broadcasting in Belgium: Elements from a Political-Sociological Approach." *Media, Culture & Society* 11(2): 167–93.

Bustamante, Enrique (1989). "TV and Public Service in Spain: A Difficult Encounter." *Media, Culture & Society* 11: 67–87.

——— (2000). "Spain's Interventionist and Authoritarian Communication Policy: Telefónica as a Political Battering Ram of the Spanish Right." *Media, Culture & Society* 22: 433–55.

Butler, David and Dennis Kavanagh (1997). *The British General Election of 1997.* London: Macmillan.

Butler, David and Austin Ranney (1992). *Electioneering.* Oxford: Clarendon.

Canel, María José and Antoni M. Piqué (1998). "Journalists in Emerging Democracies: The Case of Spain." In David H. Weaver, ed., *The Global Journalist: News People Around the World*, pp. 299–319. Creskill, NJ: Hampton Press.

Canel, María José, Roberto Rodríguez, and José Javier Sánchez (2000). *Periodistas al descubierto.* CIS.

Carr, Raymond (1980). *Modern Spain, 1875–1980*. New York: Oxford University Press.

Carty, R. K. (1981). *Party and Parish Pump: Electoral Politics in Ireland*. Waterloo, Ontario: Wilfred Laurier University Press.

Caruso, Maria Pia (2000). "La 'Par Condicio' in Francia, Germania, Regno Unito e Spagna." *Comunicazione Politica* 1: 99–109.

Cassese, Sabino (1984). "The Higher Civil Service in Italy." In E. Suleiman, ed., *Bureaucrats and Policy-Making*. New York: Holmes and Meier.

Castronovo, Valerio (1976). *La stampa italiana dall'unità al fascismo*. Bari: Laterza.

Castronovo, Valerio and Nicola Tranfaglia, eds. (1994). *La stampa italiana nell'età della TV, 1975–1994*. Bari: Laterza.

Chalaby, Jean K. (1996). "Journalism as an Anglo-American Invention: A Comparison of the Development of French and Anglo-American Journalism, 1830s–1920s." *European Journal of Communication* 11(3): 303–26.

———— (1998). *The Invention of Journalism*. London: Macmillan.

Charon, Jean-Marie (1990). "Decline of a Polemical Press: The Case of France." *Gannett Center Journal* 4(4): 103–9.

Cheesman, Robin and Carsten Kyhn (1991). "The Structure of Danish Mass Media." *Nordicom Review* 2: 3–19.

Chiarenza, Franco (2002). *Il cavallo morente*. Milano: Angeli.

Cipolla, Carlo M. (1969). *Literacy and Development in the West*. Middlesex: Penguin.

Clark, Charles E. (1994). *The Public Prints: The Newspaper in Anglo-American Culture, 1665–1740*. New York: Oxford University Press.

Clift, Dominique (1981). "Press Councils and Ombudsmen." In Royal Commission on the Press, *The Journalists*. Ottawa: Minister of Supply and Services Canada.

Collier, David (1993). "The Comparative Method." In Ada W. Finifter, ed, *Political Science: The State of the Discipline II*. Washington, DC: American Political Science Association.

Collins, Randall (1990). "Changing Conceptions in the Sociology of the Professions." In R. Torstendahl and M. Burrage, eds., *The Formation of Professions: Knowledge, State and Strategy*. London: Sage.

Colomer, Josep M. (1996). "Spain and Portugal: Rule by Party Leadership." In J. Colomer, ed., *Political Institutions in Europe*. London: Routledge.

Cook, Timothy E. (1998). *Governing with the News: The News Media as a Political Institution*. Chicago: University of Chicago Press.

Curran, Catherine (1996). "Fianna Fáil and the Origins of *The Irish Press*." *Irish Communications Review* 6: 7–17.

Curran, James (1978). "The Press as an Agency of Social Control: An Historical Perspective." In G. Boyce, J. Curran, and P. Wingate, eds., *Newspaper History: From the Seventeenth Century to the Present Day*, pp. 51–75. London: Constable.

———— (1979). "Capitalism and Control of the Press, 1800–1975." In J. Curran, M. Gurevitch, and J. Woolacott, eds., *Mass Communication and Society*, pp. 195–230. Beverly Hills: Sage.

———— (1991). "Rethinking the Media as a Public Sphere." In P. Dahlgren and C. Sparks, eds., Communication and Citizenship: *Journalism and the Public Sphere in the New Media Age*. London: Routledge: 27–57.

Curran, James and Colin Leys (2000). "Media and the Decline of Liberal Corporatism in Britain." In J. Curran and M. Park., eds., *De-Westernizing Media Studies*, pp. 221–36. London: Routledge.

Curran, James and Myung-Jin Park (2000). *De-Westernizing Media Studies*. London: Routledge.

Curran, James and Jean Seaton (1997). *Power Without Responsibility: The Press and Broadcasting in Britain*. London: Routledge.

Curry, Jane Leftwich (1990). *Poland's Journalists: Professionalization and Politics*. Cambridge: Cambridge University Press.

Dader, José Luis (1998). "European Political Communication in Comparison: Some Perspectives about Spain." Paper presented at Workshop on Media and Politics in Europe, Center for German and European Studies, University of California, Berkeley, April 16–18.

Dagnaud, Monique (2000). *L'État et les Médias: Fin de Partie*. Paris: Éditions Odile Jacob.

Dahl, Robert A. and Charles E. Lindblom (1976). *Politics, Economics, and Welfare*. Chicago: University of Chicago Press.

Dalton, Robert (1988). *Citizen Politics in Western Democracies*. New York: Chatham House.

Dalton, Russell J. and Martin P. Wattenberg (2000). *Parties without Partisans: Political Change in Advanced Industrial Democracies*. New York: Oxford University Press.

Danziger, Charles (1986). "The Right of Reply in the United States and Europe." *New York University Journal of International Law and Politics* 19(1–2): 171–201.

Dardano, M. (1976). *Il linguaggio dei giornali italiano*. Bari: Laterza.

Dauncy, Hugh and Geoff Hare (1999). "French Youth Talk Radio: The Free Market and Free Speech." *Media, Culture & Society* 21(1).

De Bens, Els and Vibeke Petersen (1992). "Models of Local Media Development." In K. Siune and W. Truetzschler, eds., *Dynamics of Media Politics: Broadcast and Electronic Media in Western Europe*, pp. 154–78. London: Sage.

de Carvalho, Arons (1999). *A Censura à Imprensa na Época Marcelista*. Coimbra: Livraria Minerva Editora.

Delberghe, Michel (2000). "Le lectorat de la presse nationale reste dépendent du niveau d'études." *Le Monde*, December 15.

De Mateo, Rosario (1997). "Spain." In B. Østergaard, ed., *The Media in Western Europe: The Euromedia Handbook*, 2nd ed. London: Sage.

De Mauro, Tullio (1979). "La cultura." In AA. VV. *Dal 68 ad oggi, Come siamo e come eravamo*, pp. 168–218. Bari: Laterza.

de Tocqueville, Alexis (1969). *Democracy in America*. Garden City: Doubleday.

Deutsch, Karl (1966). *The Nerves of Government: Models of Political Communication and Control*. New York: Free Press.

Dicken-Garcia, Hazel (1989). *Journalistic Standards in Nineteenth-Century America*. Madison: University of Wisconsin Press.

Díez Nicolas, Juan and Holli Semetko (1995). "La Televisión y las elecciones de 1993." In A. Muñoz-Alonso and J. Rospir, eds., *Comunicación Política*. Madrid: Editorial Universitas.

Dimitras, Panayote Elias (1997). "Greece." In B. Østergaard, ed., *The Media in Western Europe: The Euromedia Handbook*, 2nd ed. London: Sage.

Dimock, Michael A. and Samuel L. Popkin (1997). Political Knowledge in Comparative Perspective. In S. Iyengar and R. Reeves, eds., *Do the Media Govern? Politicians, Voters and Reporters in America*, pp. 217–24. Thousand Oaks, CA: Sage Publications.

Djerf-Pierre, Monika (2000). "Squaring the Circle: Public Service and Commercial News on Swedish Television, 1956–99." *Journalism Studies* 1(2): 239–60.

Djerf-Pierre, Monika and Lennart Weibull (2000). *News and Current Affairs Journalism in Sweden 1925–1995*. Working Paper presented at the European Science Foundation Seminar, Changing Media, Changing Europe, Paris, May 25–8.

Dogan, Mattei and Dominique Pelassy (1984). *How to Compare Nations: Strategies in Comparative Politics*. Chatham, NJ: Chatham House.

Donsbach, Wolfgang (1995). "Lapdogs, Watchdogs and Junkyard Dogs." *Media Studies Journal* 9(4): 17–31.

Donsbach, Wolfgang and Bettina Klett (1993). "Subjective Objectivity: How Journalists in Four Countries Define a Key Term of Their Profession." *Gazette* 51: 53–83.

Donsbach, Wolfgang and Thomas Patterson (1992). "Journalists' Roles and Newsroom Practices: A Cross-National Comparison." Paper presented at 42nd Conference of the International Communication Association, Miami.

Donsbach, Wolfgang, J. Wolling, and Constanze von Blomberg (1996). "Repräsentation politischer Positionen im Mediensystem aus der Sicht deutscher und amerikanischer Journalisten." In W. Hömberg and H. Pürer, eds., *Medien-Transformation: Zehn Jahre dualer Rundfunk in Deutschland*. Konstanz: UVK Medien.

Drake, William J. and Kalypso Nicolaïdis (1992). "Ideas, Interests and Institutionalization: 'Trade in Services' and the Uruguay Round." *International Organization* 46(1): 37–100.

Durkheim, Émile (1965). *The Rules of Sociological Method*. New York: Free Press.

Edelstein, Alex. S. (1982). *Comparative Communication Research*. Beverly Hills: Sage.

Edwards, Mark U. (1994). *Printing, Propaganda and Martin Luther*. Berkeley: University of California Press.

Eisendrath, C. R. (1982). "Press Freedom in France: Private Ownership and State Controls." J. L. Curry and J. R. Dassin, eds., *Press Control Around the World*. New York: Praeger.

Eisenstadt, S. N. and René Lemarchand, eds. (1981). *Political Clientelism, Patronage and Development*. Beverly Hills: Sage.

Eisenstein, Elizabeth (1979). *The Printing Press as an Agent of Change*. Cambridge: Cambridge University Press.

——— (1983). *The Printing Revolution in Early Modern Europe*. Cambridge: Cambridge University Press.

Ekecrantz, Jan (1997). "Journalism's 'Discursive Events' and Sociopolitical Change in Sweden 1925–87." *Media, Culture & Society* 19(3): 393–412.

Emery, Michael and Edwin Emery (1996). *The Press and America: An Interpretive History of the Mass Media*. Boston: Allyn and Bacon.

Ericson, Richard V., Patricia M. Baranek, and Janet B. L. Chan (1987). *Visualizing Deviance: A Study of News Organization*. Toronto: University of Toronto Press.

Errera, Roger (1993). "Press Law in France," in Article XIX, *Press Law and Practice: A Comparative Study of Press Freedom in European and Other Democracies*. London: Article XIX.

312

Esping-Andersen, Gøsta (1985). *Politics Against Markets: The Social Democratic Road to Power*. Princeton: Princeton University Press.

Esser, Frank (1998). "Editorial Structures and Work Principles in British and German Newsrooms." In *European Journal of Communication* 13(3): 375–405.

Etzioni-Halevy, Eva (1987). *National Broadcasting Under Siege: A Comparative Study of Australia, Britain, Israel and West Germany*. London: Macmillan.

European Commission (2001). *Eurobarometer: Public Opinion in the European Union*. Report No. 55. Brussels: European Commission.

Evans, Peter (1997). *Embedded Autonomy: States and Industrial Transformation*. Princeton: Princeton University Press.

Fagen, Richard (1966). *Politics and Communication*. Boston: Little, Brown and Company.

Farinelli, G., E. Paccagnini, G. Santambrogio, and A. I. Villa (1997). *Storia del giornalismo italiano*. Torino: Utet.

Farrell, David M. and Paul Webb (2000). "Political Parties as Campaign Organizations." In R. J. Dalton and M. P. Wattenberg, eds., *Parties Without Partisans: Political Change in Advanced Industrial Democracies*, pp. 102–12. New York: Oxford University Press.

Featherling, Douglas (1990). *The Rise of the Canadian Newspaper*. Toronto: Oxford University Press.

Ferenczi, Thomas (1993). *L'Invention du journalisme en France*. Paris: Librairie Plon.

Fernández, Isabel and Fernanda Santana (2000). *Estado y Medios de Comunicación en la España Democrática*. Madrid: Alianza Editorial.

Fernández, Raquel (1997). "Communication Workers in Spain: The Reward of Appearance." *The Communication Review* 2(3): 381–93.

Flanagan, Scott and Russell J. Dalton (1990). "Parties under Stress." In P. Maier, ed., *The West European Party System*, pp. 232–46. New York: Oxford University Press.

Forcella, Enzo (1959). "Milleciquecento lettori." *Tempo Presente*, no. 6.

Franklin, Bob (1997). *Newzak and News Media*. London: Arnold.

Franklin, Bob and John Richardson (2002). "A Journalists Duty? Continuity and Change in Local Newspaper Reporting of Recent UK General Elections." *Journalism Studies* 3(1): 35–52.

Frieberg, J. W. (1981). *The French Press: Class, State and Ideology*. New York: Praeger.

Gagnon, Lysane (1981). "Journalism and Ideologies in Québec." In Royal Commission on the Press, *The Journalists*. Ottawa: Minister of Supply and Services Canada.

Galli, G. (1968). *Il comportamento elettorale in Italia*. Bologna: Il Mulino.

Gans, Herbert (1979). *Deciding What's News: A Study of CBS Evening News, NBC Nightly News, Newsweek and Time*. New York: Pantheon.

Garcia, José Luís (1995). "Os jornalistas portugeses enquanto actores do espaço público: Legitimidade, poder e interpermutação." *Revista de Comunicação e Linguagens*, 21–2.

George, Alexander L. (1979). "Case Studies and Theory Development: The Method of Structured Focussed Comparison." In P. G. Lauren, ed., *Diplomatic History: New Approaches*. New York: The Free Press.

George, Alexander L. and Timothy J. McKeown (1985). "Case Studies and Theories of Organizational Decision Making." In *Advances in Information Processing in Organizations* 2: 21–58.

Gerth, H. H. and C. Wright Mills (1946). *From Max Weber: Essays in Sociology*. New York: Oxford University Press.

Geyer, Robert, Christine Ingebritsen, and Jonathan W. Moses, eds. (2000). *Globalization, Europeanization and the End of Scandinavian Social Democracy?* New York: St. Martins.

Giddens, Anthony (1990). *The Consequences of Modernity.* Stanford: Stanford University Press.

Gitlin, Todd (1980). *The Whole World Is Watching: Mass Media in the Making and Unmaking of the New Left.* Berkeley: University of California Press.

Golding, Peter (1977). "Media Professionalism in the Third World: The Transfer of an Ideology." In J. Curran, M. Gurevitch, and J. Woollacott, eds., *Mass Communication and Society*, pp. 291–308. London: Sage.

Grossman, Michael Baruch and Sandra Joynt Kumar (1981). *Portraying the President: The White House and the News Media.* Baltimore: Johns Hopkins University Press.

Gundle, Stephen (2000). *Between Hollywood and Moscow: The Italian Communists and the Challenge of Mass Culture, 1943–1991.* Durham NC: Duke University Press.

Gunther, Richard and José Ramón Montero (2001). "The Multidimensionality of Attitudinal Support for New Democracies: Conceptual Redefinition and Empirical Refinement." Paper presented at the annual meeting of the American Political Science Association, San Francisco.

Gunther, Richard, P. Nikiforos Diamandouros, and Hans-Jürgen Puhle, eds. (1995). *The Politics of Democratic Consolidation: Southern Europe in Comparative Perspective.* Baltimore: Johns Hopkins University Press.

Gunther, Richard, José Ramón Montero, and José Ignacio Wert (2000). "The Media and Politics in Spain: From Dictatorship to Democracy." In R. Gunther and A. Mughan, eds., *Democracy and the Media: A Comparative Perspective.* Cambridge: Cambridge University Press.

Gustafsson, Karl-Erik (1980). "The Press Subsidies of Sweden: A Decade of Experiment." In A. Smith, ed., *Newspapers and Democracy. International Essays on a Changing Medium*, pp. 104–26. Cambridge, MA: MIT Press.

Gustafsson, Karl-Erik and Stig Hadenius (1976). *Swedish Press Policy.* Stockholm: The Swedish Institute.

Gustafsson, Karl-Erik and Olaf Hulten (1997). "Sweden." Euromedia Research Group, ed., *The Media in Western Europe.* London: Sage.

Gustafsson, Karl-Erik and Lennart Weibull (1997). "European Newspaper Readership: Structure and Development." *The European Journal of Communication Research* 22(3): 249–73.

Hachten, William A. (1996). *The World News Prism: Changing Media of International Communication.* Ames: Iowa State University Press.

Hackett, Robert A. and Yuezhi Zhao (1998). *Sustaining Democracy? Journalism and the Politics of Objectivity.* Toronto: Garamond Press.

Hadenius, Stig (1983). "The Rise and Possible Fall of the Swedish Party Press." *Communication Research* 10:3: 287–311.

Hadenius, Stig and Lennart Weibull (1999). "The Swedish Newspaper System in the Late 1990s." *Nordicom Review* 20(1): 129–52.

Hagen, Lutz M. (1993). "Opportune Witnesses: An Analysis of Balance in the Selection of Sources and Arguments in the Leading German Newspapers' Coverage of the Census Issue." *European Journal of Communication* 8: 317–43.

Hall, Stuart, C. Chrichter, T. Jefferson, J. Clarke, and B. Roberts (1978). *Policing the Crisis: Mugging, the State, and Law and Order.* London: Macmillan.

Hallin, Daniel C. (1986). *The "Uncensored War": The Media and Vietnam.* New York: Oxford University Press.

——— (1992). "Sound Bite News: Television Coverage of Elections, 1968–1988." *Journal of Communication* 42(2): 5–24.

——— (2000). "Commercialism and Professionalism in the American News Media." In J. Curran and M. Gurevitch, eds., *Mass Media and Society*, pp. 218–37. London: Arnold.

Hallin, Daniel C. and Paolo Mancini (1984). "Speaking of the President: Political Structure and Representational Form in U.S. and Italian TV News." *Theory and Society* 13: 829–50.

——— (1994). "Summits and the Constitution of an International Public Sphere: The Reagan-Gorbachev Meetings as Televised Media Events." In D. C. Hallin, ed., *We Keep America on Top of the World: Television Journalism and the Public Sphere*, pp. 153–69. London: Routledge.

Hallin, Daniel C. and Stylianos Papathanassopoulos (2002). "Political Clientelism and the Media: Southern Europe and Latin America in Comparative Perspective." *Media Culture & Society* 24(2): 175–95.

Harcup, Tony and Dierdre O'Neill (2001). "What is News: Galtung and Ruge Revisited." *Journalism Studies* 2(2): 261–80.

Hardt, Hanno (1979). *Social Theories of the Press: Early German and American Perspectives.* Beverly Hills: Sage.

——— (1988). "Comparative Media Research: The World According to America." *Critical Studies in Mass Communication* 5: 129–43.

——— (1996). "Sites of Reality: Constructing Press Photography in Weimar Germany: 1928–33." *The Communication Review* 1(3): 373–402.

Harris, Michael (1978). "The Structure, Ownership and Control of the Press, 1620–1780." In G. Boyce, J. Curran, and P. Wingate, eds., *Newspaper History: From the Seventeenth Century to the Present Day*, pp, 82–97. London: Constable.

Hartz, Louis (1955). *The Liberal Tradition in America.* New York: Harcourt Brace and World.

Hazel, Kathryn-Jane (2001). "The Media and Nationalism in Québec: A Complex Relationship." *Journalism Studies* 2(1): 93–107.

Heclo, Hugh (1984). "In Search of a Role: America's Higher Civil Service." In E. N. Suleiman, ed., *Bureaucrats and Policy Making: A Comparative Overview*, pp. 8–34. New York: Holmes and Meier.

Heinonen, Ari (1998). "The Finnish Journalist: Watchdog with a Conscience." In D. H. Weaver, ed., *The Global Journalist: News People Around the World*, pp. 161–213. Cresskill, NJ: Hampton Press.

Henningham, John and Anthony Delano (1998). "British Journalists." In D. H. Weaver, ed., *The Global Journalist: News People Around the World*, pp. 143–60. Cresskill, NJ: Hampton Press.

Herman, Edward S. and Noam Chomsky (1988). *Manufacturing Consent: The Political Economy of Mass Media.* New York: Pantheon.

Herman, Edward and Robert McChesney (1997). *The Global Media: The New Missionaries of Corporate Capitalism.* London: Cassel.

Herstgaard, Mark (1988). *On Bended Knee: The Press and the Reagan Presidency.* New York: Farrar Straus Giroux.

Hibberd, Matthew (2001). "The Reform of Public Service Broadcasting in Italy." *Media, Culture & Society* 23(2): 233–52.

Hickey, Neil (1998). "Is Fox News Fair?" *Columbia Journalism Review* March/April: 30–5.

Hill, Christopher (1961). *The Century of Revolution, 1603–1714.* New York: W. W. Norton.

Hoffmann-Riem, Wolfgang (1996). *Regulating Media: The Licensing and Supervision of Media in Six Countries.* New York: Guilford.

Holz-Bacha, Christina (2002). "Internal Press Freedom in Germany: What Has Been Achieved after Struggling for More Than 30 Years?" Paper presented at the annual meeting of the Intenational Communication Association, Seoul, July 14.

Hoover, Stewart M. (1988). *Mass Media Religion: The Social Sources of the Electronic Church.* Newbury Park: Sage.

Horgan, John (2001). *Irish Media: A Critical History Since 1922.* London: Routledge.

Horwitz, G. (1966). "Conservatism, Liberalism and Socialism in Canada: An Interpretation." *Canadian Journal of Economics and Political Science* 32:2: 143–71.

Horwitz, Robert (1989). *The Irony of Regulatory Reform: The Deregulation of American Telecommunications.* New York: Oxford University Press.

——— (1997). "Broadcast Reform Revisited: Reverend Everett C. Parker and the WLBT Case (Office of Communications of the United Church of Christ v. FCC)." *The Communication Review* 2(3): 311–48.

Høst, Sigurd (1999). "Newspaper Growth in the Television Era." *Nordicom Review* 20(1): 31–76.

Høyer, Svennik and Pål E. Lorentzen (1977). "The Politics of Professionalization in Scandinavian Journalism." In M. Berg, P. Hemanus, J. Ekecrantz, F. Mortensen, and P. Sepstrup, eds., *Current Theories in Scandinavian Mass Communication Research.* Grenaa: GMT.

Hoynes, William (1994). *Public Television for Sale: Media, the Market and the Public Sphere.* Boulder, CO: Westview Press.

Humphreys, Peter (1994). *Media and Media Policy in Germany: The Press and Broadcasting Since 1945.* Oxford: Berg.

——— (1996). *Mass Media and Media Policy in Western Europe.* Manchester: Manchester University Press.

Inglehart, Ronald (1977). *The Silent Revolution: Changing Values and Political Styles among Western Publics.* Princeton: Princeton University Press.

Jacobson, Gary (2001). "A House and Senate Divided: The Clinton Legacy and the Congressional Elections of 2000." *Political Science Quarterly* 116: 5–27.

Johansson, Egil (1981). "The History of Literacy in Sweden." In H. Graff, ed., *Literacy and Social Development in the West.* Cambridge: Cambridge University Press.

Johnson, Terence J. (1972). *Professions and Power.* London: Macmillan.

Jones, Nicholas (1997). *Campaign 1997: How the General Election Was Won and Lost.* London: Indigo.

Katz, Richard and Peter Mair (1994). *How Parties Organize.* London: Sage.

Katzenstein, Peter J. (1985). *Small States in World Markets: Industrial Policy in Europe.* Ithaca: Cornell University Press.

Kelly, Mary (1983). "Influences on Broadcasting Policies for Election Coverage." In J. Blumler, ed., *Communicating to Voters: Television in the First European Parliamentary Elections*, pp. 65–82. London: Sage.

Kelly, Mary and Wolfgang Treutzschler (1992). "Ireland." In Euromedia Research Group, *The Media in Western Europe*. London: Sage.

Keman, Hans (1996). "The Low Countries: Confrontation and Coalition in Segemented Societies." In J. Colomer, ed., *Political Institutions in Europe*, pp. 211–53. London: Routledge.

Kepplinger, Hans Mathias, Hans-Bernd Brosius, and Joachim Friedrich Staab (1991). "Instrumental Actualization: A Theory of Mediated Conflicts." *European Journal of Communication* 6: 263–90.

Kernell, Samuel (1986). *Going Public: New Strategies of Presidential Leadership*. Washington, DC: Congressional Quarterly Press.

Kindelmann, K. (1994). *Kanzlerkandidaten in den Medien*. Opladen: Westdeutscher Verlag.

Kirchheimer, Otto (1966). "The Transformation of the West European Party Systems." In J. LaPalombara and M. Weiner, eds., *Political Parties and Political Development*, pp. 50–60. Princeton: Princeton University Press.

Kitschelt, Herbert (2000). "Citizens, Politicians and Party Cartelization: Political Representation and State Failure in Post-Industrial Democracies." *European Journal of Political Research* 37: 149–79.

Kleinsteuber, Hans (1997). "Federal Republic of Germany." In Euromedia Research Group, ed., *The Media in Western Europe*. London, Sage.

Kluger, Richard (1986). *The Paper: The Life and Death of the New York Herald Tribune*. New York: Alfred A. Knopf.

Köcher, Renate (1986). "Bloodhounds or Missionaires: Role Definitions of German and British Journalists." *European Journal of Communication* 1(1): 43–65.

Koss, Stephen (1981). *The Rise and Fall of the Political Press in Britain*, 2 vols. Chapel Hill: University of North Carolina Press.

Kruuse, Helle Nissen (n.d.). "Press Ethics in Denmark." Danish School of Journalism: www.djh.dk [downloaded February 2002].

Kuhn, Raymond (1995). *The Media in France*. London: Routledge.

Lægried, Per and Johan P. Olsen (1984). "Top Civil Servants in Norway." In E. Suleiman, ed., *Bureaucrats and Policymaking: A Comparative Overview*, pp. 206–41. New York: Holmes and Meyer.

Laitila, T. (1995). "Journalistic Codes in Europe." *European Journal of Communication* 10(4): 527–44.

Lane, Jan-Erik and Svante O. Ersson (1991). *Politics and Society in Western Europe*. London: Sage.

Lawson, Linda (1993). *Truth in Publishing: Federal Regulation of the Press's Business Practices, 1880–1920*. Carbondale, IL: Southern Illinois University Press.

Legg, K. R. (1975). "Patrons, Clients and Politicians: New Perspectives on Clientelism." Berkeley, CA: Institute of International Studies, Working Papers on Development 3.

Leurdijk, Ardra (1997). "Common Sense Versus Political Discourse: Debating Racism and Multicultural Society in Dutch Talk Sows." *European Journal of Communication* 12(2): 147–68.

Levy, Leonard W. (1985). *The Emergence of a Free Press*. New York: Oxford University Press.

Lewis, Charles (2000). "Media Money: How Corporate Spending Blocked Political Ad Reform and Other Tales of Influence." *Columbia Journalism Review* September/October, pp. 20–7.

Lijphart, Arend (1968). *The Politics of Accommodation*. Berkeley: University of California Press.

———— (1971). "Comparative Politics and the Comparative Method." *American Political Science Review* 65(3): 682–93.

———— (1977). *Democracy in Plural Societies*. New Haven: Yale University Press.

———— (1999). *Patterns of Democracy: Government Forms and Performance in Thirty-Six Countries*. New Haven: Yale University Press.

Lindblom, Charles E. (1977). *Politics and Markets: The World Political and Economic Systems*. New York: Basic Books.

Lipset, Seymour M. and Rokkan Stein (1967). *Party Systems and Voter Alignments: Cross-National Perspectives*. New York: Free Press.

Listhaug, O. and M. Wiberg (1995). "Confidence in Political and Private Institutions." In H. D. Klingeman and D. Fuchs, eds., *Citizens and the State*. Oxford: Oxford University Press.

Lorimer, Rowland and Mike Gasher (2001). *Mass Communication in Canada*. New York: Oxford University Press.

Lorwin, V. (1971). "Segmented Pluralism: Ideological Clevages and Political Cohesion in the Smaller European Democracies." *Comparative Politics* 3(2): 141–77.

Luhmann, Niklas (1978). *Stato di diritto e sistema sociale*. Napoli: Guida.

———— (2000). *The Reality of the Mass Media*. Stanford, CA: Stanford University Press.

Lukes, Stephen (1974). *Power: A Radical View*. London: Macmillan.

Mair, Peter (1997). *Party System Change: Approaches and Interpretations*. Oxford: Clarendon Press.

Mair, Peter, ed. (1990). *The West Euroepan Party System*. Oxford: Oxford University Press.

Malefakis, Edward (1992). "Southern Europe in the 19th & 20th Centuries: An Historical Overview." Madrid: Juan March Institute.

———— (1995). "Contours of Southern European History." In R. Gunther, P. N. Diamandouros, and H.-J. Puhle, eds., *The Politics of Democratic Consolidation: Southern Europe in Comparative Perspective*, pp. 33–76. Baltimore: Johns Hopkins University Press.

Mancini, Paolo (1991). "The Public Sphere and the Use of News in a 'Coalition' System of Government.' " In P. Dahlgren and C. Sparks, eds., *Communication and Citizenship: Journalism and the Public Sphere in the New Media Age*, 137–54. London: Routledge.

———— (2000a). "How to Combine Media Commercialization and Party Affiliation: The Italian Experience." *Political Communication* 17(4): 319–24.

———— (2000b). *Il sistema fragile: I mass media in Italia tra politica e mercato*. Roma: Carocci.

———— (2000c). "Political Complexity and Alternative Models of Journalism: The Italian Case." In J. Curran and M.-J. Park, eds., *De-Westernizing Media Studies*, pp. 265–78. London: Routledge.

———— (2002). "Parliament and the News." Paper presented at the annual meeting of the American Political Science Association, Boston.

Mannheimer, Renato and Giacomo Sani (1987). *Il mercato elettorale*. Bologna: Il Mulino.

Marchetti, Dominique (2000). "Les Révélations du 'Journalisme d'Investigation.' " *Actes de la recherche en sciences sociales*, 131–2.

Marletti, Carlo (1985). *Prima e dopo*. Torino: Eri.

Marletti, Carlo, ed. (1999). *Politica e società in Italia*. Milano: Angeli.

Marletti, Carlo and Franca Roncarolo (2000). "Media Influence in the Italian Transition from a Consensual to a Majoritarian Democracy." In R. Gunther and A. Mughan, eds., *Democracy and the Media: A Comparative Perspective*. Cambridge: Cambridge University Press.

Marlière, Philippe (1998). "The Rules of the Journalistic Field: Pierre Bourdieu's Contribution to the Sociology of the Media." *European Journal of Communication* 13(2): 219–34.

Marsh, Robert M. (1964). "The Bearing of Comparative Analysis on Sociological Theory." *Social Forces* 20(2): 188–96.

Martin, L. John and Anju Grover Chaudhary (1983). *Comparative Mass Media Systems*. New York: Longman.

Marzolf, Marion Tuttle (1991). *Civilizing Voices: American Press Criticism 1880–1950*. New York: Longman.

Maxwell, Kenneth, ed. (1983). *The Press and the Rebirth of Iberian Democracy*. Westport, CT: Geenwood Press.

Maxwell, Richard (1995). *The Spectacle of Democracy: Spanish Television, Nationalism and Political Transition*. Minneapolis: University of Minnesota Press.

Mazzoleni, Gianpietro (1987). "Media Logic and Party Logic in Campaign Coverage: The Italian General Election of 1983." *European Journal of Communication* 2(1): 81–103.

McChesney, Robert W. (1994). *Telecommunications, Mass Media & Democracy: The Battle for Control of U.S. Broadcasting, 1928–1935*. New York: Oxford University Press.

McClelland, Charles E. (1990). "Escape from Freedom: Reflections on German Professionalization, 1870–1933." In R. Torstendahl and M. Burrage, eds., *The Formation of Professions: Knowledge, State and Strategy*, pp. 97–113. London: Sage.

McLachlan, Shelly and Peter Golding (2000). "Tabloidization and the British Press: A Quantitative Investigation into Changes in British Newspapers, 1952–1997." In C. Sparks and J. Tulloch, eds., *Tabloid Tales: Global Debates Over Media Standards*, pp. 75–90. Oxford: Rowman and Littlefield.

McMane, Aralyn Abare (1998). "The French Journalist." In D. H. Weaver, ed., *The Global Journalist*, pp. 191–212. Cresskill, NJ: Hampton Press.

McQuail, Denis (1993). "Dutch Public Service Broadcasting." In R. K. Avery, ed., *Public Service Broadcasting in a Multichannel Environment: The History and Survival of an Ideal*, pp. 75–92. New York: Longman.

——— (1994). *Mass Communication Theory. An Introduction*. London: Sage.

Mendes, Victor (1999). *Legislação sobre Comunicação Social*. Porto: Legis Editora.

Menduni, Enrico (1998). "Televisione e radio." In Istituto di Economia dei Media, ed., *L'industria della comunicazione in Italia. Quarto rapporto Iem*. Milano: Guerrini e Associati.

Merrill, John C. and Harold Fisher (1980). *The World's Great Dailies: Profiles of Fifty Newspapers*. New York: Hastings House.

Michnik, Adam (1995). "*Samizdat* Goes Public." *Media Studies Journal* 9(3): 69–78.

Miliband, Ralph (1969). *The State in Capitalist Society*. New York: Basic Books.

Monteleone, Franco (1992). *Storia della radio e della televisione in Italia*. Venezia: Marsilio.

Moog, Sandra and Jeffrey Sluyter-Beltrao (in press). "The Transformation of Political Communication?" In B. Axelrod and R. Huggins., eds., *New Media and Politics*. London: Sage.

Morlino, Leonardo and José R. Montero (1995). "Legitimacy and Democracy in Southern Europe." In R. Gunther, P. N. Diamandouros, and H.-J. Puhle, eds., *The Politics of Democratic Consolidation: Southern Europe in Comparative Perspective*, pp. 231–60. Baltimore: Johns Hopkins University Press.

Mouzelis, Nicos (1980). "Capitalism and the Development of the Greek State." In R. Scase, ed. *The State in Western Europe*. London: Croom Helm.

——— (1995). "Greece in the Twenty-First Century: Institutions and Political Culture." In D. Constas and T. Stavrou, eds., *Greece Prepares for the Twenty-First Century*. Baltimore: Johns Hopkins University Press.

Mundt, Whitney R. (1991). "Global Media Philosophies." In J. C. Merrill, ed., *Global Journalism: Survey of International Communication*, pp. 11–27. White Plains, NY: Longman.

Murdock, Graham and Peter Golding (1977). "Capitalism, Communication and Class Relations." In J. Curran, M. Gurevitch, and J. Woollacott, eds., *Mass Communication and Society*, pp. 12–43. London: Sage.

Murialdi, Paolo (1986). *Storia del giornalismo italiano*. Torino: Gutenberg.

Murschetz, Paul (1998). "State Support for the Daily Press in Europe: A Critical Appraisal; Austria, France, Norway and Sweden Compared." *European Journal of Communication* 13(3): 291–313.

Nacos, Brigitte Lebens (1990). *The Press, Presidents and Crises*. New York: Columbia University Press.

Negrine, Ralph (1994). *Politics and the Mass Media in Britain*. London: Routledge.

——— (1998). *Parliament and the Media: A Study of Britain, Germany and France*. London: Chatham House.

Negrine, Ralph and Stylianos Papathanassopoulos (1996). "The 'Americanization' of Political Communication." *Harvard International Journal of Press/Politics* 1(2): 45–62.

Nerone, John C., ed. (1995). *Last Rights: Revisiting Four Theories of the Press*. Urbana: University of Illinois Press.

Neveu, Erik (1999). "Politics on French Television: Toward a Renewal of Political Journalism and Debate Frames?" *European Journal of Communication* 14(3): 379–409.

——— (2001). *Sociologie du journalisme*. Paris: La Découverte.

——— (2002). "The Four Generations of Political Journalism." In R. Kuhn and E. Neveu, eds., *Political Journalism. New Challenges. New Practices*. London: Routledge.

Newton, Kenneth and Nigel Artingstall (1994). "Government and Private Censorship in Nine Western Democracies in the 1970s and 1980s." In I. Budge and D. McKay, eds., *Developing Democracy: Comparative Research in Honor of J. F. P. Blondel*, pp. 297–321. London: Sage.

Nieuwenhuis, J. (1992). "Media Policy in The Netherlands: Beyond the Market." *European Journal of Communication* 7(2): 195–218.

Nimmo, Dan and Michael W. Mansfield (1982). *Government and the News Media: Comparative Dimensions*. Waco, TX: Baylor University Press.

Nobre-Correia, J. M. (1997). "Portugal." In B. Østergaard, ed., *The Media in Western Europe: The Euromedia Handbook*, 2nd ed. London: Sage.

Nobre-Correia, J.-M. and Suzy Collard (1999). "Bélgica: la federalización radiotelevisiva y la televisión comunitaria." In M. de Moragas, C. Garitaonandia, and B. López, eds., *Televisión de Proximidad en Europa*, pp. 95–112. Barcelona: Bellatera Castellón.

Nord, David Paul (2001). *Communities of Journalism: A History of American Newspapers and Their Readers*. Urbana: University of Illinois Press.

North, Douglass C. (1990). *Institutions, Institutional Change, and Economic Performance*. New York: Cambridge University Press.

Olsson, Tom (2002). "The Right to Talk Politics in Swedish Journalism 1925–1995." In M. Hurd, T. Olsson, and P. Åker, eds., *Storylines: Media, Power and Identity in Modern Europe. Festschrift for Jan Ekecrantz*. Stockholm: Hjalmarson and Högberg.

Ortega, Félix and M. Luisa Humanes (2000). *Algo Mas Que Periodistas: Sociología de una Profesión*. Barcelona: Editorial Ariel.

Ortiz, David (1995). *Opposition Voices in Regency Spain: Liberalism, the Press and the Public Sphere, 1885–1902*. Ph.D. diss., University of California, San Diego.

Osler, Andrew M. (1993). *News: The Evolution of Journalism in Canada*. Toronto: Copp Clark Pitman.

Østbye, Helge (1991). "Norwegian Media in the 1980s." *The Nordicom Review* 2: 10–37.

——— (1997). "Norway." In Euromedia Research Group, ed., *The Media in Western Europe*. London: Sage.

Padioleau, Jean G. (1985). *Le Monde et Le Washington Post: Précepteurs et Mousquetaires*. Paris: Presses Universitaires de France.

Padovani, Cinzia and Andrew Calabrese (1996). "Berlusconi, RAI and the Modernization of Italian Feudalism." *The Public* vol. 3.

Palmer, Michael and Claude Sorbets (1997). "France." In B. Østergaard ed., *The Media in Western Europe: The Euromedia Handbook*, 2nd ed. London: Sage.

Panebianco, Angelo (1988). *Political Parties: Organization and Power*. Cambridge: Cambridge University Press.

Pansa, Gianpaolo (1977). *Comprati e venduti*. Milano: Bompiani.

Papathanassopoulos, Stylianos (1997). "The Politics and the Effects of the Deregulation of Greek Television." *European Journal of Communication*, 12(3).

——— (1999). "The Effects of Media Commercialization on Journalism and Politics in Greece." *The Communication Review* (3)4: 379–402.

——— (2000). "Election Campaigning in the Television Age: The Case of Contemporary Greece." *Political Communication* 17: 47–60.

——— (2001a). "Media Commercialization and Journalism in Greece." *European Journal of Communication* 16(4): 505–21.

——— (2001b). "The Decline of Newspapers: The Case of the Greek Press." *Journalism Studies* 2(1): 109–23.

Parsons, Talcott (1939). "The Professions and Social Structure." *Social Forces* 17(4): 457–67.

——— (1971). *The System of Modern Societies*. Englewood Cliffs, NJ: Prentice-Hall.

Patterson, Thomas C. (1993). *Out of Order*. New York: A. Knopf.

Patterson, Thomas E. and Wolfgang Donsbach (1993). "Press-Party Parallelism: A Cross-National Comparison." Paper presented at the annual meeting of the International Communication Association, Washington, DC.

——— (1996). "Decisions: Journalists as Partisan Actors." *Political Communication* 13: 455–68.

Pedelty, Mark (1995). *War Stories: The Culture of Foreign Correspondents*. London: Routledge.

Petersen, Vibeke G. and Karen Siune (1997). "Denmark." In Stubbe Østergaard, ed., *The Media in Western Europe: The Euromedia Handbook*, 2nd ed. London: Sage.

Pew Research Center for the People and the Press (2003). "Public Wants Neutrality *and* Pro-American Point of View." [News Release.] Washington, DC, July 13.

Pfetsch, Barbara (1996). "Convergence Through Privatization? Changing Media Environments and Televised Politics in Germany." *European Journal of Communication* 11(4): 427–51.

——— (2001). "Political Communication Culture in the United States and Germany." *Press/Politics* 6(1): 46–68.

Piattoni, Simona (2001). *Clientelism, Interests and Democratic Representation: The European Experience in Historical and Comparative Perspective.* Cambridge: Cambridge University Press.

Picard, Robert G. (1984). "Levels of State Intervention in the Western Press." *Mass Comm Review* 11(1–2): 27–35.

——— (1985). *The Press and the Decline of Democracy: The Democratic Response in Public Policy.* Westport, CT: Greenwood Press.

——— (1988). *The Ravens of Odin: The Press in the Nordic Nations.* Ames: Iowa State University Press.

Pilati, Antonio (1987). *Il nuovo sistema dei media.* Milano: Edizioni di Comunità.

——— (1990). *L'Industria dei Media.* Milano: Il Sole 24 Ore.

Pizzorno, Alessandro (1998). *Il potere dei giudici.* Bari: Laterza.

Plasser, Fritz (2000). "American Campaign Techniques Worldwide." *Harvard International Journal of Press/Politics* 5(4): 33–54.

Poggioli, Sylvia (1991). "The Media in Europe after 1992: A Case Study of *La Repubblica.*" Cambridge, MA: Joan Shorenstein Barone Center on Press, Politics and Public Policy, Discussion Paper D-11.

Popkin, Jeremy D. (1990). *Revolutionary News: The Press in France, 1789–1799.* Durham, NC: Duke University Press.

Porter, Vincent and Suzanne Hasselbach (1991). *Pluralism, Politics, and the Marketplace: The Regulation of German Broadcasting.* London: Routledge.

Porter, William E. (1976). *Assault on the Media: The Nixon Years.* Ann Arbor: University of Michigan Press.

——— (1983). *The Italian Journalist.* Ann Arbor: University of Michigan Press.

Prior, Markus (2002). "Liberated Viewers, Polarized Voters: The Implications of Increased Media Choice for Democratic Politics." *The Good Society* 11(3).

Pritchard, David and Florian Savageau (1998). "The Journalists and Journalisms of Canada." In D. H. Weaver, ed., *The Global Journalist: News People Around the World*, pp. 373–93. Cresskill, NJ: Hampton Press.

Przeworski, Adam and Henry Teune (1970). *The Logic of Comparative Social Inquiry.* Malabar, FL: Robert E. Krieger Publishing Company.

Putnam, Robert D. (1973). *The Beliefs of Politicians: Ideology, Conflict and Democracy in Britain and Italy.* New Haven: Yale University Press.

——— (1993). *Making Democracy Work: Civic Traditions in Modern Italy.* Princeton: Princeton University Press.

Pye, Lucian W., ed. (1963). *Communications and Political Development.* Princeton: Princeton University Press.

Reese, Stephen D. (1990). "The News Paradigm and the Ideology of Objectivity: A Socialist at *The Wall Street Journal.*" *Critical Studies in Mass Communication* 7: 390–409.

Reig, Ramón (1998). *Medios de Comunicación y Poder en España: Prensa, Radio, Televisión y Mundo Editorial.* Barcelona: Paidós.

Ricuperati, G. (1981). "I giornalisti italiani fra poteri e cultura dalle origini all'Unità." In AA.VV., *Storia d'Italia*, pp. 1085–132. Torino: Einaudi.

Rieffel, Rémy (1984). *L'Élite des Journalistes: Les Hérauts de L'Information.* Paris: Presses Universitaires de France.

Rodriguez, América (1999). *Making Latino News: Race, Language, Class.* Thousand Oaks, CA: Sage.

Roidi, Vittorio (2001). *La fabbrica delle notizie.* Bari: Laterza.

Roniger, Luis and Ayse Günes-Ayata, eds. (1994). *Democracy, Clientelism and Civil Society.* Boulder, CO: Lynne Rienner.

Rooney, Dick (2000). "Thirty Years of Competition in the British Tabloid Press: The Mirror and the Sun 1968–1988." In C. Sparks and J. Tulloch, eds., *Tabloid Tales: Global Debates over Media Standards*, pp. 91–109. Oxford: Rowman and Littlefield.

Rose, Richard (1984). "The Political Status of Higher Civil Servants in Britain." In E. N. Suleiman, ed., *Bureaucrats and Policy Making: A Comparative Overview*, pp. 136–73. New York: Holmes and Meier.

Rospir, Juan I. (1996). "Political Communication and Electoral Campaigns in the Young Spanish Democracy." In D. Swanson and P. Mancini eds., *Politics, Media and Modern Democracy*, pp. 155–69. Westport, CT: Praeger.

Rutenberg, Jim (2002). "Cable TV Serves Business News with Opinions." *The New York Times*, April 3: C1.

Saint-Jean, Armande (1998). "Journalistic Ethics and Referendum Coverage in Montreal." In G. Robinson, ed., *Constructing the Quebec Referendum: French and English Media Voices*, pp. 37–51. Toronto: University of Toronto Press.

Salokangas, Raimo (1999). "From Political to National, Regional and Local." In *Nordicom Review* 20(1): 31–76.

Sampedro Blanco, Víctor (1997). *Movimientos sociales: debates sin mordaza.* Madrid: Centro de Estudios Constitucionales.

Sandford, J. (1976). *The Mass Media of German Speaking Countries.* London: Oswald Wolff.

Sani, Giacomo (1980). "The Political Culture of Italy: Continuity and Change." In G. Almond and S. Verba, eds. *The Civic Culture Revisited.* New York: Sage.

Sani, Giacomo, ed. (2001) *Mass Media ed Elezioni.* Mulino.

Sartori, Giovanni (1976). *Parties and Party Systems: A Framework for Analysis.* Cambridge: Cambridge University Press.

Scammell, Margaret and Martin Harrop (1997). "The Press." In D. Butler and D. Kavanaugh, *The British General Election of 1997.* London: Macmillan.

Schiller, Dan (1981). *Objectivity and the News: The Public and the Rise of the Commercial Journalism.* Philadelphia: University of Pennsylvania Press.

Schiller, Herbert I. (1969). *Mass Communications and American Empire.* Boston: Beacon Press.

——— (1973). *The Mind Managers.* Boston: Beacon Press

——— (1976). *Communication and Cultural Domination.* White Plains, NY: International Arts and Sciences Press.

Schlesinger, Philip (1987). *Putting "Reality" Together: BBC News.* London: Methuen.

——— (1999). "Changing Spaces of Political Communication: The Case of the European Union." *Political Communication* 16(3): 263–79.

Schmidt, Manfred G. (1996). "Germany. The Grand Coalition State." In J. Colomer, ed., *Political Institutions in Europe.* London: Routledge.

Schoenbach, Klaus, Dieter Stuerzebecher, and Beate Schneider (1998). "German Journalists in the Early 1990s: East and West." In D. H. Weaver, ed., *The Global Journalist,* pp. 213–27. Cresskill, NJ: Hampton Press.

Schou, Søren (1992). "Postwar Americanisation and the Revitalisation of European Culture." In M. Skovmand and K. C. Schroder, eds., *Media Cultures: Reappraising Transnational Media,* pp. 142–58. London and New York: Sage.

Schudson, Michael (1978). *Discovering the News: A Social History of American Newspapers.* New York: Basic Books.

——— (1995). "Question Authority: A History of the News Interview." In *The Power of News.* Cambridge, MA: Harvard University Press.

——— (2001). "The Objectivity Norm in American Journalism." *Journalism* 2(2): 149–70.

Schulz, Winfried (1996). "A Study of the Success of the Chancellor Candidates' Strategies during the 1990 German Bundstag Elections." *European Journal of Communiction* 11(1): 33–57.

Sciolla, Loredana (1990). "Identità mutamento culturale nell'Italia di oggi." In Cesareo, Vincenzo, ed., *La cultura dell'Italia contemporanea.* Torino: Edizioni della Fondazione Agnelli.

Seaton, Jean and Ben Pimlott (1980). "The Role of the Media in the Portuguese Revolution." In A. Smith, ed., *Newspapers and Democracy,* pp. 174–99. Cambridge, MA: MIT Press.

Seaton, Jean and Ben Pimlott, eds. (1987). *The Media in British Politics.* Aldershot: Avebury.

Semetko, Holli and Kaus Schoenbach (1994). *Germany's "Unity Elecion": Voters and the Media.* Cresskill, NJ: Hampton.

Semetko, Holli, Jay G. Blumler, Michael Gurevitch, and David H. Weaver (1991). *The Formation of Campaign Agendas: A Comparative Analysis of Party and Media Roles in Recent American and British Elections.* Hillside, NJ: Lawrence Erlbaum Associates.

Seymour-Ure, Colin (1974). *The Political Impact of Mass Media.* London: Constable.

——— (1996). *The British Press and Broadcasting Since 1945.* Oxford: Blackwell.

Shawcross, William (1992). *Murdoch.* New York: Simon and Schuster.

Shefter, Martin (1977). "Party and Patronage: Germany, England and Italy." *Politics and Society* 7(1): 403–35.

Siebert, Fred S., Theodore Peterson, and Wilbur Schramm (1956). *Four Theories of the Press.* Urbana: University of Illinois Press.

Sigal, Leon V. (1973). *Reporters and Officials: The Organization and Politics of Newsmaking.* Lexington, MA: D. C. Heath.

Smith, A. C. H. with Elizabeth Immirzi and Trevor Blackwell (1975). *Paper Voices: The Popular Press and Social Change 1935–1965.* Totowa, NJ: Rowman and Littlefield.

Smith, Culver H. (1977). *The Press, Politics, and Patronage: The American Government's Use of Newspapers, 1789–1875*. Athens, GA: University of Georgia Press.

Smythe, Ted Curtis (1980). "The Reporter, 1880–1900: Working Conditions and Their Influence on the News." *Journalism History* 7.

Søllinge, Jette Drachmann (1999). "Danish Newspapers." *Nordicom Review* 20(1): 31–76.

Sonninen, P. and T. Laitila (1995). "Press Councils in Europe." University of Tampere: Department of Journalism and Mass Communication.

Splichal, Slavko and Colin Sparks (1994). *Journalists for the 21ˢᵗ Century*. Norwood, NJ: Ablex.

Squires, James (1993). *Read All About It: The Corporate Takeover of America's Newspapers*. New York: Random House.

Steele, Janet E. (1990). "The 19th Century *World* Versus the *Sun*: Promoting Consumption (Rather than the Working Man)." *Journalism Quarterly* 67(3): 592–600.

Suleiman, Ezra N. (1984). *Bureaucrats and Policy Making: A Comparative Overview*. New York: Holmes and Meier.

Swanson, David and Paolo Mancini, eds. (1996). *Politics, Media and Modern Democracy*. Westport: Praeger.

Taras, David (1999). *Power and Betrayal in Canadian Media*. Peterborough, Ontario: Broadview Press.

Taylor, Paul (1992). "Political Coverage in the 1990s: Teaching the Old News New Tricks." In Twentieth Century Fund, *The New News v. the Old News*. New York: Twentieth Century Fund.

Thogmartin, Clyde (1998). *The National Daily Press of France*. Birmingham, AL: Summa Publications.

Thompson, John B. (1995). *The Media and Modernity*. Cambridge: Polity.

Tilly, Charles (1984). *Big Structures, Large Processes, Huge Comparison*. New York: Russell Sage Foundation.

Tracey, Michael (1998). *The Decline and Fall of Public Service Broadcasting*. New York: Oxford University Press.

Traquina, Nelson (1995). "Portuguese Television: The Politics of Savage Deregulation." *Media, Culture & Society* 17(2): 223–38.

——— (1997). *Big Show Media: Viagem pelo Mundo do Audiovisual Português*. Lisboa: Editorial Noticícias.

Trigilia, C. (1981). "Le subculture politiche territoriali." In *Sviluppo economico e trasformazioni socio-politiche dei sistemi territoriali a economia diffusa, Quaderni della Fondazione Feltrinelli*, 16.

Tsan-Kuo, Chang with Pat Berg, Anthony Ying-Him Fung, Kent D. Kedl, Catherine A. Luther, and Janet Szuba (2001). "Comparing Nations in Mass Communication Research, 1970–97: A Critical Assessment of How We Know What We Know." *Gazzette* 63(5): 415–34.

Tuchman, Gaye (1978). *Making News: A Study in the Construction of Reality*. New York: Free Press.

Tunstall, Jeremy (1971). *Journalists at Work*. London: Constable.

——— (1977). *The Media Are American*. London: Constable.

——— (1993). *Television Producers*. London: Routledge.

Tunstall Jeremy and Michael Palmer (1991). *Media Moguls*. London: Routledge.

Twentieth Century Fund (1993). *Quality Time? The Report of the Twentieth Century Fund Task Force on Public Television.* New York: Twentieth Century Fund Press.

Underwood, Doug (1993). *When MBAs Rule the Newsroom: How the Marketers and Managers are Reshaping Today's Media.* New York: Columbia University Press.

van der Eijk, Cees (2000). "The Netherlands: Media and Politics between Segmented Pluralism and Market Forces." In R. Gunther and A. Mughan, eds., *Democracy and the Media*, pp. 303–42. Cambridge: Cambridge University Press.

Van Gompel, R. (1998). "Political Control, Market Logic and Public Responsibility." Paper presented at 21st Scientific Conference of IAMCR, Glasgow, July 26–30.

Van Lenthe, Francine and Ineke Boerefin (1993). "Press Law in the Netherlands." In *Press Law and Practice.* London: Article XIX.

Vedel, Thierry and Jérome Bourdon (1993). "French Public Service Broadcasting: From Monopoly to Marginalization." In R. K. Avery, ed., *Public Service Broadcasting in a Multichannel Environment: The History and Survival of an Ideal*, pp. 29–52. New York: Longman.

Vincent, David (2000). *The Rise of Mass Literacy: Reading and Writing in Modern Europe.* Cambridge: Polity Press.

Waisbord, Silvio (2000). *Watchdog Journalism in South America: News, Accountability and Democracy.* New York: Columbia University Press.

Weaver, David H., ed. (1998). *The Global Journalist: News People Around the World.* Cresskill, NJ: Hampton Press.

Weaver, David and G. Cleveland Wilhoit (1991). "Journalists in the United States." In D. H. Weaver, ed., *The Global Journalist*, pp. 395–414. Cresskill, NJ: Hampton Press.

Weber, Eugen Joseph (1976). *Peasants into Frenchmen: The Modernization of Rural France, 1870–1914.* Stanford, CA: Stanford University Press.

Weber, Max (1946). "Politics as a Vocation." In H. H. Gerth and C. Wright Mills, eds., *From Max Weber: Essays in Sociology.* New York: Oxford University Press.

Weibull, Lennart (1983). "Political Factors in Newspaper Readership." *Communication Research* 10(3): 311–33.

Weibull, Lennart and M. Anshelm (1991). "Signs of Change. Swedish Media in Transition." *Nordicom Review* 2: 37–63.

——— (1992). "Indications of Change: Developments in Swedish Media 1980–1990." *Gazette* 49(1–2): 41–73.

Weibull, Lennart and Britt Börjesson (1991). "The Swedish Media Accountability System: A Research Perspective." *European Journal of Communication* 7:121–39.

Weischenberg, Siegfried, Martin Löffelholz and Armin Scholl (1998). "Journalism in Germany." In D. H. Weaver, ed., *The Global Journalist*, pp. 229–56. Cresskill, NJ: Hampton Press.

Westergaard, John (1977). "Power, Class and the Media." In J. Curran, M. Gurevitch, and J. Woollacott, eds., *Mass Communication and Society*, pp. 15–115. London: Sage.

Weymouth, Anthony and Bernard Lamizet, eds. (1996). *Markets and Myths: Forces for Change in the Media of Western Europe.* New York: Longman.

Wiebe, Robert H. (1967). *The Search for Order, 1877–1920.* New York: Hill and Wang.

Wigbold, Herman (1979). "Holland: The Shaky Pillars of Hilversum." In A. Smith, ed., *Television and Political Life: Studies in Six European Countries*, pp. 191–231. London: Macmillan.

Wilensky, Harold L. (1964). "The Professionalization of Everyone?" *American Journal of Sociology* 70(2): 137–58.

Winston, Brian (2002). "Towards Tabloidization? Glasgow Revisited, 1975–2001." *Journalism Studies* 3(1): 5–20.

Wolland, Steingrim (1993). "Press Law in Norway." In *Press Law and Practice*. London: Article XIX.

World Association of Newspapers (2001). *World Press Trends*. Paris.

Youm, Kyu Ho (1993). "Right of Reply Under Korean Press Law: A Statutory and Judicial Perspective." *The American Journal of Comparative Law* 61(1): 49–71.

Zaharopoulos, Thimios and Manny E. Paraschos (1993). *Mass Media in Greece: Power, Politics and Privatization*. Westport, CT: Prager.

# Index

Lightning Source UK Ltd.
Milton Keynes UK
UKOW03f2350130814

236874UK00001B/106/P

9 780521 543088